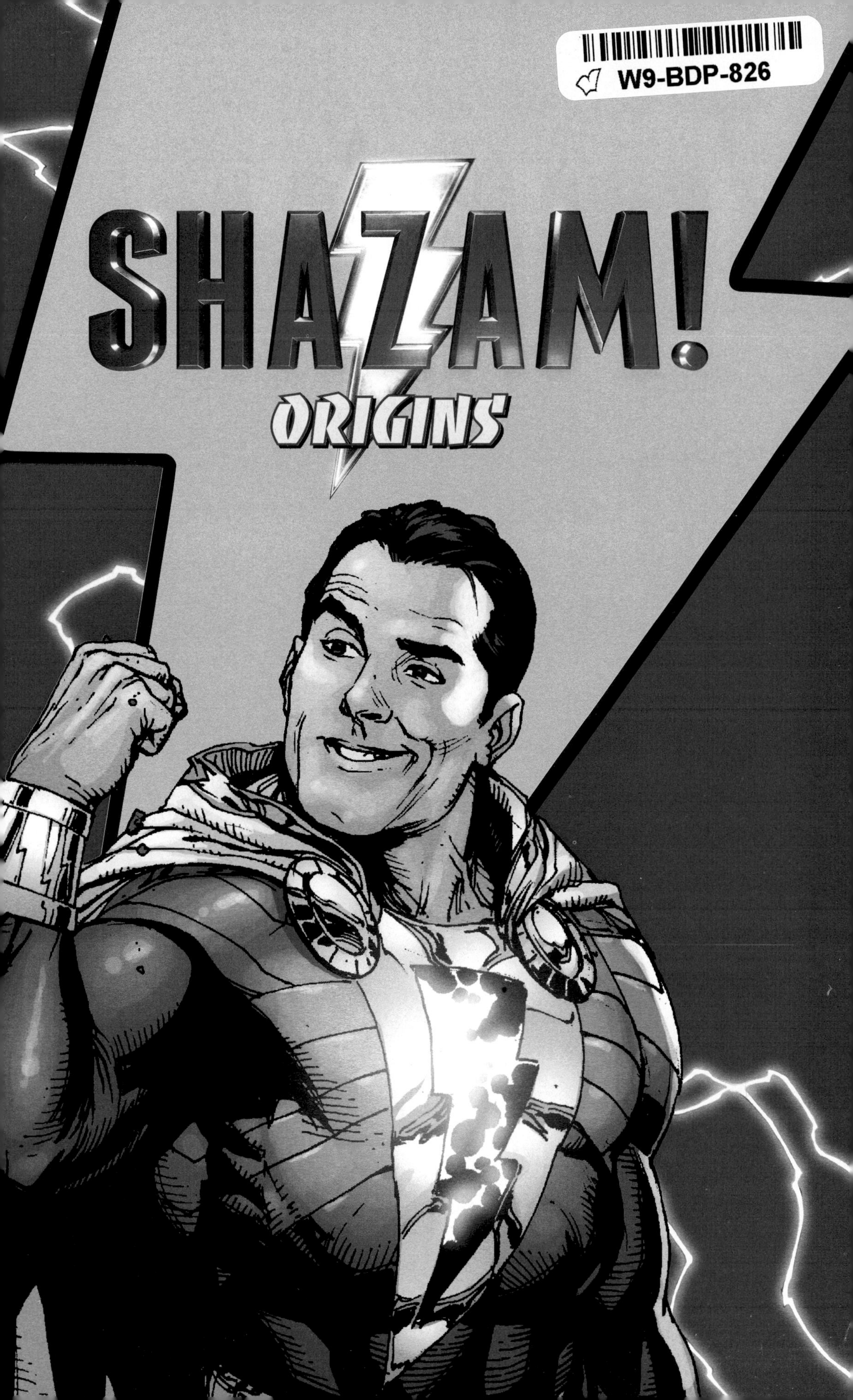
SHAZAM!
ORIGINS

SHAZAM! ORIGINS

GEOFF JOHNS
writer

GARY FRANK
artist

BRAD ANDERSON
colorist

NICK J. NAPOLITANO
DEZI SIENTY
letterers

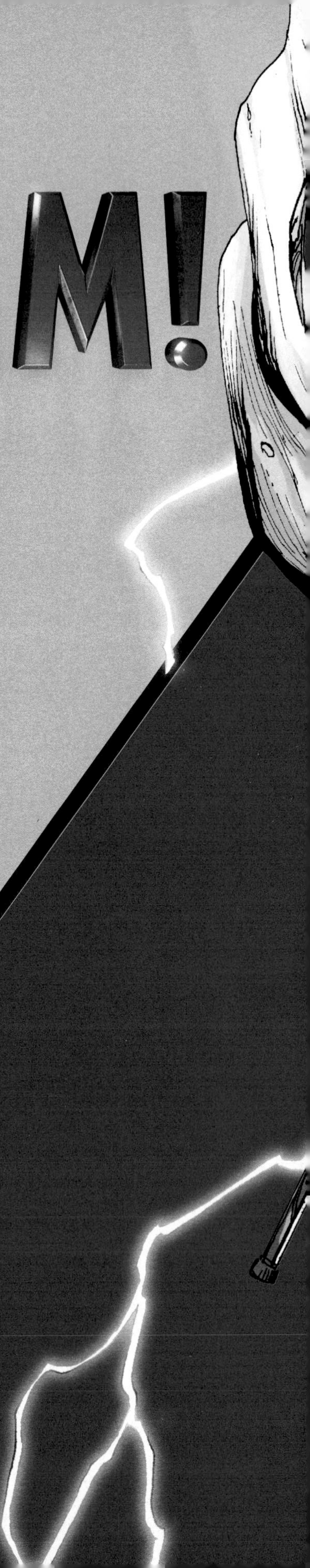

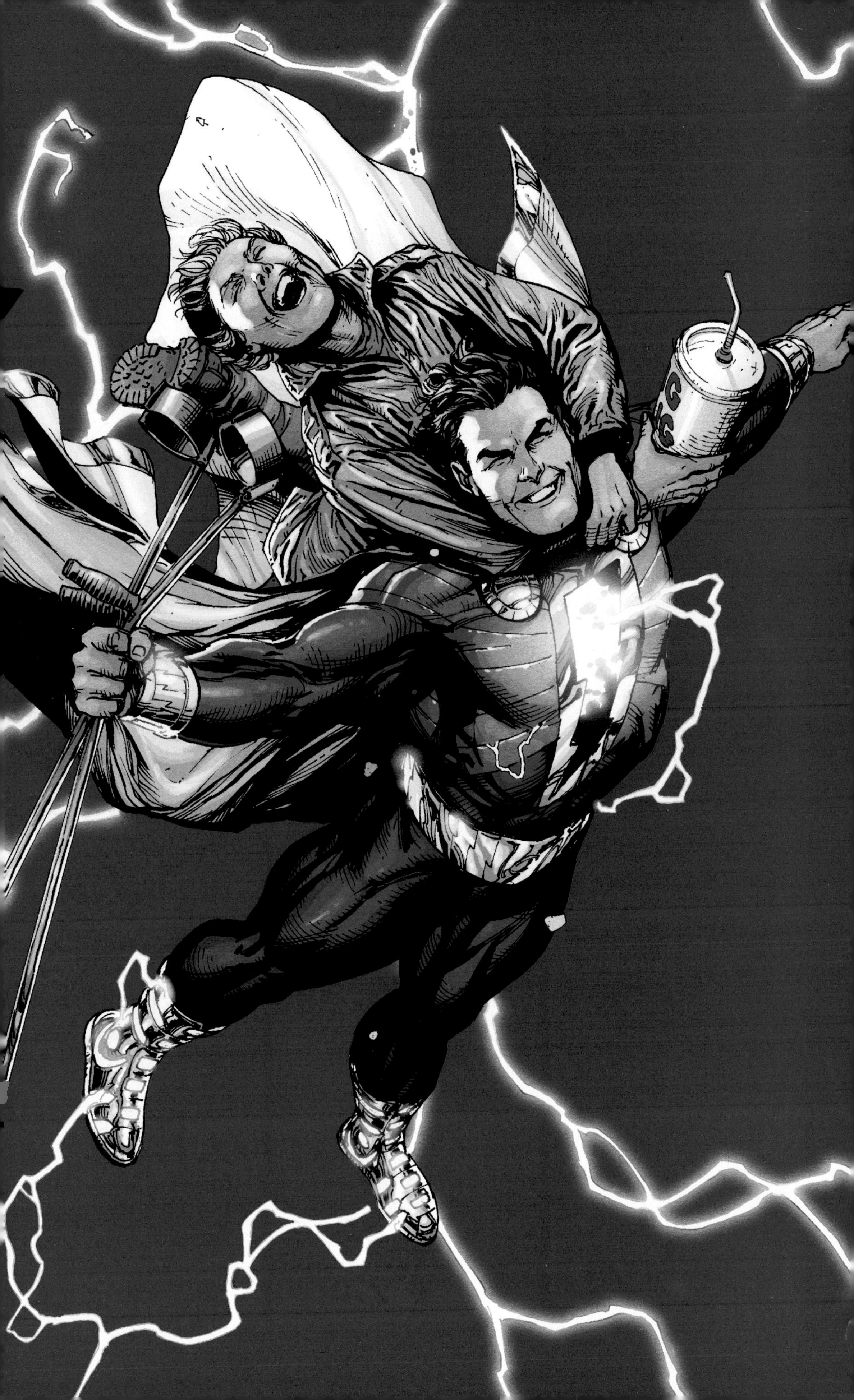

BRIAN CUNNINGHAM Editor – Original Series **KATIE KUBERT** Associate Editor – Original Series
DARREN SHAN, KATE DURRÉ Assistant Editors – Original Series
JEB WOODARD Group Editor – Collected Editions **ERIC SEARLEMAN** Editor – Collected Edition
STEVE COOK Design Director – Books **DAMIAN RYLAND** Publication Design

BOB HARRAS Senior VP – Editor-in-Chief, DC Comics **PAT McCALLUM** Executive Editor, DC Comics

DAN DiDIO Publisher
JIM LEE Publisher & Chief Creative Officer
AMIT DESAI Executive VP – Business & Marketing Strategy, Direct to Consumer & Global Franchise Management
BOBBIE CHASE VP & Executive Editor, Young Reader & Talent Development
MARK CHIARELLO Senior VP – Art, Design & Collected Editions
JOHN CUNNINGHAM Senior VP – Sales & Trade Marketing
BRIAR DARDEN VP – Business Affairs
ANNE DePIES Senior VP – Business Strategy, Finance & Administration
DON FALLETTI VP – Manufacturing Operations
LAWRENCE GANEM VP – Editorial Administration & Talent Relations
ALISON GILL Senior VP – Manufacturing & Operations
JASON GREENBERG VP – Business Strategy & Finance
HANK KANALZ Senior VP – Editorial Strategy & Administration
JAY KOGAN Senior VP – Legal Affairs
NICK J. NAPOLITANO VP – Manufacturing Administration
LISETTE OSTERLOH VP – Digital Marketing & Events
EDDIE SCANNELL VP – Consumer Marketing
COURTNEY SIMMONS Senior VP – Publicity & Communications
JIM (SKI) SOKOLOWSKI VP – Comic Book Specialty Sales & Trade Marketing
NANCY SPEARS VP – Mass, Book, Digital Sales & Trade Marketing
MICHELE R. WELLS VP – Content Strategy

SHAZAM!: ORIGINS

DC Comics, 2900 West Alameda Ave., Burbank, CA 91505
Printed by LSC Communications, Kendallville, IN, USA. 1/25/19.
First Printing. ISBN: 978-1-4012-8789-4

Library of Congress Cataloging-in-Publication Data
is available.

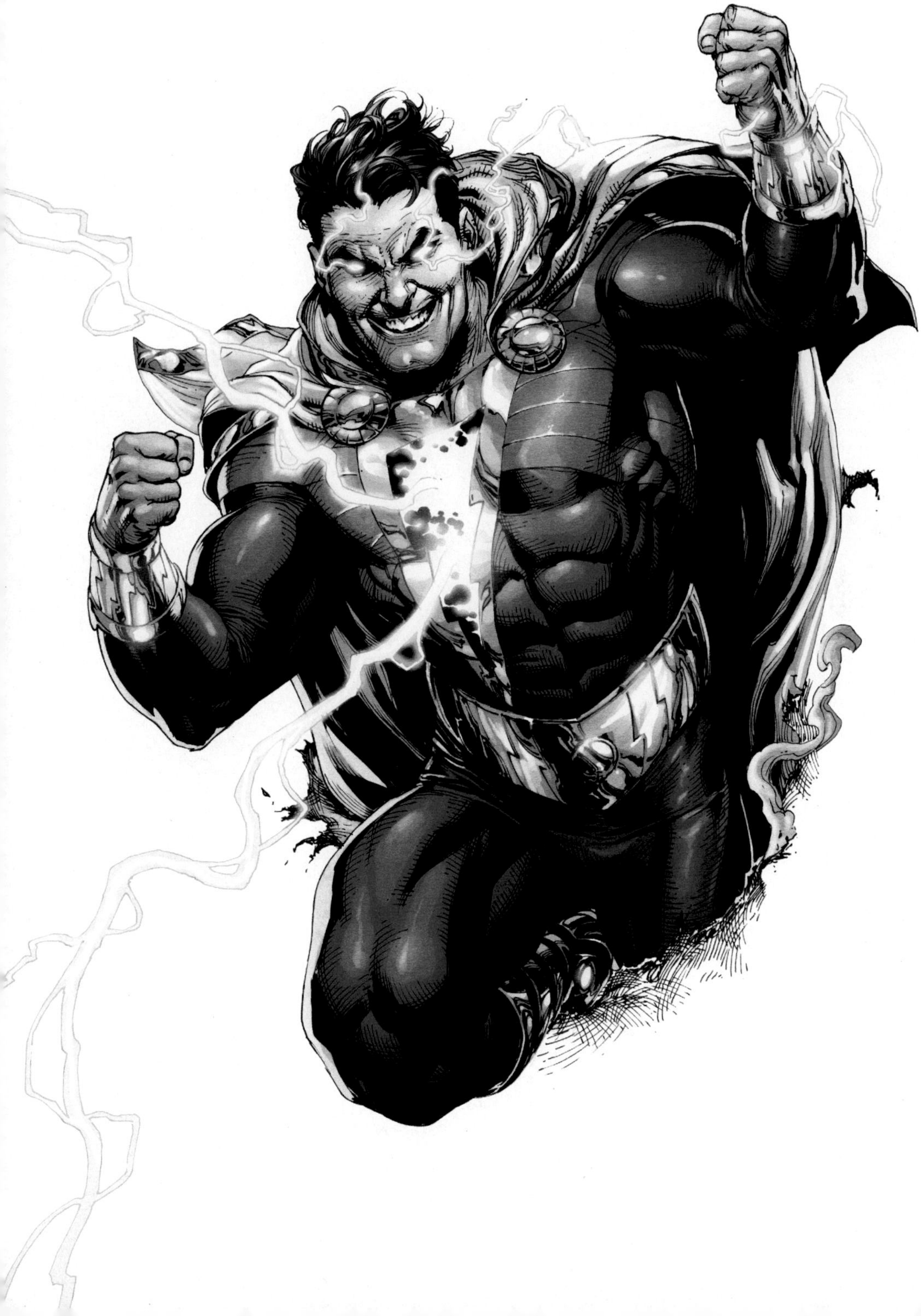

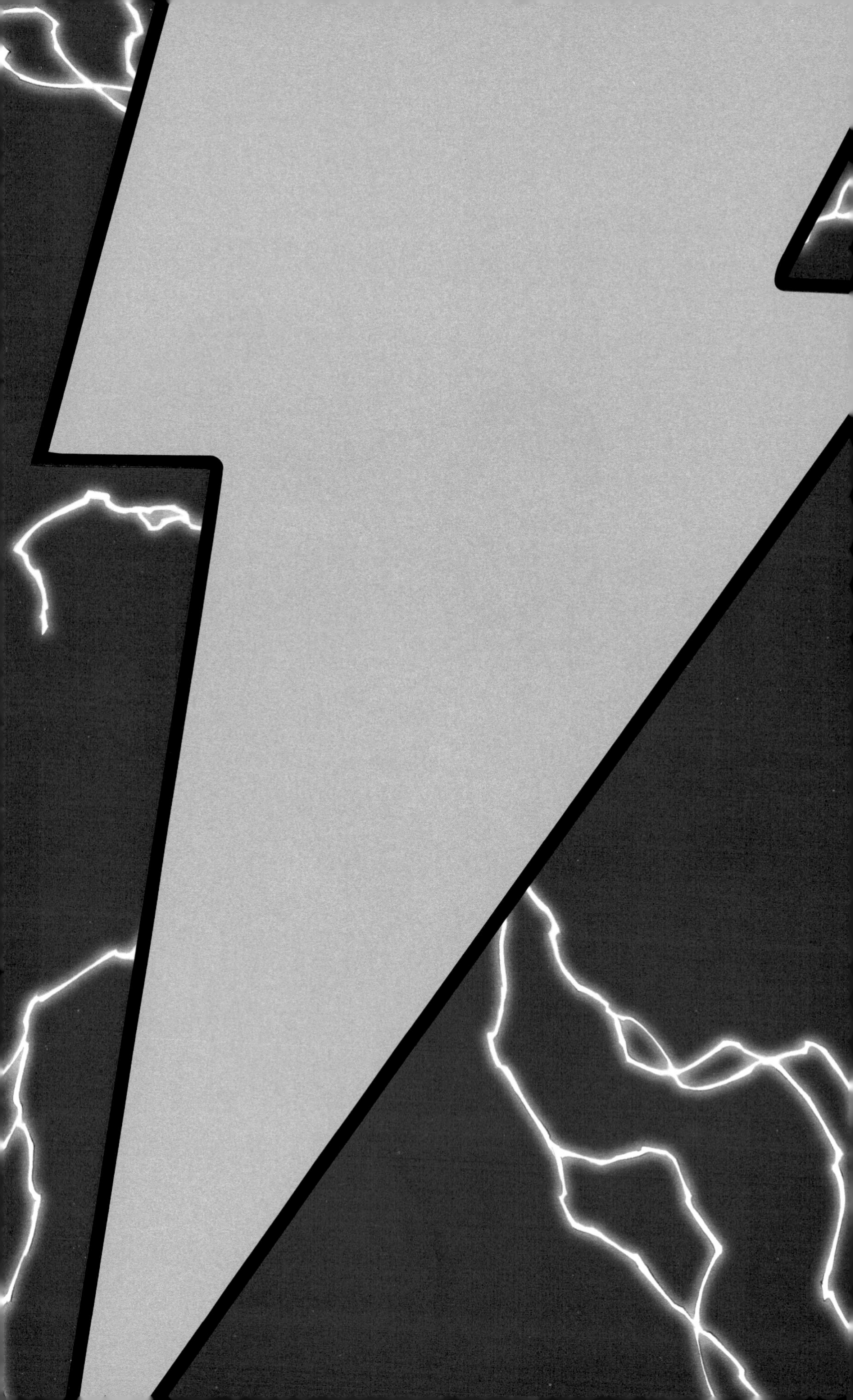

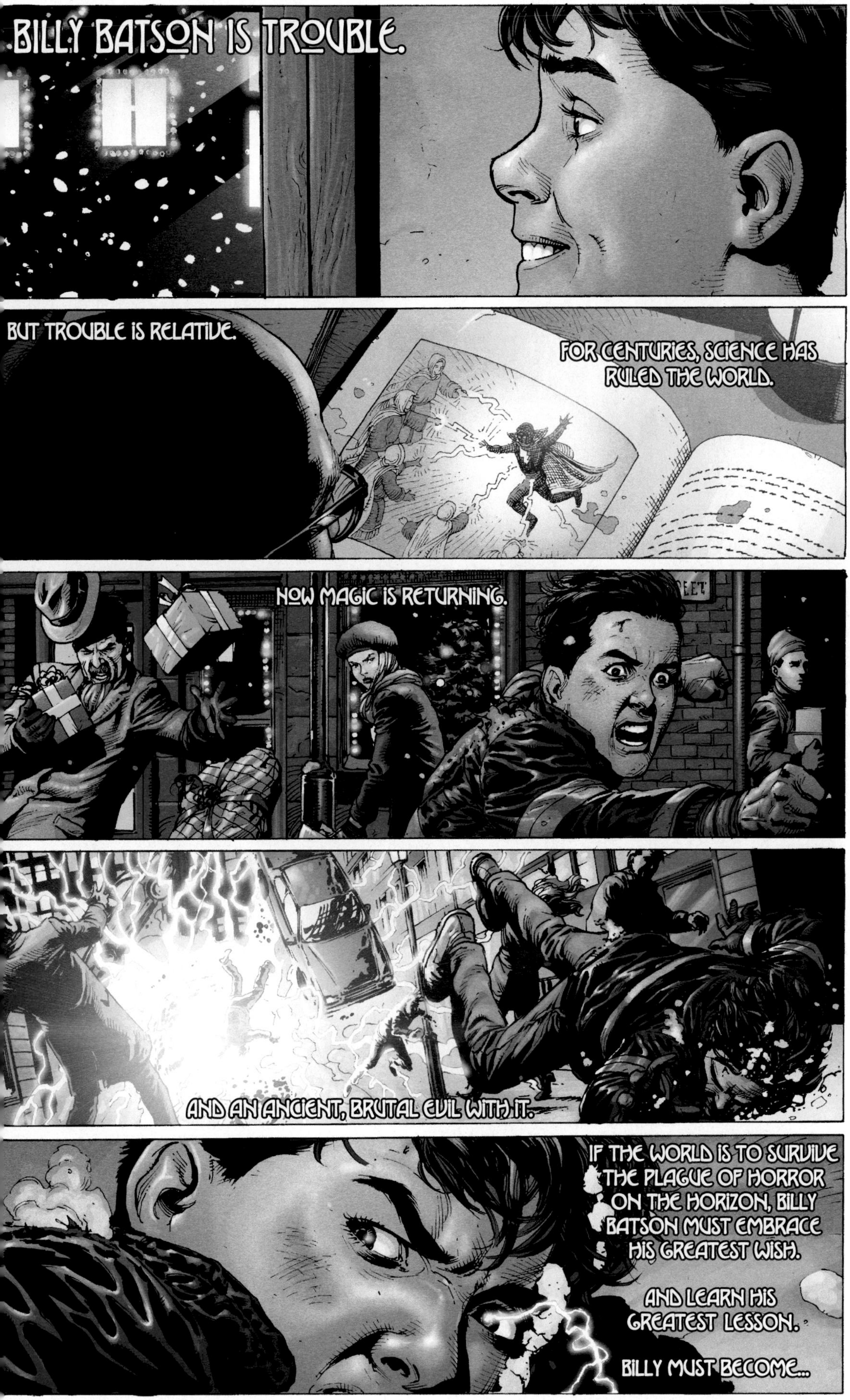
BILLY BATSON IS TROUBLE.
BUT TROUBLE IS RELATIVE.
FOR CENTURIES, SCIENCE HAS RULED THE WORLD.
NOW MAGIC IS RETURNING.
AND AN ANCIENT, BRUTAL EVIL WITH IT.
IF THE WORLD IS TO SURVIVE THE PLAGUE OF HORROR ON THE HORIZON, BILLY BATSON MUST EMBRACE HIS GREATEST WISH.
AND LEARN HIS GREATEST LESSON.
BILLY MUST BECOME...

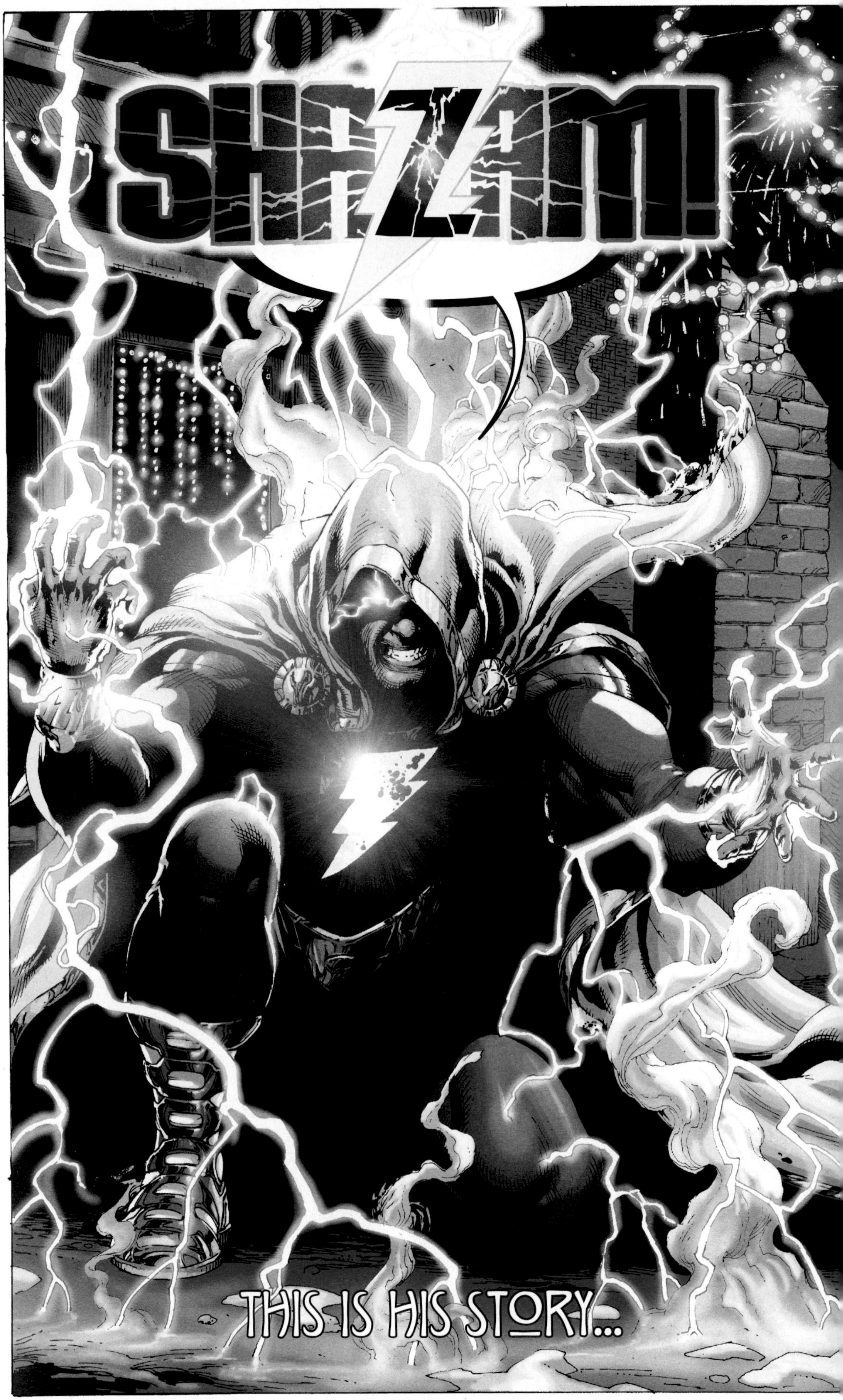
SHAZAM!
THIS IS HIS STORY...

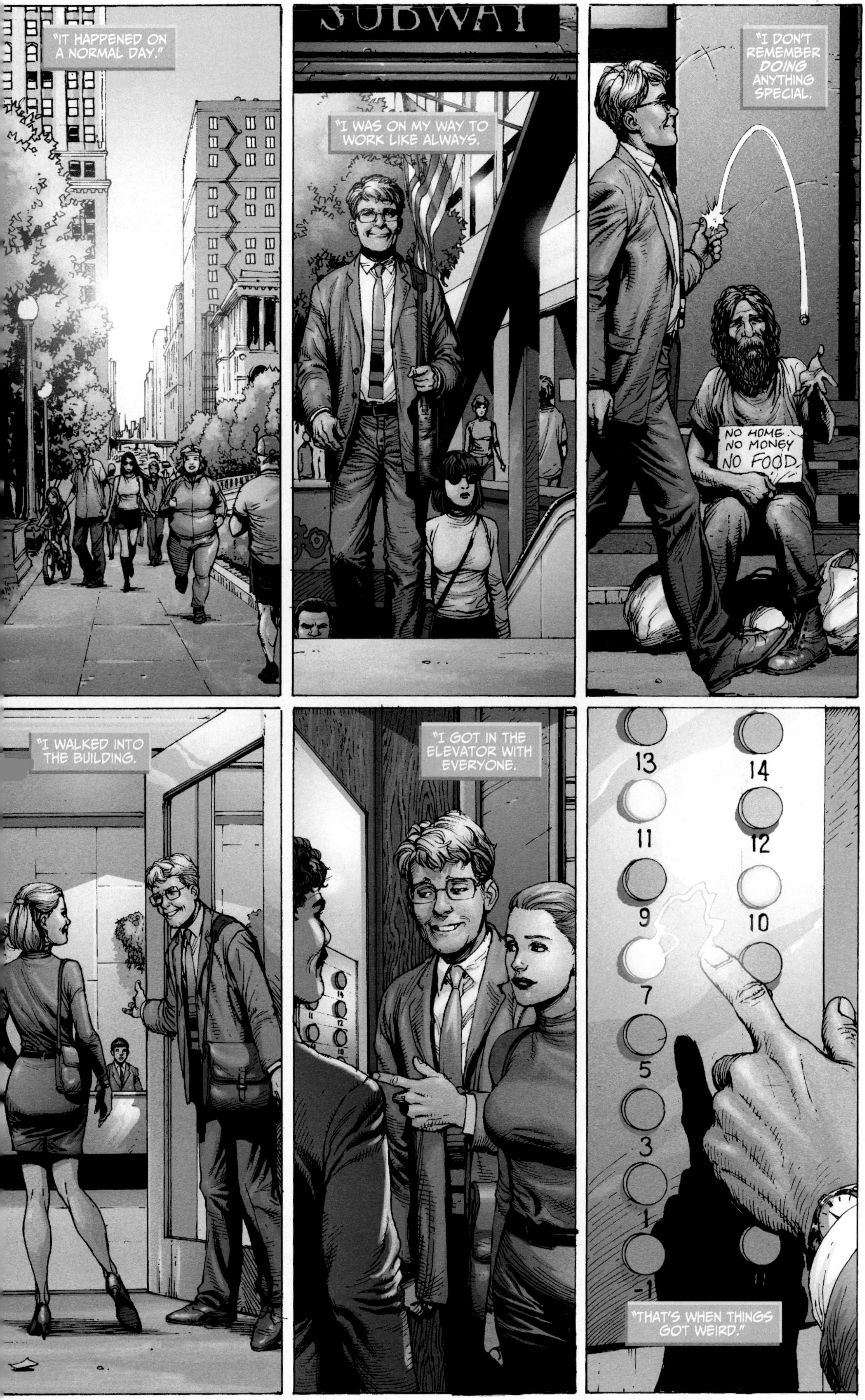
"IT HAPPENED ON A NORMAL DAY."
SUBWAY
"I WAS ON MY WAY TO WORK LIKE ALWAYS.
"I DON'T REMEMBER DOING ANYTHING SPECIAL.
NO HOME. NO MONEY NO FOOD
"I WALKED INTO THE BUILDING.
"I GOT IN THE ELEVATOR WITH EVERYONE.
13
14
11
12
9
10
7
5
3
1
-1
"THAT'S WHEN THINGS GOT WEIRD."

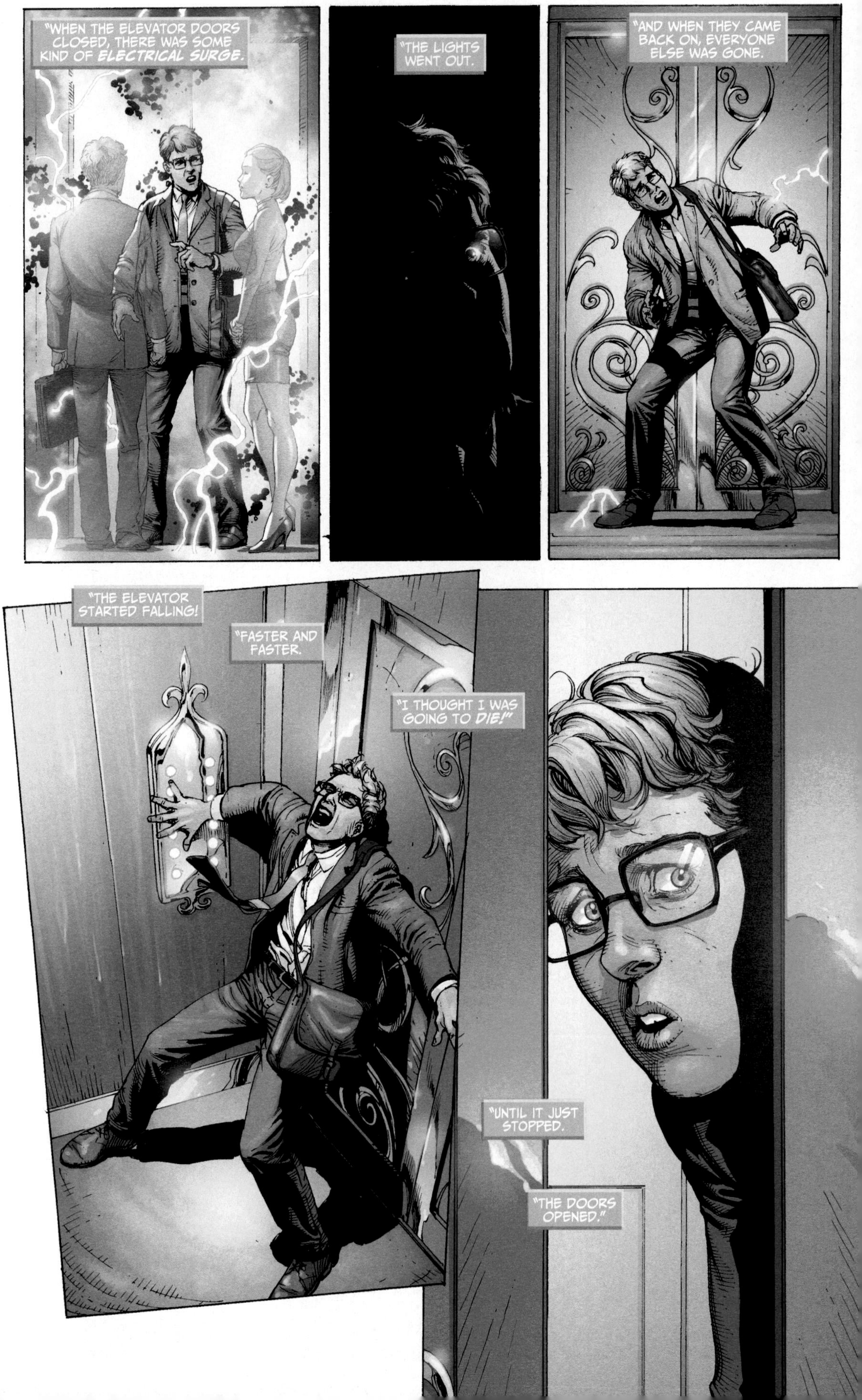

"WHEN THE ELEVATOR DOORS CLOSED, THERE WAS SOME KIND OF ELECTRICAL SURGE.
"THE LIGHTS WENT OUT.
"AND WHEN THEY CAME BACK ON, EVERYONE ELSE WAS GONE.
"THE ELEVATOR STARTED FALLING!
"FASTER AND FASTER.
"I THOUGHT I WAS GOING TO DIE!"
"UNTIL IT JUST STOPPED.
"THE DOORS OPENED."

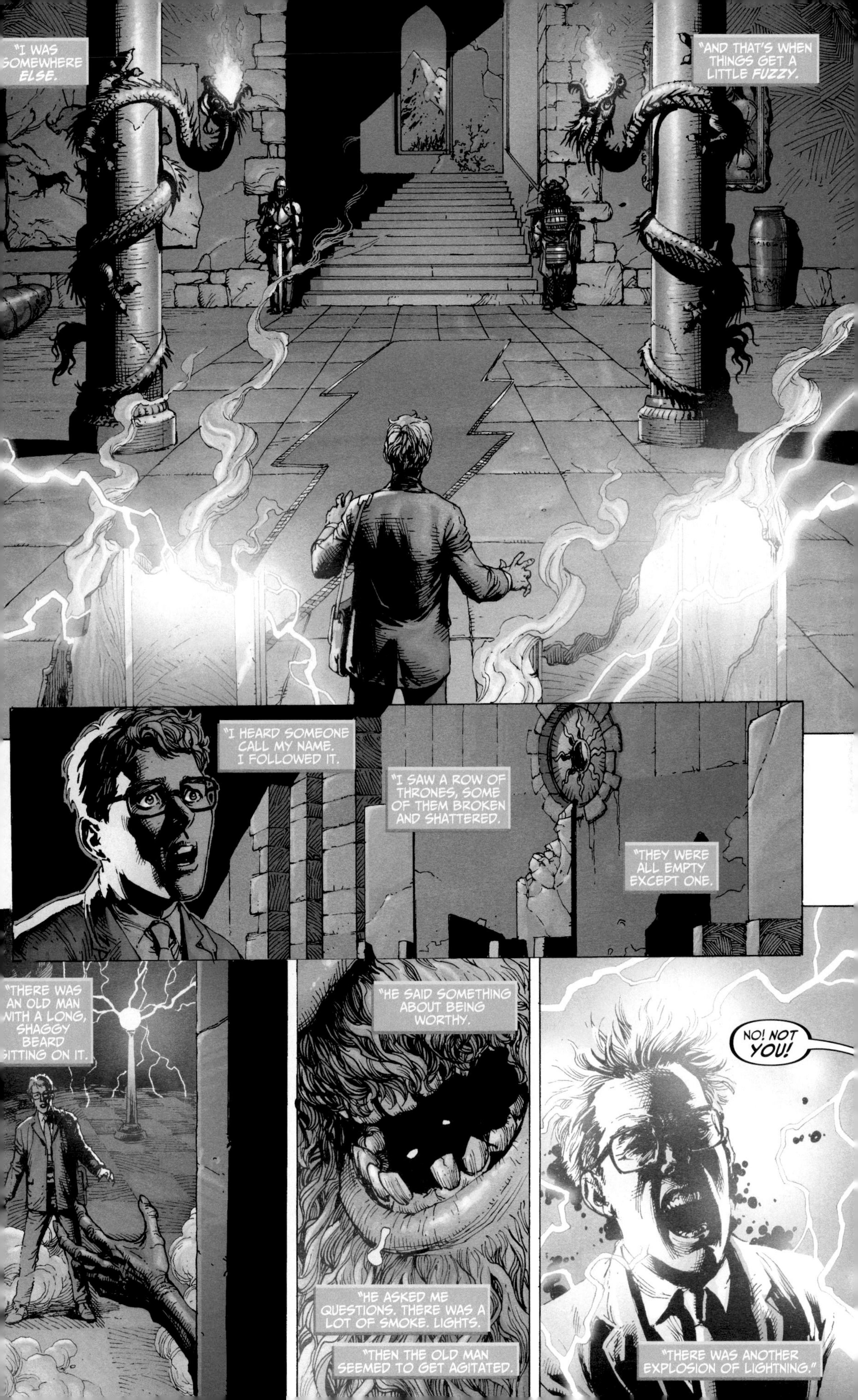
"I WAS SOMEWHERE ELSE.
"AND THAT'S WHEN THINGS GET A LITTLE FUZZY.
"I HEARD SOMEONE CALL MY NAME. I FOLLOWED IT.
"I SAW A ROW OF THRONES, SOME OF THEM BROKEN AND SHATTERED.
"THEY WERE ALL EMPTY EXCEPT ONE.
"THERE WAS AN OLD MAN WITH A LONG, SHAGGY BEARD SITTING ON IT.
"HE SAID SOMETHING ABOUT BEING WORTHY.
"HE ASKED ME QUESTIONS. THERE WAS A LOT OF SMOKE. LIGHTS.
"THEN THE OLD MAN SEEMED TO GET AGITATED.
NO! NOT YOU!
"THERE WAS ANOTHER EXPLOSION OF LIGHTNING."

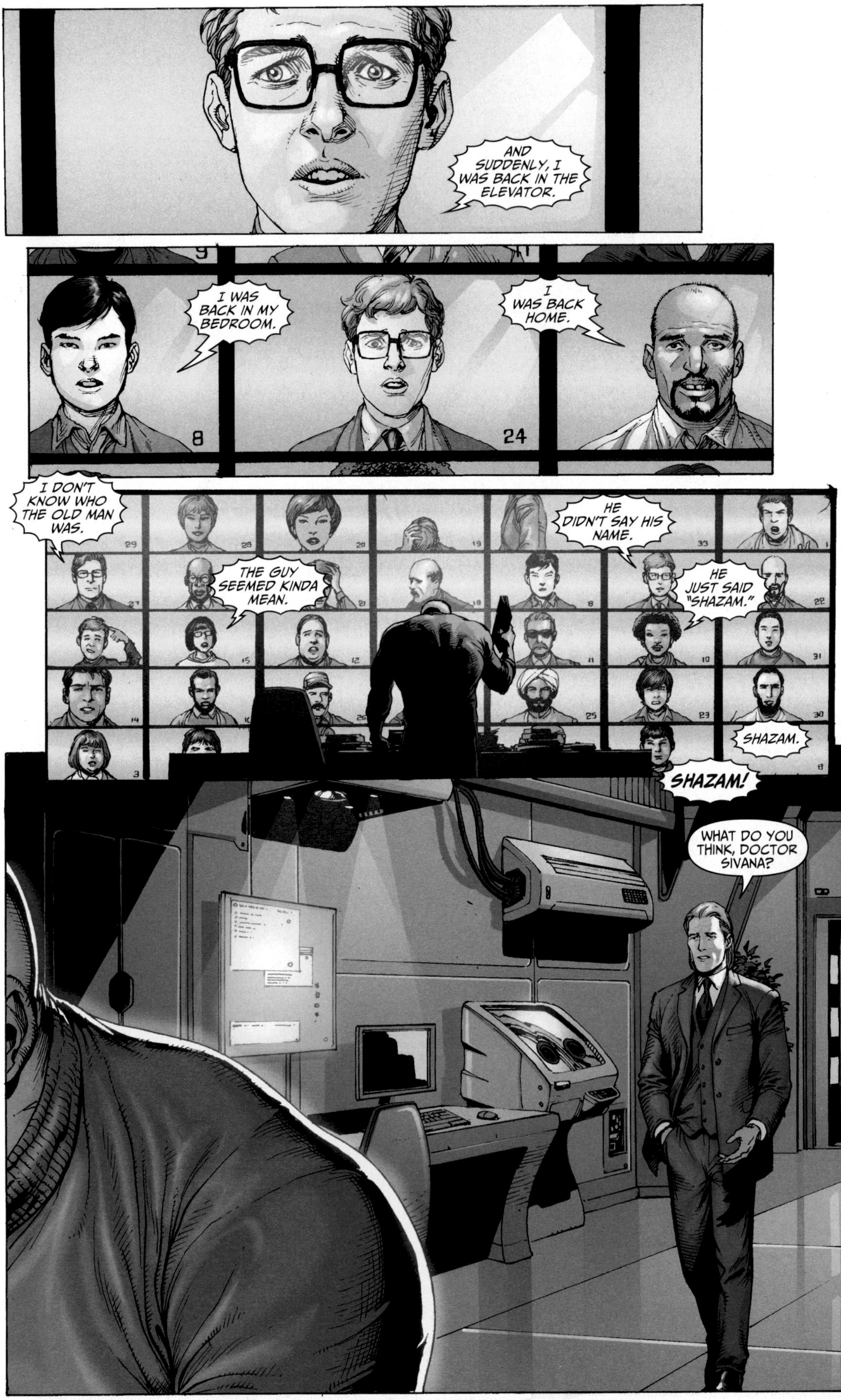
AND SUDDENLY, I WAS BACK IN THE ELEVATOR.
I WAS BACK IN MY BEDROOM.
I WAS BACK HOME.
I DON'T KNOW WHO THE OLD MAN WAS.
THE GUY SEEMED KINDA MEAN.
HE DIDN'T SAY HIS NAME.
HE JUST SAID "SHAZAM."
SHAZAM.
SHAZAM!
WHAT DO YOU THINK, DOCTOR SIVANA?

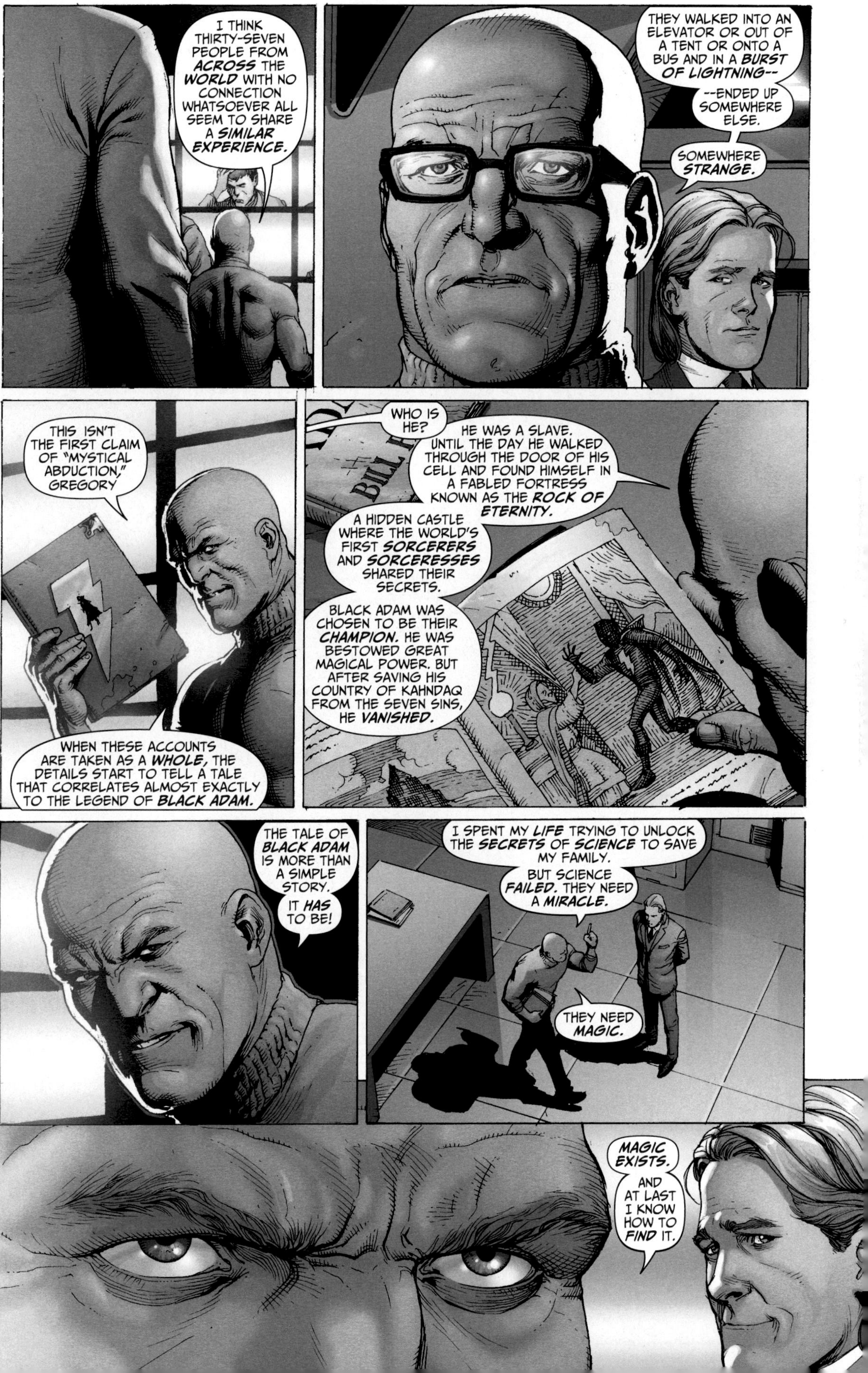
I THINK THIRTY-SEVEN PEOPLE FROM ACROSS THE WORLD WITH NO CONNECTION WHATSOEVER ALL SEEM TO SHARE A SIMILAR EXPERIENCE.
THEY WALKED INTO AN ELEVATOR OR OUT OF A TENT OR ONTO A BUS AND IN A BURST OF LIGHTNING--
--ENDED UP SOMEWHERE ELSE.
SOMEWHERE STRANGE.
THIS ISN'T THE FIRST CLAIM OF "MYSTICAL ABDUCTION," GREGORY
WHEN THESE ACCOUNTS ARE TAKEN AS A WHOLE, THE DETAILS START TO TELL A TALE THAT CORRELATES ALMOST EXACTLY TO THE LEGEND OF BLACK ADAM.
WHO IS HE?
HE WAS A SLAVE. UNTIL THE DAY HE WALKED THROUGH THE DOOR OF HIS CELL AND FOUND HIMSELF IN A FABLED FORTRESS KNOWN AS THE ROCK OF ETERNITY.
A HIDDEN CASTLE WHERE THE WORLD'S FIRST SORCERERS AND SORCERESSES SHARED THEIR SECRETS.
BLACK ADAM WAS CHOSEN TO BE THEIR CHAMPION. HE WAS BESTOWED GREAT MAGICAL POWER. BUT AFTER SAVING HIS COUNTRY OF KAHNDAQ FROM THE SEVEN SINS, HE VANISHED.
THE TALE OF BLACK ADAM IS MORE THAN A SIMPLE STORY.
IT HAS TO BE!
I SPENT MY LIFE TRYING TO UNLOCK THE SECRETS OF SCIENCE TO SAVE MY FAMILY.
BUT SCIENCE FAILED. THEY NEED A MIRACLE.
THEY NEED MAGIC.
MAGIC EXISTS.
AND AT LAST I KNOW HOW TO FIND IT.

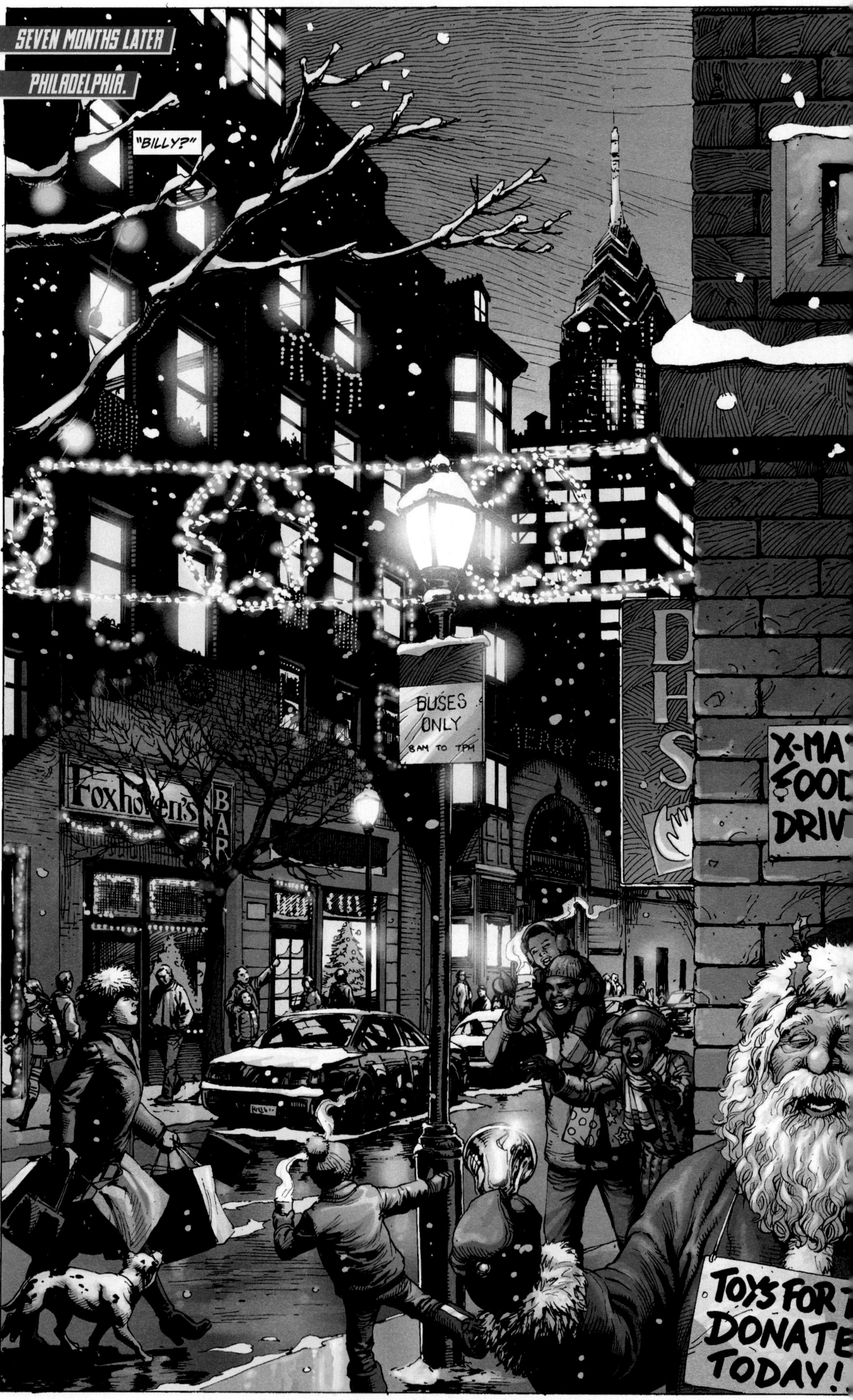
SEVEN MONTHS LATER
PHILADELPHIA.
"BILLY?"
BUSES ONLY 8AM TO 7PM
Foxhoven's
BAR
X-MA
FOOD
DRIV
TOYS FOR T
DONATE
TODAY!

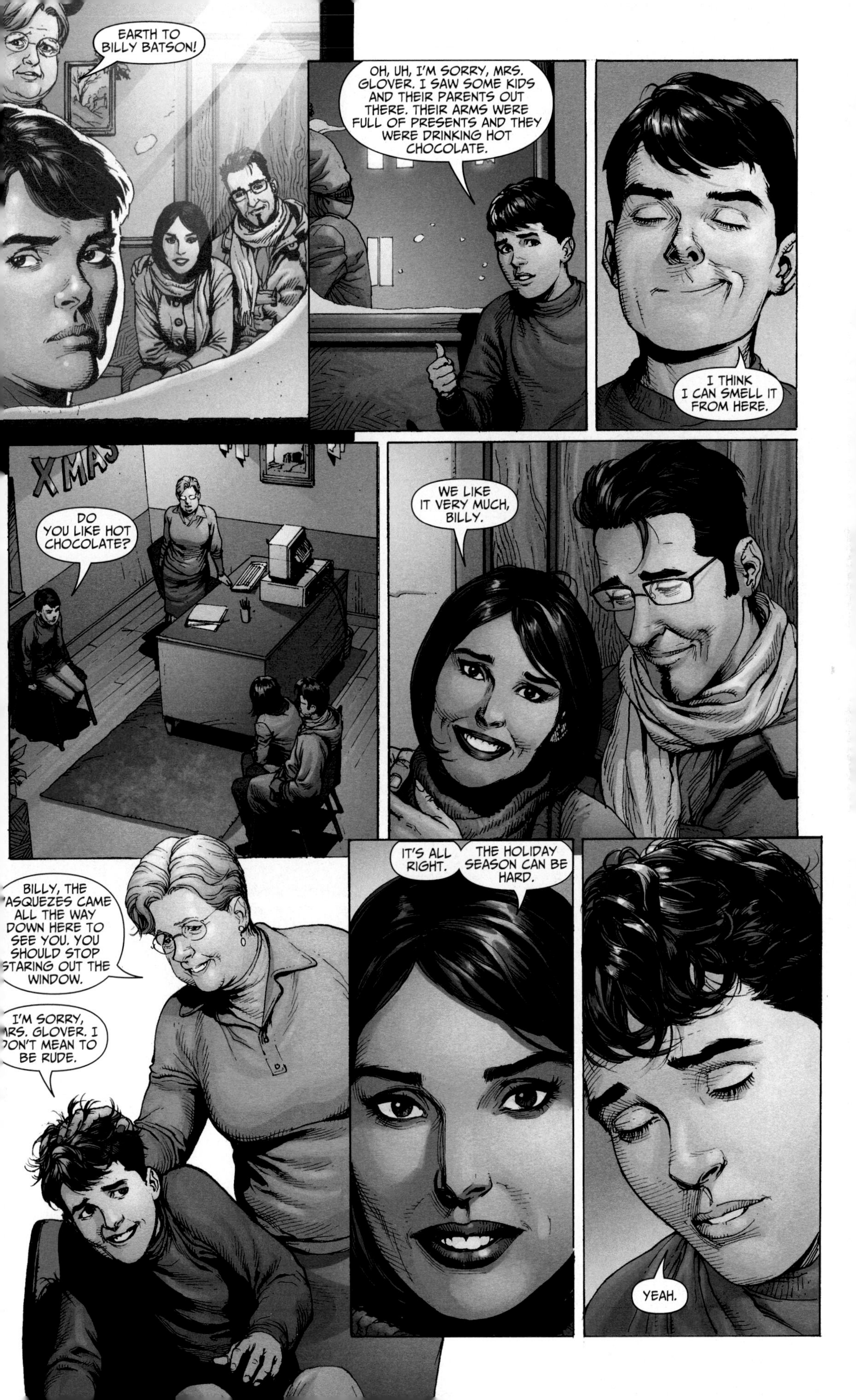
EARTH TO BILLY BATSON!
OH, UH, I'M SORRY, MRS. GLOVER. I SAW SOME KIDS AND THEIR PARENTS OUT THERE. THEIR ARMS WERE FULL OF PRESENTS AND THEY WERE DRINKING HOT CHOCOLATE.
I THINK I CAN SMELL IT FROM HERE.
XMAS
DO YOU LIKE HOT CHOCOLATE?
WE LIKE IT VERY MUCH, BILLY.
BILLY, THE VASQUEZES CAME ALL THE WAY DOWN HERE TO SEE YOU. YOU SHOULD STOP STARING OUT THE WINDOW.
I'M SORRY, MRS. GLOVER. I DON'T MEAN TO BE RUDE.
IT'S ALL RIGHT.
THE HOLIDAY SEASON CAN BE HARD.
YEAH.

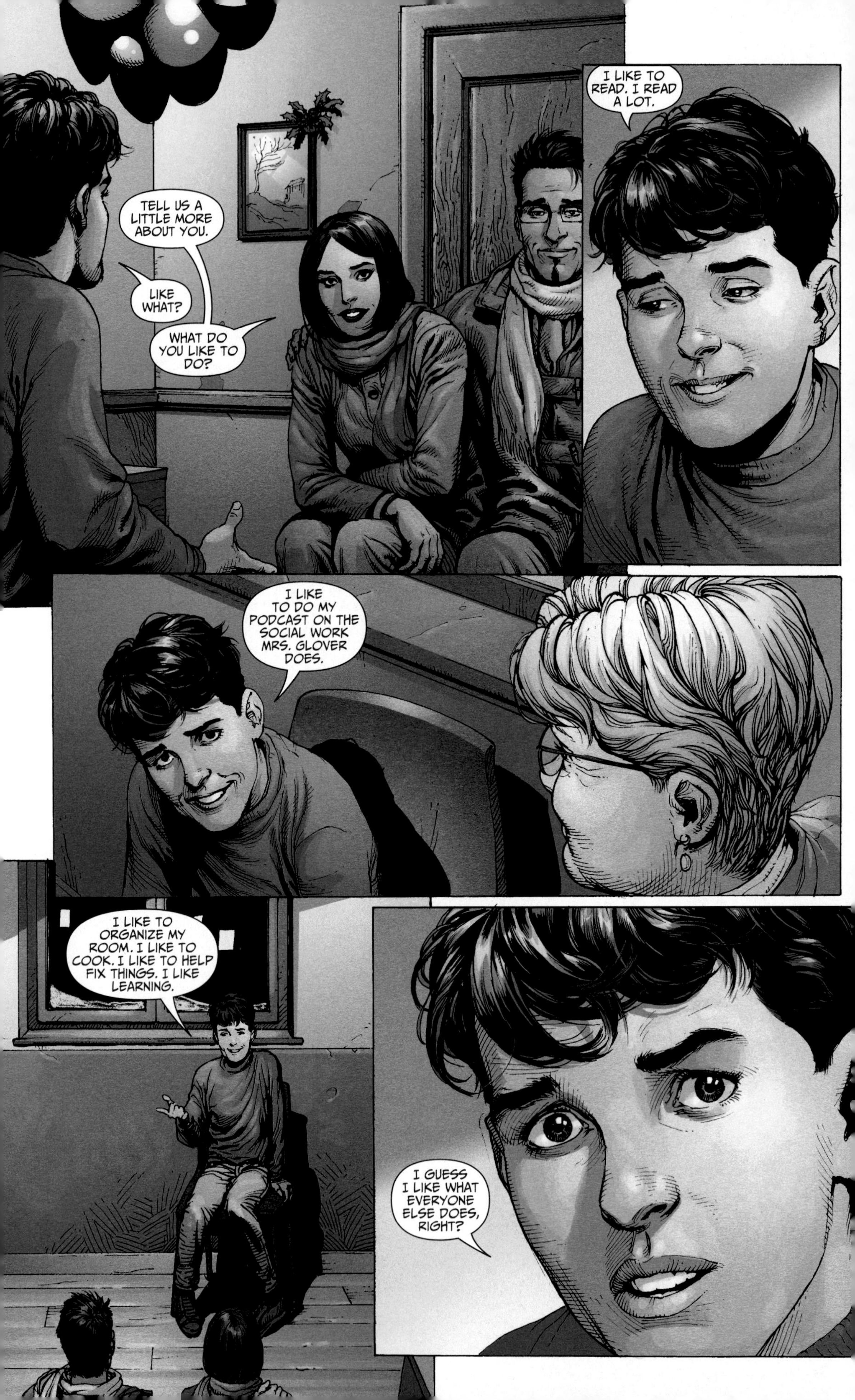
TELL US A LITTLE MORE ABOUT YOU.
LIKE WHAT?
WHAT DO YOU LIKE TO DO?
I LIKE TO READ. I READ A LOT.
I LIKE TO DO MY PODCAST ON THE SOCIAL WORK MRS. GLOVER DOES.
I LIKE TO ORGANIZE MY ROOM. I LIKE TO COOK. I LIKE TO HELP FIX THINGS. I LIKE LEARNING.
I GUESS I LIKE WHAT EVERYONE ELSE DOES, RIGHT?

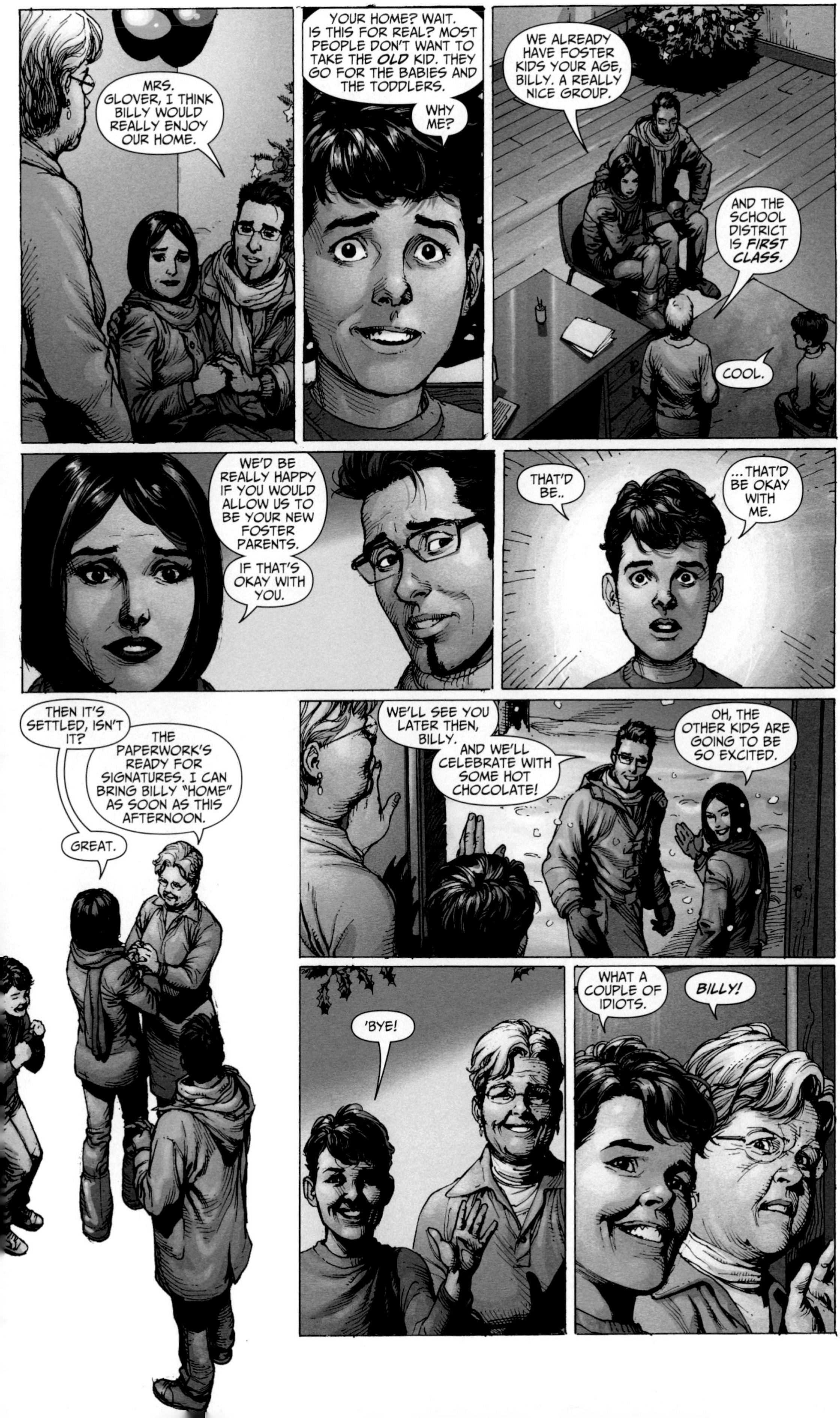
MRS. GLOVER, I THINK BILLY WOULD REALLY ENJOY OUR HOME.
YOUR HOME? WAIT. IS THIS FOR REAL? MOST PEOPLE DON'T WANT TO TAKE THE OLD KID. THEY GO FOR THE BABIES AND THE TODDLERS.
WHY ME?
WE ALREADY HAVE FOSTER KIDS YOUR AGE, BILLY. A REALLY NICE GROUP.
AND THE SCHOOL DISTRICT IS FIRST CLASS.
COOL.
WE'D BE REALLY HAPPY IF YOU WOULD ALLOW US TO BE YOUR NEW FOSTER PARENTS.
IF THAT'S OKAY WITH YOU.
THAT'D BE..
...THAT'D BE OKAY WITH ME.
THEN IT'S SETTLED, ISN'T IT?
THE PAPERWORK'S READY FOR SIGNATURES. I CAN BRING BILLY "HOME" AS SOON AS THIS AFTERNOON.
GREAT.
WE'LL SEE YOU LATER THEN, BILLY.
AND WE'LL CELEBRATE WITH SOME HOT CHOCOLATE!
OH, THE OTHER KIDS ARE GOING TO BE SO EXCITED.
'BYE!
WHAT A COUPLE OF IDIOTS.
BILLY!

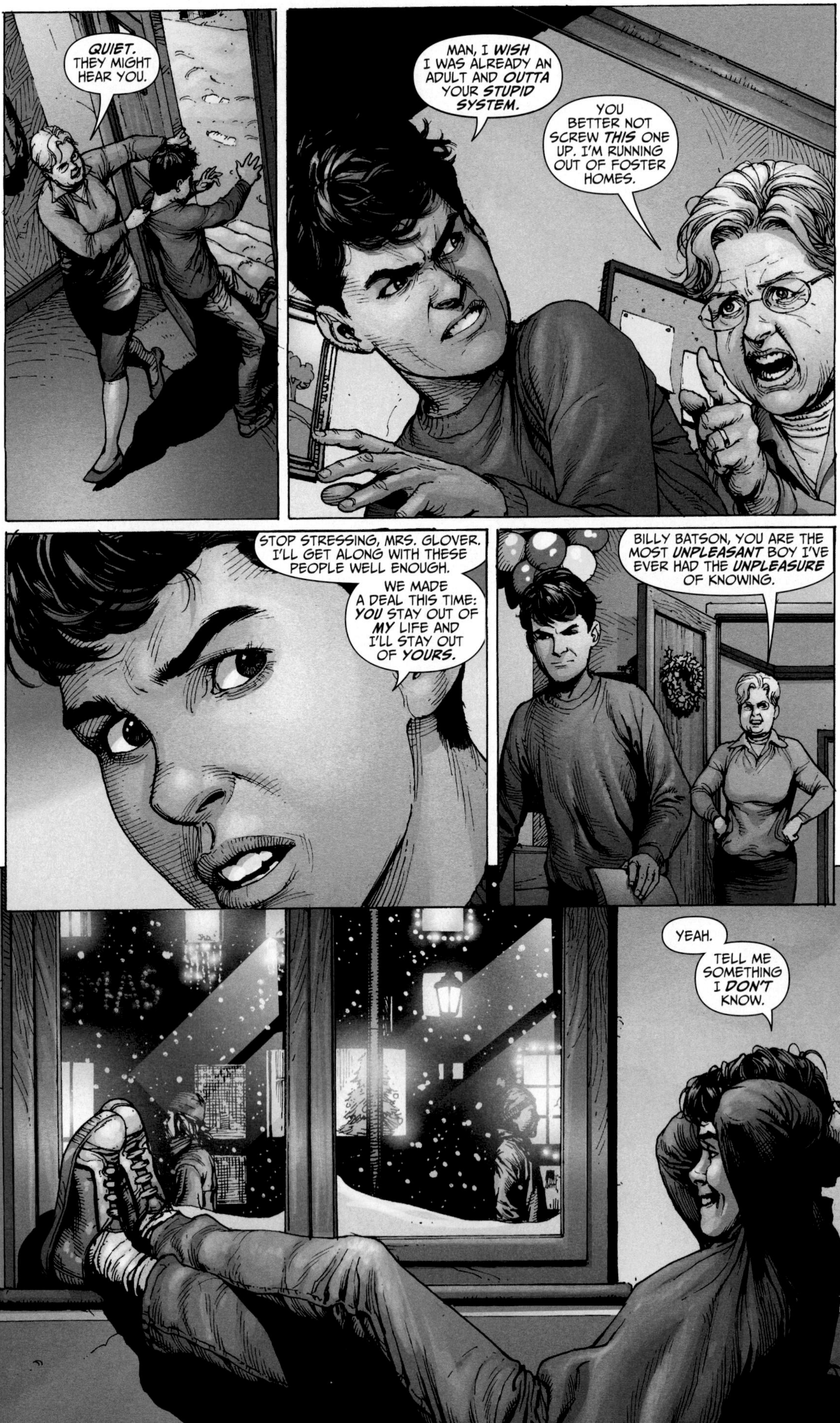
QUIET. THEY MIGHT HEAR YOU.
MAN, I WISH I WAS ALREADY AN ADULT AND OUTTA YOUR STUPID SYSTEM.
YOU BETTER NOT SCREW THIS ONE UP. I'M RUNNING OUT OF FOSTER HOMES.
STOP STRESSING, MRS. GLOVER. I'LL GET ALONG WITH THESE PEOPLE WELL ENOUGH.
WE MADE A DEAL THIS TIME: YOU STAY OUT OF MY LIFE AND I'LL STAY OUT OF YOURS.
BILLY BATSON, YOU ARE THE MOST UNPLEASANT BOY I'VE EVER HAD THE UNPLEASURE OF KNOWING.
YEAH.
TELL ME SOMETHING I DON'T KNOW.

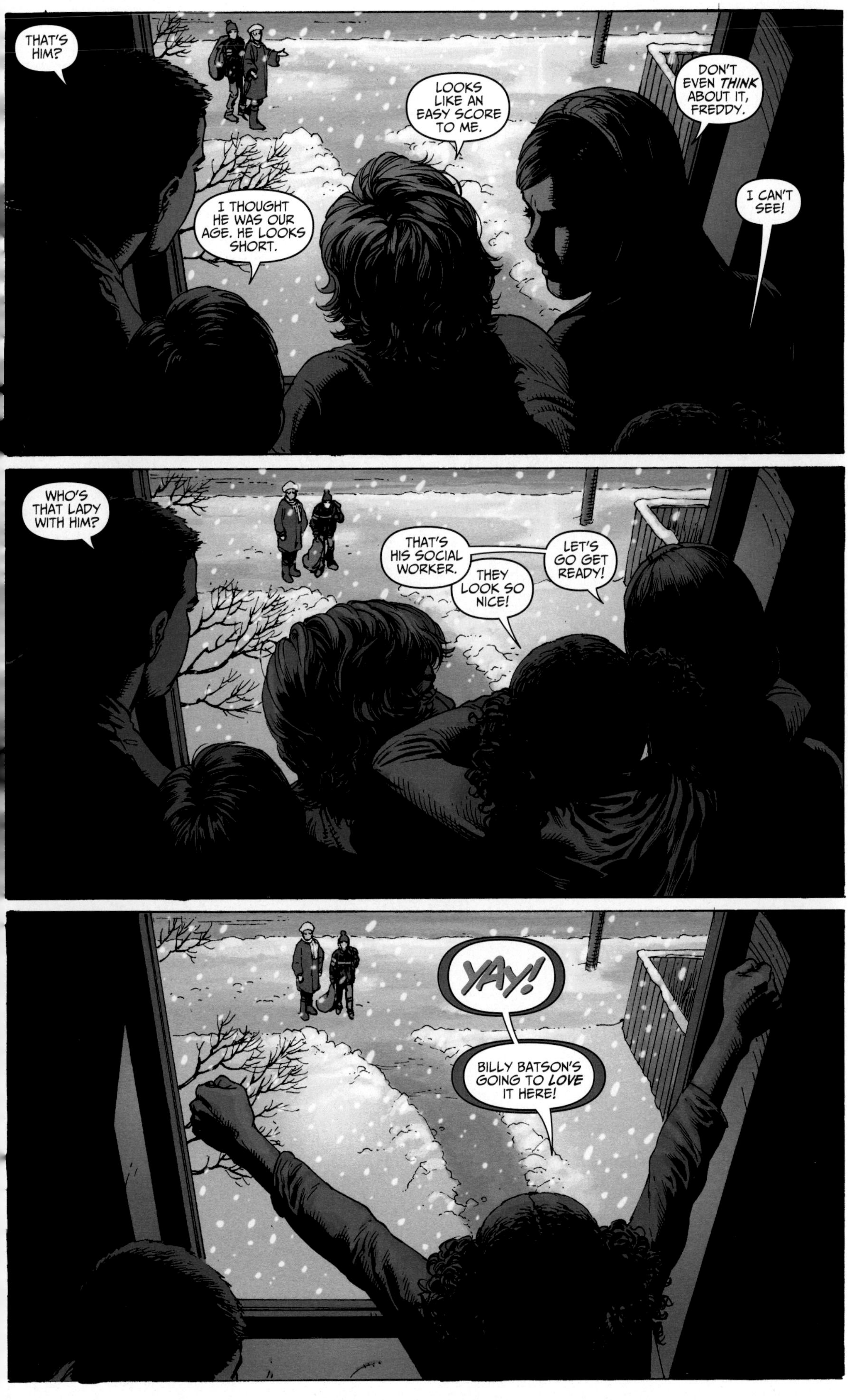
THAT'S HIM?
LOOKS LIKE AN EASY SCORE TO ME.
DON'T EVEN THINK ABOUT IT, FREDDY.
I THOUGHT HE WAS OUR AGE. HE LOOKS SHORT.
I CAN'T SEE!
WHO'S THAT LADY WITH HIM?
THAT'S HIS SOCIAL WORKER.
LET'S GO GET READY!
THEY LOOK SO NICE!
YAY!
BILLY BATSON'S GOING TO LOVE IT HERE!

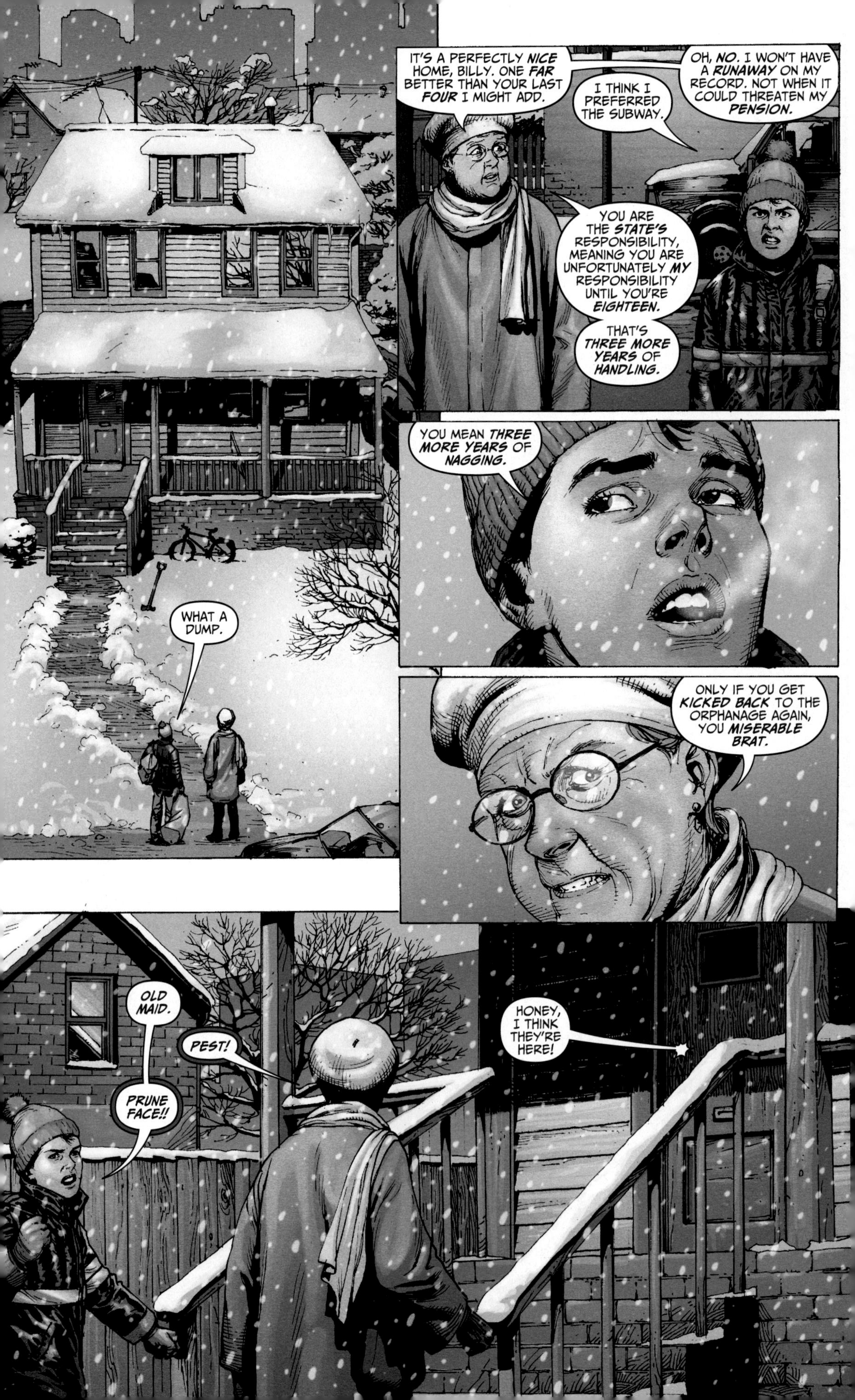
WHAT A DUMP.
IT'S A PERFECTLY NICE HOME, BILLY. ONE FAR BETTER THAN YOUR LAST FOUR I MIGHT ADD.
I THINK I PREFERRED THE SUBWAY.
OH, NO. I WON'T HAVE A RUNAWAY ON MY RECORD. NOT WHEN IT COULD THREATEN MY PENSION.
YOU ARE THE STATE'S RESPONSIBILITY, MEANING YOU ARE UNFORTUNATELY MY RESPONSIBILITY UNTIL YOU'RE EIGHTEEN.
THAT'S THREE MORE YEARS OF HANDLING.
YOU MEAN THREE MORE YEARS OF NAGGING.
ONLY IF YOU GET KICKED BACK TO THE ORPHANAGE AGAIN, YOU MISERABLE BRAT.
OLD MAID.
PEST!
PRUNE FACE!!
HONEY, I THINK THEY'RE HERE!

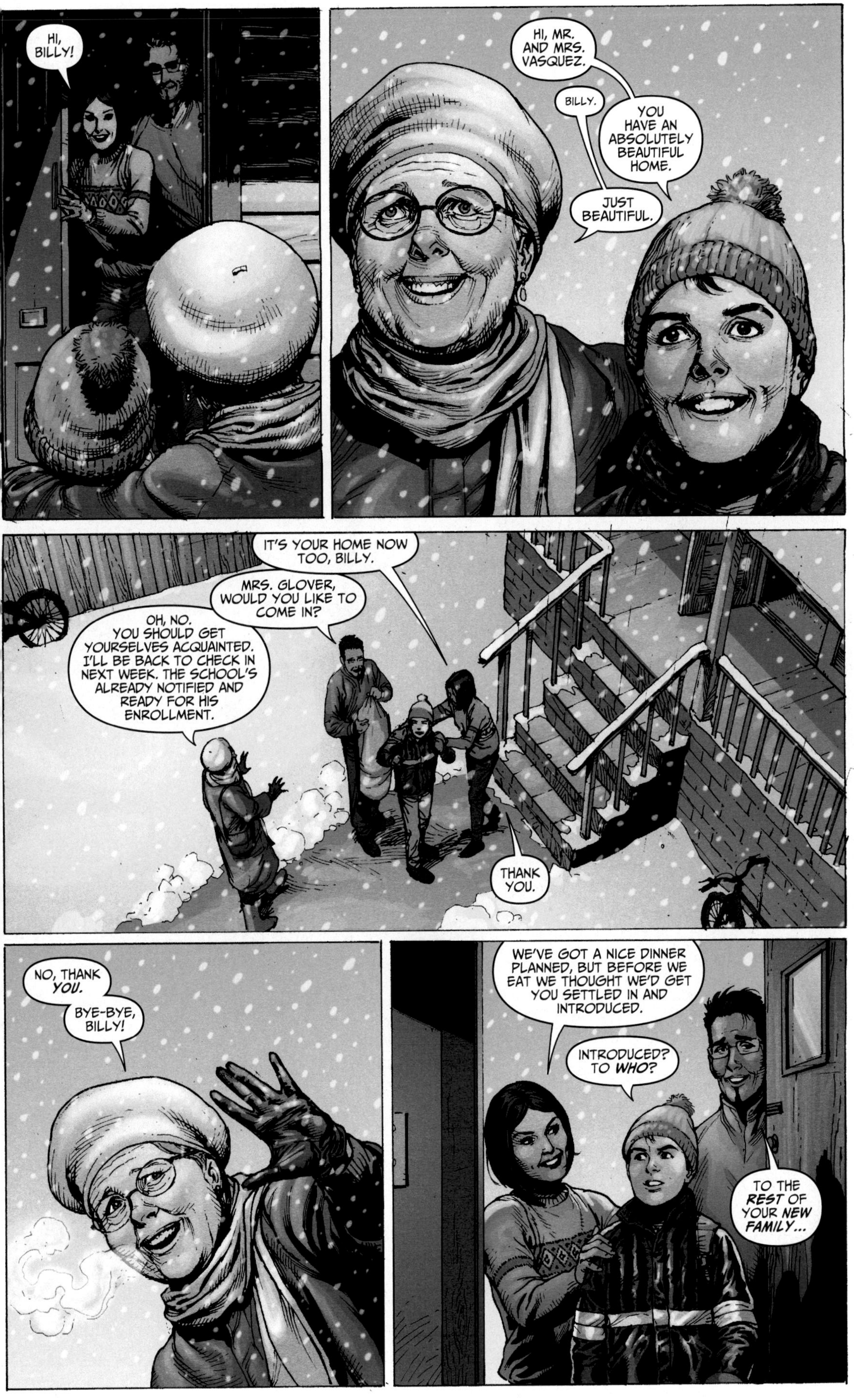
HI, BILLY!
HI, MR. AND MRS. VASQUEZ.
BILLY.
YOU HAVE AN ABSOLUTELY BEAUTIFUL HOME.
JUST BEAUTIFUL.
IT'S YOUR HOME NOW TOO, BILLY.
MRS. GLOVER, WOULD YOU LIKE TO COME IN?
OH, NO. YOU SHOULD GET YOURSELVES ACQUAINTED. I'LL BE BACK TO CHECK IN NEXT WEEK. THE SCHOOL'S ALREADY NOTIFIED AND READY FOR HIS ENROLLMENT.
THANK YOU.
NO, THANK *YOU.*
BYE-BYE, BILLY!
WE'VE GOT A NICE DINNER PLANNED, BUT BEFORE WE EAT WE THOUGHT WE'D GET YOU SETTLED IN AND INTRODUCED.
INTRODUCED? TO *WHO*?
TO THE *REST* OF YOUR *NEW FAMILY...*

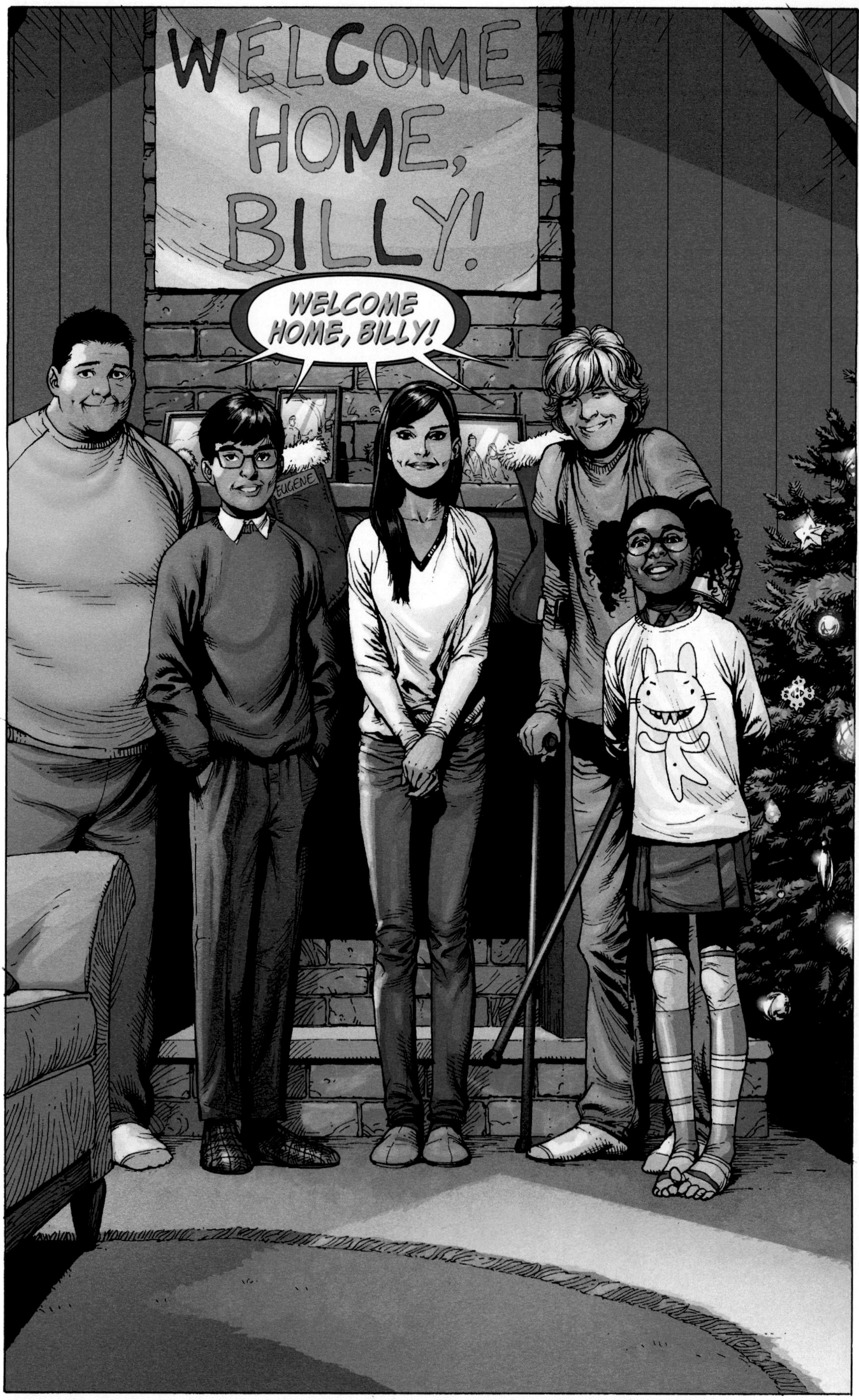
WELCOME HOME, BILLY!
WELCOME HOME, BILLY!
EUGENE

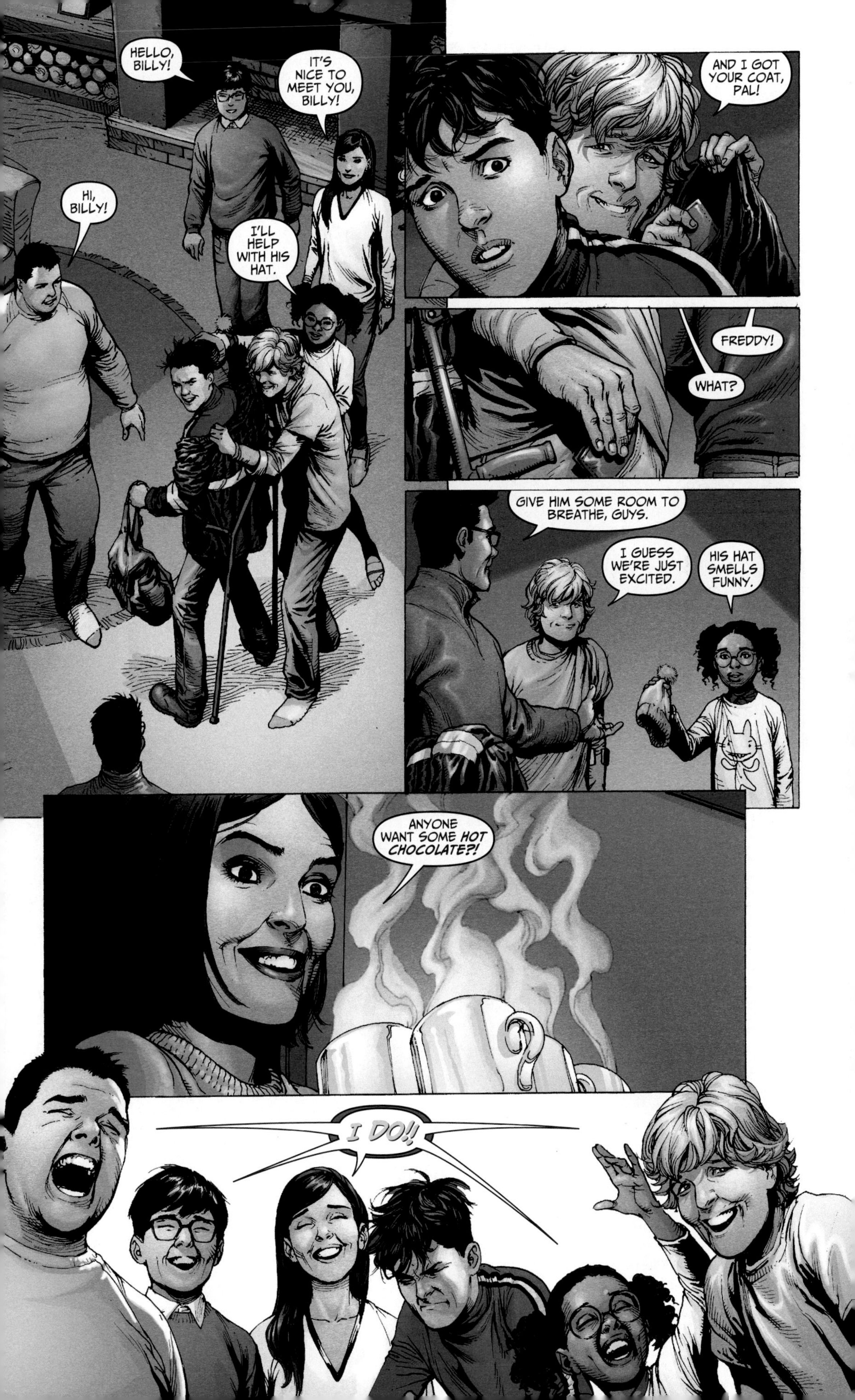
HELLO, BILLY!
IT'S NICE TO MEET YOU, BILLY!
HI, BILLY!
I'LL HELP WITH HIS HAT.
AND I GOT YOUR COAT, PAL!
FREDDY!
WHAT?
GIVE HIM SOME ROOM TO BREATHE, GUYS.
I GUESS WE'RE JUST EXCITED.
HIS HAT SMELLS FUNNY.
ANYONE WANT SOME HOT CHOCOLATE?!
I DO!!

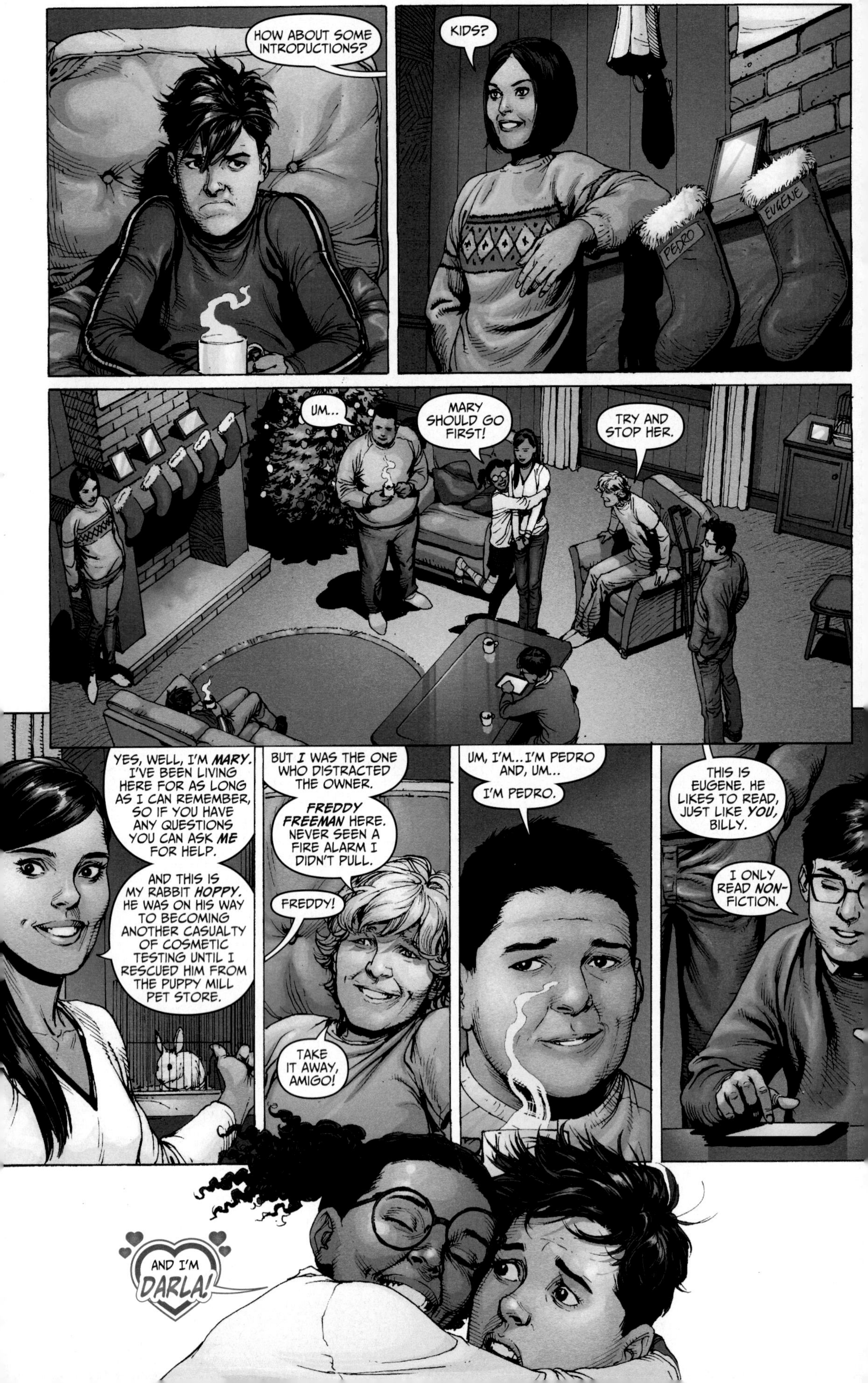
HOW ABOUT SOME INTRODUCTIONS?
KIDS?
PEDRO
EUGENE
UM...
MARY SHOULD GO FIRST!
TRY AND STOP HER.
YES, WELL, I'M MARY. I'VE BEEN LIVING HERE FOR AS LONG AS I CAN REMEMBER, SO IF YOU HAVE ANY QUESTIONS YOU CAN ASK ME FOR HELP.
AND THIS IS MY RABBIT HOPPY. HE WAS ON HIS WAY TO BECOMING ANOTHER CASUALTY OF COSMETIC TESTING UNTIL I RESCUED HIM FROM THE PUPPY MILL PET STORE.
BUT I WAS THE ONE WHO DISTRACTED THE OWNER.
FREDDY FREEMAN HERE. NEVER SEEN A FIRE ALARM I DIDN'T PULL.
FREDDY!
TAKE IT AWAY, AMIGO!
UM, I'M...I'M PEDRO AND, UM...
I'M PEDRO.
THIS IS EUGENE. HE LIKES TO READ, JUST LIKE YOU, BILLY.
I ONLY READ NON-FICTION.
AND I'M DARLA!

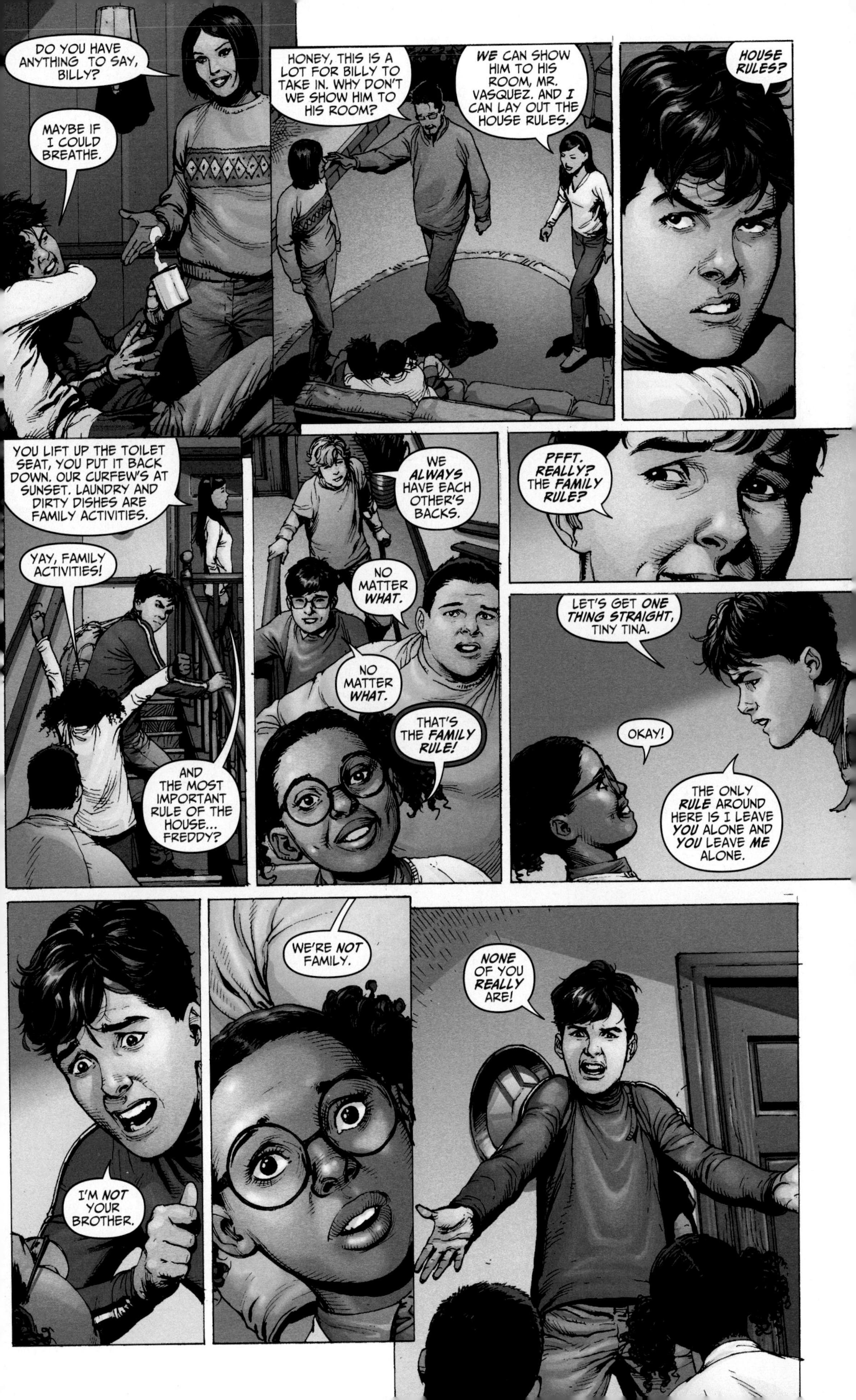

DO YOU HAVE ANYTHING TO SAY, BILLY?
MAYBE IF I COULD BREATHE.
HONEY, THIS IS A LOT FOR BILLY TO TAKE IN. WHY DON'T WE SHOW HIM TO HIS ROOM?
WE CAN SHOW HIM TO HIS ROOM, MR. VASQUEZ. AND I CAN LAY OUT THE HOUSE RULES.
HOUSE RULES?
YOU LIFT UP THE TOILET SEAT, YOU PUT IT BACK DOWN. OUR CURFEW'S AT SUNSET. LAUNDRY AND DIRTY DISHES ARE FAMILY ACTIVITIES.
YAY, FAMILY ACTIVITIES!
AND THE MOST IMPORTANT RULE OF THE HOUSE... FREDDY?
WE ALWAYS HAVE EACH OTHER'S BACKS.
NO MATTER WHAT.
NO MATTER WHAT.
THAT'S THE FAMILY RULE!
PFFT. REALLY? THE FAMILY RULE?
LET'S GET ONE THING STRAIGHT, TINY TINA.
OKAY!
THE ONLY RULE AROUND HERE IS I LEAVE YOU ALONE AND YOU LEAVE ME ALONE.
I'M NOT YOUR BROTHER.
WE'RE NOT FAMILY.
NONE OF YOU REALLY ARE!

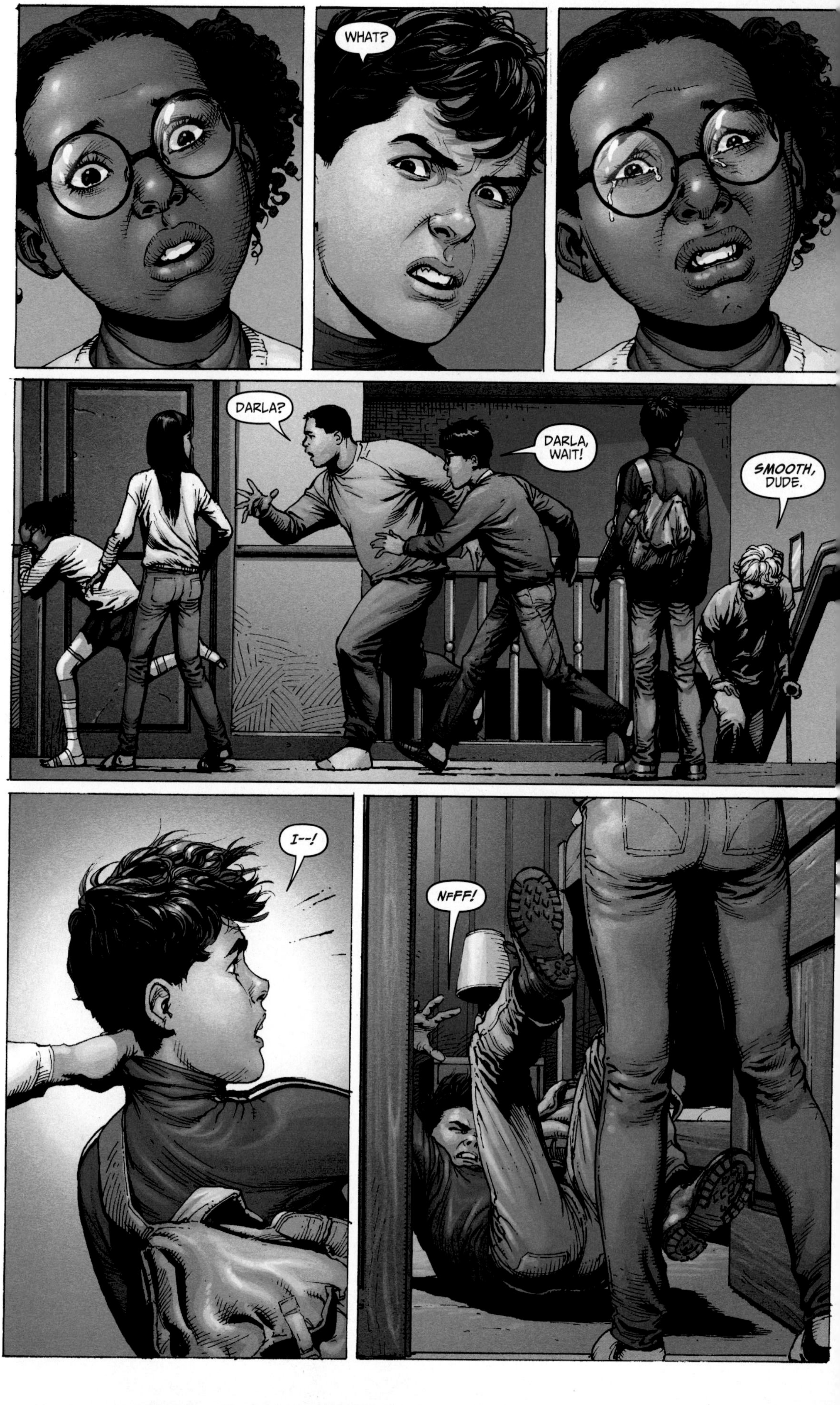
WHAT?
DARLA?
DARLA, WAIT!
SMOOTH, DUDE.
I--!
NFFF!

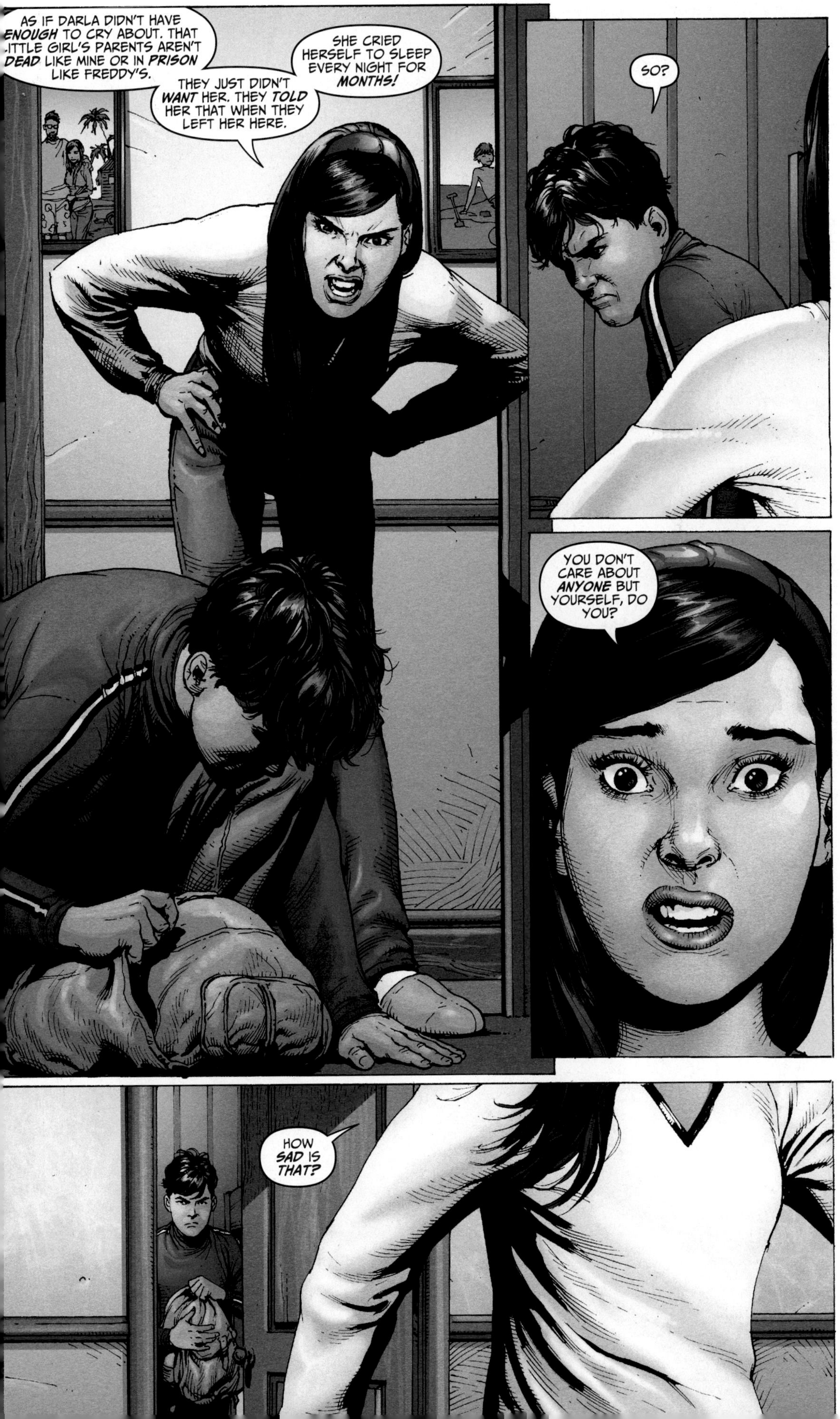
AS IF DARLA DIDN'T HAVE ENOUGH TO CRY ABOUT. THAT LITTLE GIRL'S PARENTS AREN'T DEAD LIKE MINE OR IN PRISON LIKE FREDDY'S.
SHE CRIED HERSELF TO SLEEP EVERY NIGHT FOR MONTHS!
THEY JUST DIDN'T WANT HER. THEY TOLD HER THAT WHEN THEY LEFT HER HERE.
SO?
YOU DON'T CARE ABOUT ANYONE BUT YOURSELF, DO YOU?
HOW SAD IS THAT?

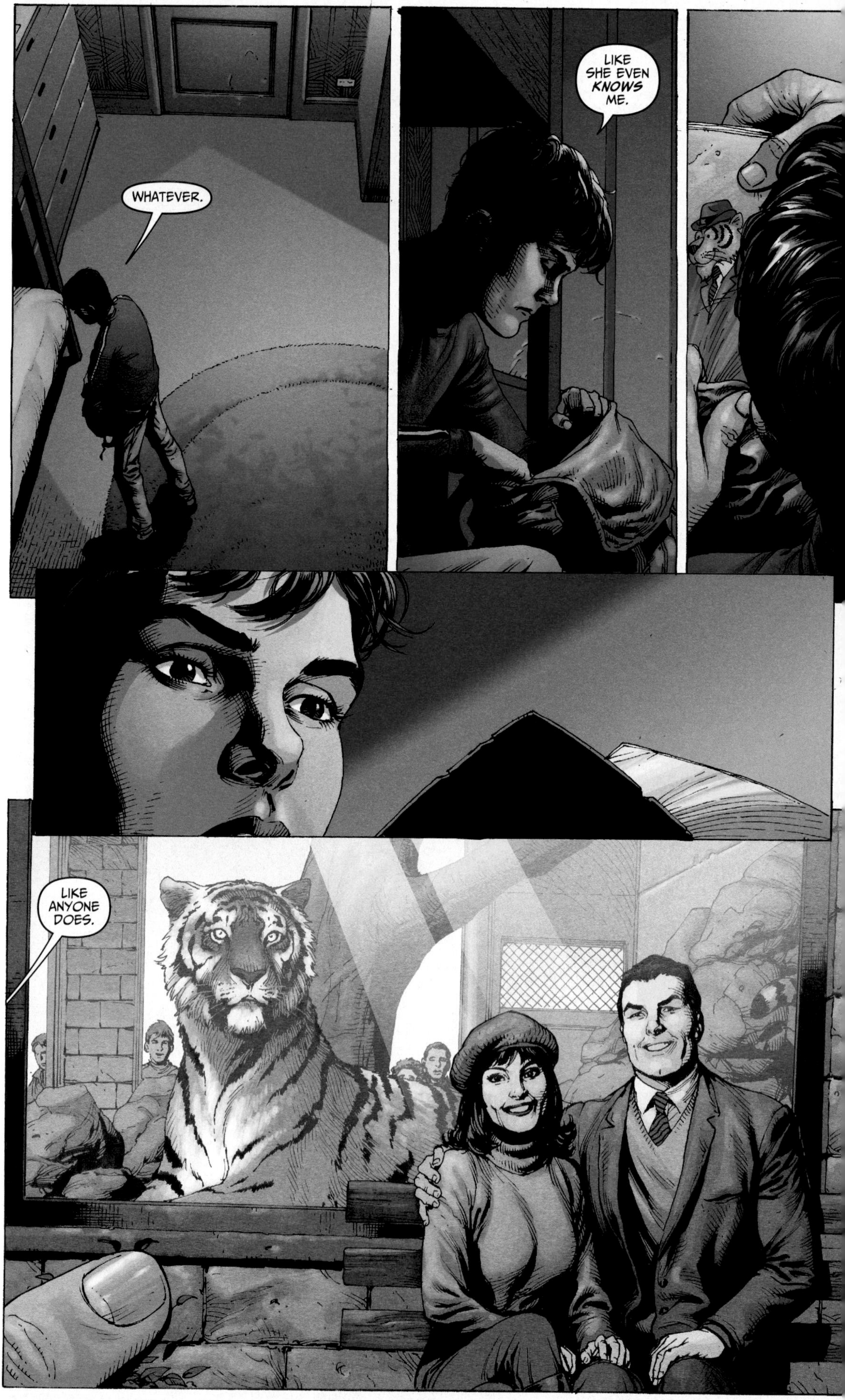
WHATEVER.
LIKE SHE EVEN KNOWS ME.
LIKE ANYONE DOES.

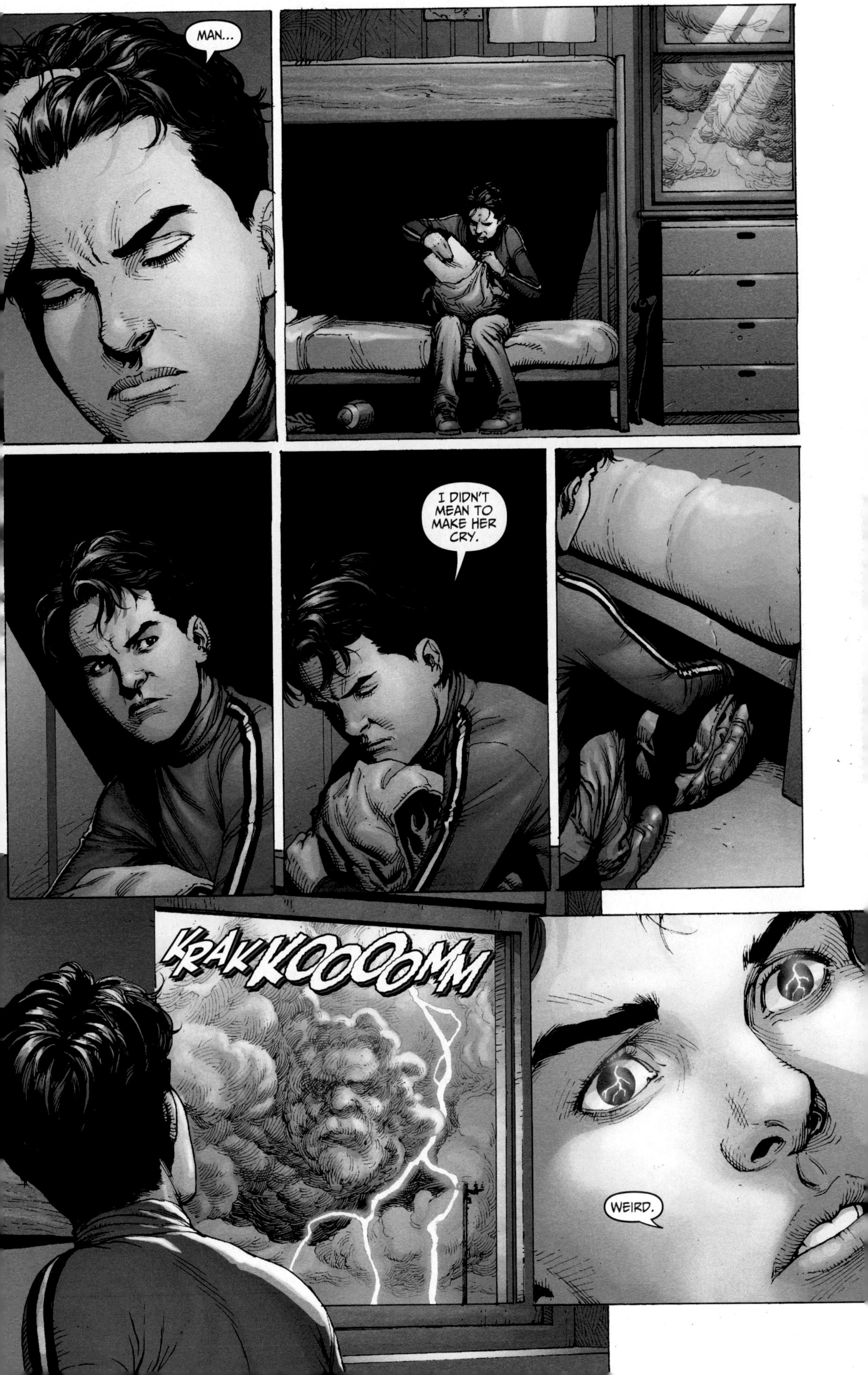
MAN...
I DIDN'T MEAN TO MAKE HER CRY.
KRAKKOOOOMM
WEIRD.

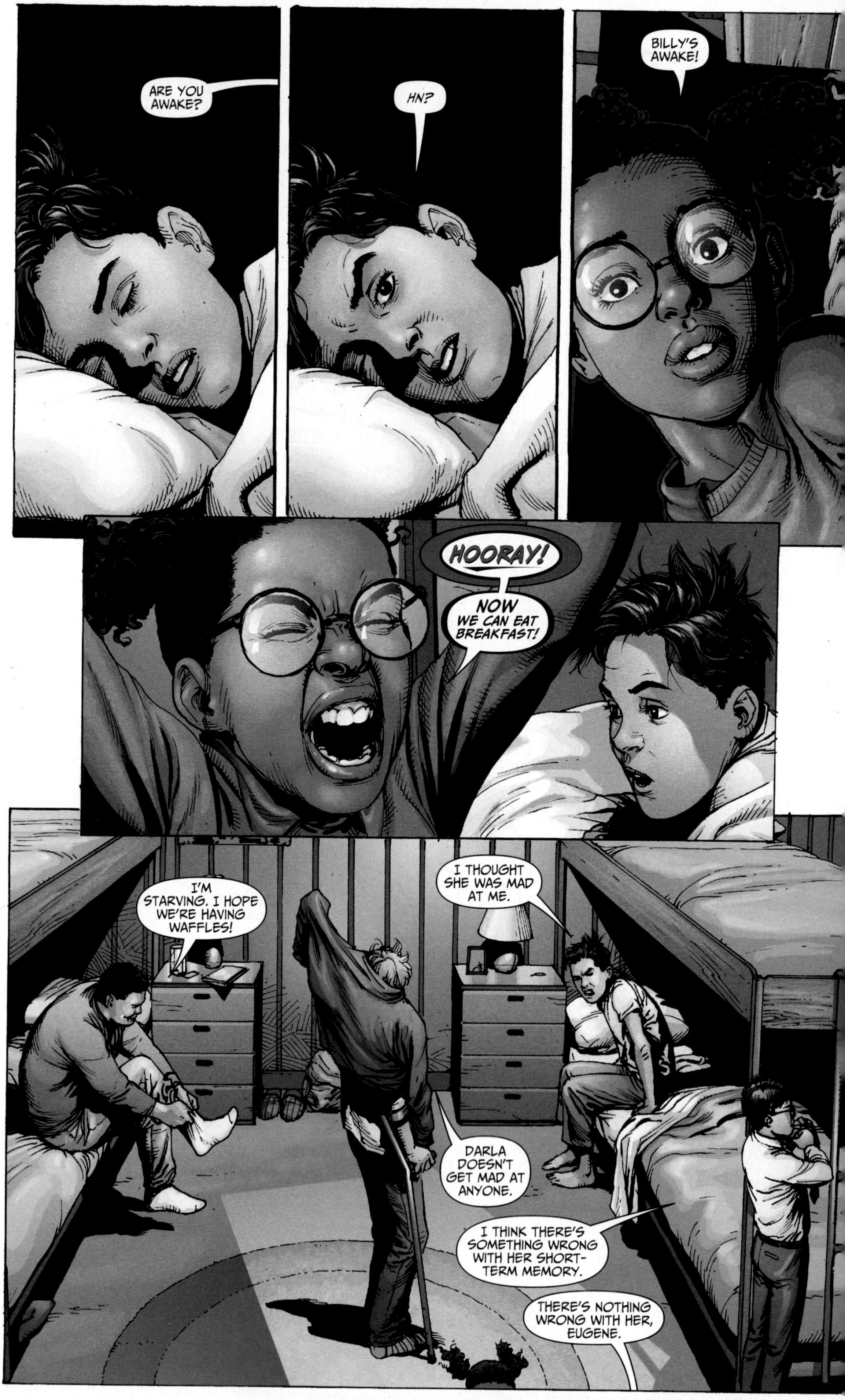
ARE YOU AWAKE?
HN?
BILLY'S AWAKE!
HOORAY!
NOW WE CAN EAT BREAKFAST!
I'M STARVING. I HOPE WE'RE HAVING WAFFLES!
I THOUGHT SHE WAS MAD AT ME.
DARLA DOESN'T GET MAD AT ANYONE.
I THINK THERE'S SOMETHING WRONG WITH HER SHORT-TERM MEMORY.
THERE'S NOTHING WRONG WITH HER, EUGENE.

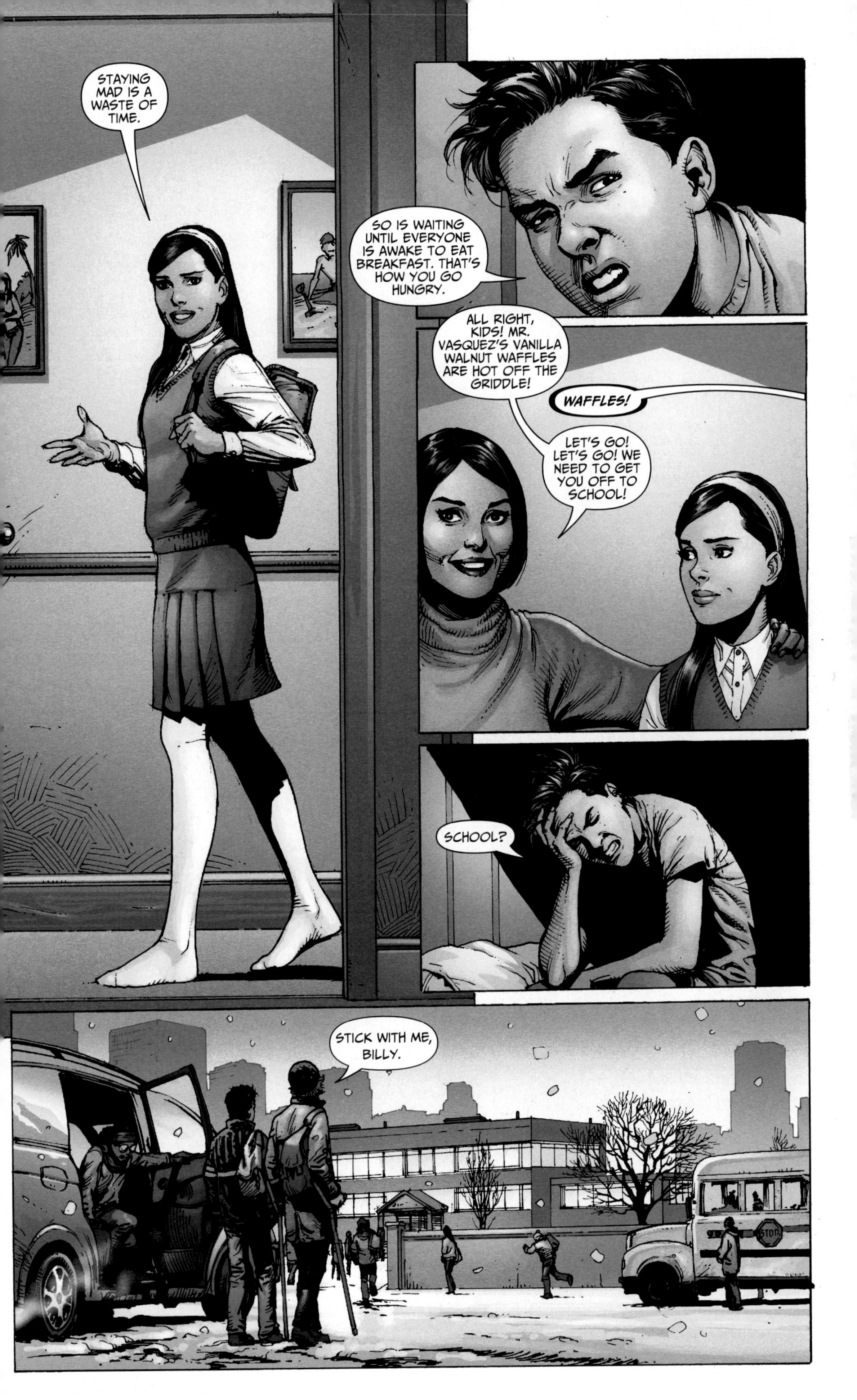
STAYING MAD IS A WASTE OF TIME.
SO IS WAITING UNTIL EVERYONE IS AWAKE TO EAT BREAKFAST. THAT'S HOW YOU GO HUNGRY.
ALL RIGHT, KIDS! MR. VASQUEZ'S VANILLA WALNUT WAFFLES ARE HOT OFF THE GRIDDLE!
WAFFLES!
LET'S GO! LET'S GO! WE NEED TO GET YOU OFF TO SCHOOL!
SCHOOL?
STICK WITH ME, BILLY.

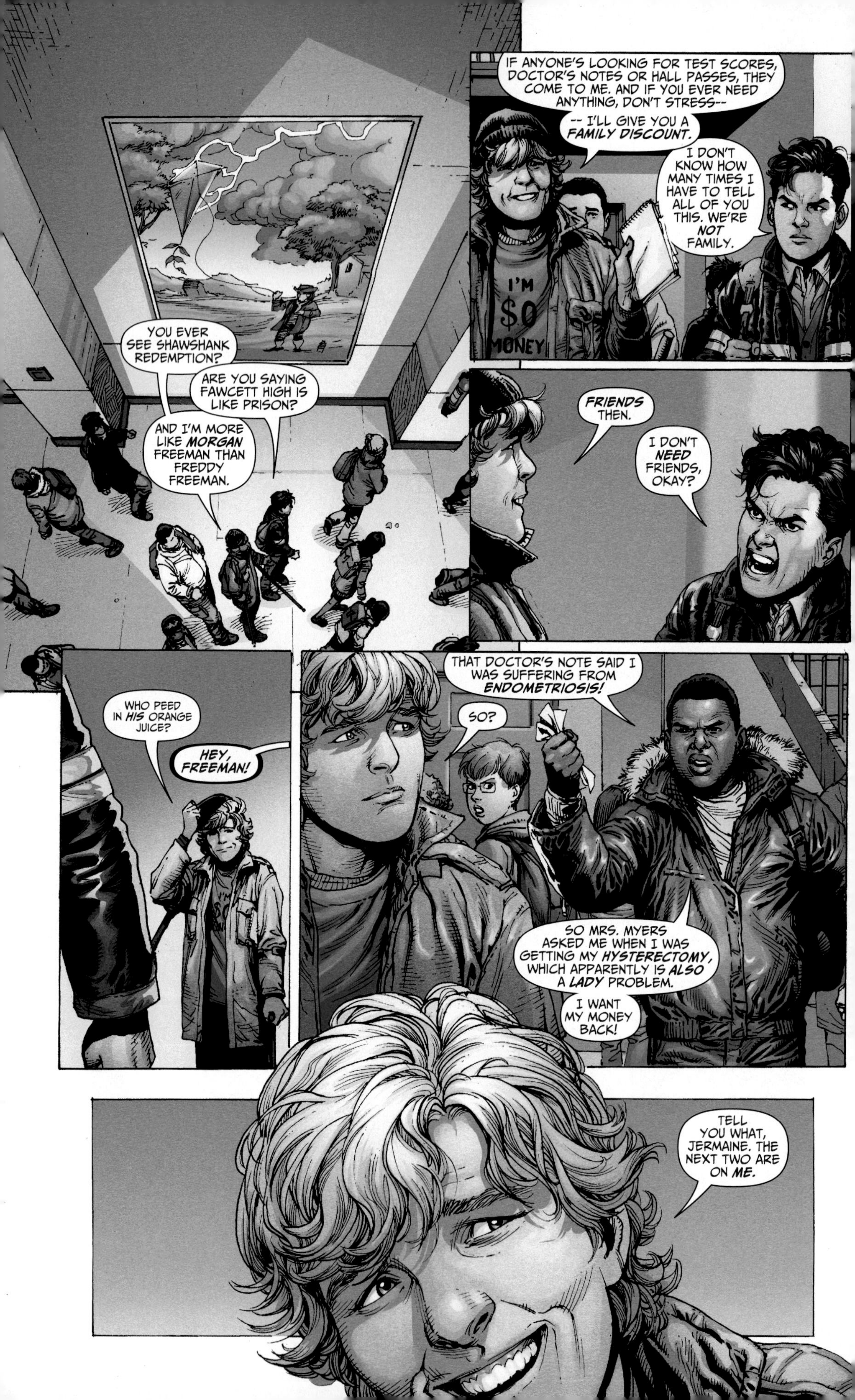

YOU EVER SEE SHAWSHANK REDEMPTION?
ARE YOU SAYING FAWCETT HIGH IS LIKE PRISON?
AND I'M MORE LIKE MORGAN FREEMAN THAN FREDDY FREEMAN.
IF ANYONE'S LOOKING FOR TEST SCORES, DOCTOR'S NOTES OR HALL PASSES, THEY COME TO ME. AND IF YOU EVER NEED ANYTHING, DON'T STRESS--
-- I'LL GIVE YOU A FAMILY DISCOUNT.
I DON'T KNOW HOW MANY TIMES I HAVE TO TELL ALL OF YOU THIS. WE'RE NOT FAMILY.
I'M $0 MONEY
FRIENDS THEN.
I DON'T NEED FRIENDS, OKAY?
WHO PEED IN HIS ORANGE JUICE?
HEY, FREEMAN!
THAT DOCTOR'S NOTE SAID I WAS SUFFERING FROM ENDOMETRIOSIS!
SO?
SO MRS. MYERS ASKED ME WHEN I WAS GETTING MY HYSTERECTOMY, WHICH APPARENTLY IS ALSO A LADY PROBLEM.
I WANT MY MONEY BACK!
TELL YOU WHAT, JERMAINE. THE NEXT TWO ARE ON ME.

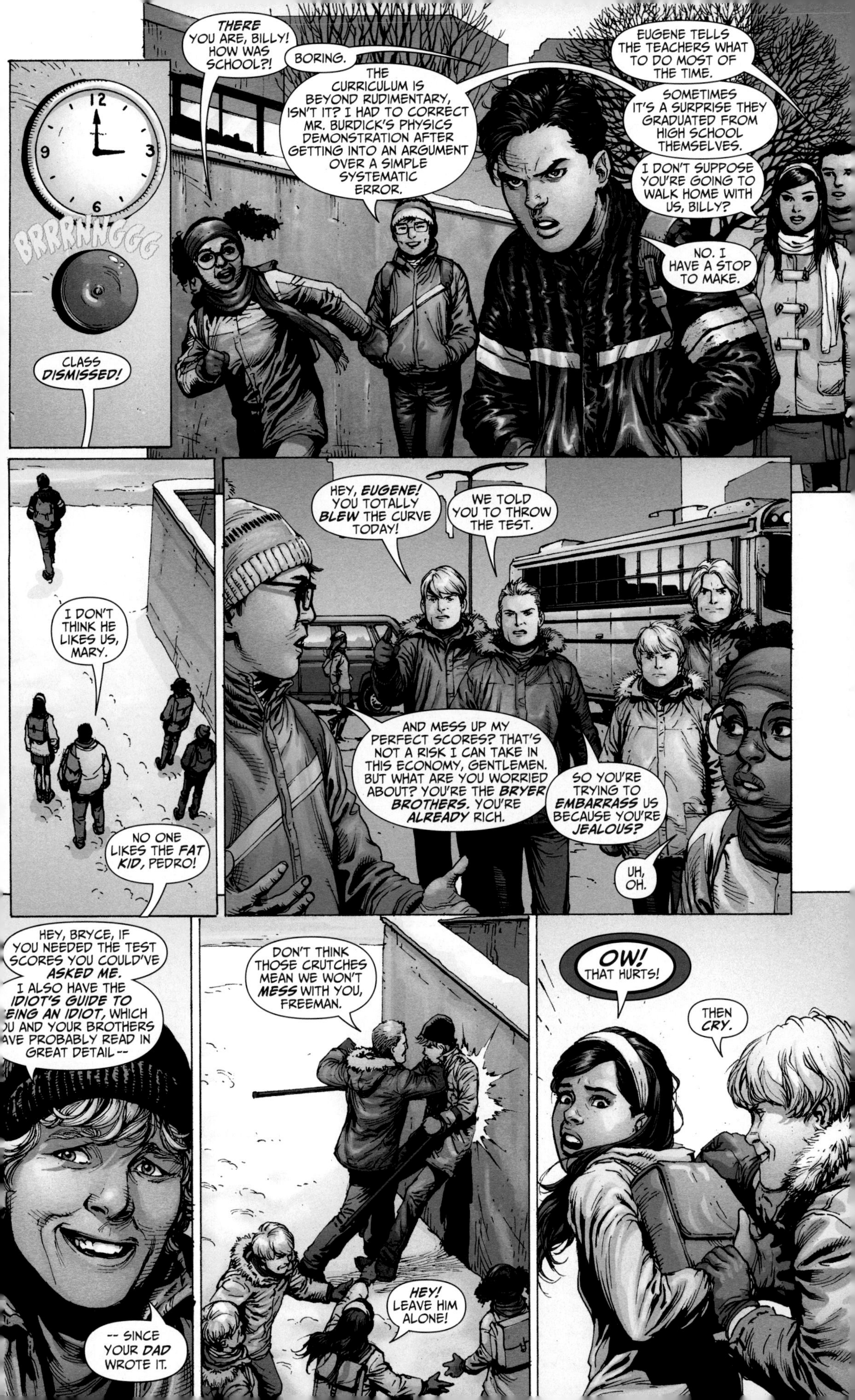
BRRRNNGGG
CLASS DISMISSED!
THERE YOU ARE, BILLY! HOW WAS SCHOOL?!
BORING.
THE CURRICULUM IS BEYOND RUDIMENTARY, ISN'T IT? I HAD TO CORRECT MR. BURDICK'S PHYSICS DEMONSTRATION AFTER GETTING INTO AN ARGUMENT OVER A SIMPLE SYSTEMATIC ERROR.
EUGENE TELLS THE TEACHERS WHAT TO DO MOST OF THE TIME.
SOMETIMES IT'S A SURPRISE THEY GRADUATED FROM HIGH SCHOOL THEMSELVES.
I DON'T SUPPOSE YOU'RE GOING TO WALK HOME WITH US, BILLY?
NO. I HAVE A STOP TO MAKE.
I DON'T THINK HE LIKES US, MARY.
NO ONE LIKES THE FAT KID, PEDRO!
HEY, EUGENE! YOU TOTALLY BLEW THE CURVE TODAY!
WE TOLD YOU TO THROW THE TEST.
AND MESS UP MY PERFECT SCORES? THAT'S NOT A RISK I CAN TAKE IN THIS ECONOMY, GENTLEMEN. BUT WHAT ARE YOU WORRIED ABOUT? YOU'RE THE BRYER BROTHERS. YOU'RE ALREADY RICH.
SO YOU'RE TRYING TO EMBARRASS US BECAUSE YOU'RE JEALOUS?
UH, OH.
HEY, BRYCE, IF YOU NEEDED THE TEST SCORES YOU COULD'VE ASKED ME. I ALSO HAVE THE IDIOT'S GUIDE TO EING AN IDIOT, WHICH U AND YOUR BROTHERS AVE PROBABLY READ IN GREAT DETAIL --
-- SINCE YOUR DAD WROTE IT.
DON'T THINK THOSE CRUTCHES MEAN WE WON'T MESS WITH YOU, FREEMAN.
HEY! LEAVE HIM ALONE!
OW! THAT HURTS!
THEN CRY.

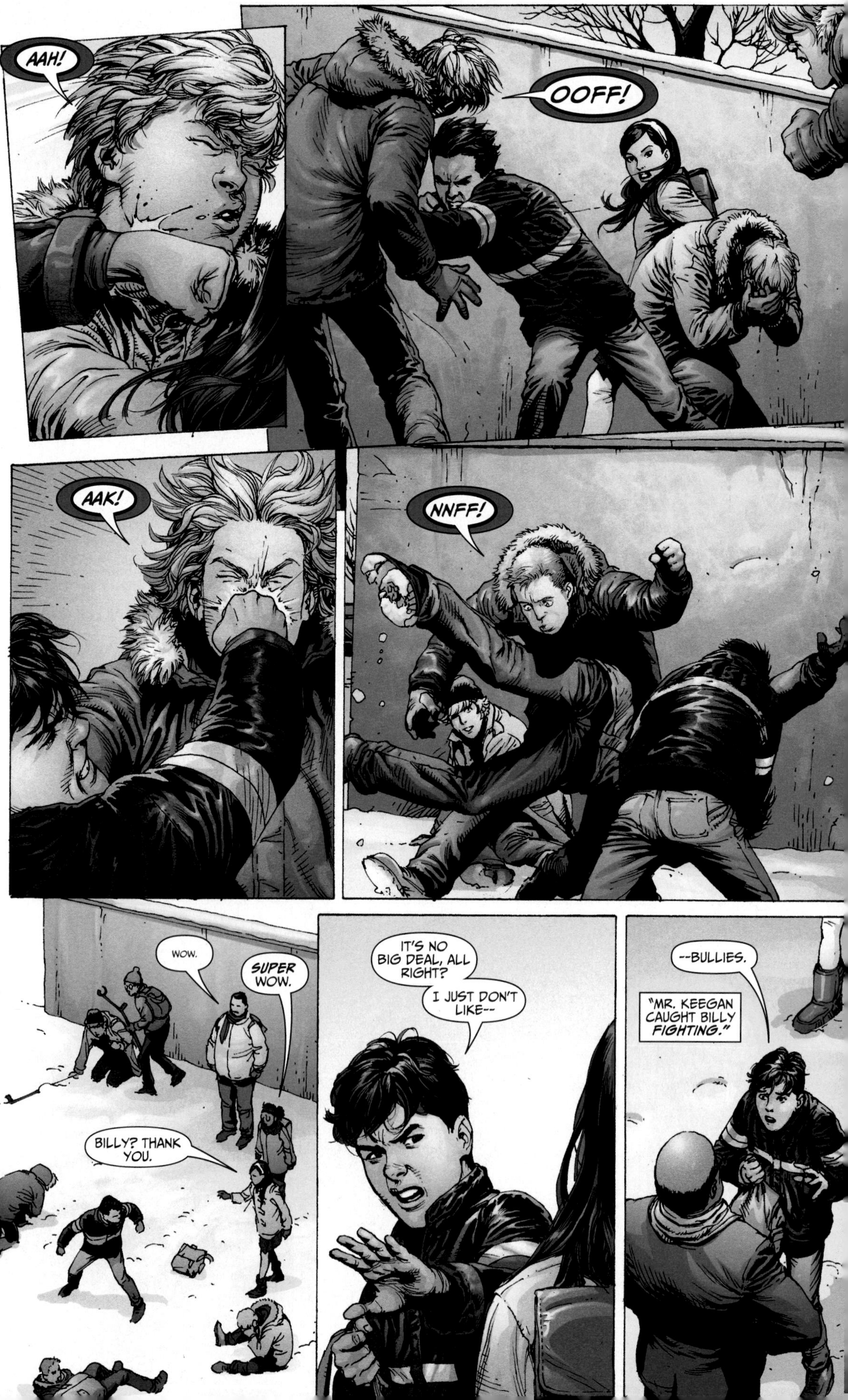
AAH!
OOFF!
AAK!
NNFF!
WOW.
SUPER WOW.
BILLY? THANK YOU.
IT'S NO BIG DEAL, ALL RIGHT?
I JUST DON'T LIKE--
--BULLIES.
"MR. KEEGAN CAUGHT BILLY FIGHTING."

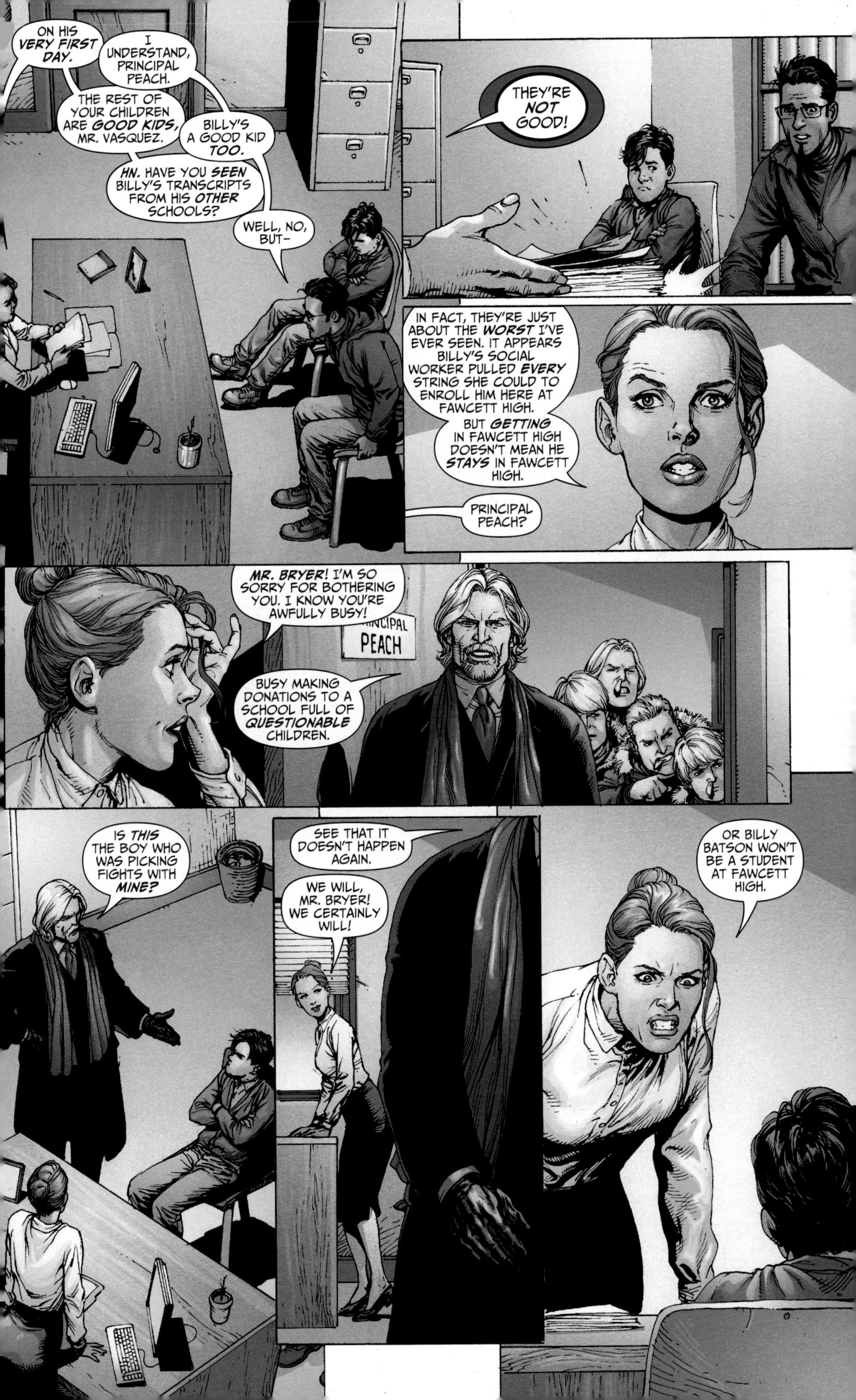

ON HIS VERY FIRST DAY.
I UNDERSTAND, PRINCIPAL PEACH.
THE REST OF YOUR CHILDREN ARE GOOD KIDS, MR. VASQUEZ.
BILLY'S A GOOD KID TOO.
HN. HAVE YOU SEEN BILLY'S TRANSCRIPTS FROM HIS OTHER SCHOOLS?
WELL, NO, BUT-
THEY'RE NOT GOOD!
IN FACT, THEY'RE JUST ABOUT THE WORST I'VE EVER SEEN. IT APPEARS BILLY'S SOCIAL WORKER PULLED EVERY STRING SHE COULD TO ENROLL HIM HERE AT FAWCETT HIGH.
BUT GETTING IN FAWCETT HIGH DOESN'T MEAN HE STAYS IN FAWCETT HIGH.
PRINCIPAL PEACH?
MR. BRYER! I'M SO SORRY FOR BOTHERING YOU. I KNOW YOU'RE AWFULLY BUSY!
PEACH
BUSY MAKING DONATIONS TO A SCHOOL FULL OF QUESTIONABLE CHILDREN.
IS THIS THE BOY WHO WAS PICKING FIGHTS WITH MINE?
SEE THAT IT DOESN'T HAPPEN AGAIN.
WE WILL, MR. BRYER! WE CERTAINLY WILL!
OR BILLY BATSON WON'T BE A STUDENT AT FAWCETT HIGH.

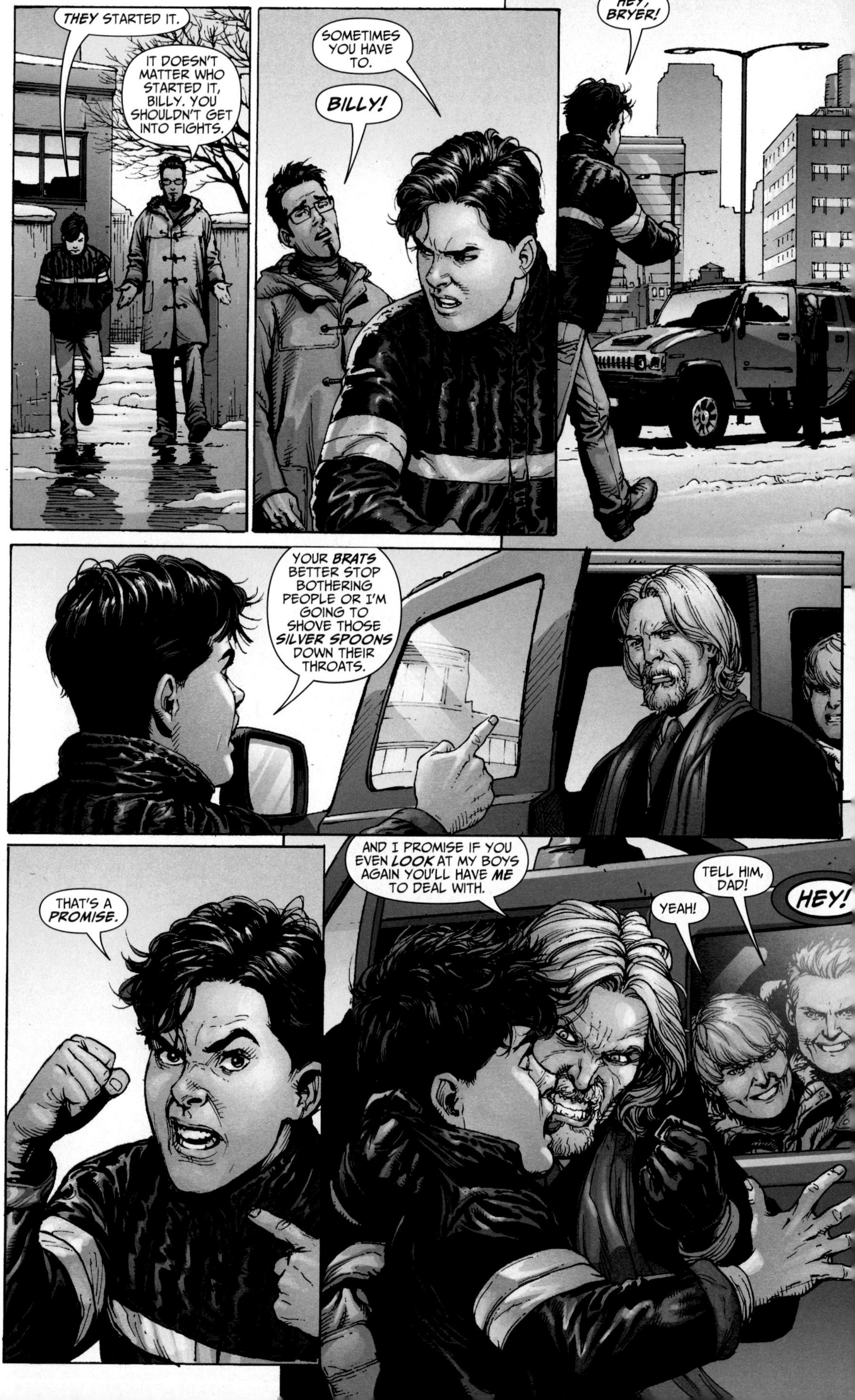
THEY STARTED IT.
IT DOESN'T MATTER WHO STARTED IT, BILLY. YOU SHOULDN'T GET INTO FIGHTS.
SOMETIMES YOU HAVE TO.
BILLY!
HEY, BRYER!
YOUR BRATS BETTER STOP BOTHERING PEOPLE OR I'M GOING TO SHOVE THOSE SILVER SPOONS DOWN THEIR THROATS.
THAT'S A PROMISE.
AND I PROMISE IF YOU EVEN LOOK AT MY BOYS AGAIN YOU'LL HAVE ME TO DEAL WITH.
YEAH!
TELL HIM, DAD!
HEY!

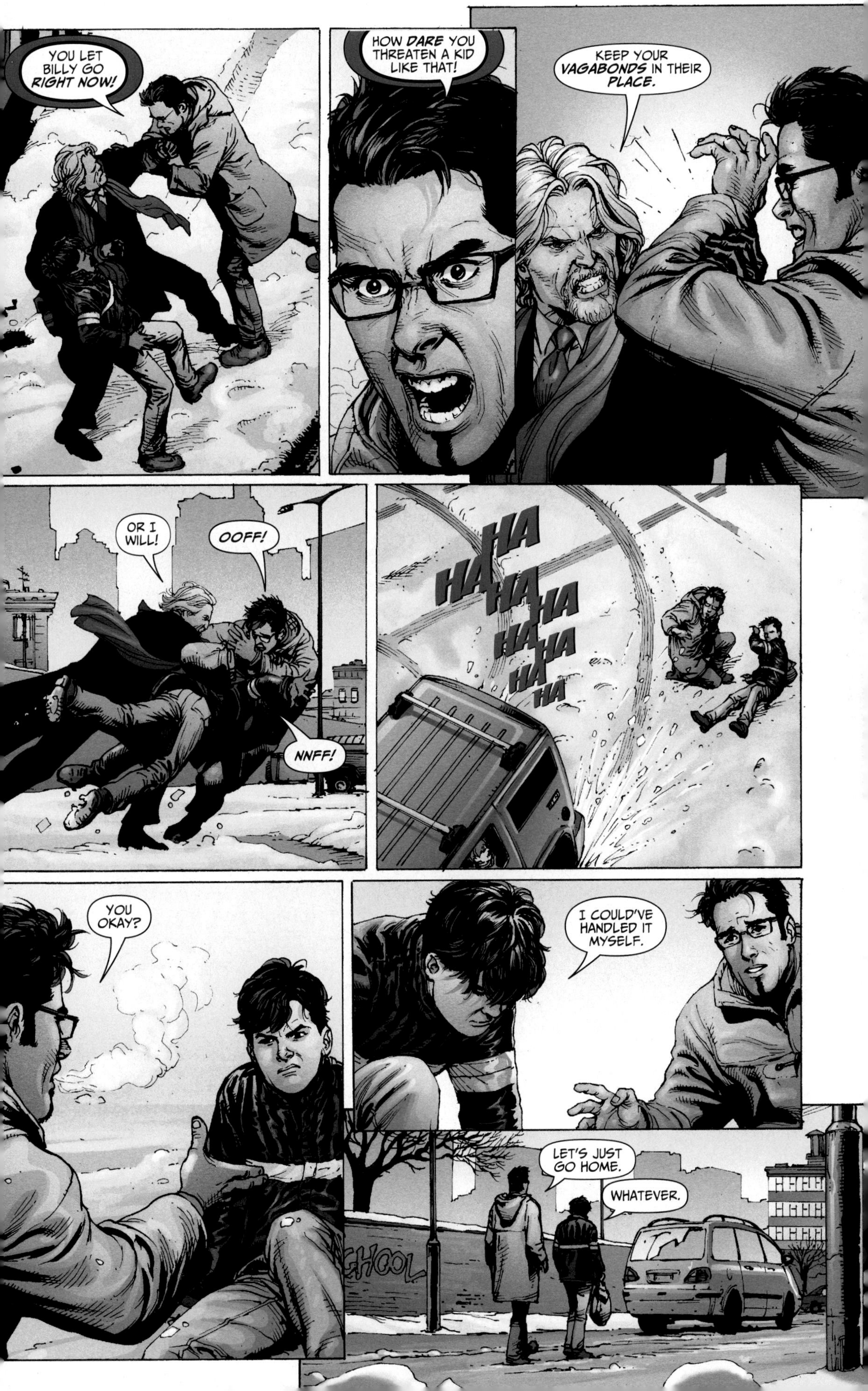
YOU LET BILLY GO RIGHT NOW!
HOW DARE YOU THREATEN A KID LIKE THAT!
KEEP YOUR VAGABONDS IN THEIR PLACE.
OR I WILL!
OOFF!
NNFF!
HA HA HA HA HA HA HA HA HA
YOU OKAY?
I COULD'VE HANDLED IT MYSELF.
LET'S JUST GO HOME.
WHATEVER.

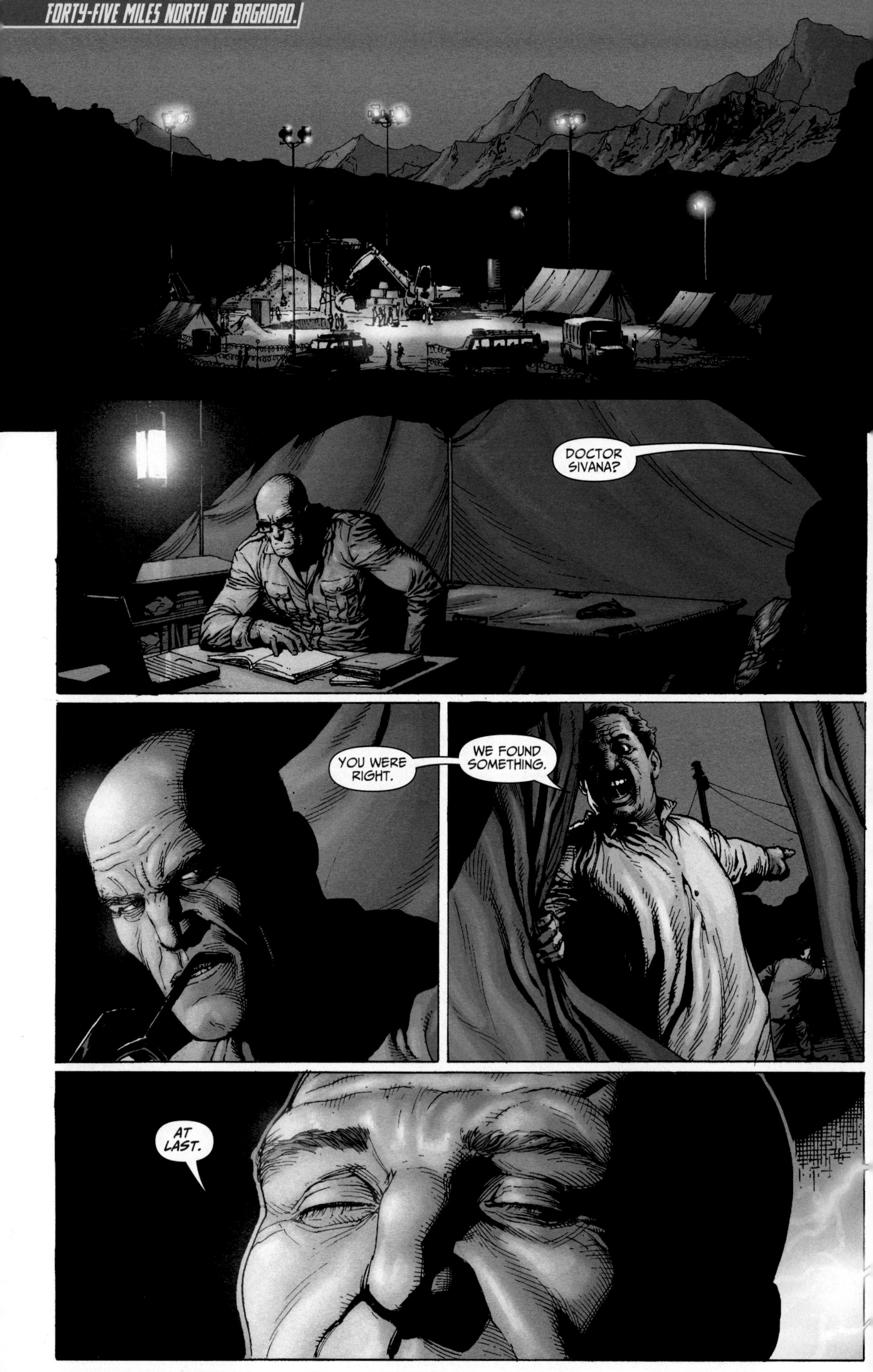
FORTY-FIVE MILES NORTH OF BAGHDAD.
DOCTOR SIVANA?
YOU WERE RIGHT.
WE FOUND SOMETHING.
AT LAST.

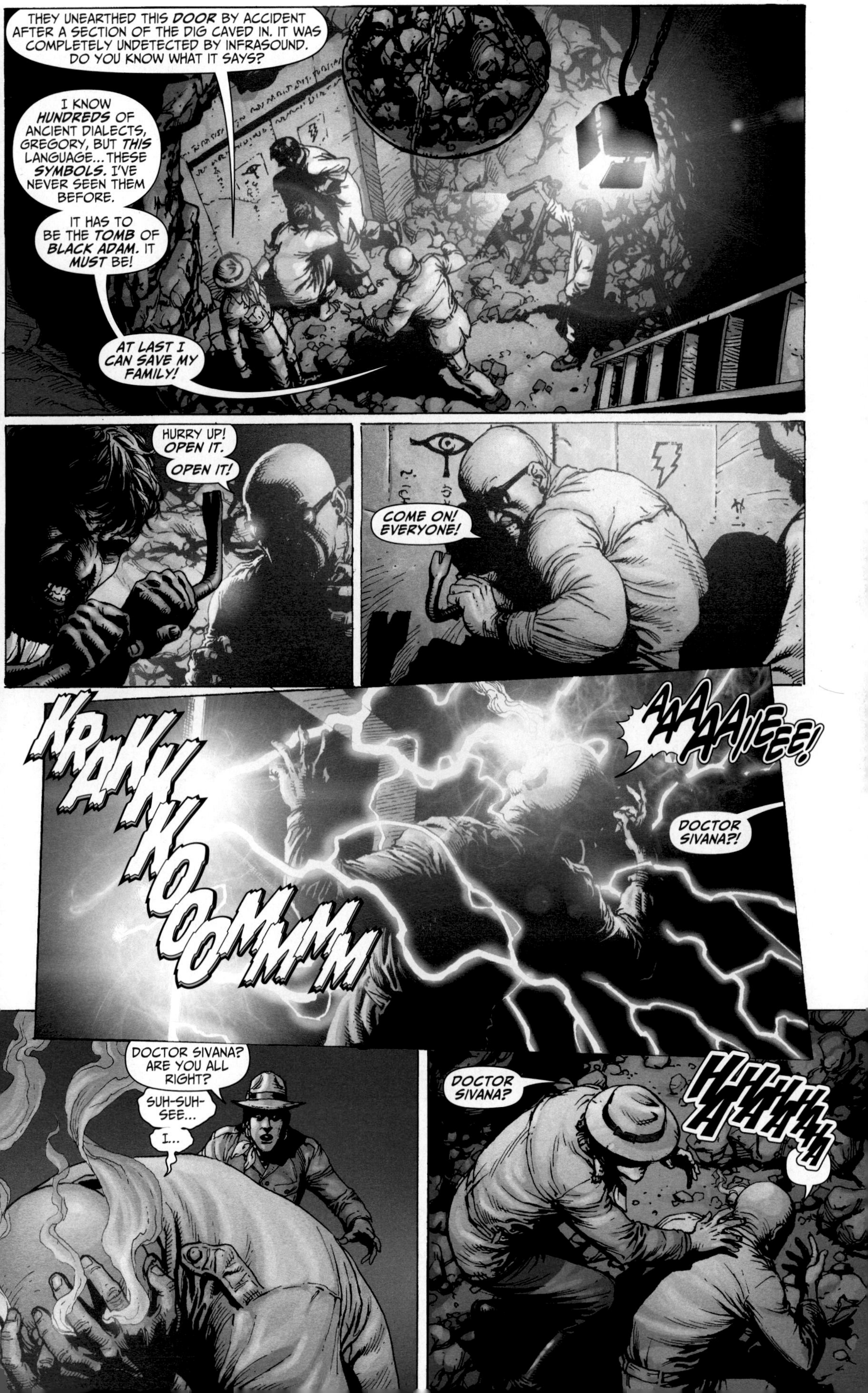
THEY UNEARTHED THIS DOOR BY ACCIDENT AFTER A SECTION OF THE DIG CAVED IN. IT WAS COMPLETELY UNDETECTED BY INFRASOUND. DO YOU KNOW WHAT IT SAYS?
I KNOW HUNDREDS OF ANCIENT DIALECTS, GREGORY, BUT THIS LANGUAGE... THESE SYMBOLS. I'VE NEVER SEEN THEM BEFORE.
IT HAS TO BE THE TOMB OF BLACK ADAM. IT MUST BE!
AT LAST I CAN SAVE MY FAMILY!
HURRY UP! OPEN IT.
OPEN IT!
COME ON! EVERYONE!
KRAKKKOOOMMMM
AAAAAIIEEE!
DOCTOR SIVANA?!
DOCTOR SIVANA? ARE YOU ALL RIGHT?
SUH-SUH-SEE...
I...
DOCTOR SIVANA?
HAHAHAHAHA

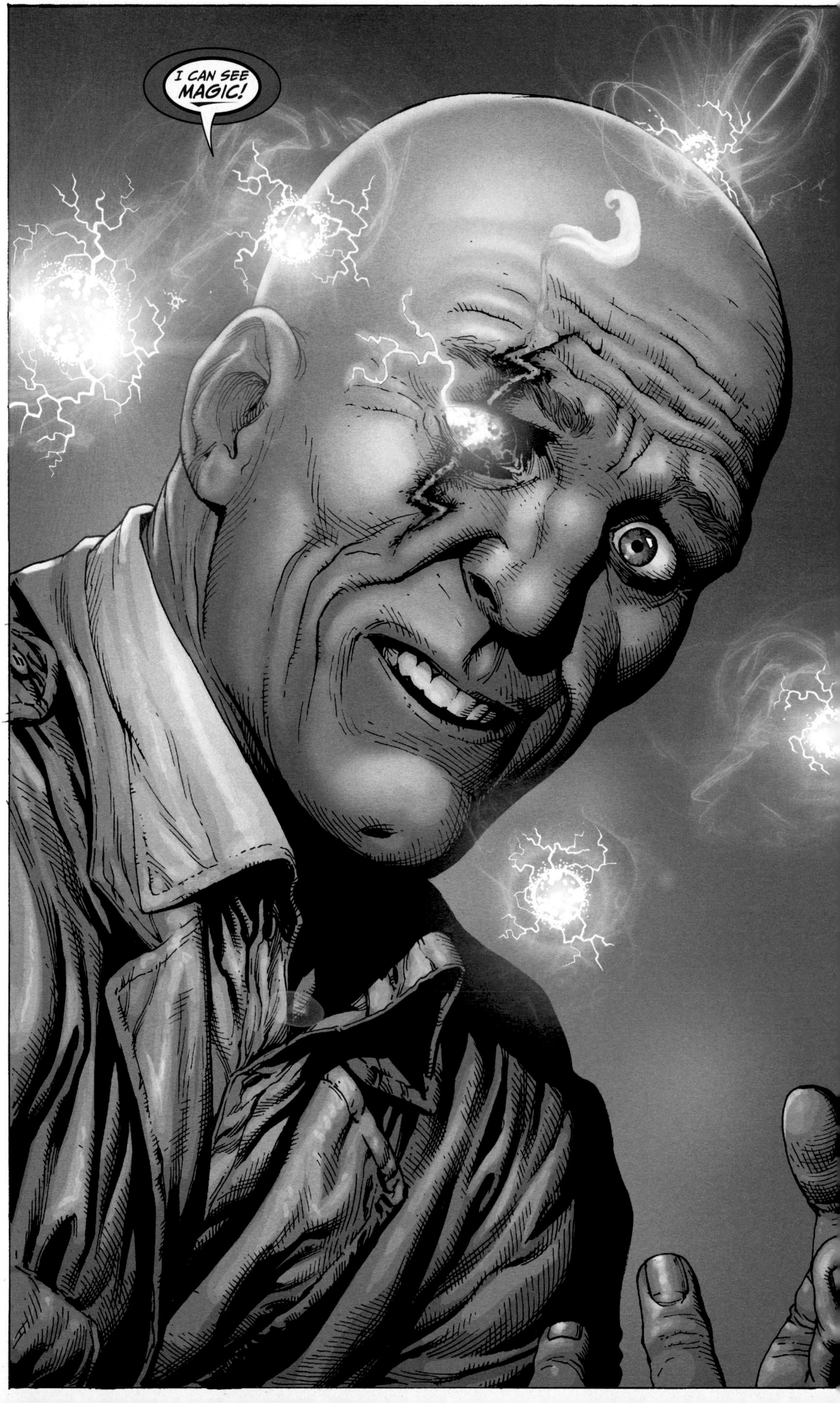
I CAN SEE MAGIC!

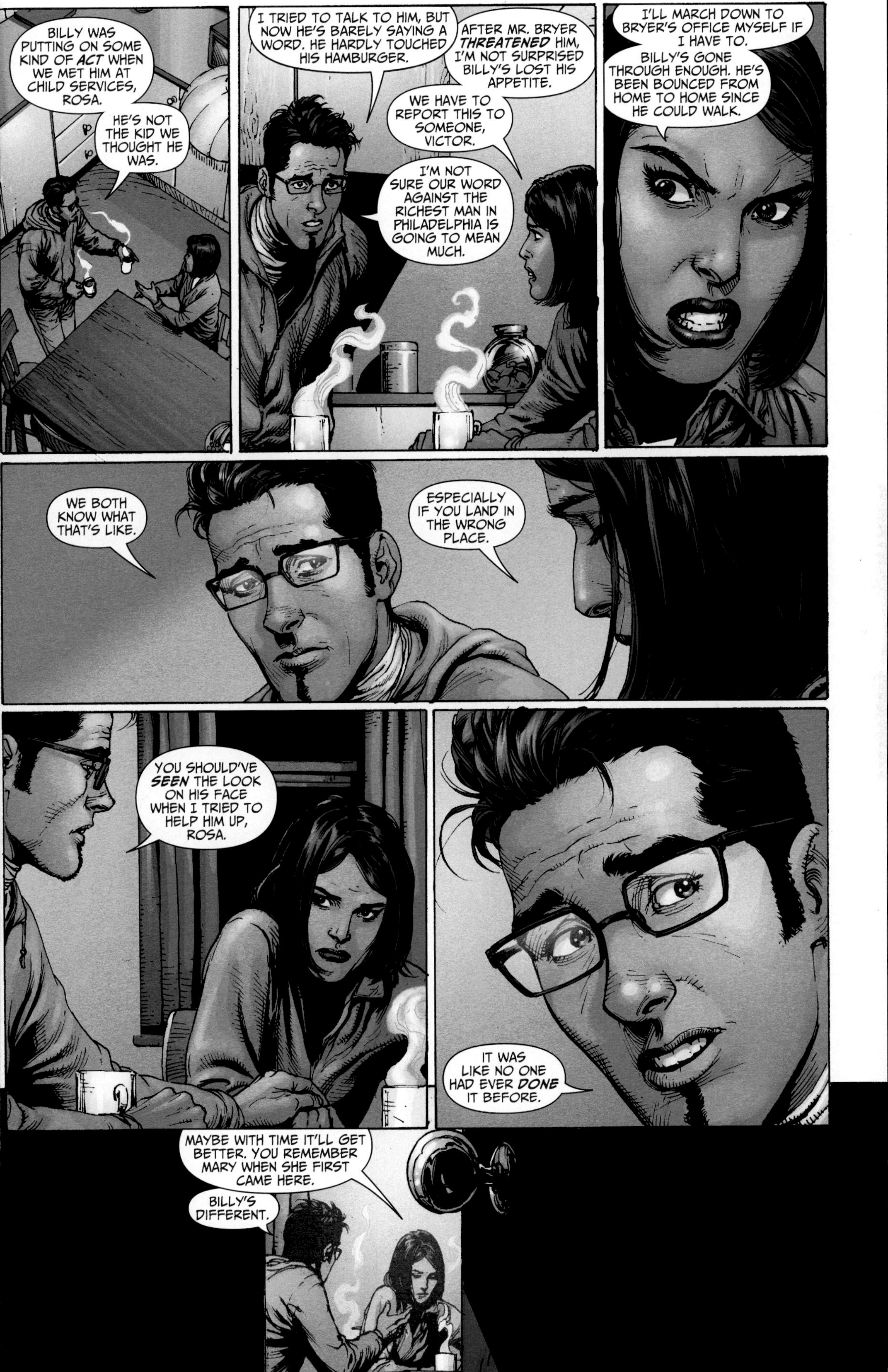

BILLY WAS PUTTING ON SOME KIND OF ACT WHEN WE MET HIM AT CHILD SERVICES, ROSA.
HE'S NOT THE KID WE THOUGHT HE WAS.
I TRIED TO TALK TO HIM, BUT NOW HE'S BARELY SAYING A WORD. HE HARDLY TOUCHED HIS HAMBURGER.
AFTER MR. BRYER THREATENED HIM, I'M NOT SURPRISED BILLY'S LOST HIS APPETITE.
WE HAVE TO REPORT THIS TO SOMEONE, VICTOR.
I'M NOT SURE OUR WORD AGAINST THE RICHEST MAN IN PHILADELPHIA IS GOING TO MEAN MUCH.
I'LL MARCH DOWN TO BRYER'S OFFICE MYSELF IF I HAVE TO.
BILLY'S GONE THROUGH ENOUGH. HE'S BEEN BOUNCED FROM HOME TO HOME SINCE HE COULD WALK.
WE BOTH KNOW WHAT THAT'S LIKE.
ESPECIALLY IF YOU LAND IN THE WRONG PLACE.
YOU SHOULD'VE SEEN THE LOOK ON HIS FACE WHEN I TRIED TO HELP HIM UP, ROSA.
IT WAS LIKE NO ONE HAD EVER DONE IT BEFORE.
MAYBE WITH TIME IT'LL GET BETTER. YOU REMEMBER MARY WHEN SHE FIRST CAME HERE.
BILLY'S DIFFERENT.

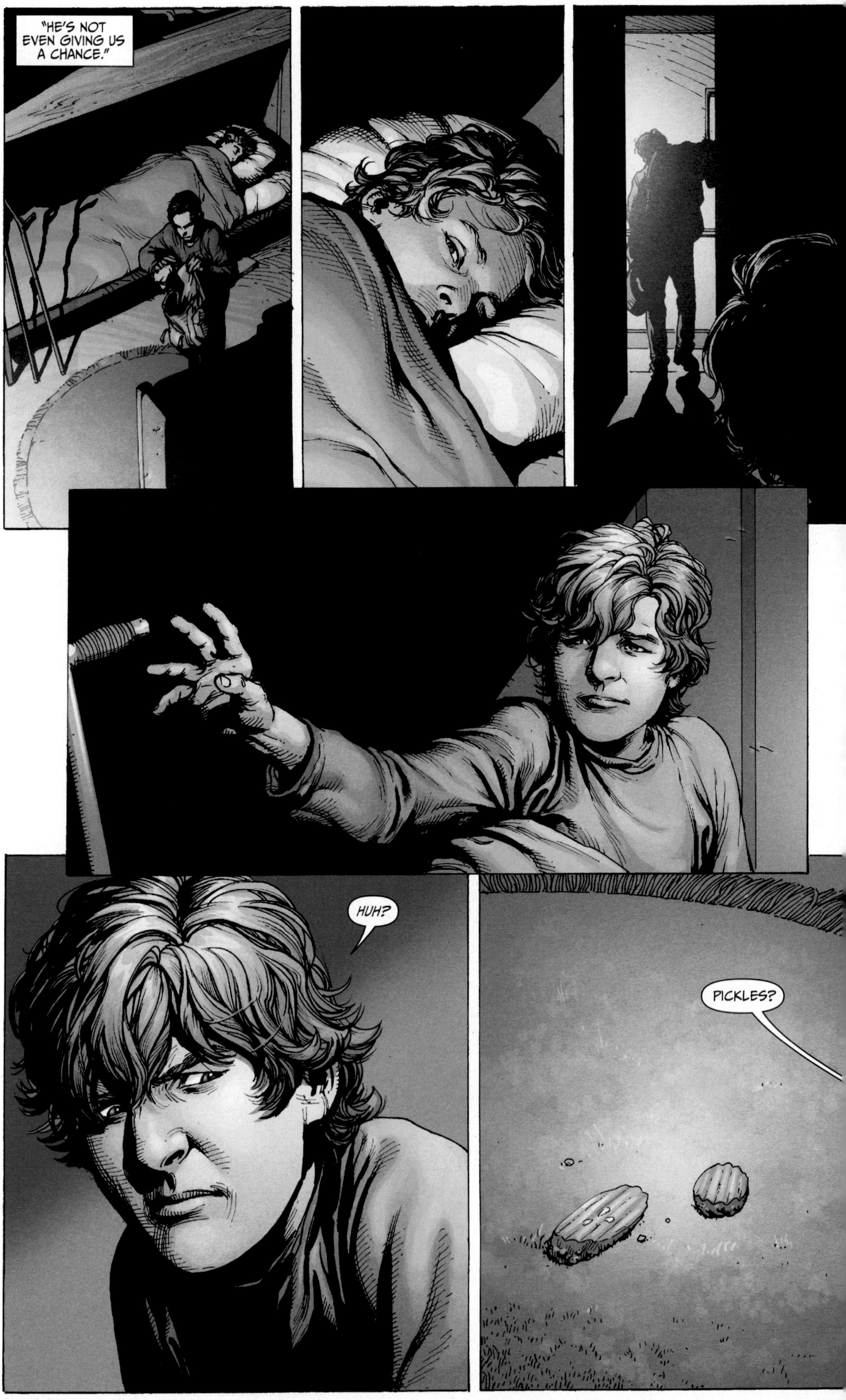
"HE'S NOT
EVEN GIVING US
A CHANCE."
HUH?
PICKLES?

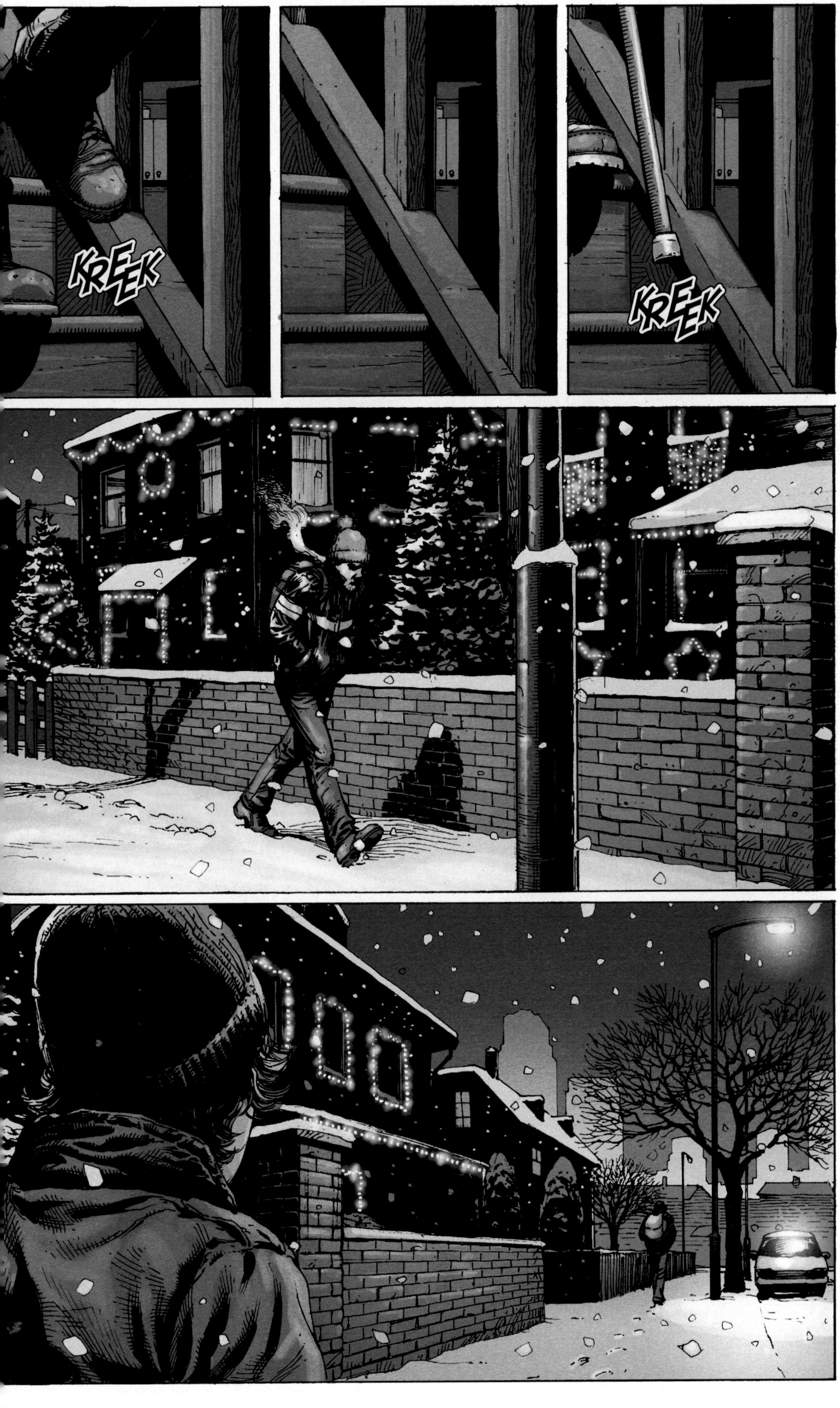
KREEEK
KREEEK

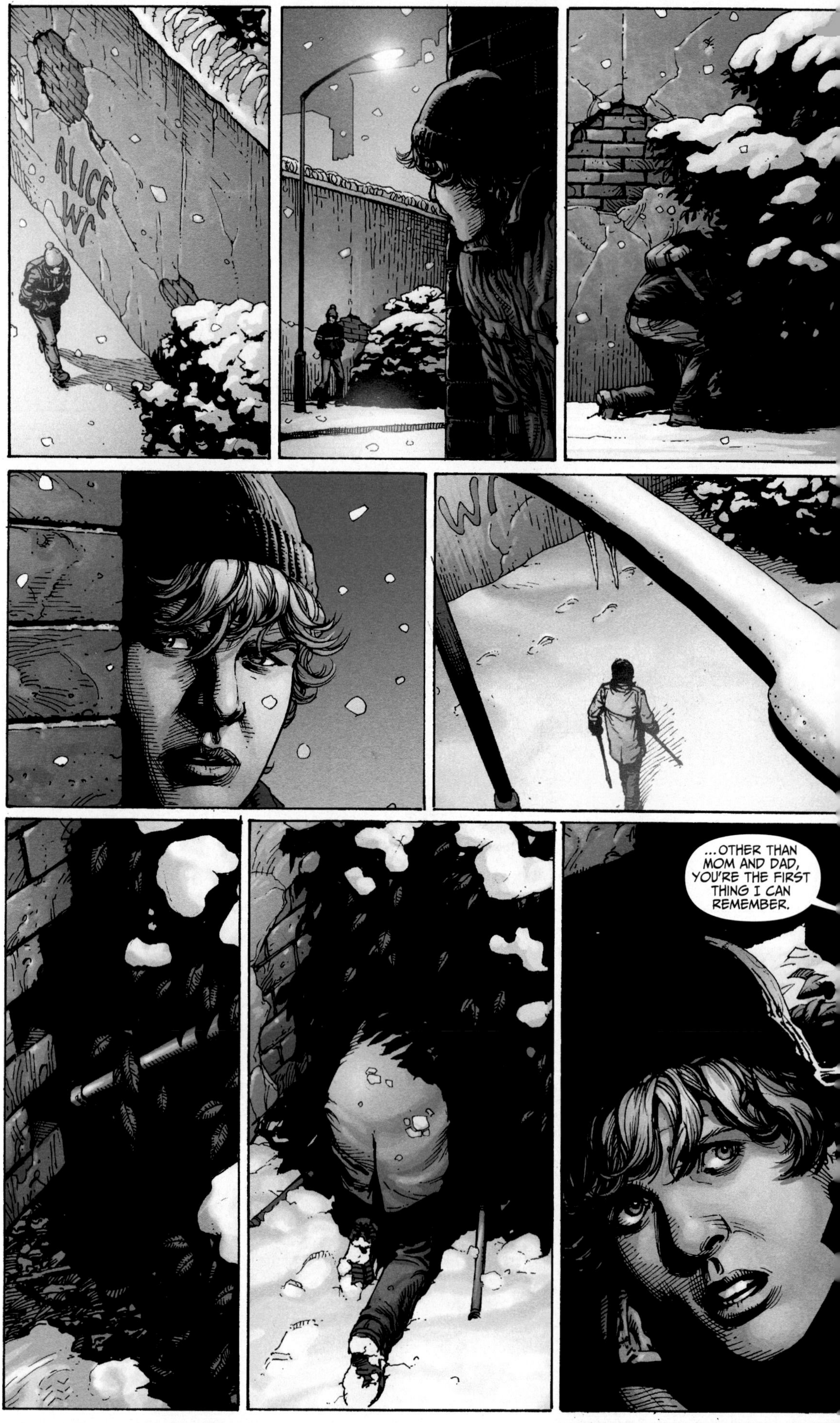
ALICE
WI
...OTHER THAN MOM AND DAD, YOU'RE THE FIRST THING I CAN REMEMBER.

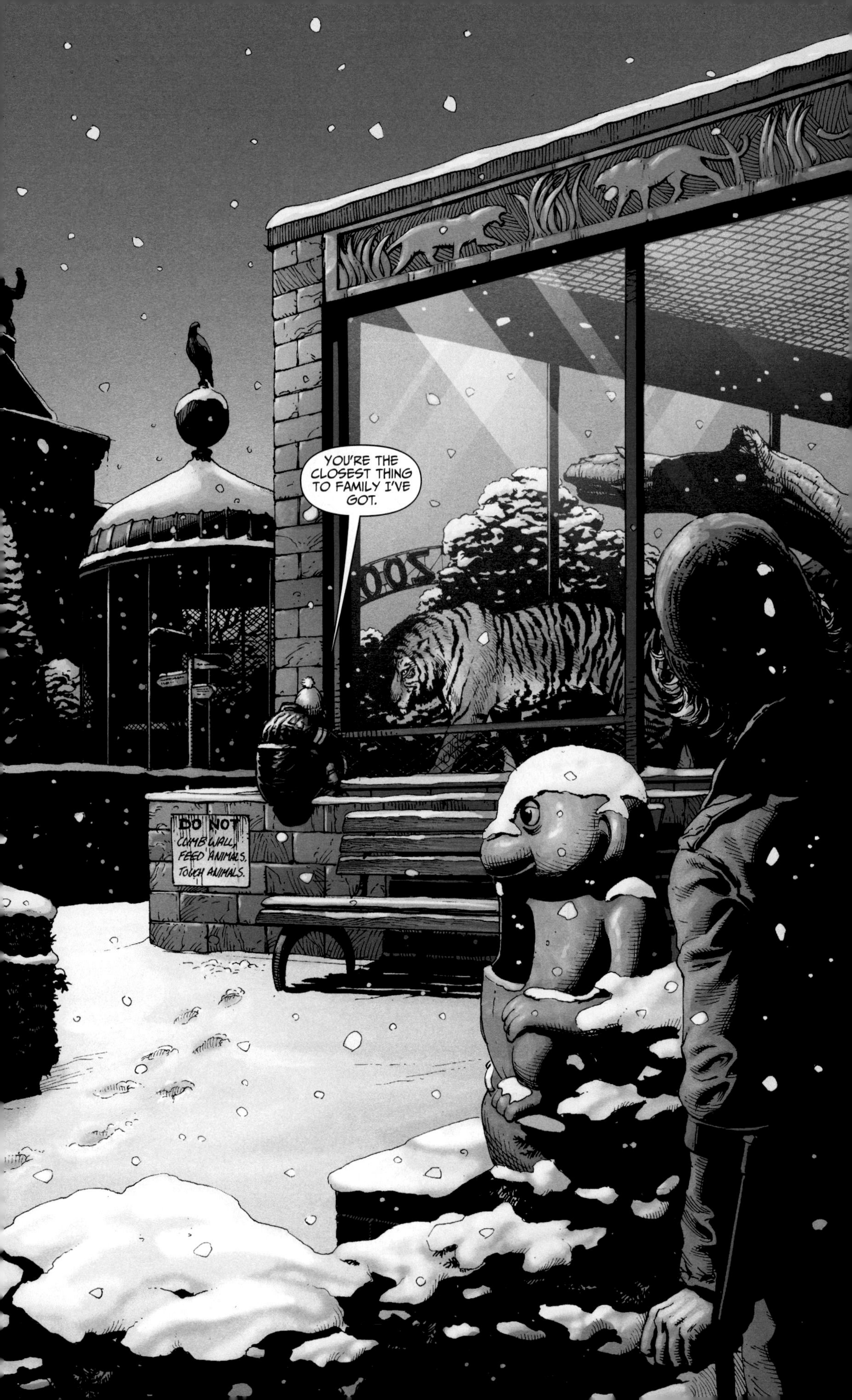
YOU'RE THE CLOSEST THING TO FAMILY I'VE GOT.
DO NOT
CLIMB WALL.
FEED ANIMALS.
TOUCH ANIMALS.
ZOO

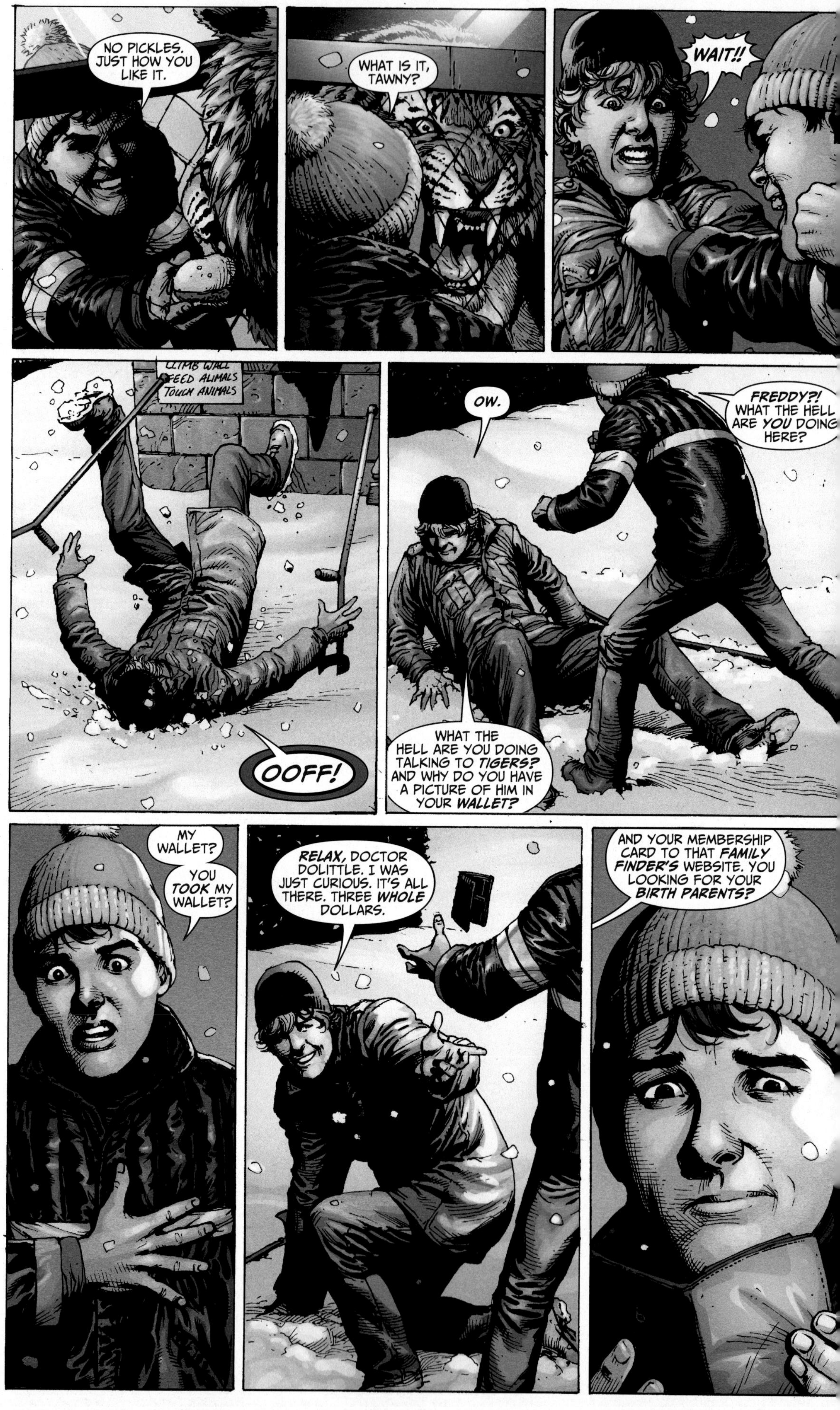
NO PICKLES. JUST HOW YOU LIKE IT.
WHAT IS IT, TAWNY?
WAIT!!
CLIMB WALL
FEED ALIMALS
TOUCH ANIMALS
OOFF!
OW.
FREDDY?! WHAT THE HELL ARE YOU DOING HERE?
WHAT THE HELL ARE YOU DOING TALKING TO TIGERS? AND WHY DO YOU HAVE A PICTURE OF HIM IN YOUR WALLET?
MY WALLET?
YOU TOOK MY WALLET?
RELAX, DOCTOR DOLITTLE. I WAS JUST CURIOUS. IT'S ALL THERE. THREE WHOLE DOLLARS.
AND YOUR MEMBERSHIP CARD TO THAT FAMILY FINDER'S WEBSITE. YOU LOOKING FOR YOUR BIRTH PARENTS?

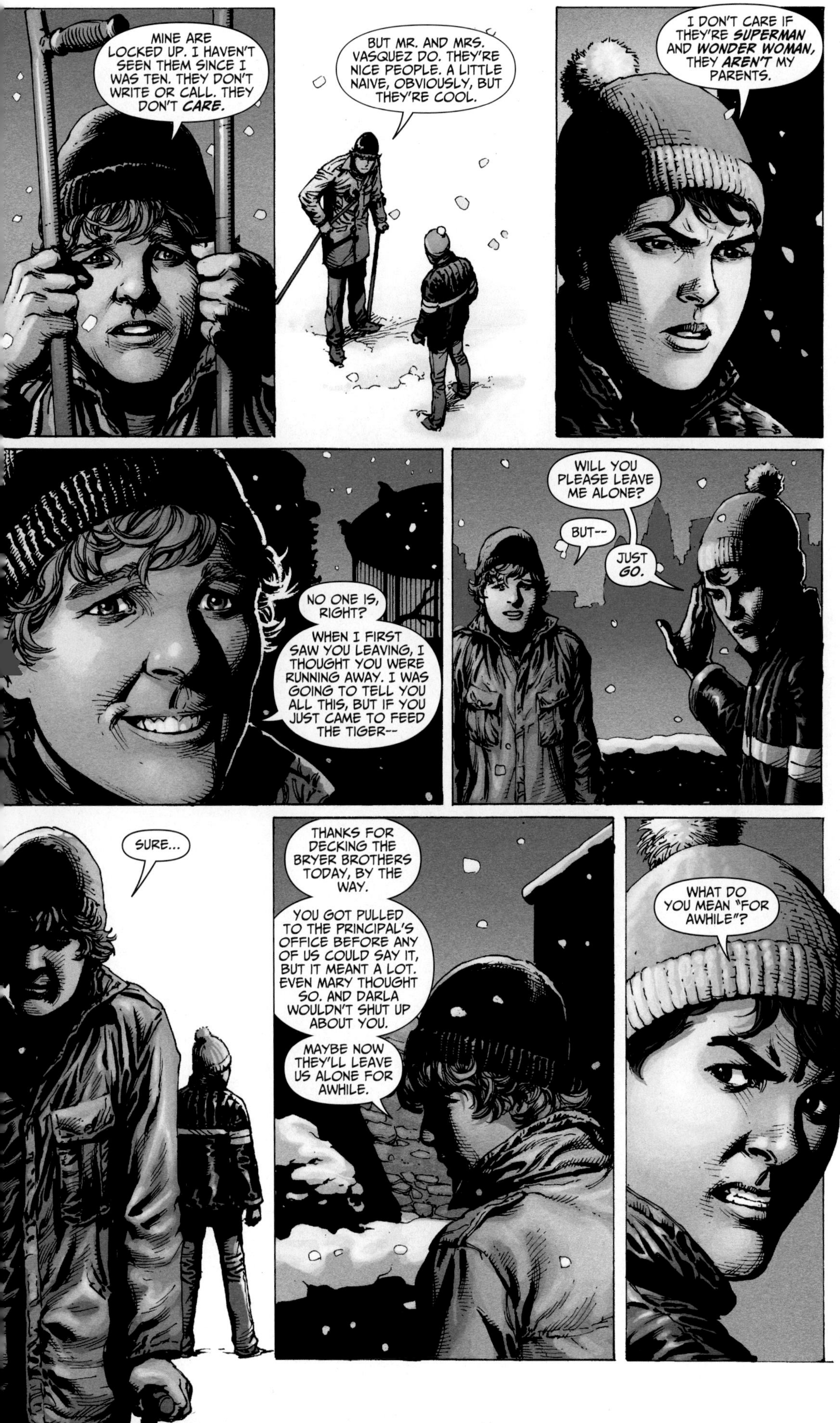
MINE ARE LOCKED UP. I HAVEN'T SEEN THEM SINCE I WAS TEN. THEY DON'T WRITE OR CALL. THEY DON'T CARE.
BUT MR. AND MRS. VASQUEZ DO. THEY'RE NICE PEOPLE. A LITTLE NAIVE, OBVIOUSLY, BUT THEY'RE COOL.
I DON'T CARE IF THEY'RE SUPERMAN AND WONDER WOMAN, THEY AREN'T MY PARENTS.
NO ONE IS, RIGHT?
WHEN I FIRST SAW YOU LEAVING, I THOUGHT YOU WERE RUNNING AWAY. I WAS GOING TO TELL YOU ALL THIS, BUT IF YOU JUST CAME TO FEED THE TIGER--
WILL YOU PLEASE LEAVE ME ALONE?
BUT--
JUST GO.
SURE...
THANKS FOR DECKING THE BRYER BROTHERS TODAY, BY THE WAY.
YOU GOT PULLED TO THE PRINCIPAL'S OFFICE BEFORE ANY OF US COULD SAY IT, BUT IT MEANT A LOT. EVEN MARY THOUGHT SO. AND DARLA WOULDN'T SHUT UP ABOUT YOU.
MAYBE NOW THEY'LL LEAVE US ALONE FOR AWHILE.
WHAT DO YOU MEAN "FOR AWHILE"?

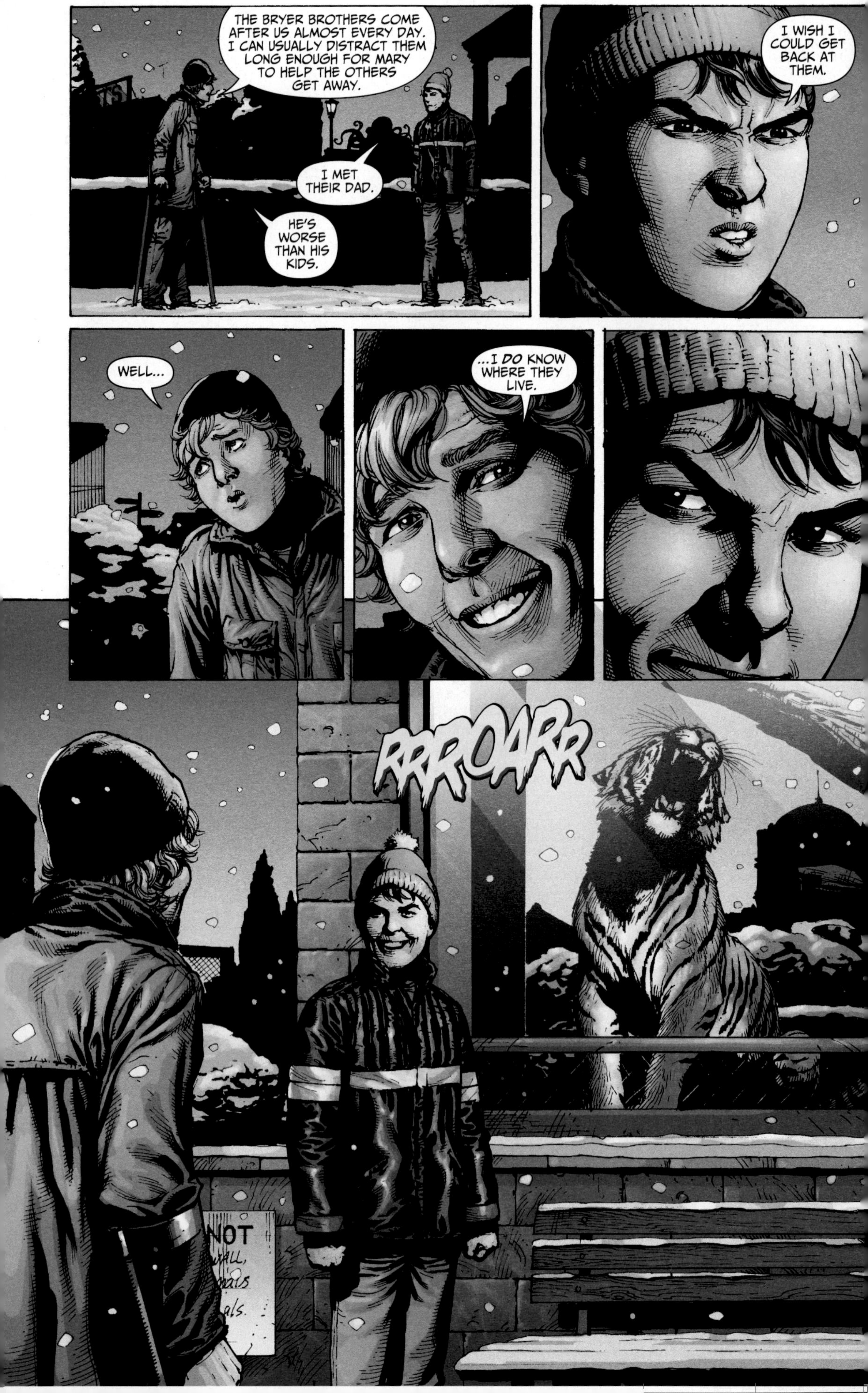
THE BRYER BROTHERS COME AFTER US ALMOST EVERY DAY. I CAN USUALLY DISTRACT THEM LONG ENOUGH FOR MARY TO HELP THE OTHERS GET AWAY.
I MET THEIR DAD.
HE'S WORSE THAN HIS KIDS.
I WISH I COULD GET BACK AT THEM.
WELL...
...I DO KNOW WHERE THEY LIVE.
RRROARR
NOT

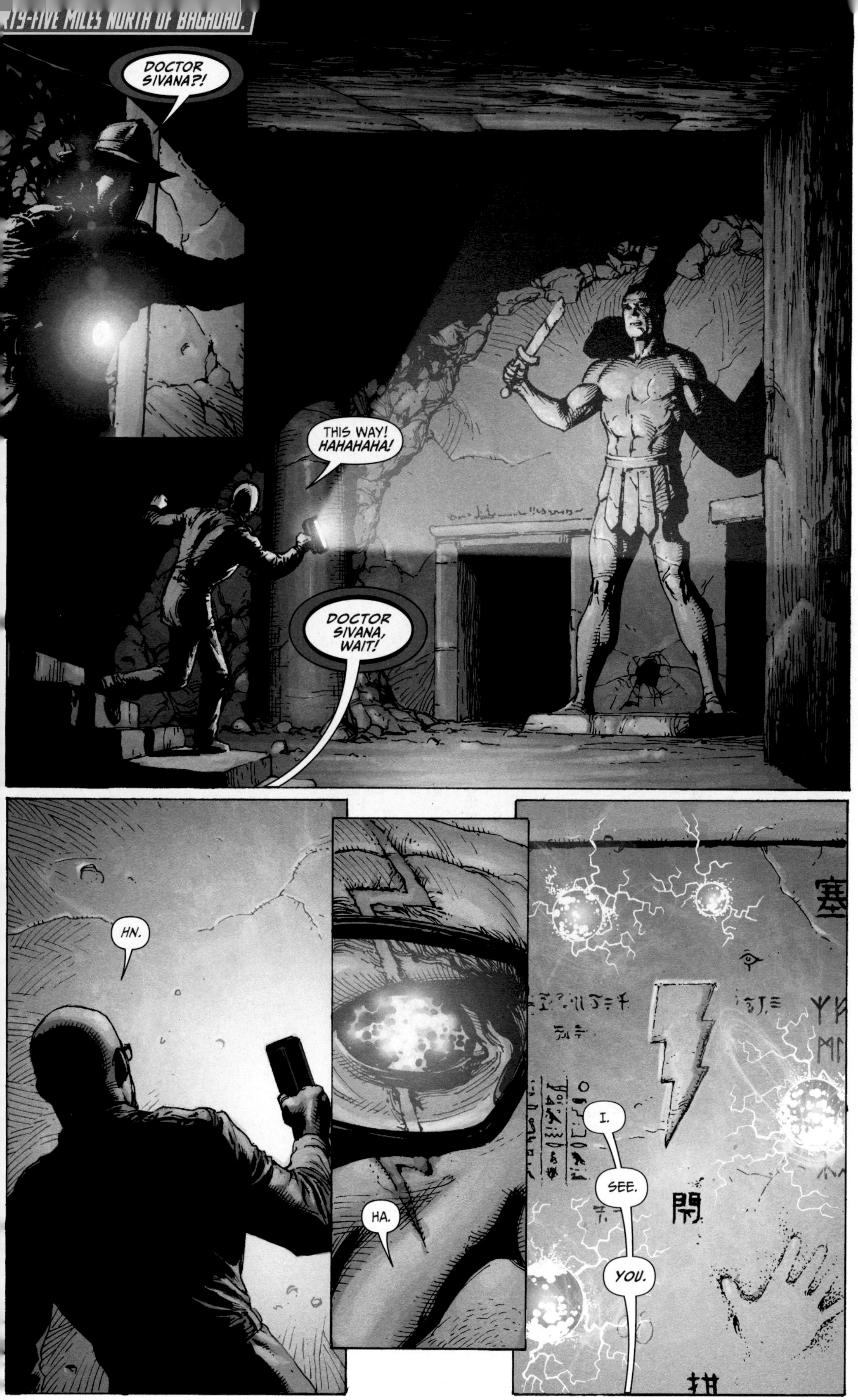

...XTY-FIVE MILES NORTH OF BAGHDAD.
DOCTOR SIVANA?!
THIS WAY! HAHAHAHA!
DOCTOR SIVANA, WAIT!
HN.
HA.
I.
SEE.
YOU.

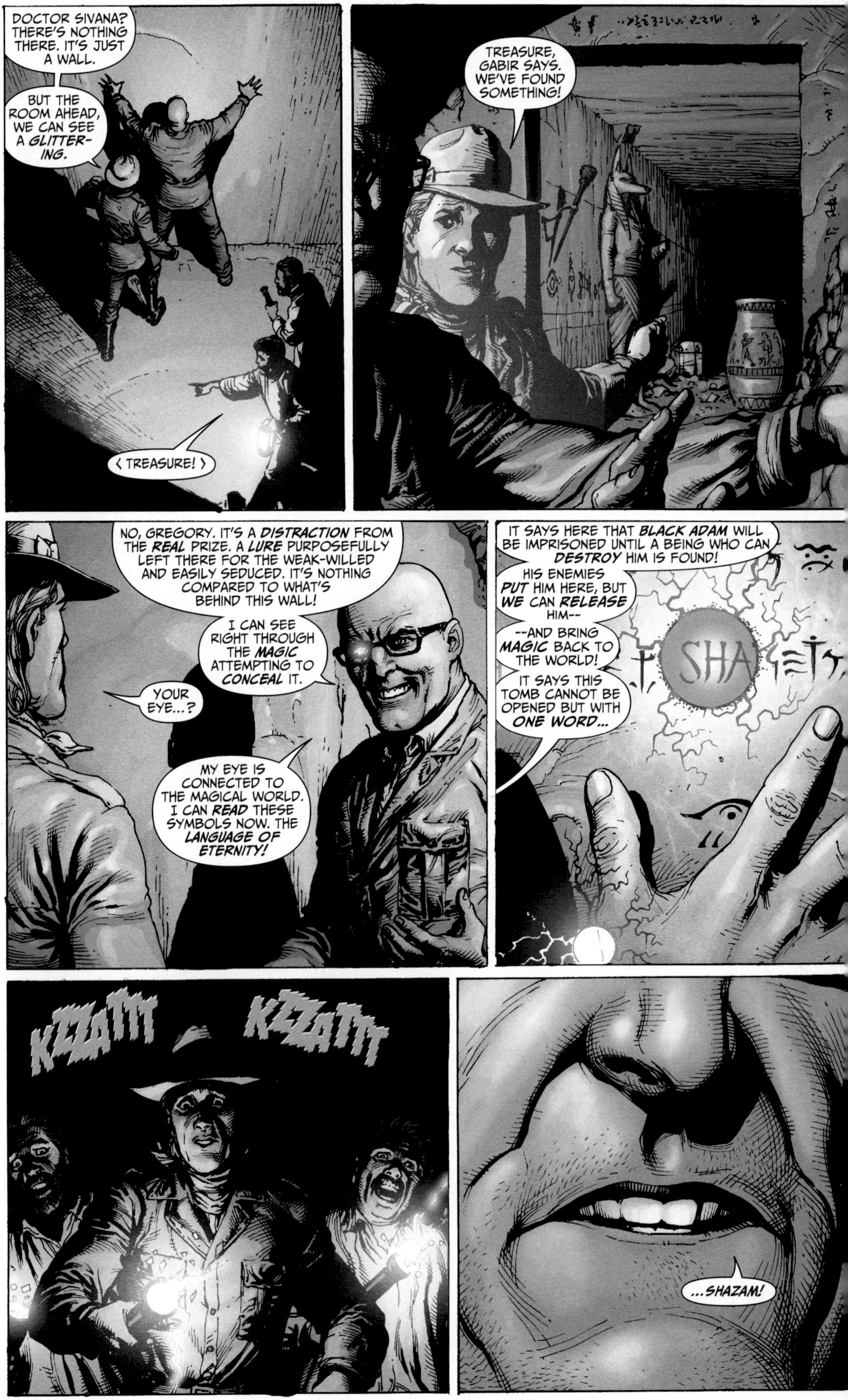
DOCTOR SIVANA? THERE'S NOTHING THERE. IT'S JUST A WALL.
BUT THE ROOM AHEAD, WE CAN SEE A GLITTERING.
‹ TREASURE! ›
TREASURE, GABIR SAYS. WE'VE FOUND SOMETHING!
NO, GREGORY. IT'S A DISTRACTION FROM THE REAL PRIZE. A LURE PURPOSEFULLY LEFT THERE FOR THE WEAK-WILLED AND EASILY SEDUCED. IT'S NOTHING COMPARED TO WHAT'S BEHIND THIS WALL!
I CAN SEE RIGHT THROUGH THE MAGIC ATTEMPTING TO CONCEAL IT.
YOUR EYE...?
MY EYE IS CONNECTED TO THE MAGICAL WORLD. I CAN READ THESE SYMBOLS NOW. THE LANGUAGE OF ETERNITY!
IT SAYS HERE THAT BLACK ADAM WILL BE IMPRISONED UNTIL A BEING WHO CAN DESTROY HIM IS FOUND!
HIS ENEMIES PUT HIM HERE, BUT WE CAN RELEASE HIM--
--AND BRING MAGIC BACK TO THE WORLD!
IT SAYS THIS TOMB CANNOT BE OPENED BUT WITH ONE WORD...
SHA
KZZATTT
KZZATTT
...SHAZAM!

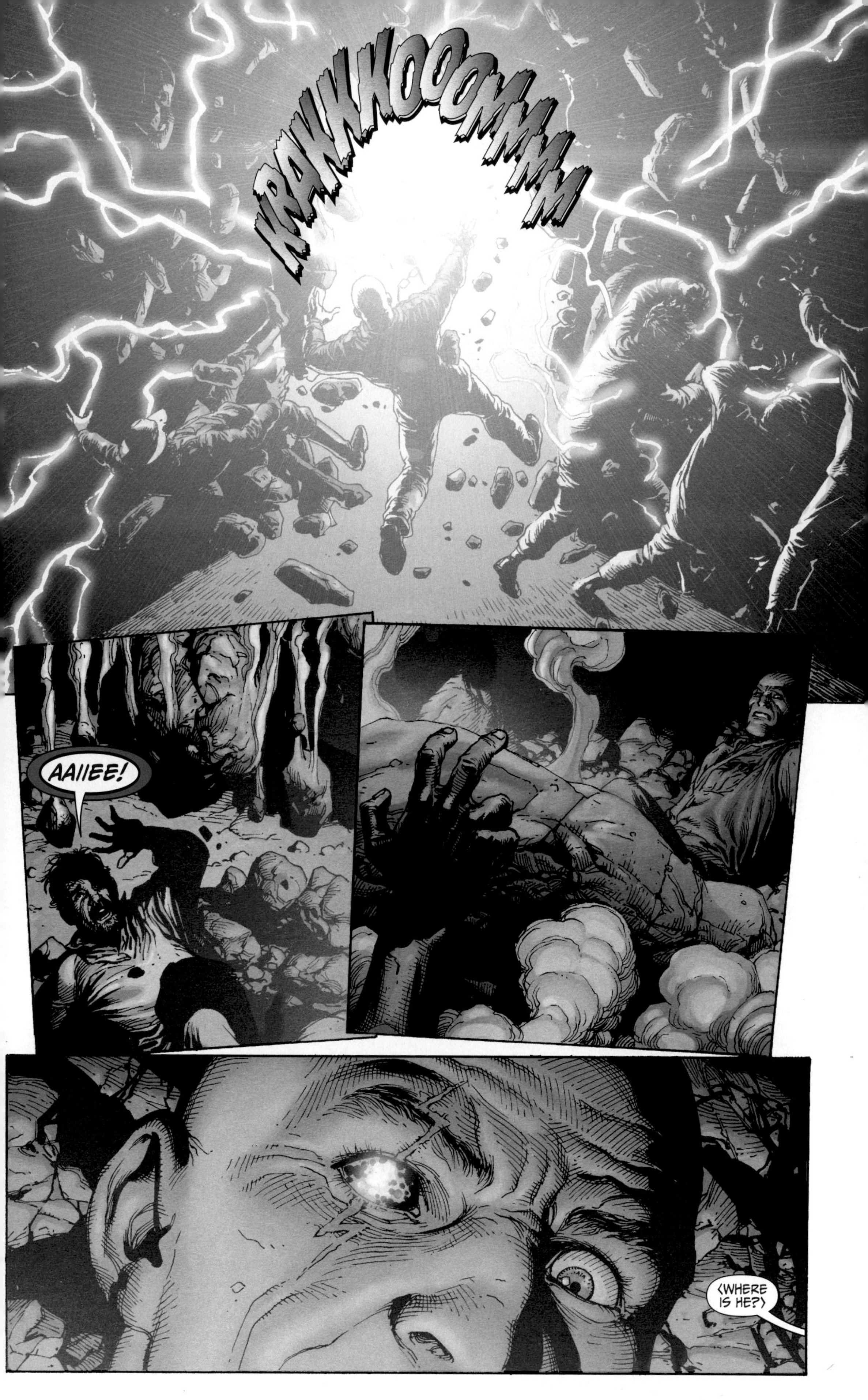
KRAKKOOOMMM
AAIIEE!
‹WHERE IS HE?›

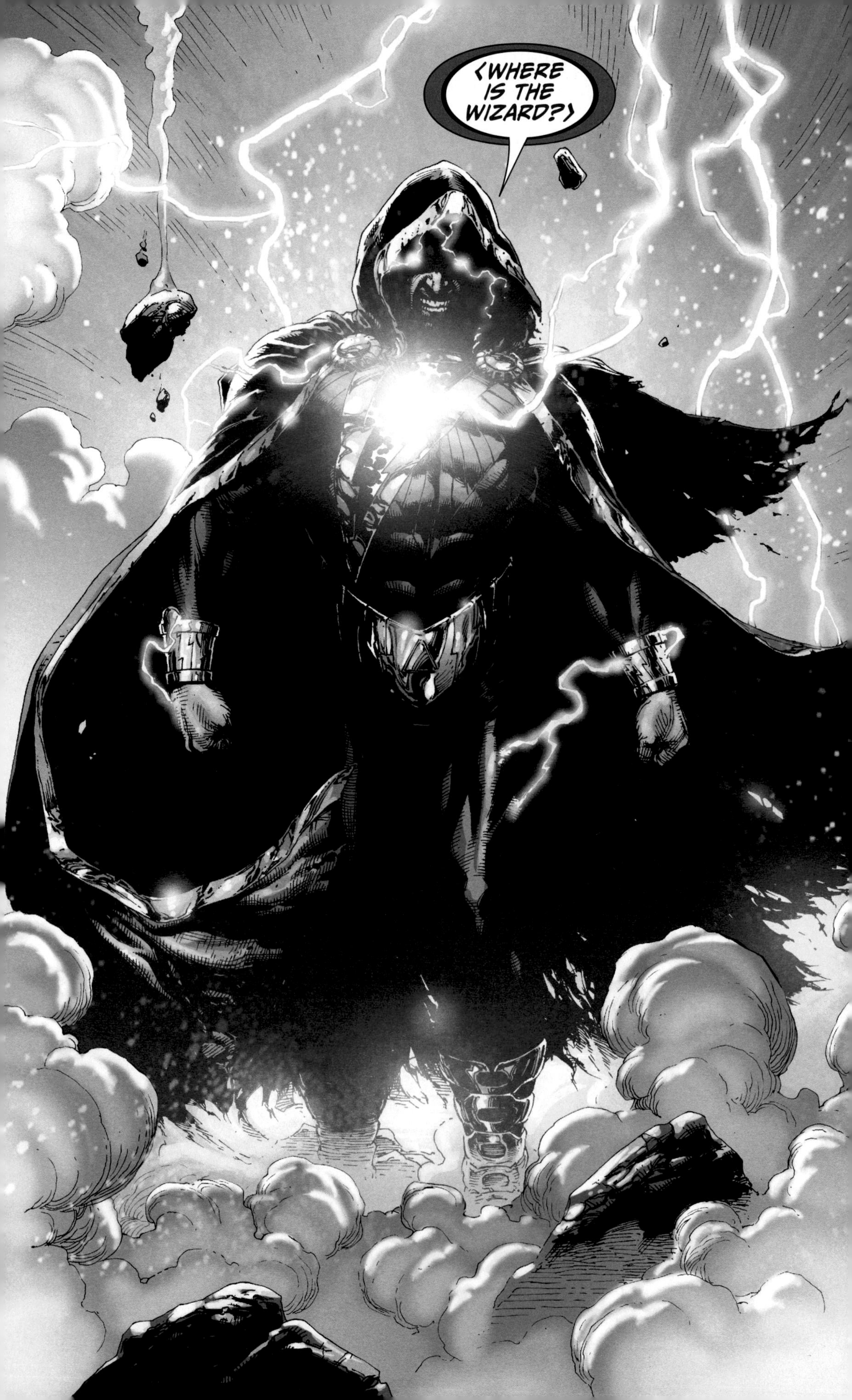
<WHERE IS THE WIZARD?>

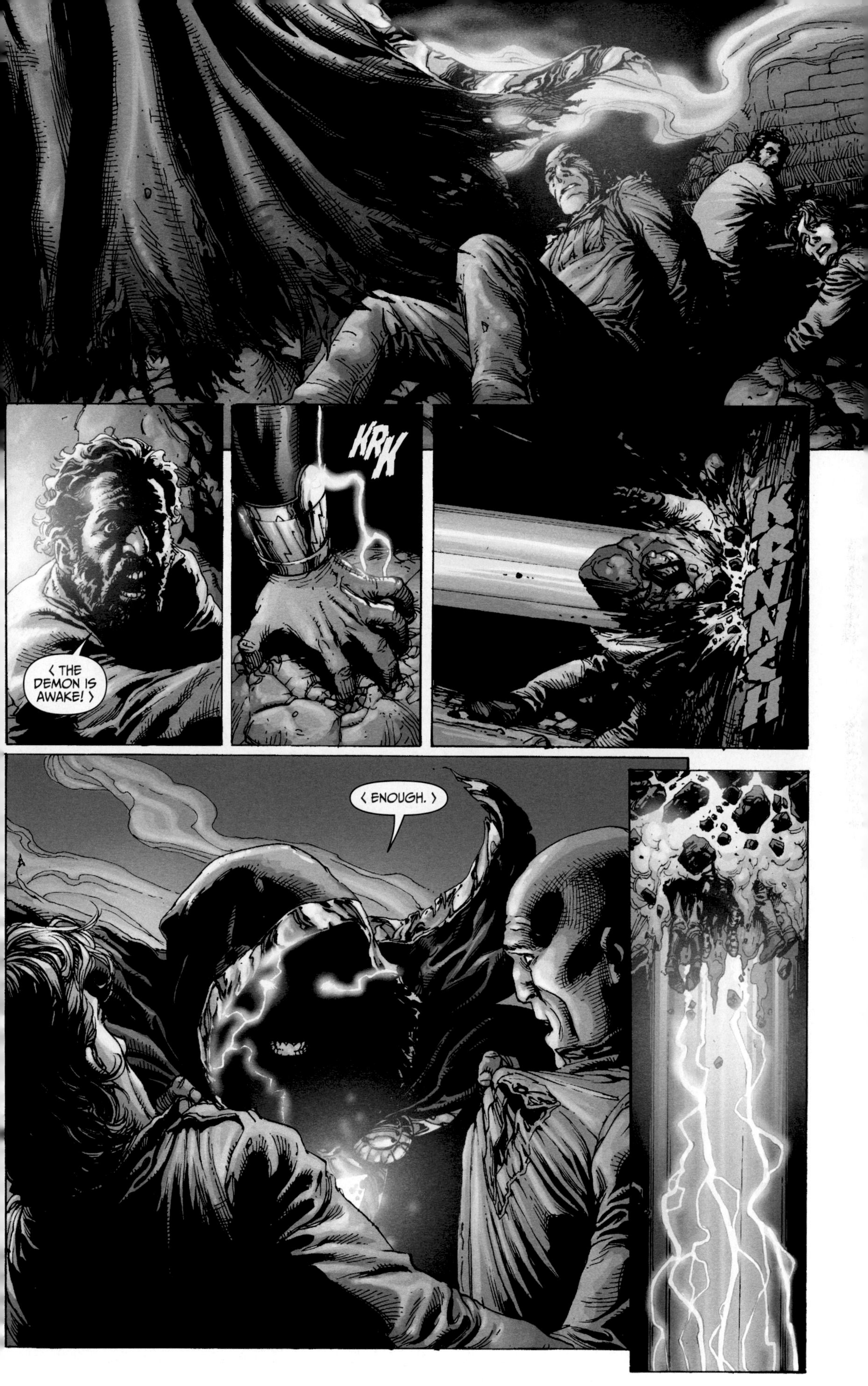

‹ THE DEMON IS AWAKE! ›
KRK
KRNNCH
‹ ENOUGH. ›

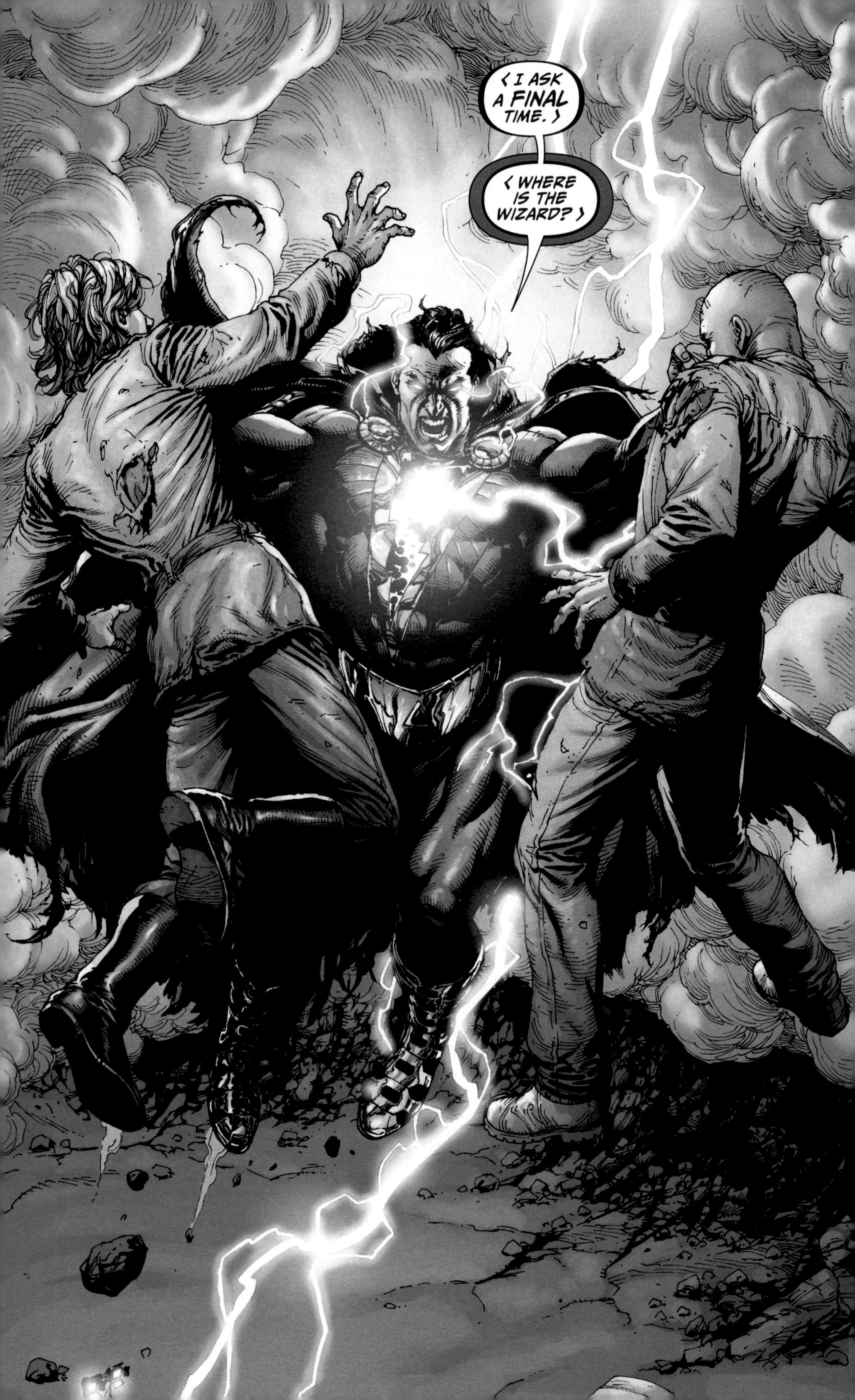
‹ I ASK A FINAL TIME. ›
‹ WHERE IS THE WIZARD? ›

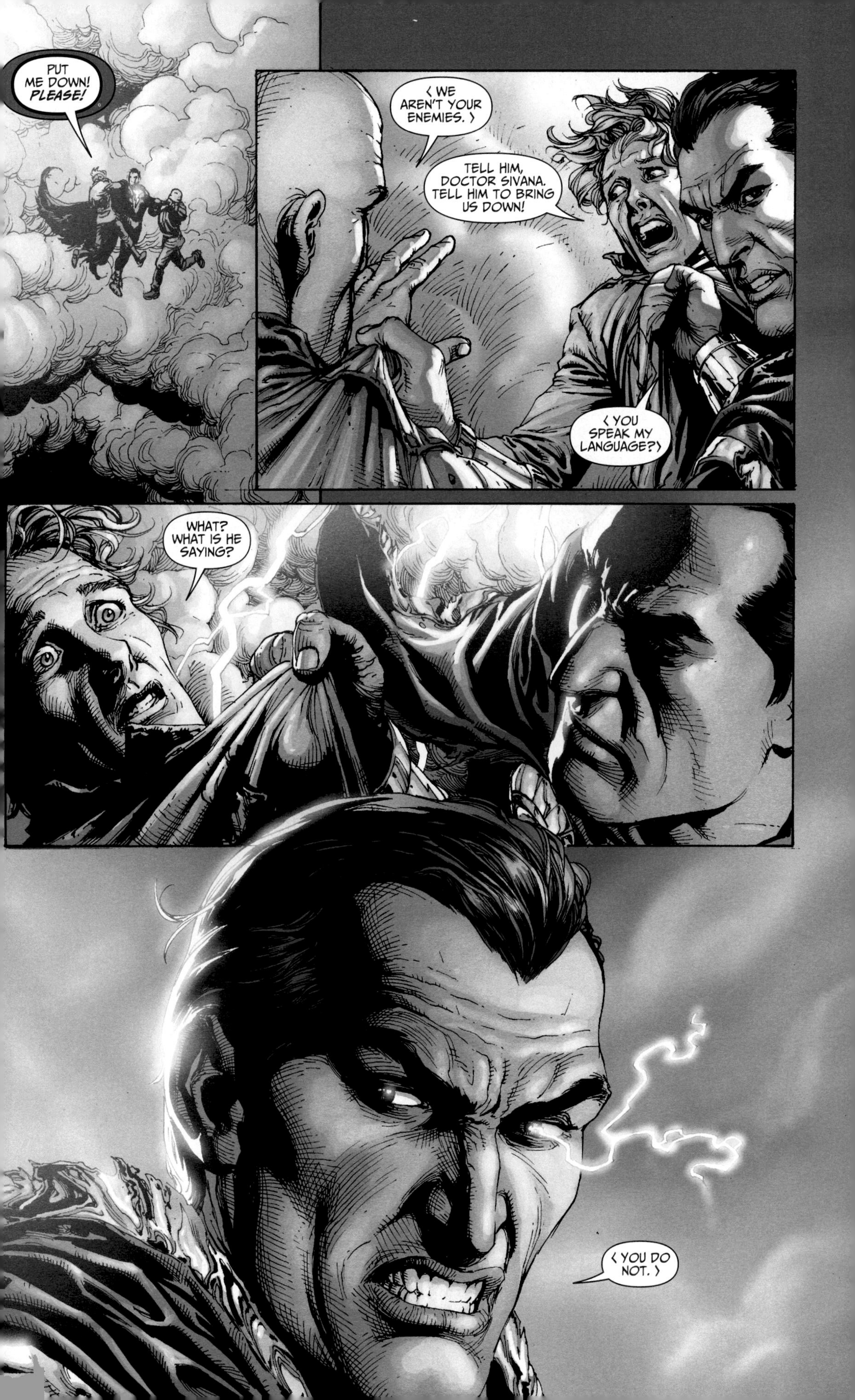
PUT ME DOWN! PLEASE!
〈 WE AREN'T YOUR ENEMIES. 〉
TELL HIM, DOCTOR SIVANA. TELL HIM TO BRING US DOWN!
〈 YOU SPEAK MY LANGUAGE? 〉
WHAT? WHAT IS HE SAYING?
〈 YOU DO NOT. 〉

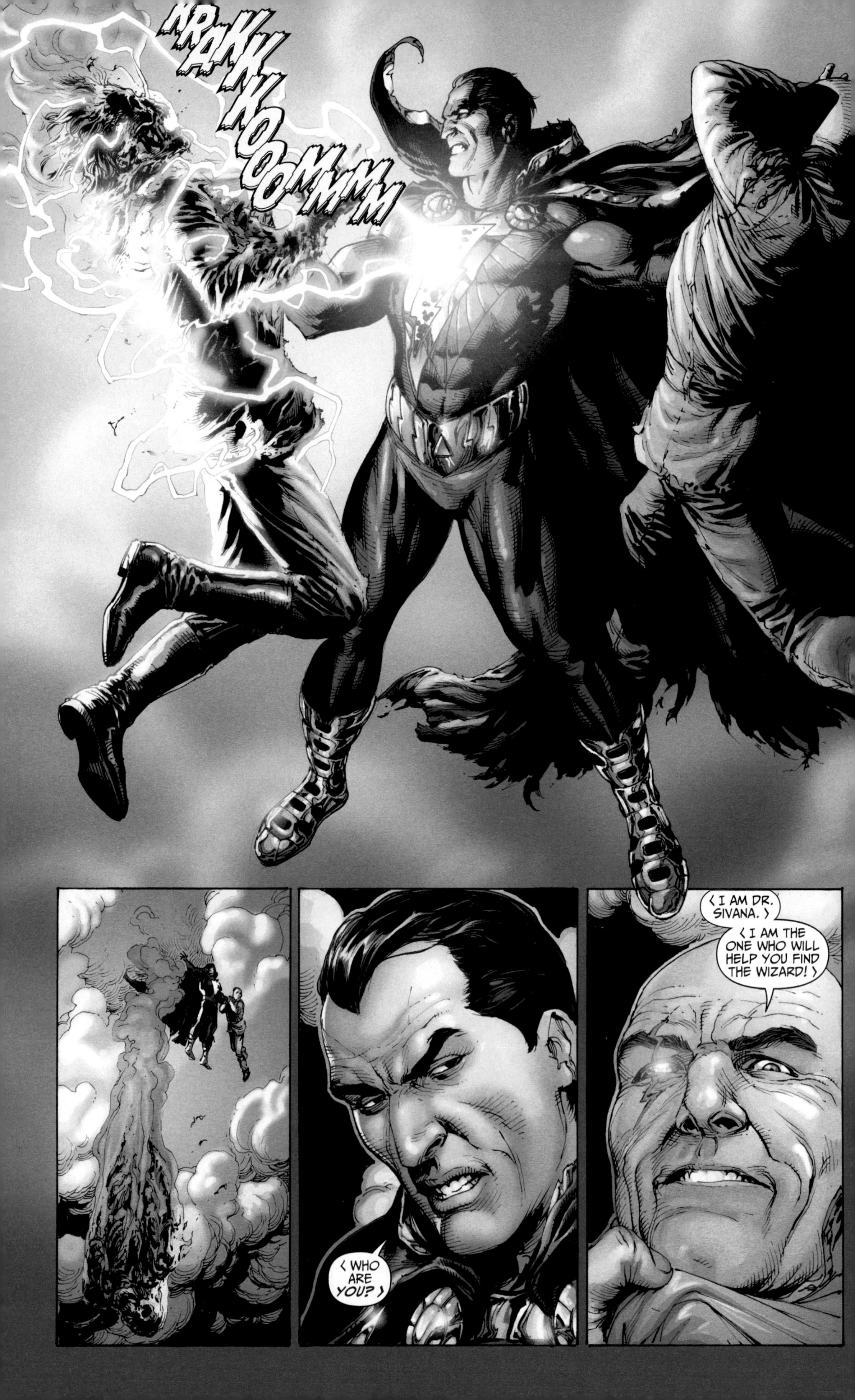
KRAKKOOOMMM
⟨ WHO ARE YOU? ⟩
⟨ I AM DR. SIVANA. ⟩
⟨ I AM THE ONE WHO WILL HELP YOU FIND THE WIZARD! ⟩

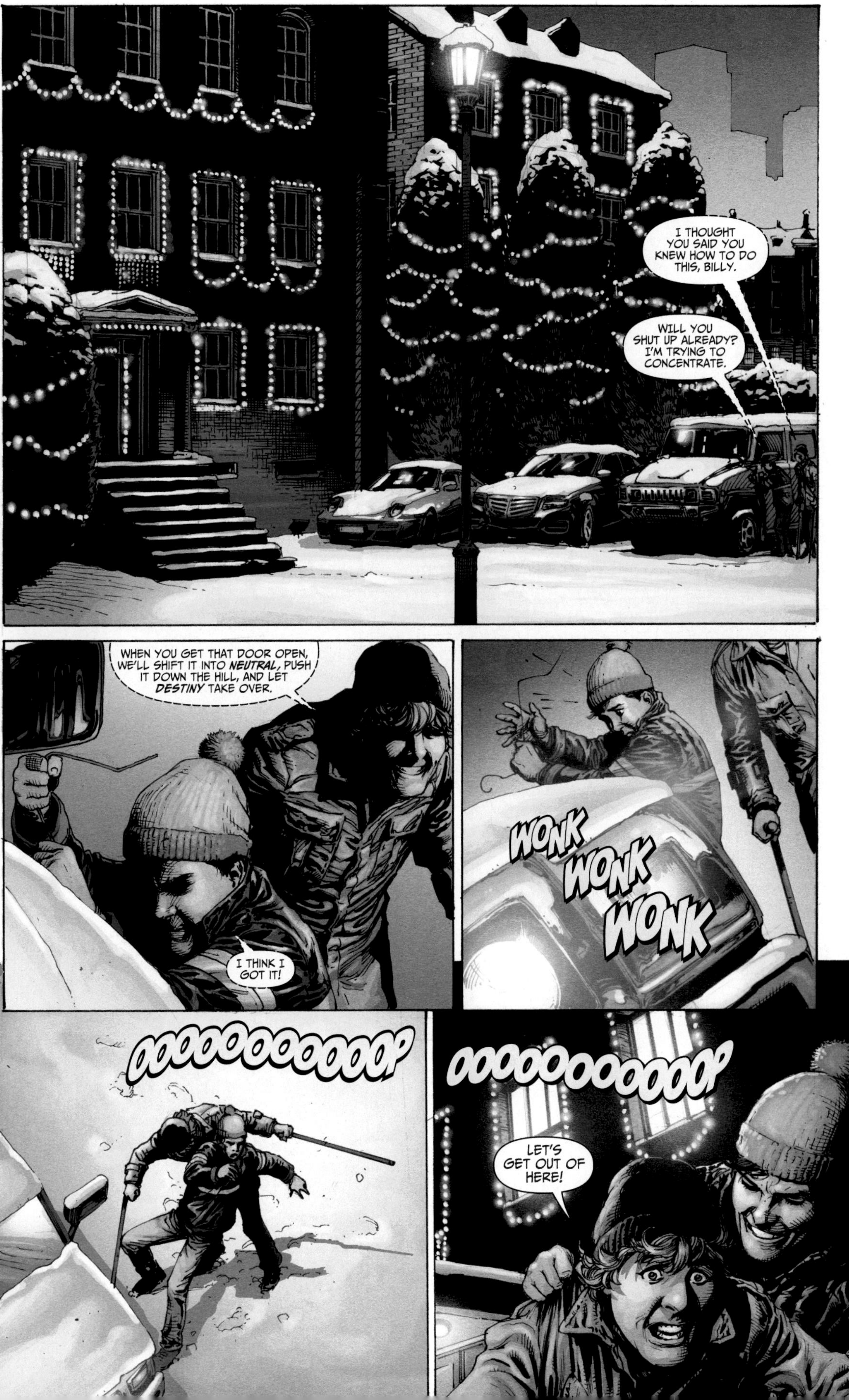
I THOUGHT YOU SAID YOU KNEW HOW TO DO THIS, BILLY.
WILL YOU SHUT UP ALREADY? I'M TRYING TO CONCENTRATE.
WHEN YOU GET THAT DOOR OPEN, WE'LL SHIFT IT INTO *NEUTRAL*, PUSH IT DOWN THE HILL, AND LET *DESTINY* TAKE OVER.
I THINK I GOT IT!
WONK
WONK
WONK
OOOOOOOOOOOP
OOOOOOOOOOOP
LET'S GET OUT OF HERE!

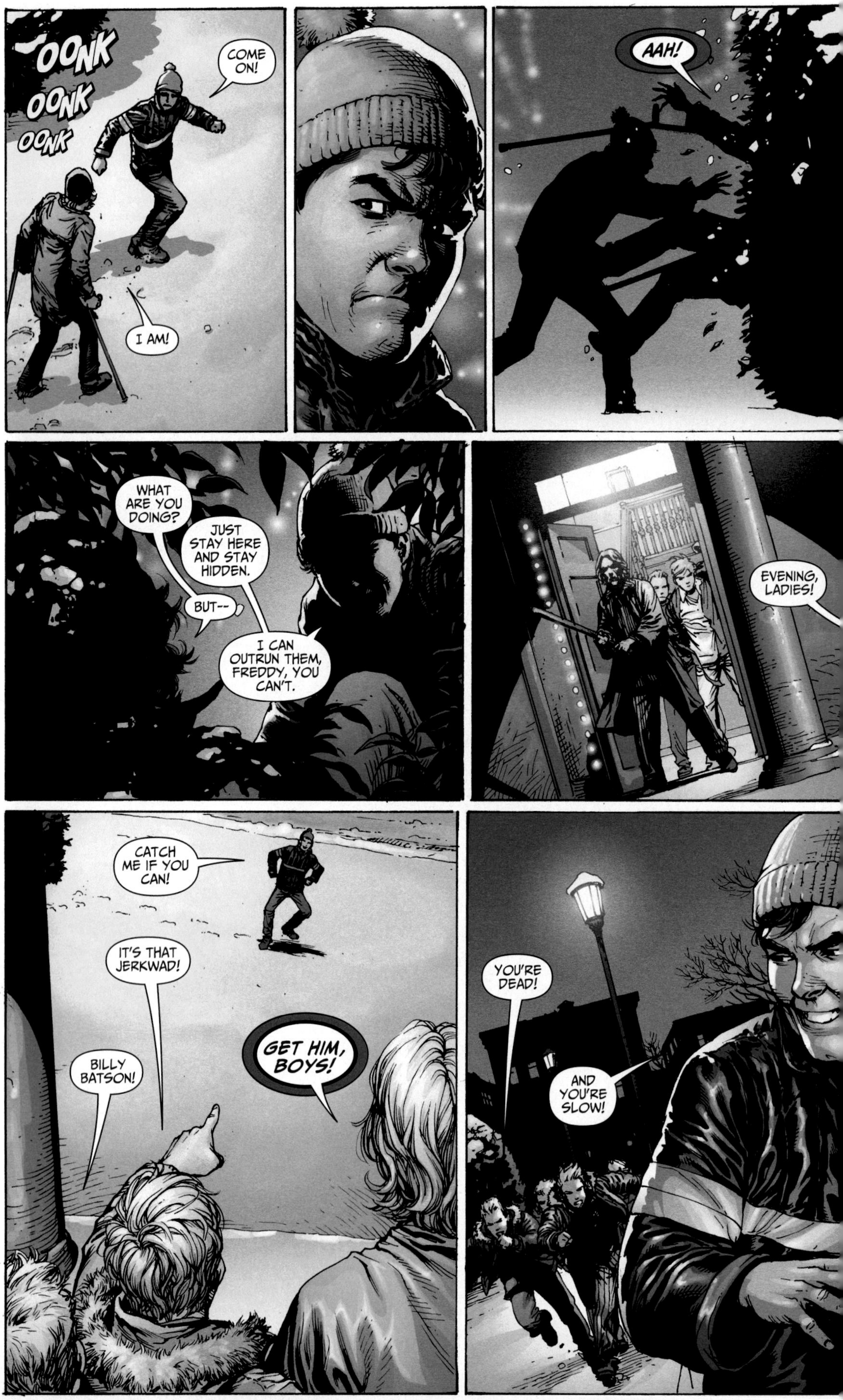
OONK
OONK
OONK
COME ON!
I AM!
AAH!
WHAT ARE YOU DOING?
JUST STAY HERE AND STAY HIDDEN.
BUT--
I CAN OUTRUN THEM, FREDDY, YOU CAN'T.
EVENING, LADIES!
CATCH ME IF YOU CAN!
IT'S THAT JERKWAD!
BILLY BATSON!
GET HIM, BOYS!
YOU'RE DEAD!
AND YOU'RE SLOW!

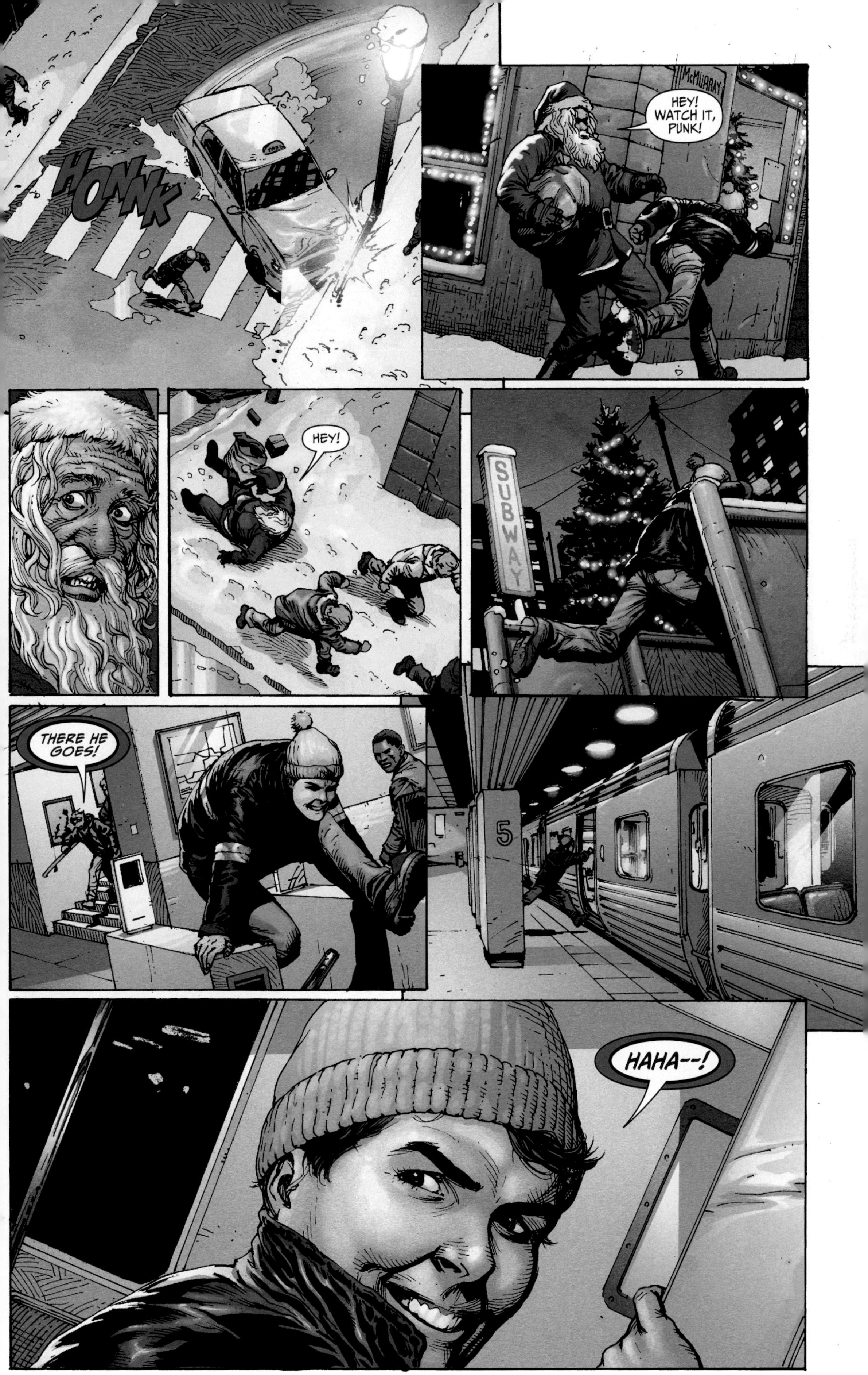
HONNK
McMURRAY
HEY! WATCH IT, PUNK!
HEY!
SUBWAY
THERE HE GOES!
5
HAHA--!

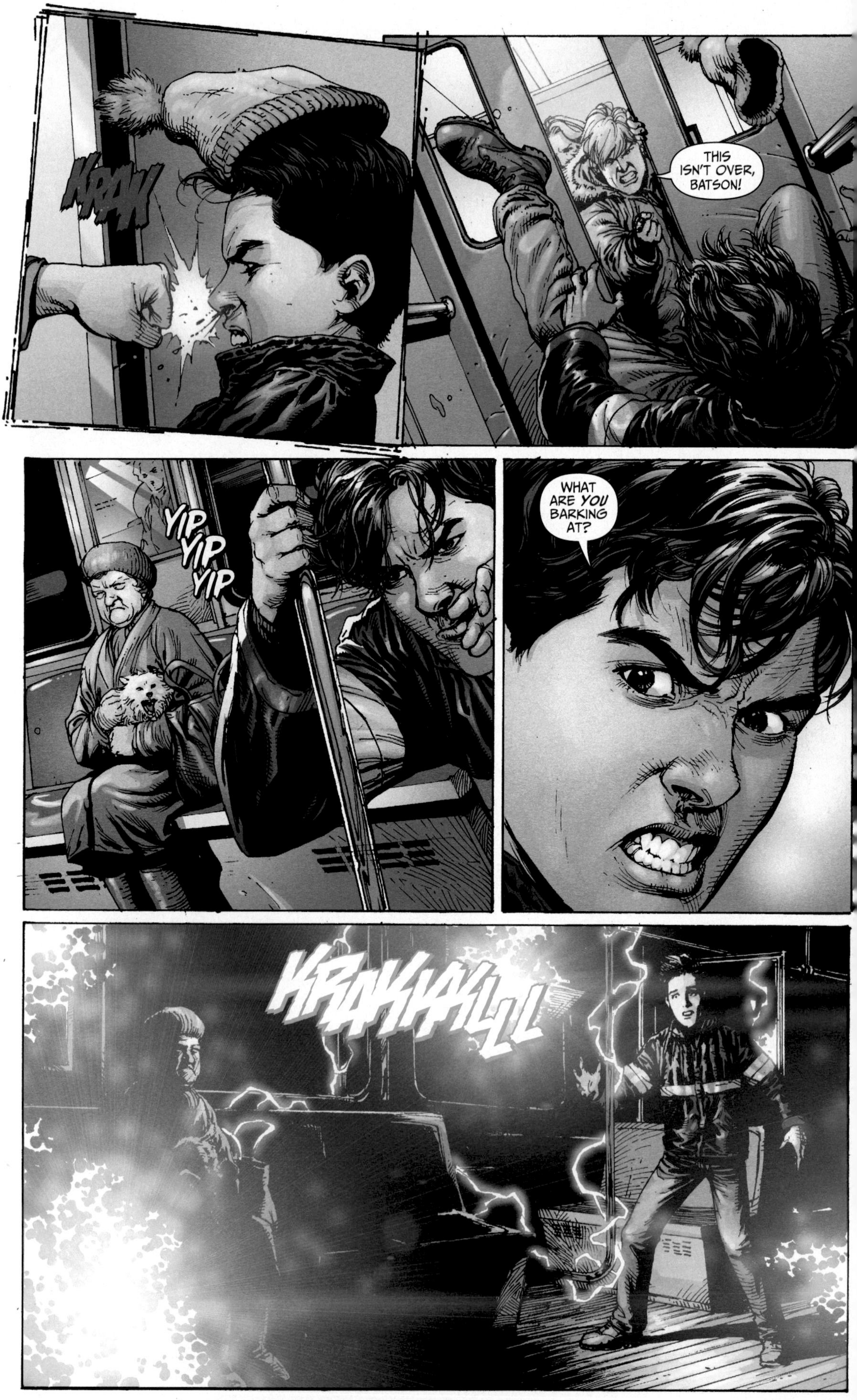
KRAK
THIS ISN'T OVER, BATSON!
YIP YIP YIP
WHAT ARE YOU BARKING AT?
KRAKKAKLLL

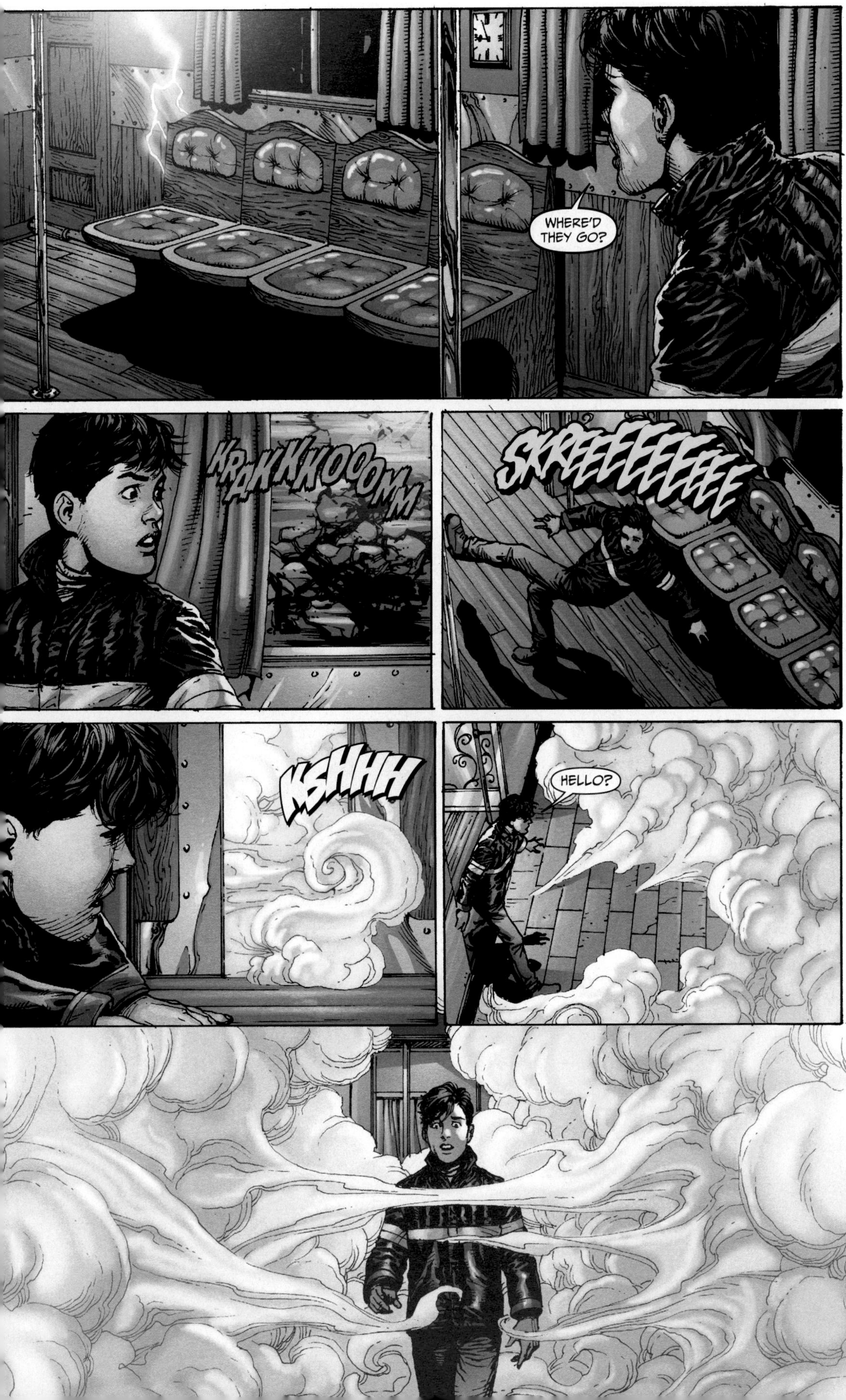
WHERE'D THEY GO?
KRAKKKOOOMM
SKREEEEEEEEEE
KSHHH
HELLO?

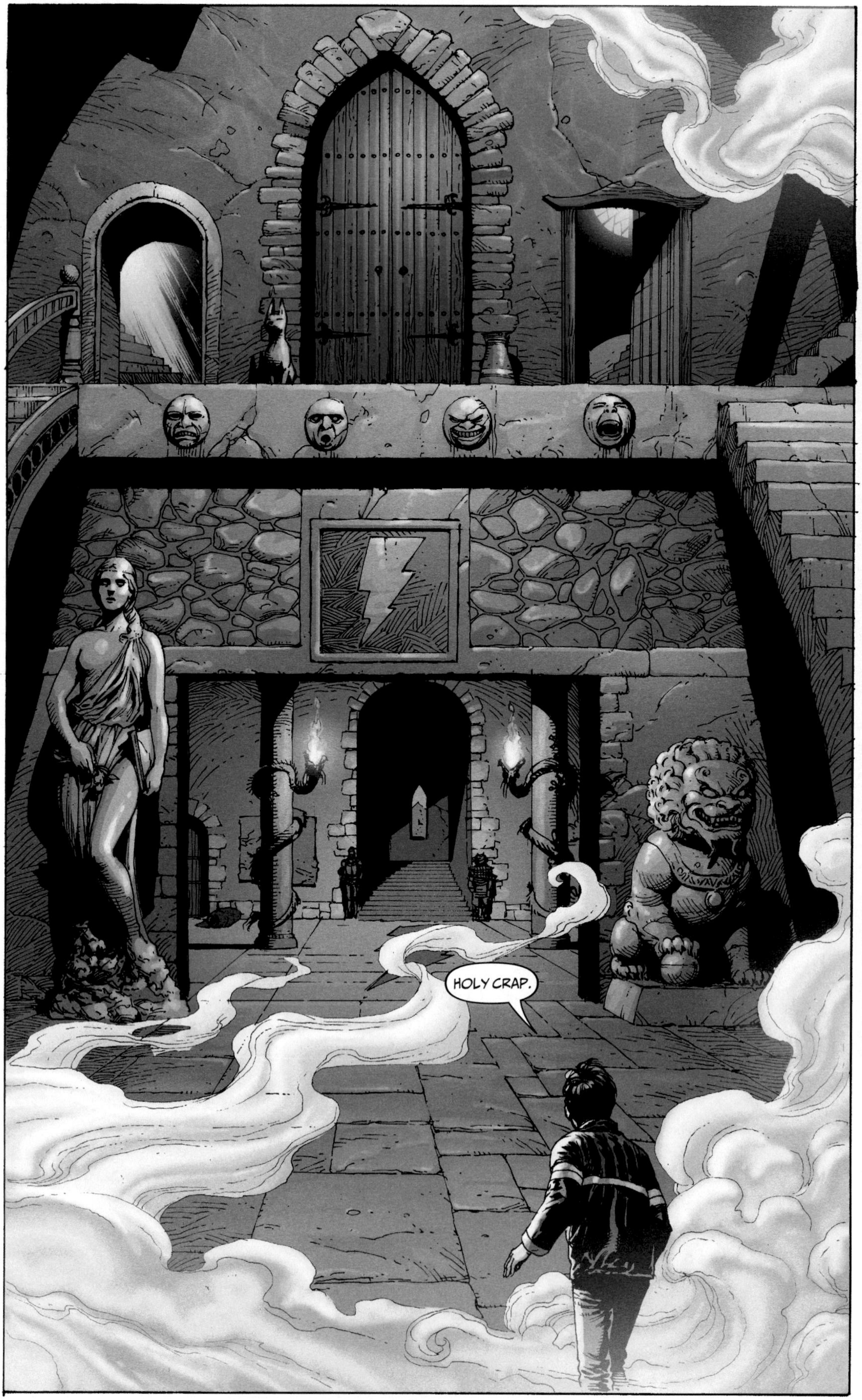
HOLY CRAP.

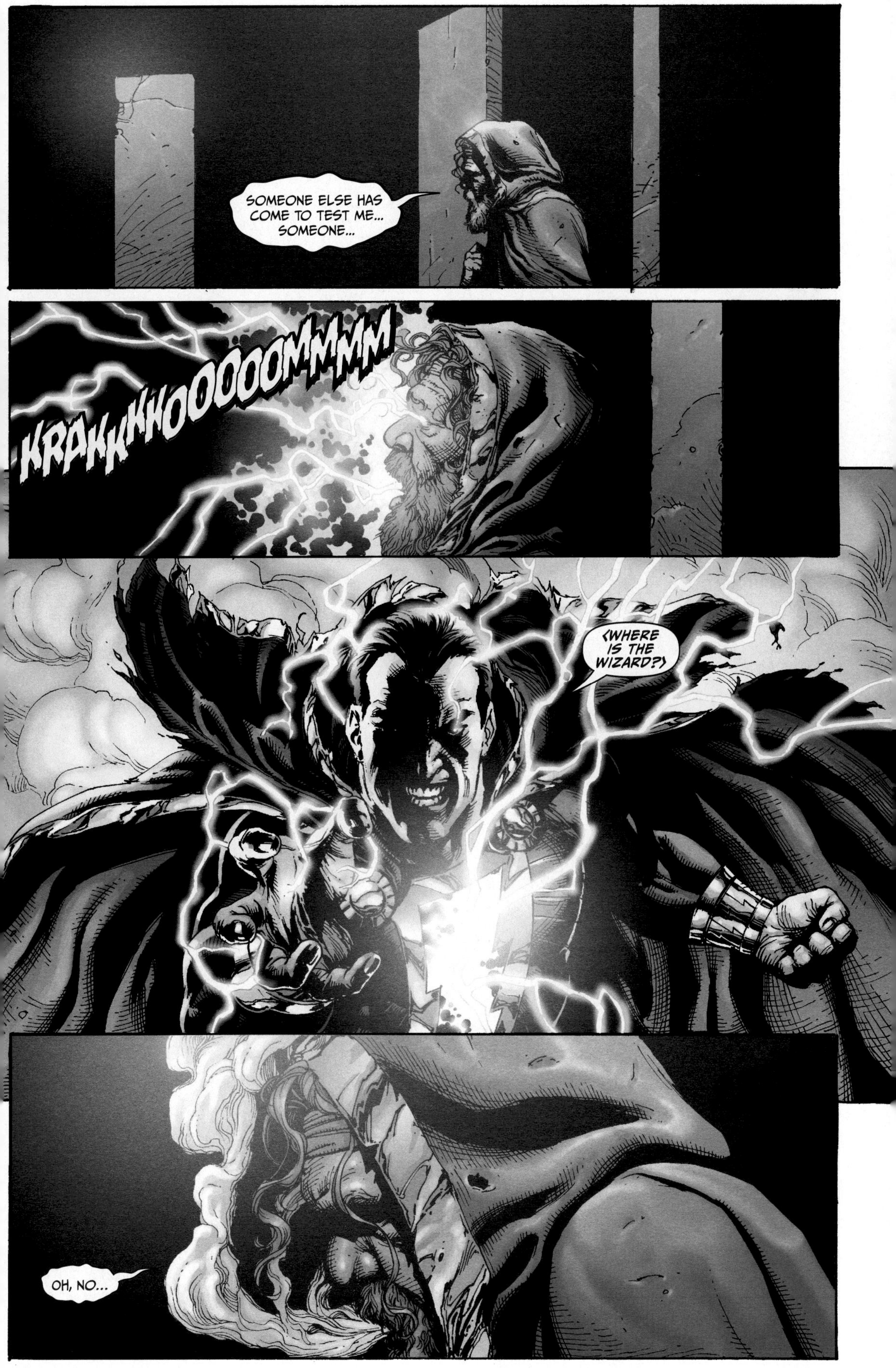
SOMEONE ELSE HAS COME TO TEST ME... SOMEONE...
KRAKKKKOOOOOMMMM
<WHERE IS THE WIZARD?>
OH, NO...

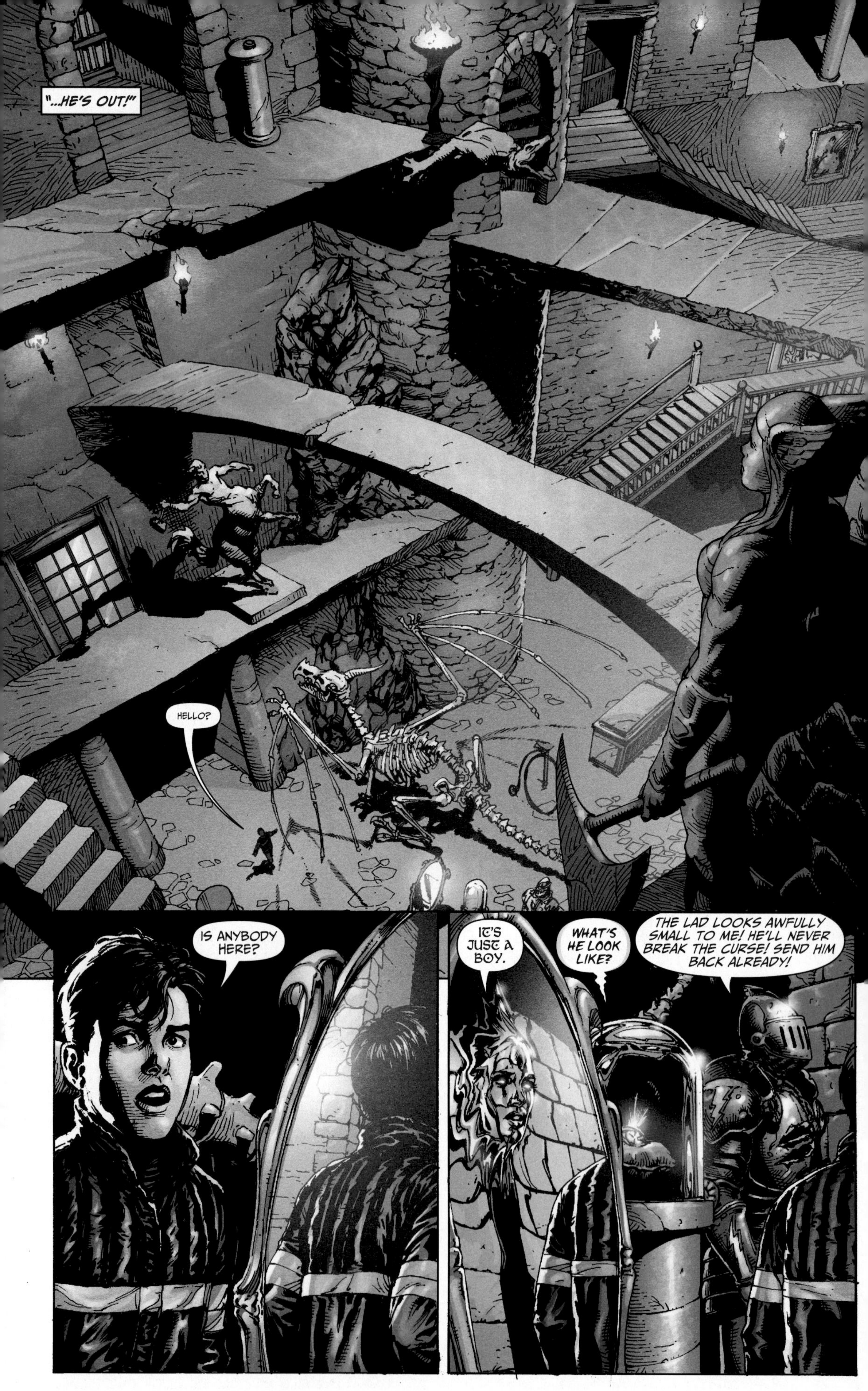
"...HE'S OUT!"
HELLO?
IS ANYBODY HERE?
IT'S JUST A BOY.
WHAT'S HE LOOK LIKE?
THE LAD LOOKS AWFULLY SMALL TO ME! HE'LL NEVER BREAK THE CURSE! SEND HIM BACK ALREADY!

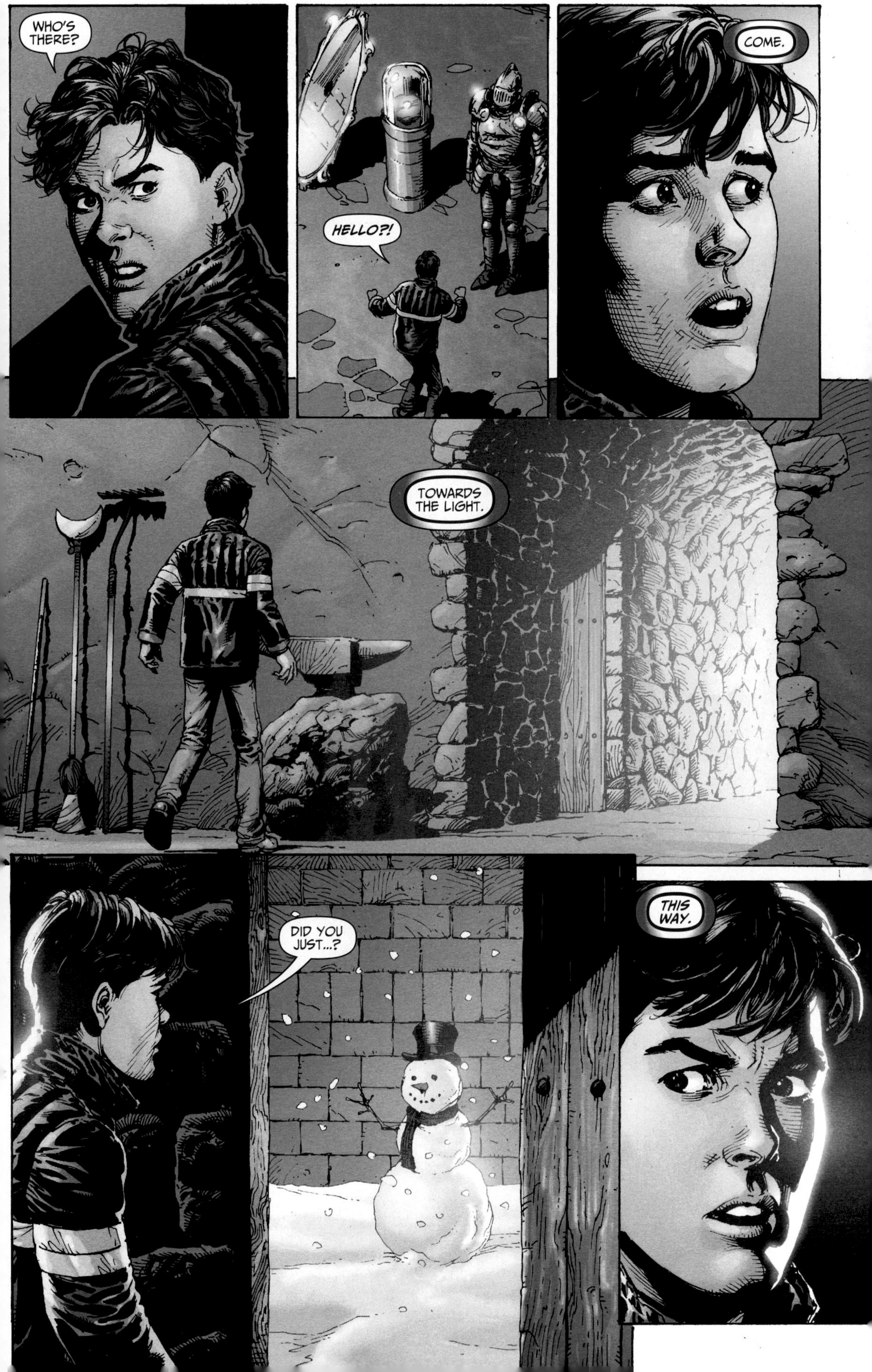
WHO'S THERE?
HELLO?!
COME.
TOWARDS THE LIGHT.
DID YOU JUST...?
THIS WAY.

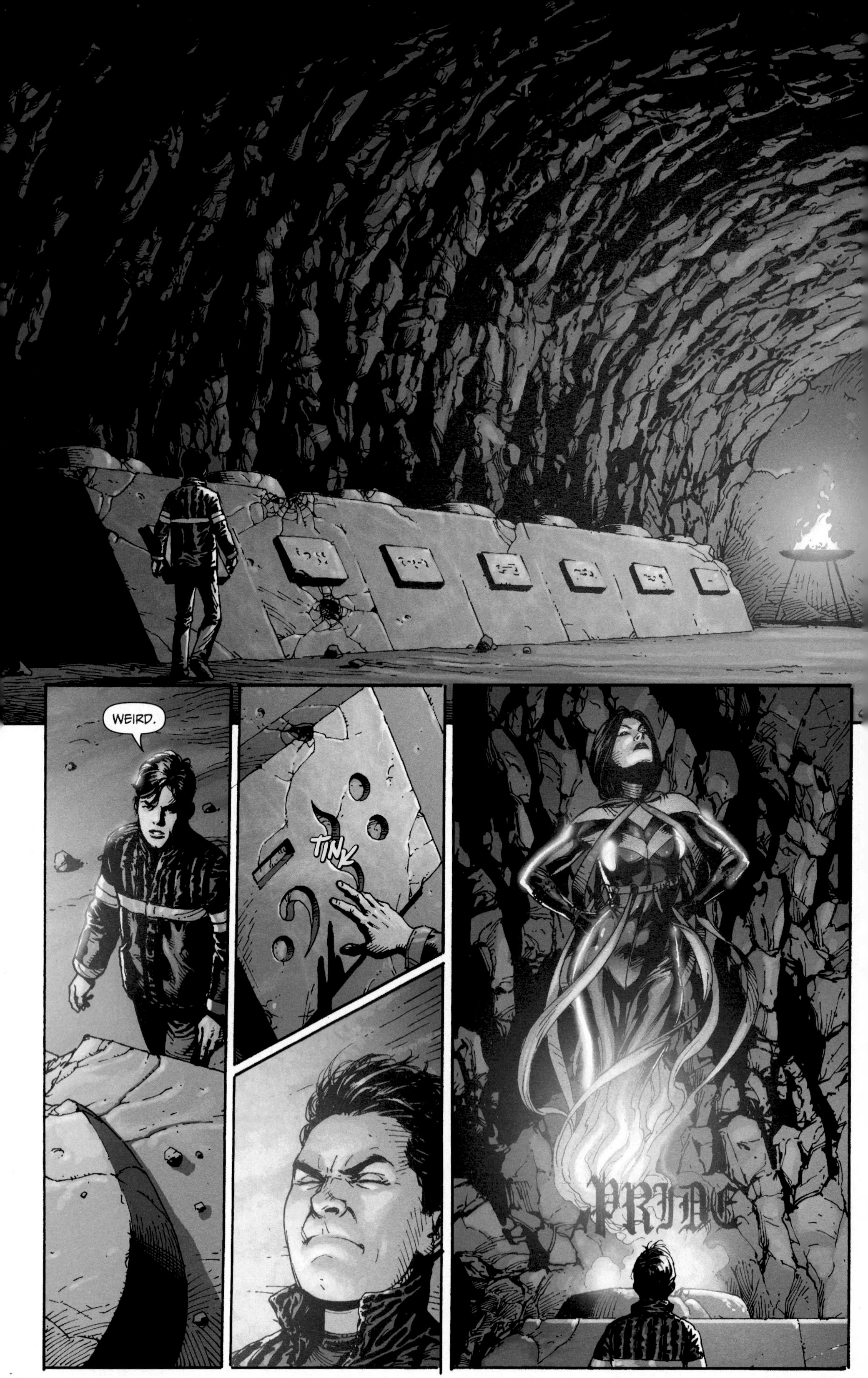
WEIRD.
TINK
PRIDE

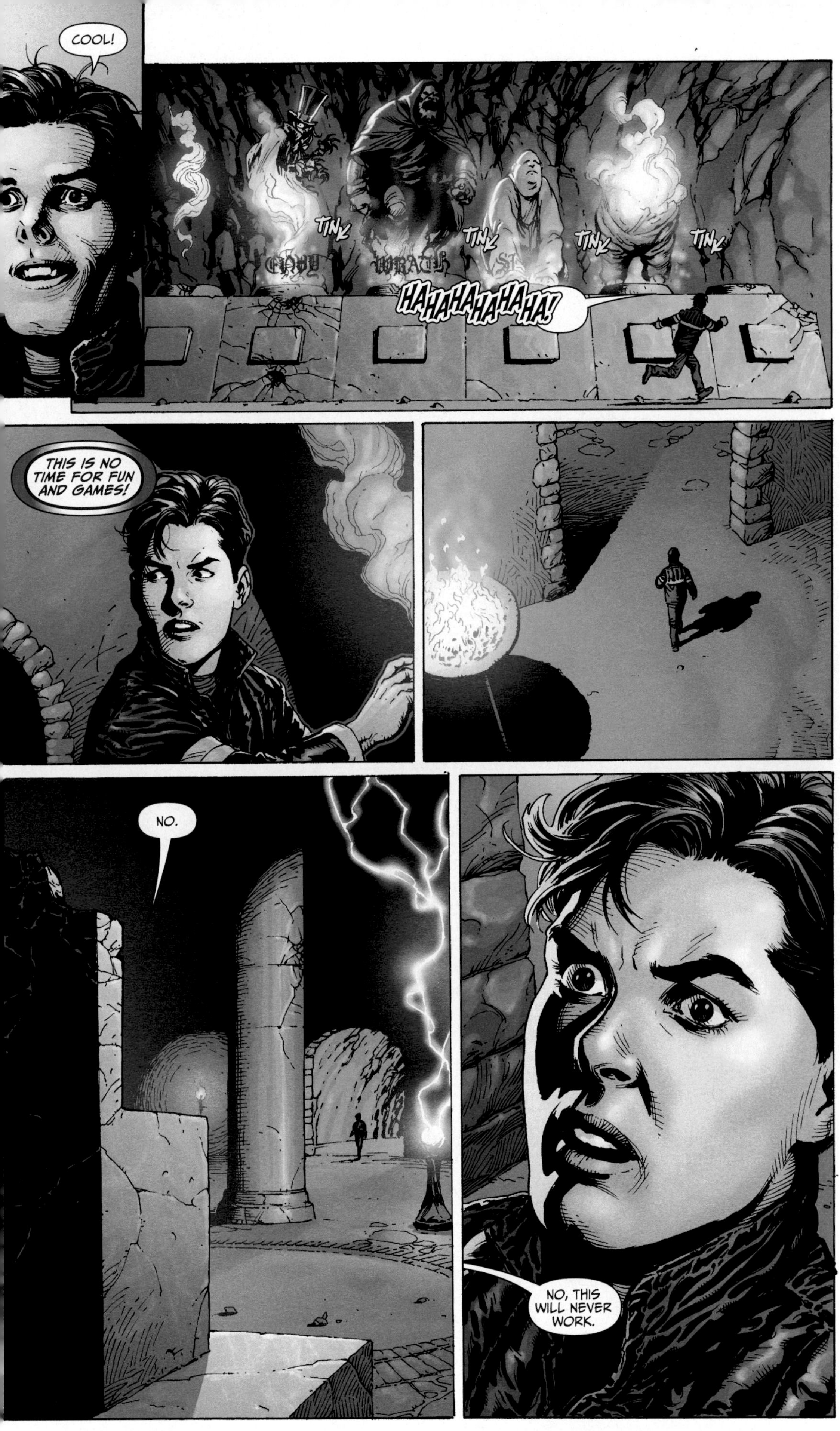
COOL!
TINK
TINK
TINK
TINK
ENVY
WRATH
HAHAHAHAHAHA!
THIS IS NO TIME FOR FUN AND GAMES!
NO.
NO, THIS WILL NEVER WORK.

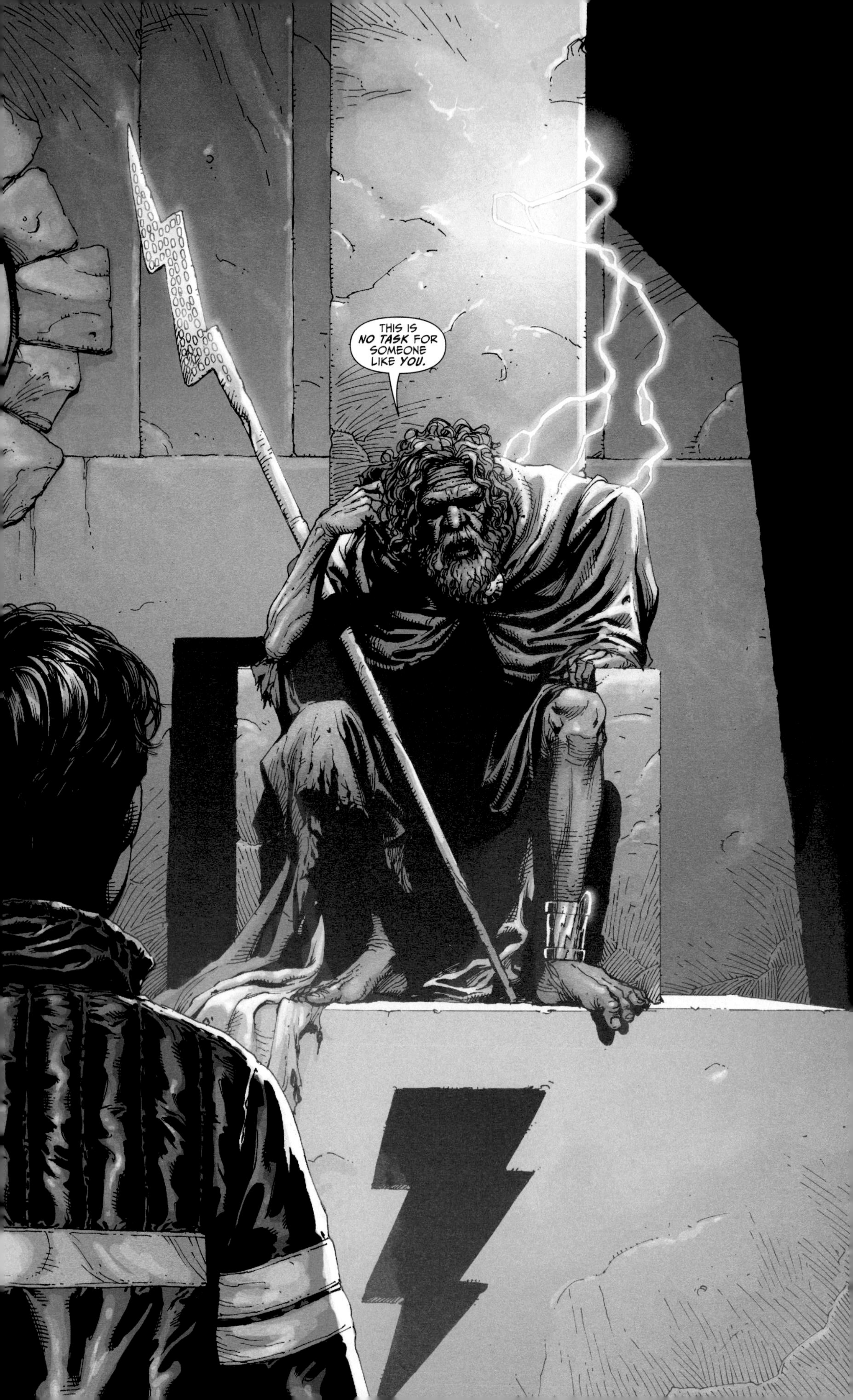
THIS IS NO TASK FOR SOMEONE LIKE YOU.

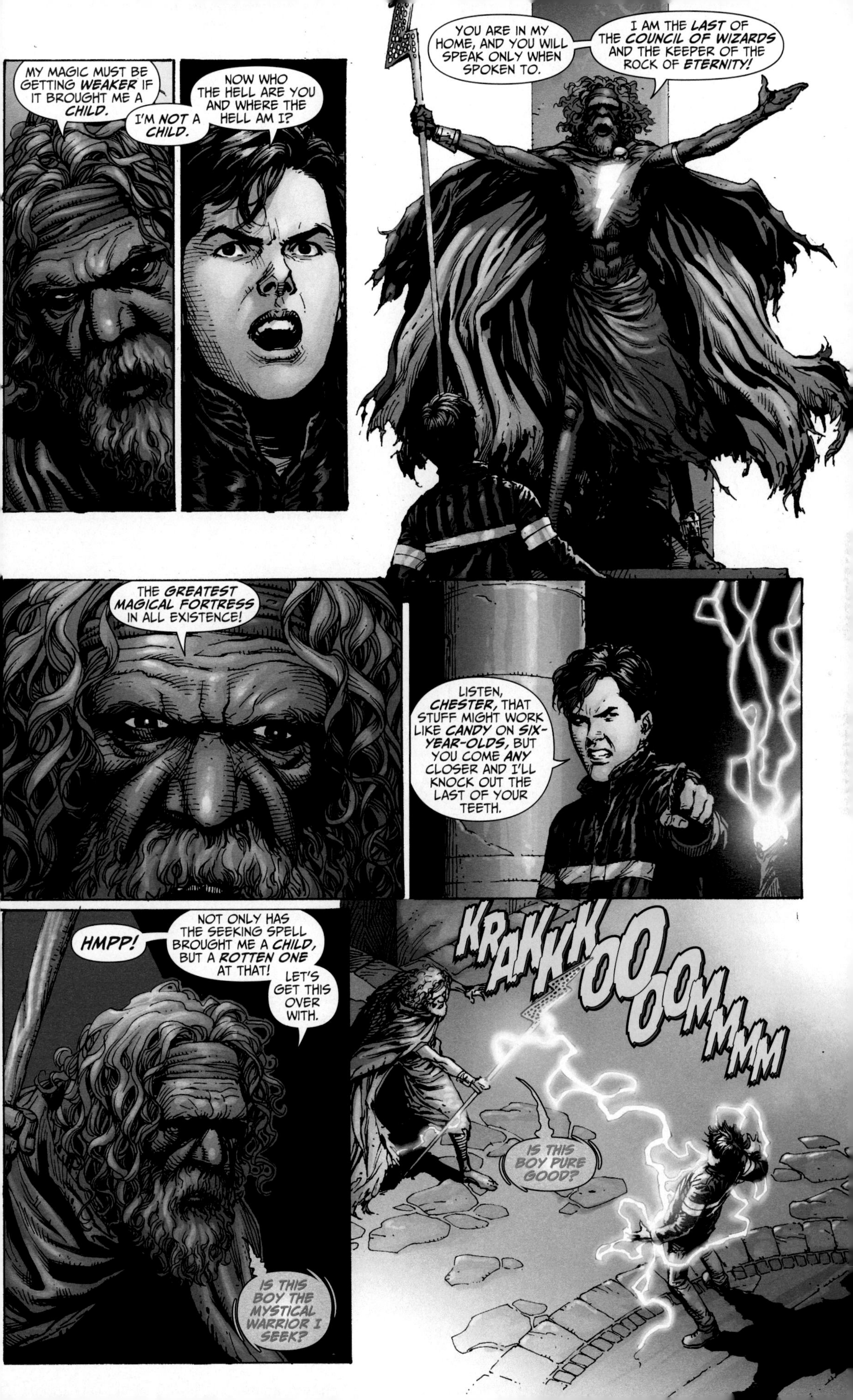

MY MAGIC MUST BE GETTING WEAKER IF IT BROUGHT ME A CHILD.
I'M NOT A CHILD.
NOW WHO THE HELL ARE YOU AND WHERE THE HELL AM I?
YOU ARE IN MY HOME, AND YOU WILL SPEAK ONLY WHEN SPOKEN TO.
I AM THE LAST OF THE COUNCIL OF WIZARDS AND THE KEEPER OF THE ROCK OF ETERNITY!
THE GREATEST MAGICAL FORTRESS IN ALL EXISTENCE!
LISTEN, CHESTER, THAT STUFF MIGHT WORK LIKE CANDY ON SIX-YEAR-OLDS, BUT YOU COME ANY CLOSER AND I'LL KNOCK OUT THE LAST OF YOUR TEETH.
HMPP!
NOT ONLY HAS THE SEEKING SPELL BROUGHT ME A CHILD, BUT A ROTTEN ONE AT THAT!
LET'S GET THIS OVER WITH.
IS THIS BOY THE MYSTICAL WARRIOR I SEEK?
KRAKKKOOOOMMMM
IS THIS BOY PURE GOOD?

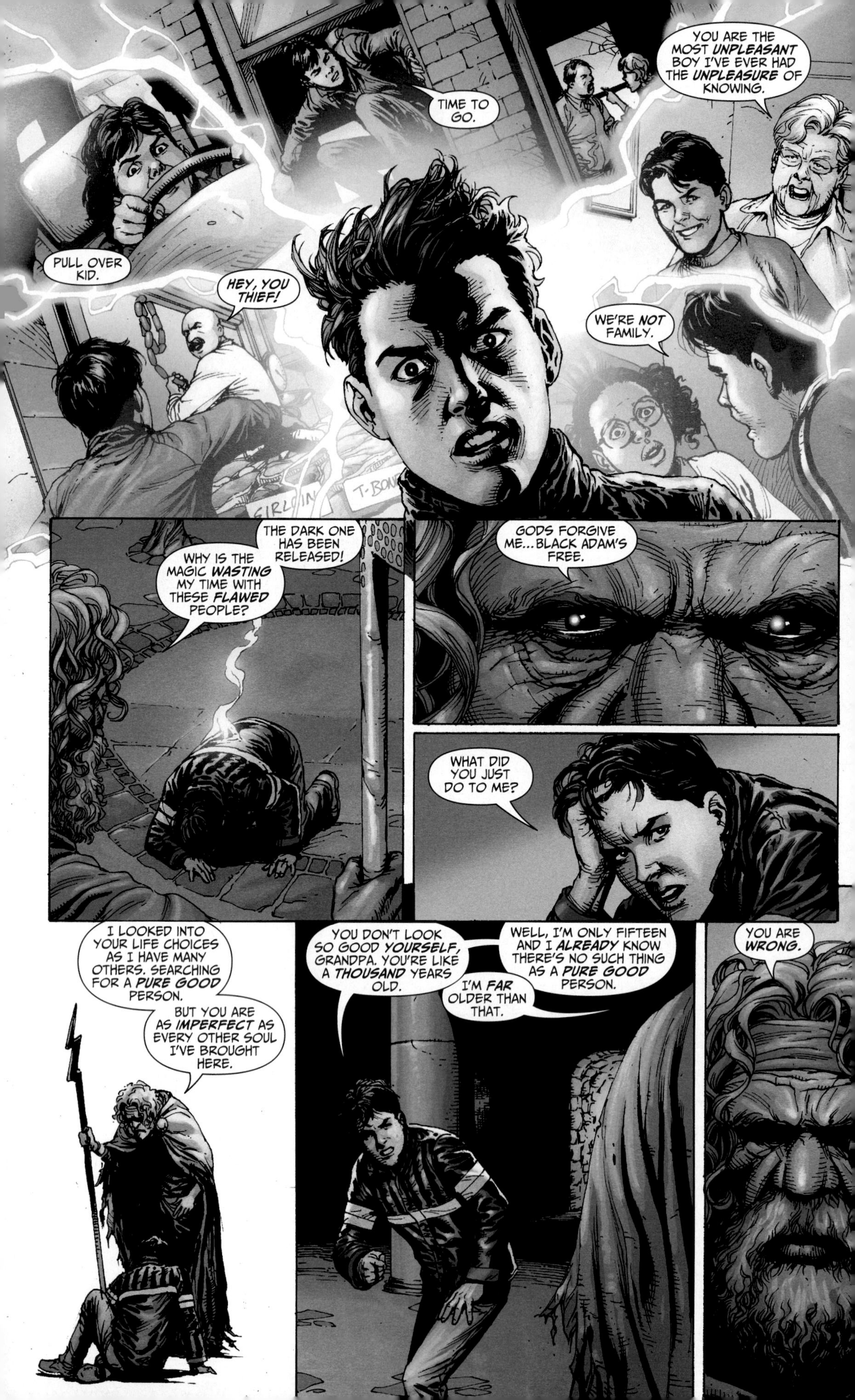
PULL OVER KID.
TIME TO GO.
YOU ARE THE MOST UNPLEASANT BOY I'VE EVER HAD THE UNPLEASURE OF KNOWING.
HEY, YOU THIEF!
WE'RE NOT FAMILY.
SIRLOIN
T-BONE
THE DARK ONE HAS BEEN RELEASED!
WHY IS THE MAGIC WASTING MY TIME WITH THESE FLAWED PEOPLE?
GODS FORGIVE ME...BLACK ADAM'S FREE.
WHAT DID YOU JUST DO TO ME?
I LOOKED INTO YOUR LIFE CHOICES AS I HAVE MANY OTHERS. SEARCHING FOR A PURE GOOD PERSON.
BUT YOU ARE AS IMPERFECT AS EVERY OTHER SOUL I'VE BROUGHT HERE.
YOU DON'T LOOK SO GOOD YOURSELF, GRANDPA. YOU'RE LIKE A THOUSAND YEARS OLD.
I'M FAR OLDER THAN THAT.
WELL, I'M ONLY FIFTEEN AND I ALREADY KNOW THERE'S NO SUCH THING AS A PURE GOOD PERSON.
YOU ARE WRONG.

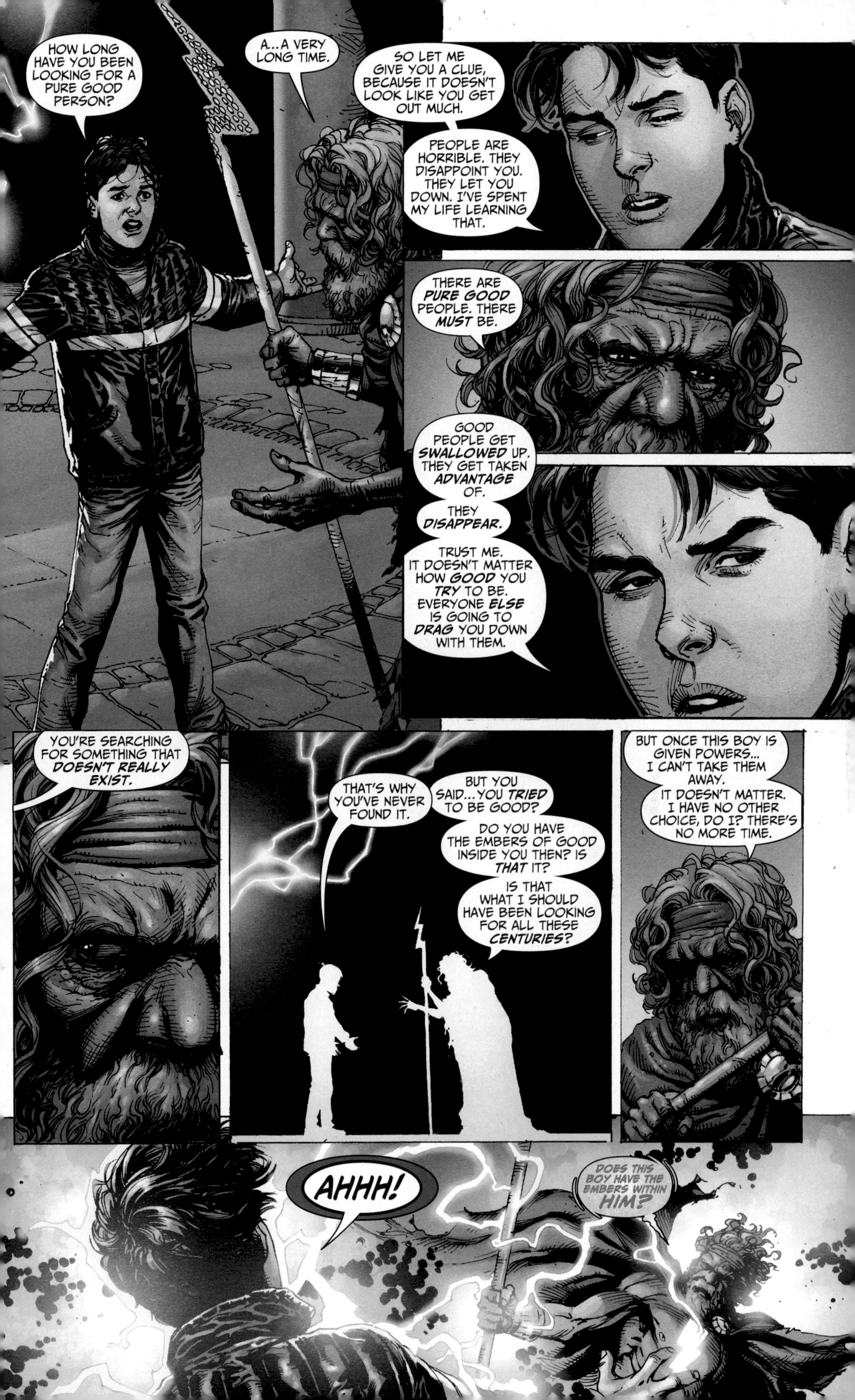
HOW LONG HAVE YOU BEEN LOOKING FOR A PURE GOOD PERSON?
A...A VERY LONG TIME.
SO LET ME GIVE YOU A CLUE, BECAUSE IT DOESN'T LOOK LIKE YOU GET OUT MUCH.
PEOPLE ARE HORRIBLE. THEY DISAPPOINT YOU. THEY LET YOU DOWN. I'VE SPENT MY LIFE LEARNING THAT.
THERE ARE PURE GOOD PEOPLE. THERE MUST BE.
GOOD PEOPLE GET SWALLOWED UP. THEY GET TAKEN ADVANTAGE OF.
THEY DISAPPEAR.
TRUST ME. IT DOESN'T MATTER HOW GOOD YOU TRY TO BE. EVERYONE ELSE IS GOING TO DRAG YOU DOWN WITH THEM.
YOU'RE SEARCHING FOR SOMETHING THAT DOESN'T REALLY EXIST.
THAT'S WHY YOU'VE NEVER FOUND IT.
BUT YOU SAID...YOU TRIED TO BE GOOD?
DO YOU HAVE THE EMBERS OF GOOD INSIDE YOU THEN? IS THAT IT?
IS THAT WHAT I SHOULD HAVE BEEN LOOKING FOR ALL THESE CENTURIES?
BUT ONCE THIS BOY IS GIVEN POWERS... I CAN'T TAKE THEM AWAY.
IT DOESN'T MATTER. I HAVE NO OTHER CHOICE, DO I? THERE'S NO MORE TIME.
AHHH!
DOES THIS BOY HAVE THE EMBERS WITHIN HIM?

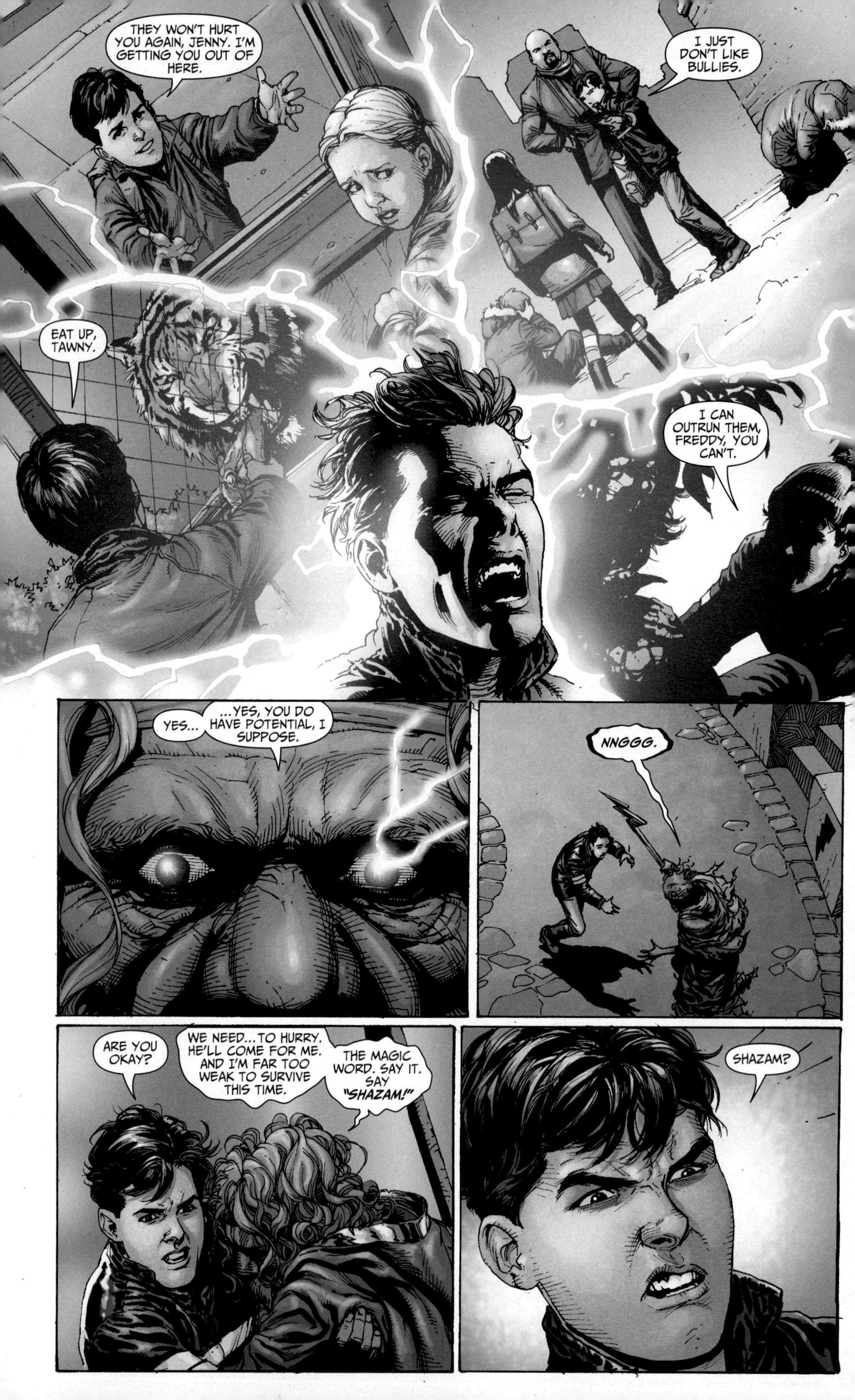
THEY WON'T HURT YOU AGAIN, JENNY. I'M GETTING YOU OUT OF HERE.
I JUST DON'T LIKE BULLIES.
EAT UP, TAWNY.
I CAN OUTRUN THEM, FREDDY, YOU CAN'T.
YES...
...YES, YOU DO HAVE POTENTIAL, I SUPPOSE.
NNGGG.
ARE YOU OKAY?
WE NEED...TO HURRY. HE'LL COME FOR ME. AND I'M FAR TOO WEAK TO SURVIVE THIS TIME.
THE MAGIC WORD. SAY IT. SAY "SHAZAM!"
SHAZAM?

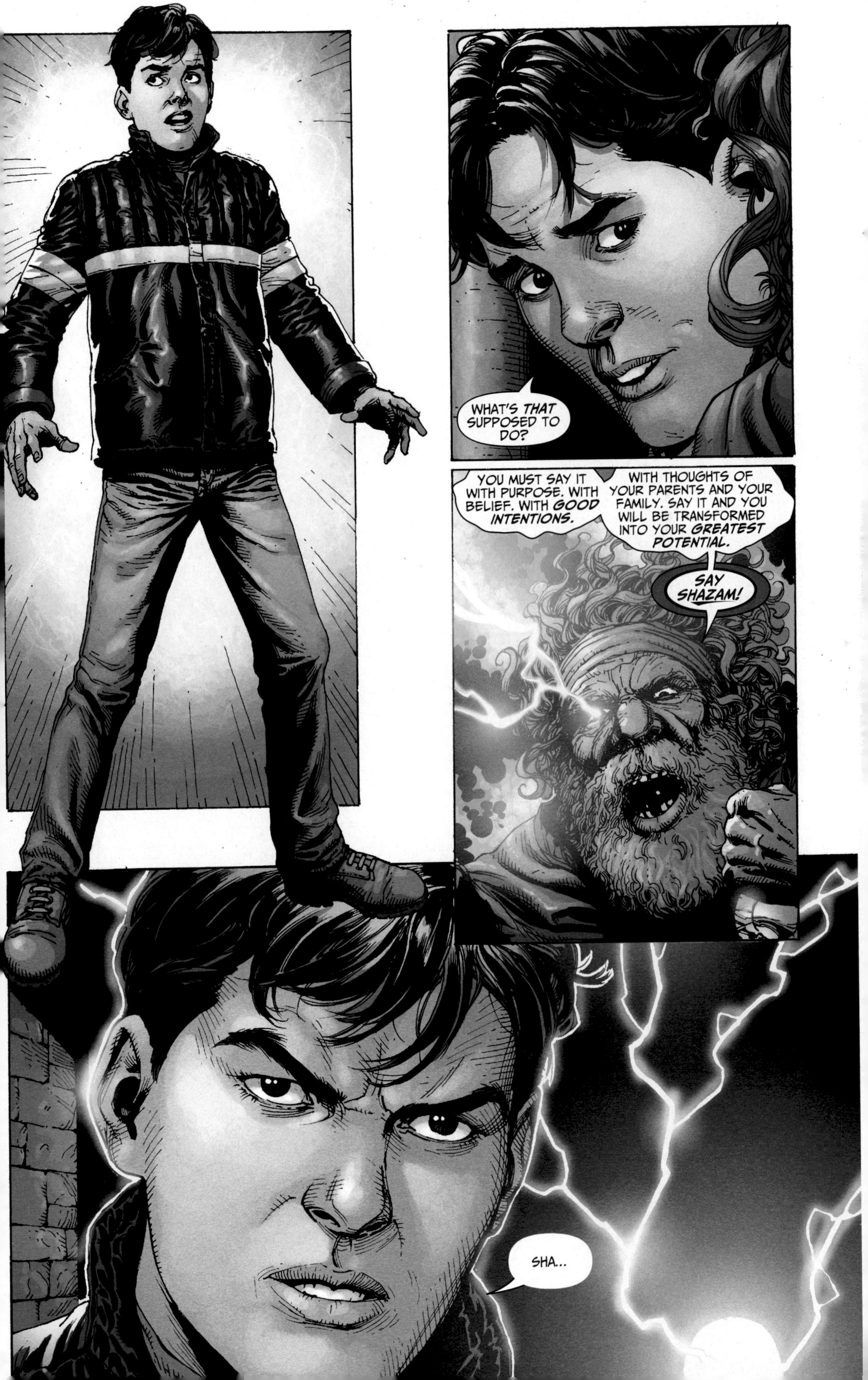
WHAT'S THAT SUPPOSED TO DO?
YOU MUST SAY IT WITH PURPOSE. WITH BELIEF. WITH GOOD INTENTIONS.
WITH THOUGHTS OF YOUR PARENTS AND YOUR FAMILY. SAY IT AND YOU WILL BE TRANSFORMED INTO YOUR GREATEST POTENTIAL.
SAY SHAZAM!
SHA...

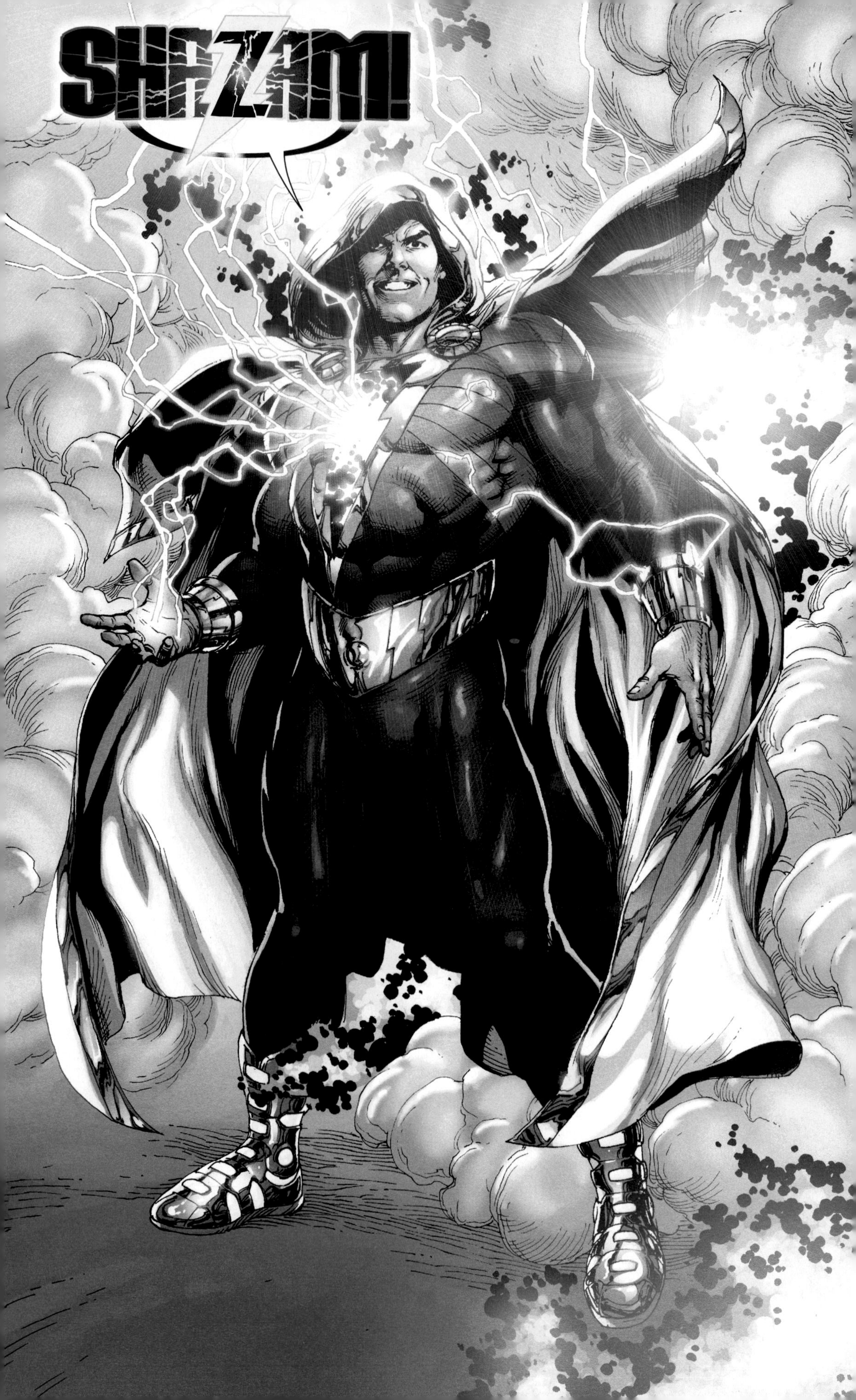
SHAZAM!

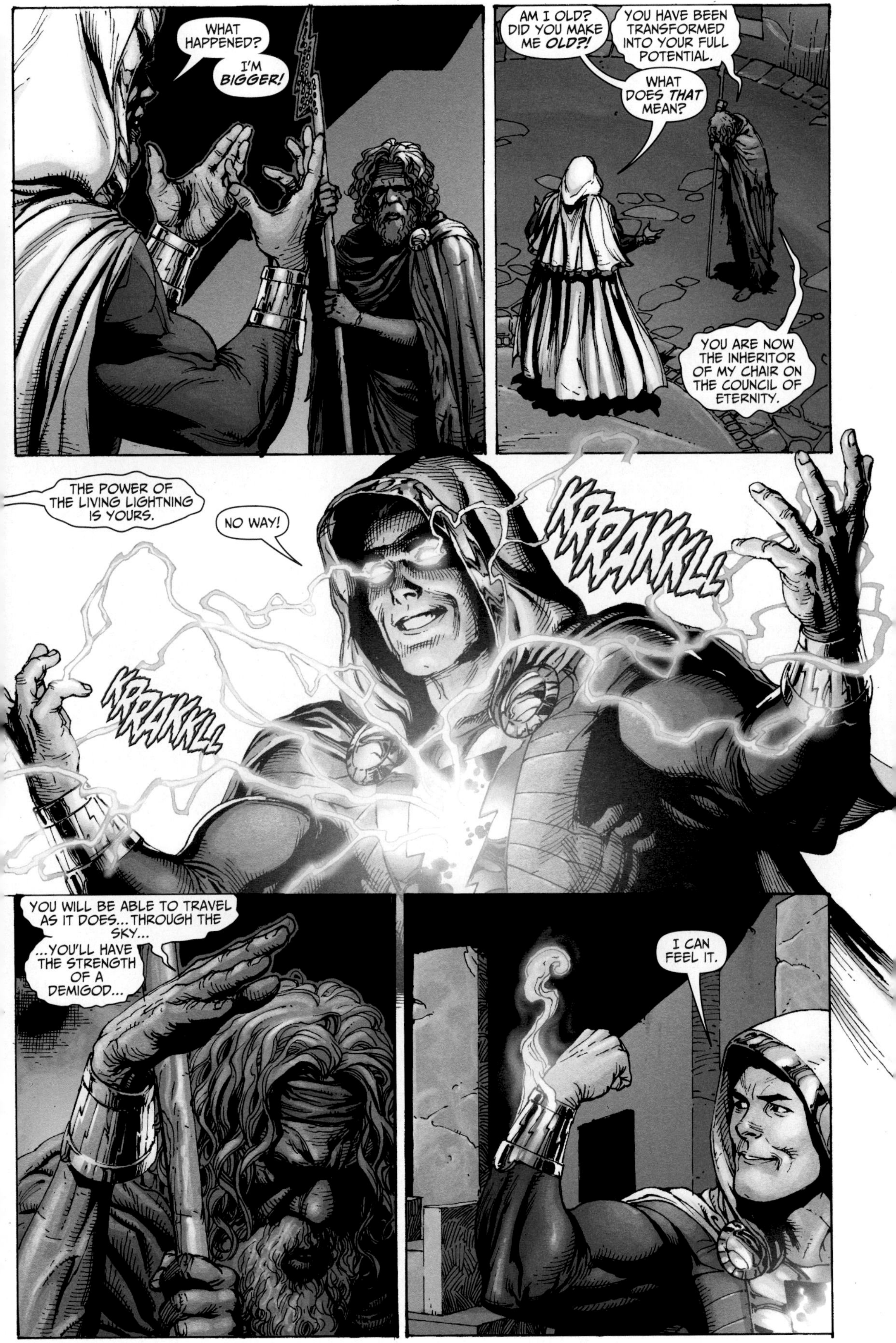
WHAT HAPPENED?
I'M BIGGER!
AM I OLD? DID YOU MAKE ME OLD?!
YOU HAVE BEEN TRANSFORMED INTO YOUR FULL POTENTIAL.
WHAT DOES THAT MEAN?
YOU ARE NOW THE INHERITOR OF MY CHAIR ON THE COUNCIL OF ETERNITY.
THE POWER OF THE LIVING LIGHTNING IS YOURS.
NO WAY!
KRRAKKLL
KRRAKKLL
YOU WILL BE ABLE TO TRAVEL AS IT DOES...THROUGH THE SKY...
...YOU'LL HAVE THE STRENGTH OF A DEMIGOD...
I CAN FEEL IT.

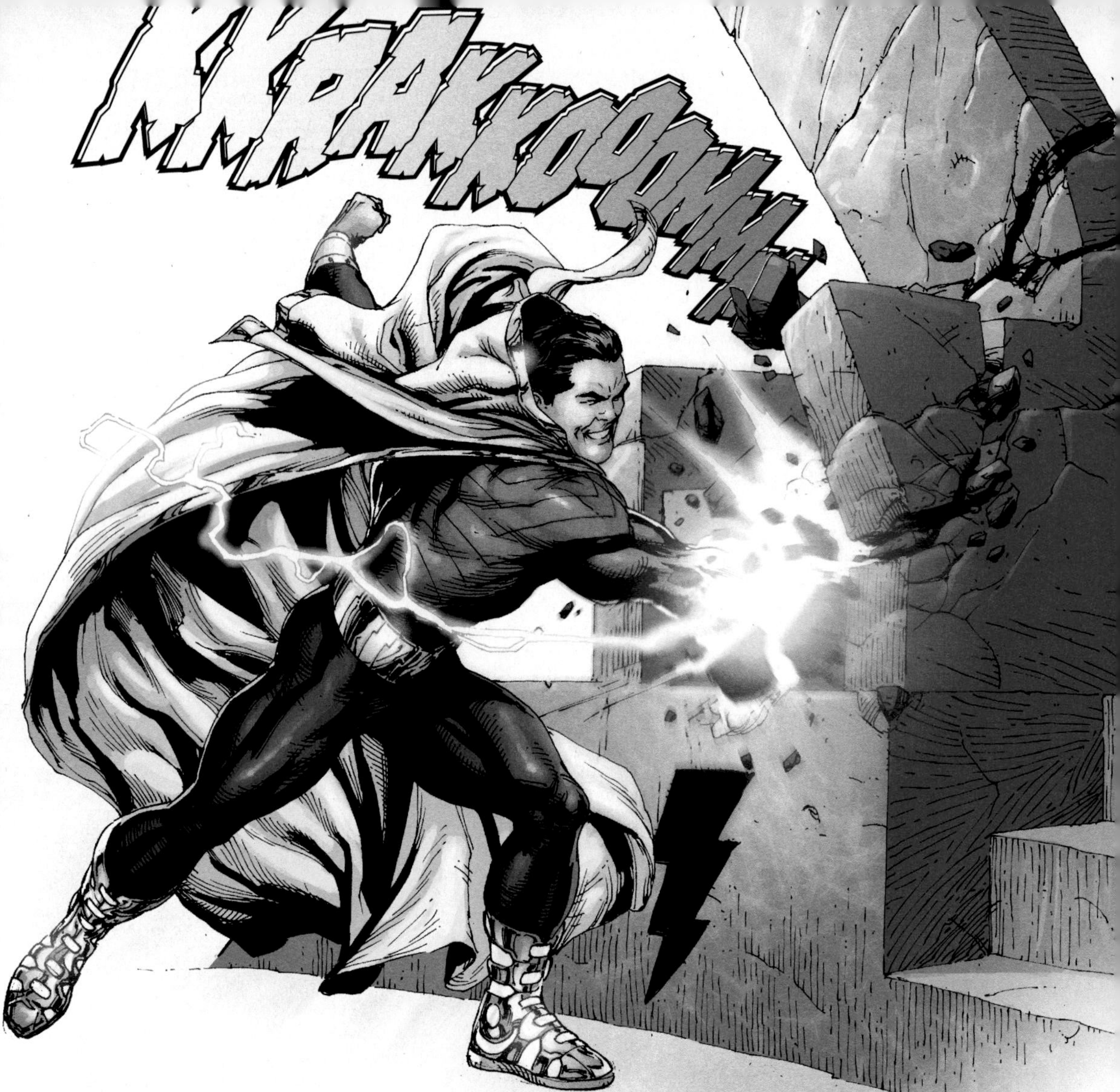
KKRAKOOMM

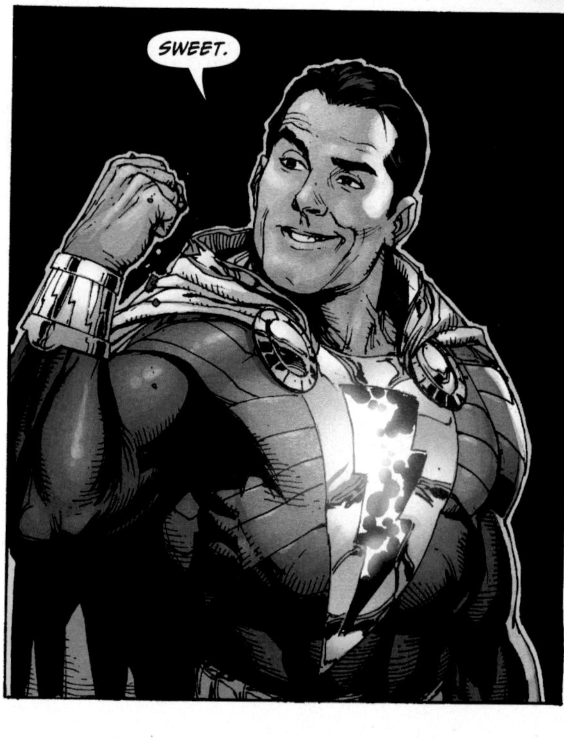
SWEET.

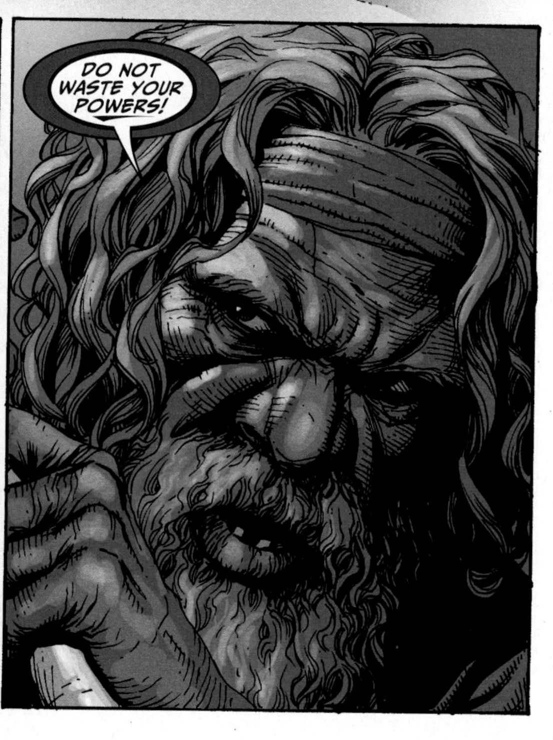
DO NOT WASTE YOUR POWERS!

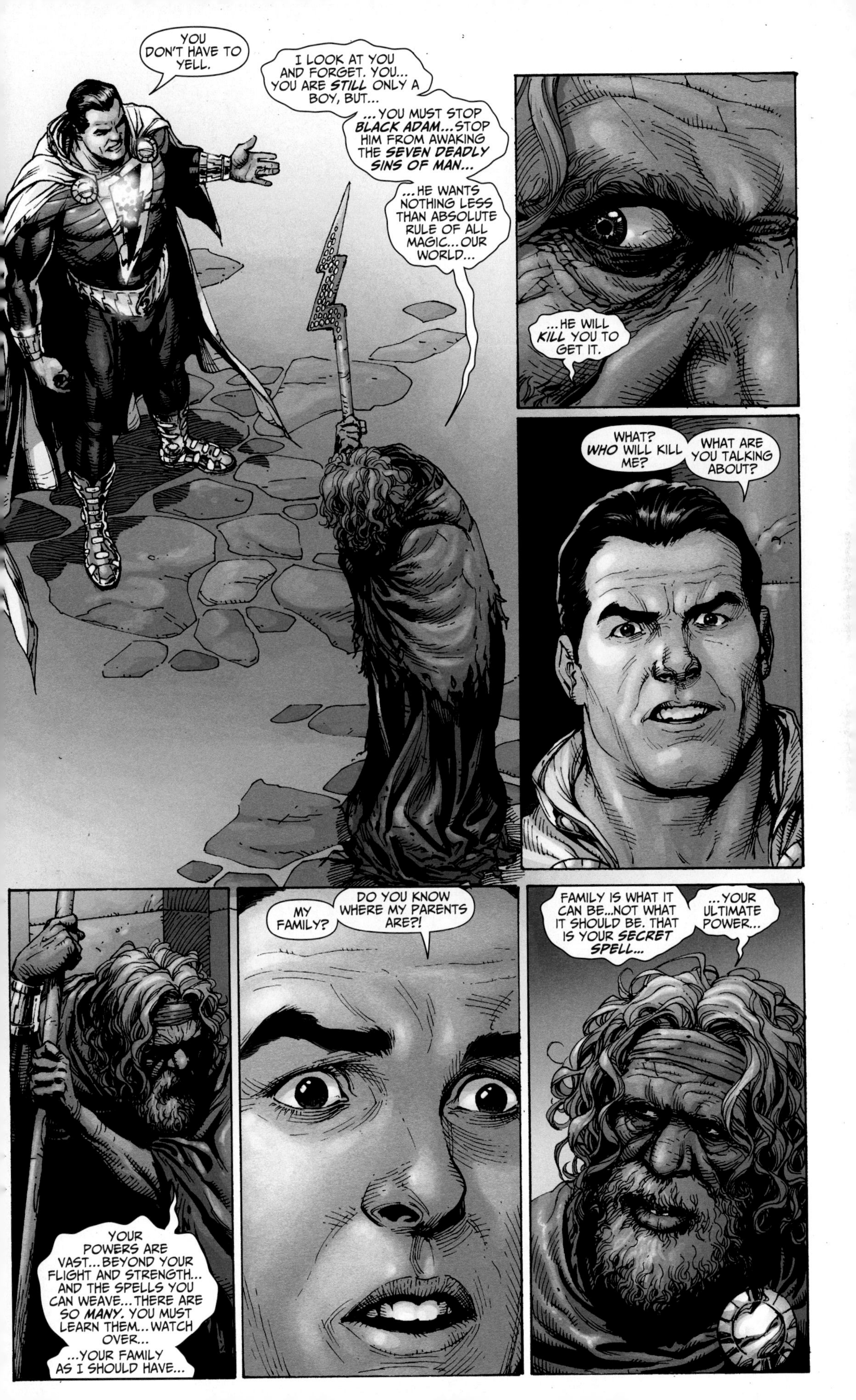
YOU DON'T HAVE TO YELL.
I LOOK AT YOU AND FORGET. YOU... YOU ARE STILL ONLY A BOY, BUT...
...YOU MUST STOP BLACK ADAM...STOP HIM FROM AWAKING THE SEVEN DEADLY SINS OF MAN...
...HE WANTS NOTHING LESS THAN ABSOLUTE RULE OF ALL MAGIC...OUR WORLD...
...HE WILL KILL YOU TO GET IT.
WHAT? WHO WILL KILL ME?
WHAT ARE YOU TALKING ABOUT?
YOUR POWERS ARE VAST...BEYOND YOUR FLIGHT AND STRENGTH... AND THE SPELLS YOU CAN WEAVE...THERE ARE SO MANY. YOU MUST LEARN THEM...WATCH OVER...
...YOUR FAMILY AS I SHOULD HAVE...
MY FAMILY?
DO YOU KNOW WHERE MY PARENTS ARE?!
FAMILY IS WHAT IT CAN BE...NOT WHAT IT SHOULD BE. THAT IS YOUR SECRET SPELL...
...YOUR ULTIMATE POWER...

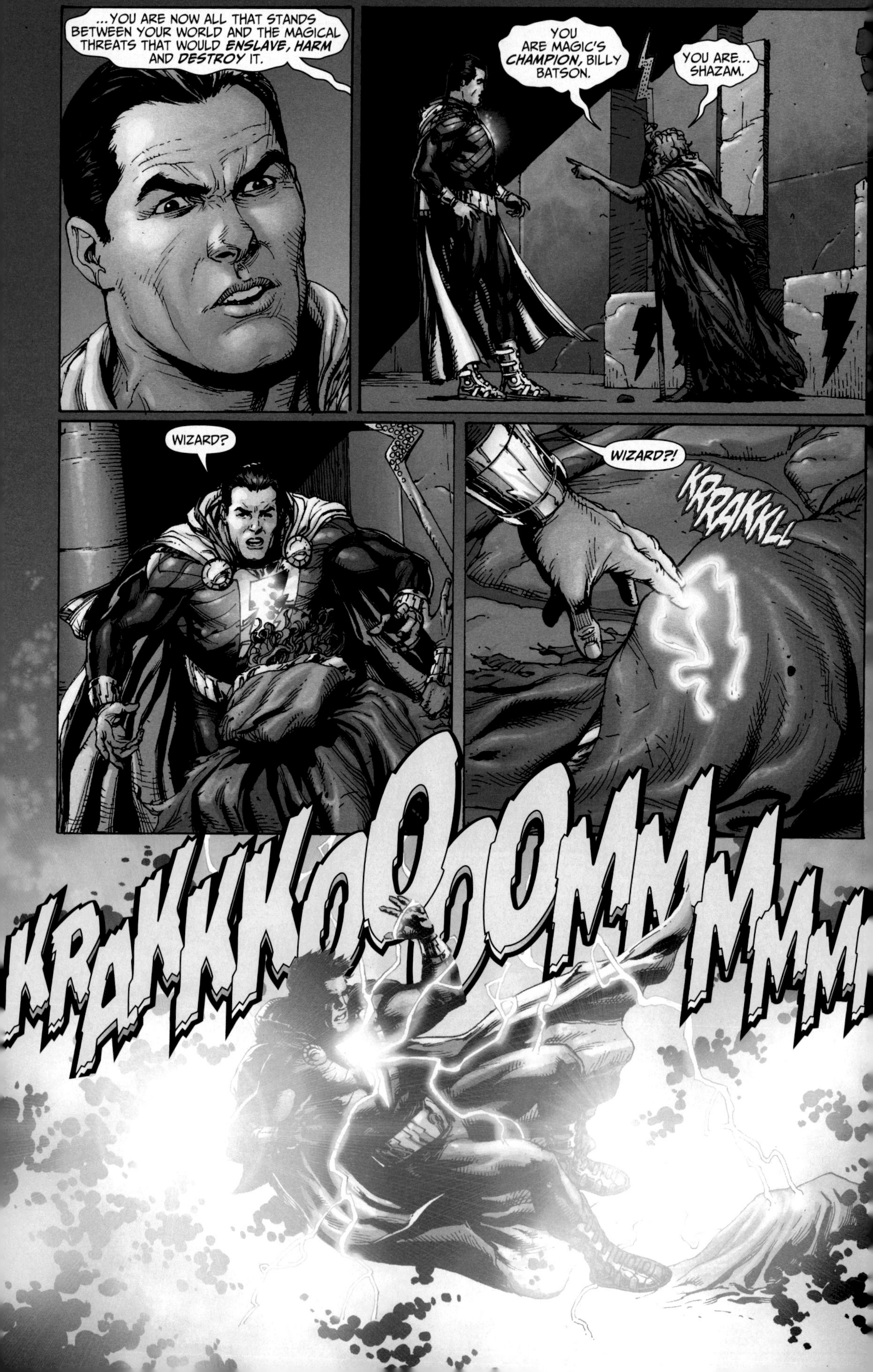
...YOU ARE NOW ALL THAT STANDS BETWEEN YOUR WORLD AND THE MAGICAL THREATS THAT WOULD ENSLAVE, HARM AND DESTROY IT.
YOU ARE MAGIC'S CHAMPION, BILLY BATSON.
YOU ARE... SHAZAM.
WIZARD?
WIZARD?!
KRRAKKLL
KRAKKKOOOOOMMMMMM

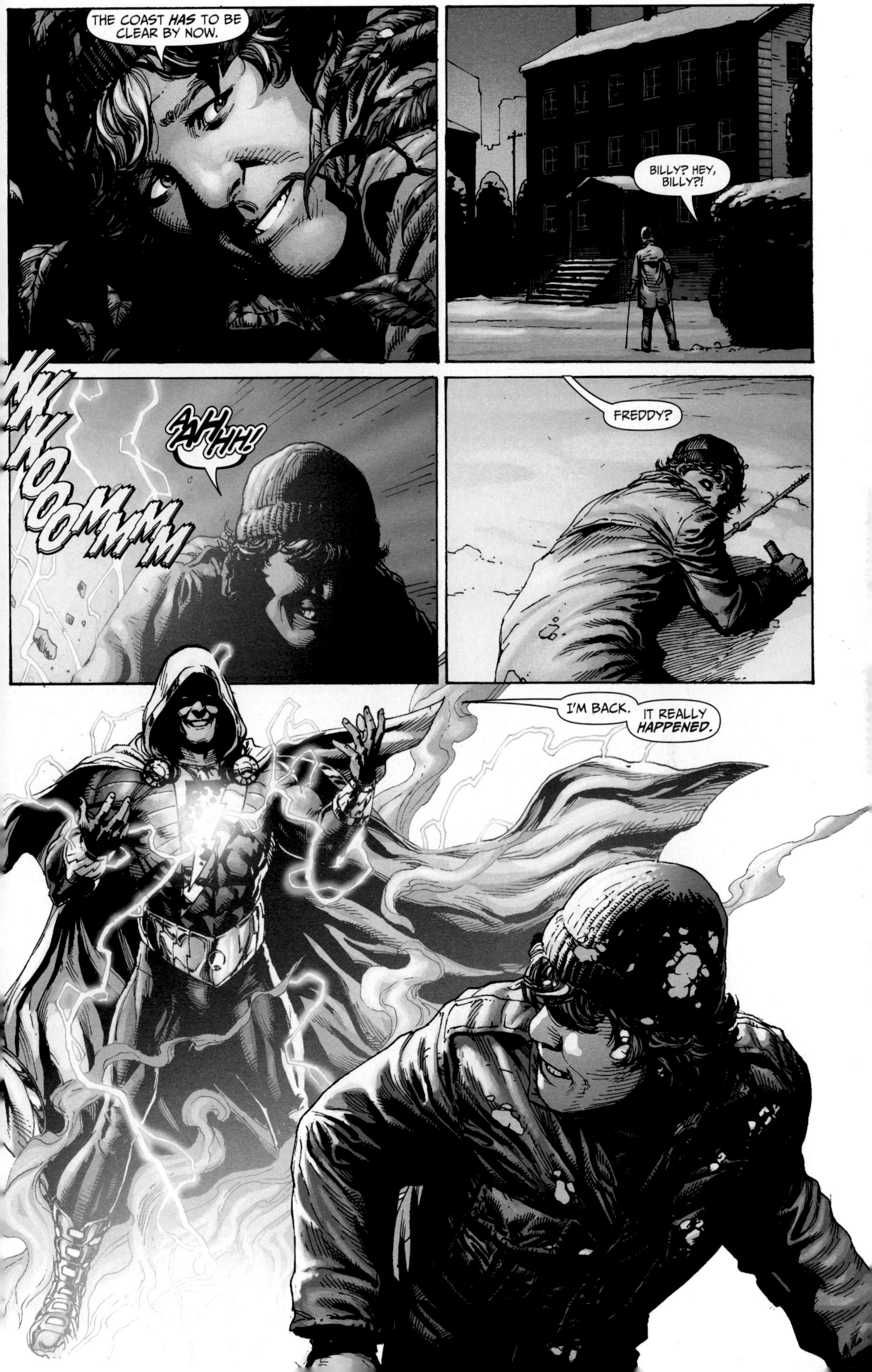
THE COAST HAS TO BE CLEAR BY NOW.
BILLY? HEY, BILLY?!
KKKHOOOMMMM
AAHHH!
FREDDY?
I'M BACK.
IT REALLY HAPPENED.

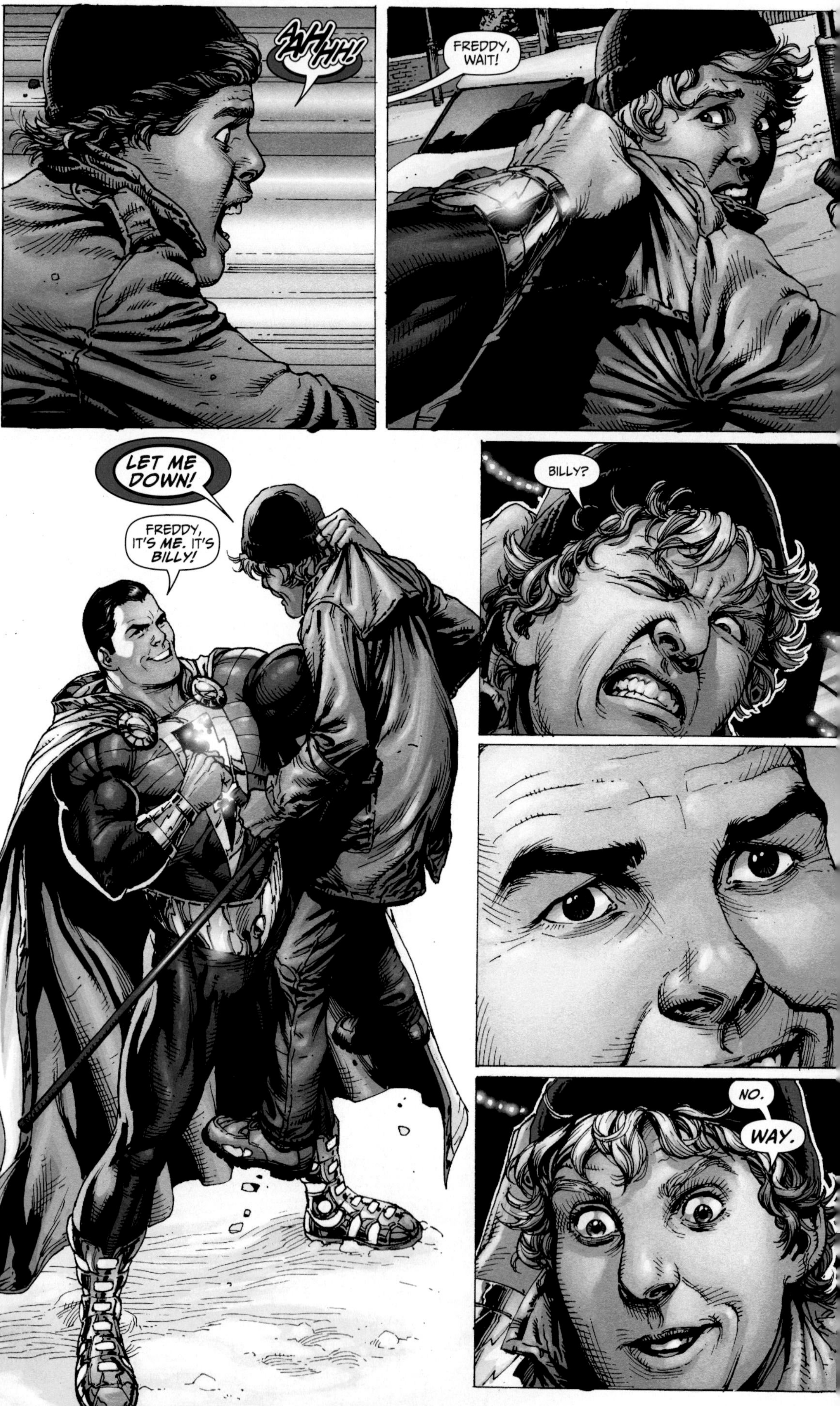
AAHHH!
FREDDY, WAIT!
LET ME DOWN!
FREDDY, IT'S ME. IT'S BILLY!
BILLY?
NO.
WAY.

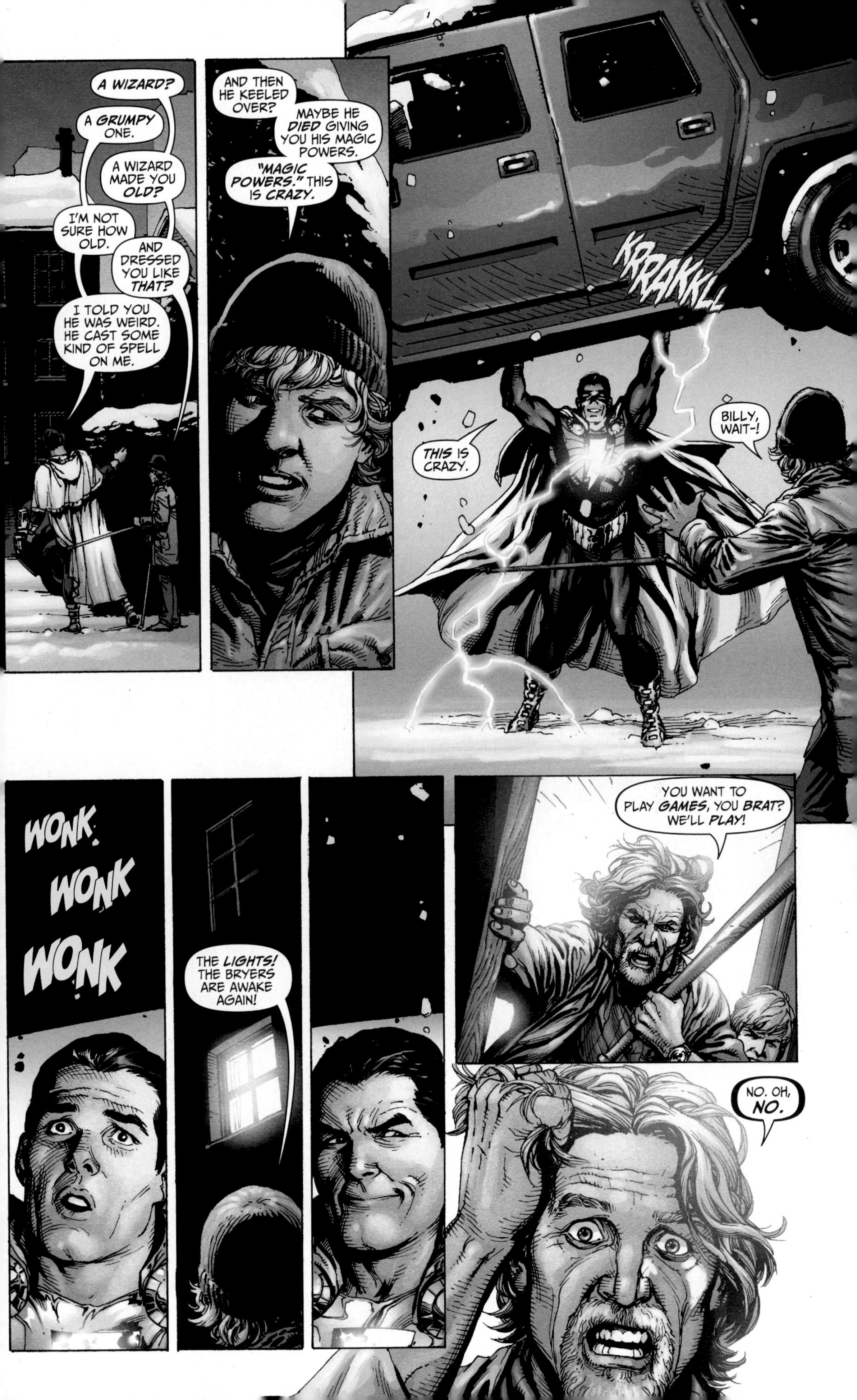

A WIZARD?
A GRUMPY ONE.
A WIZARD MADE YOU OLD?
I'M NOT SURE HOW OLD.
AND DRESSED YOU LIKE THAT?
I TOLD YOU HE WAS WEIRD. HE CAST SOME KIND OF SPELL ON ME.
AND THEN HE KEELED OVER?
MAYBE HE DIED GIVING YOU HIS MAGIC POWERS.
"MAGIC POWERS." THIS IS CRAZY.
KRRAKKL
THIS IS CRAZY.
BILLY, WAIT-!
WONK
WONK
WONK
THE LIGHTS! THE BRYERS ARE AWAKE AGAIN!
YOU WANT TO PLAY GAMES, YOU BRAT? WE'LL PLAY!
NO. OH, NO.

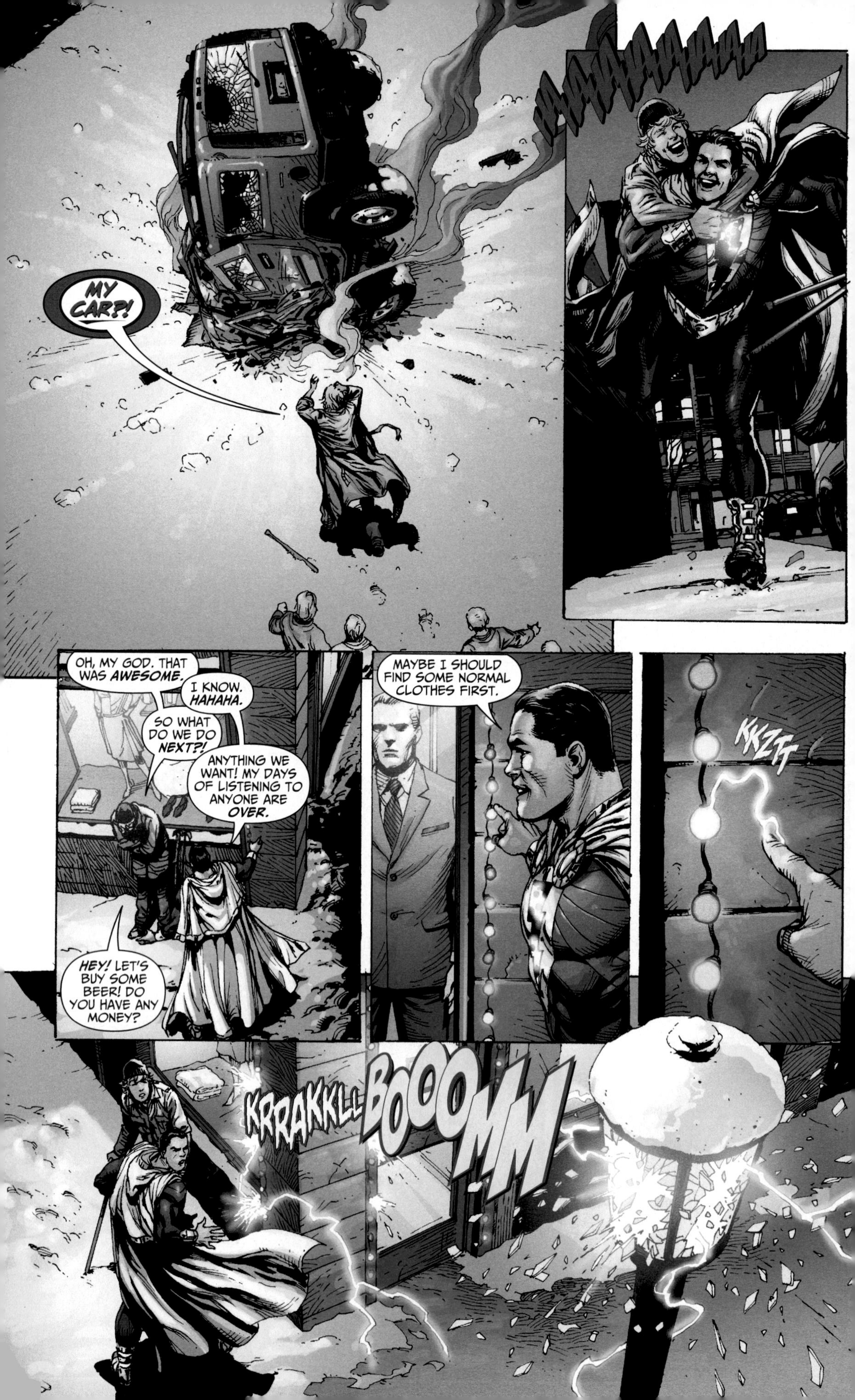

MY CAR?!
AAAAAAAAAAAAAA
OH, MY GOD. THAT WAS AWESOME.
I KNOW. HAHAHA.
SO WHAT DO WE DO NEXT?!
ANYTHING WE WANT! MY DAYS OF LISTENING TO ANYONE ARE OVER.
HEY! LET'S BUY SOME BEER! DO YOU HAVE ANY MONEY?
MAYBE I SHOULD FIND SOME NORMAL CLOTHES FIRST.
KKZTT
KRRAKKLL BOOOMM

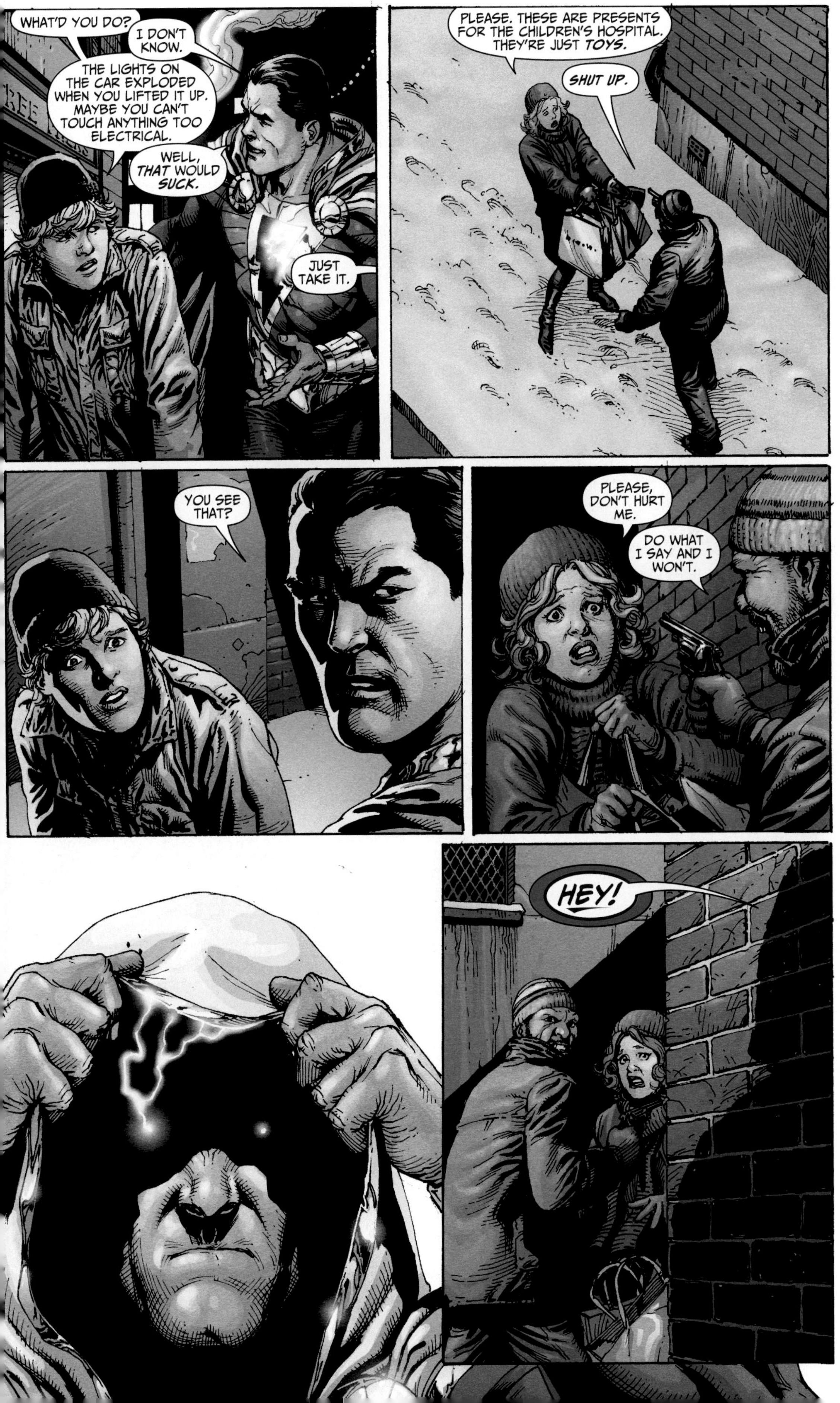
WHAT'D YOU DO?
I DON'T KNOW.
THE LIGHTS ON THE CAR EXPLODED WHEN YOU LIFTED IT UP. MAYBE YOU CAN'T TOUCH ANYTHING TOO ELECTRICAL.
WELL, *THAT* WOULD *SUCK.*
JUST TAKE IT.
PLEASE. THESE ARE PRESENTS FOR THE CHILDREN'S HOSPITAL. THEY'RE JUST *TOYS.*
SHUT UP.
YOU SEE THAT?
PLEASE, DON'T HURT ME.
DO WHAT I SAY AND I WON'T.
HEY!

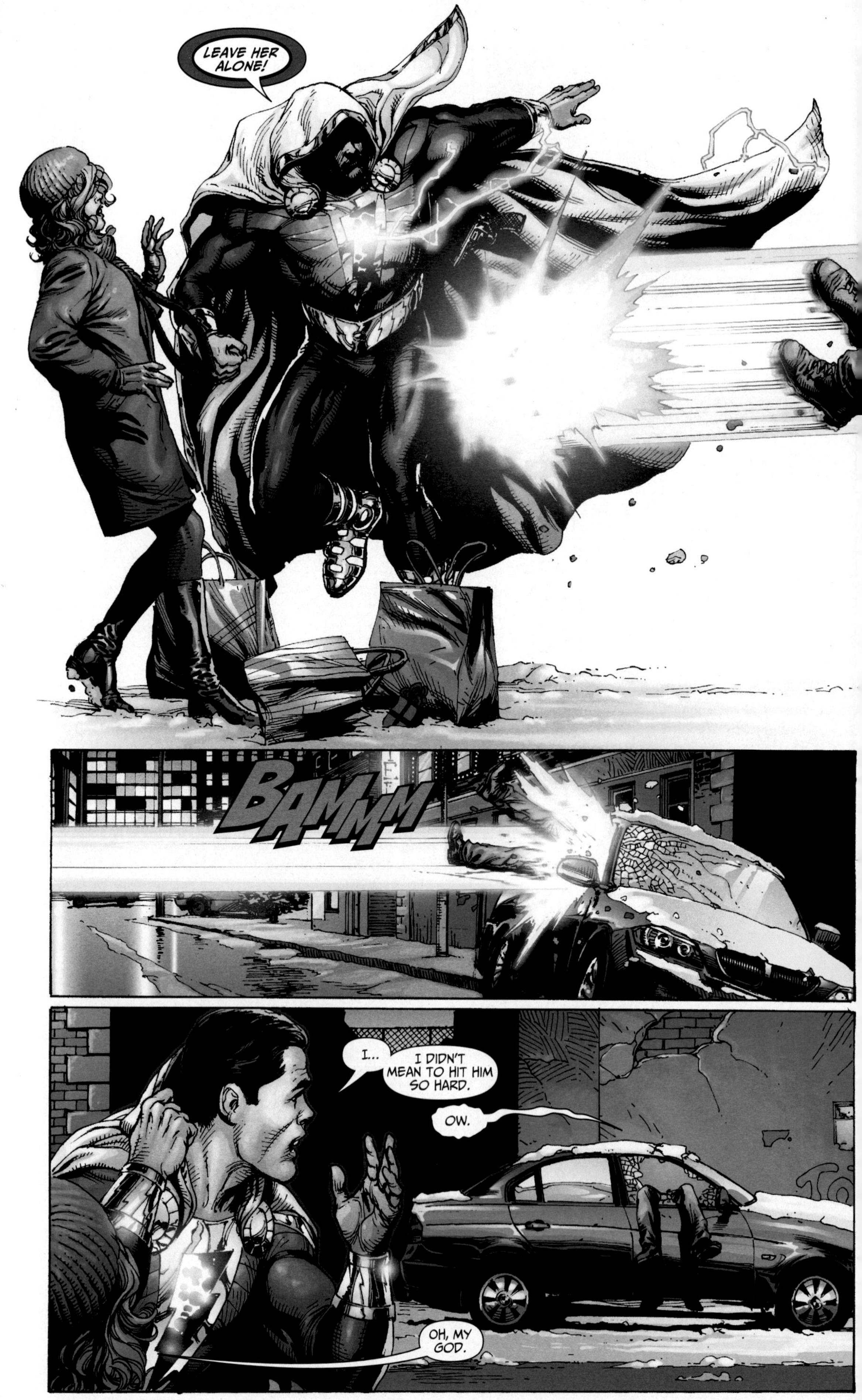
LEAVE HER ALONE!
BAMMM
I...
I DIDN'T MEAN TO HIT HIM SO HARD.
OW.
OH, MY GOD.

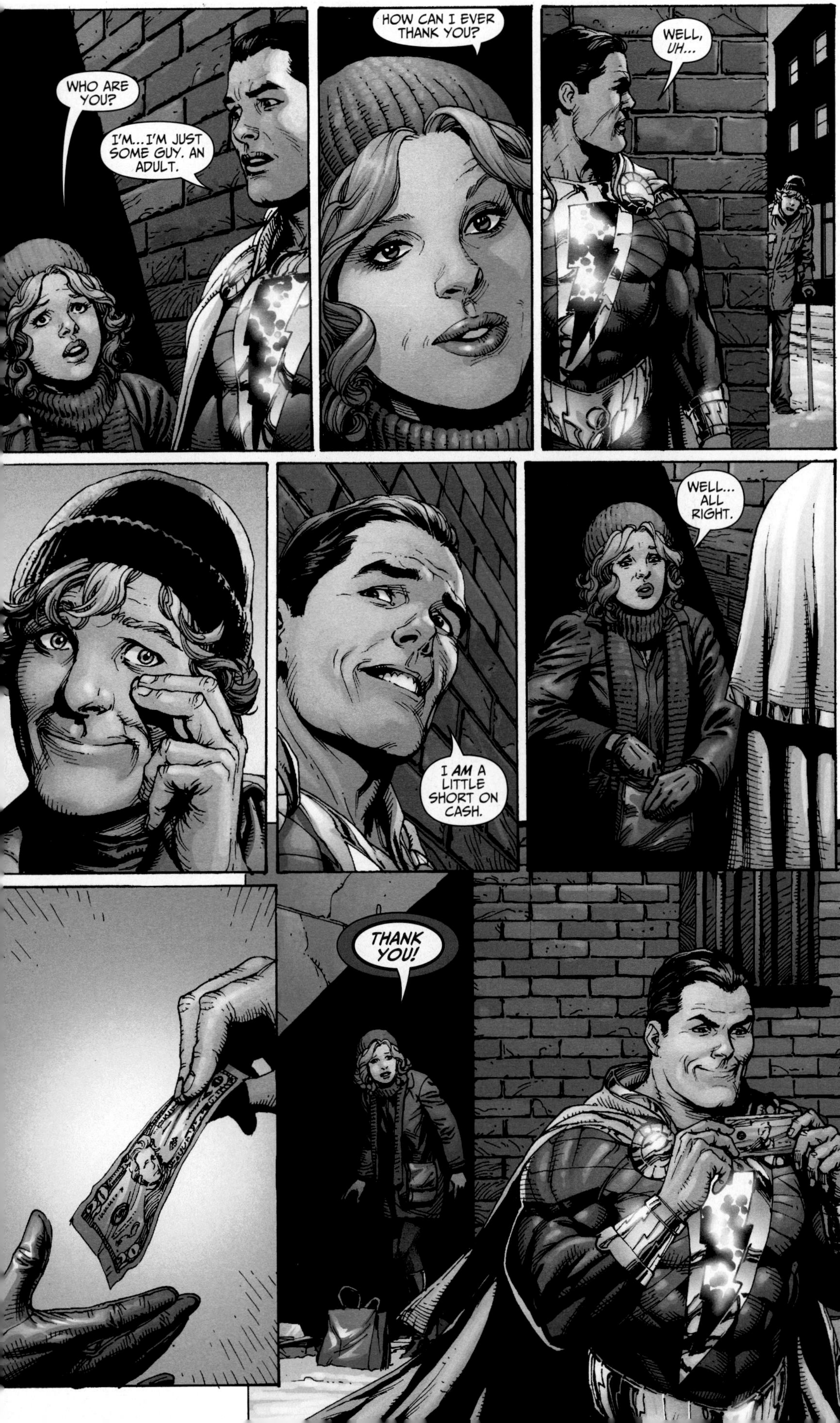
WHO ARE YOU?
I'M...I'M JUST SOME GUY. AN ADULT.
HOW CAN I EVER THANK YOU?
WELL, UH...
I AM A LITTLE SHORT ON CASH.
WELL... ALL RIGHT.
THANK YOU!

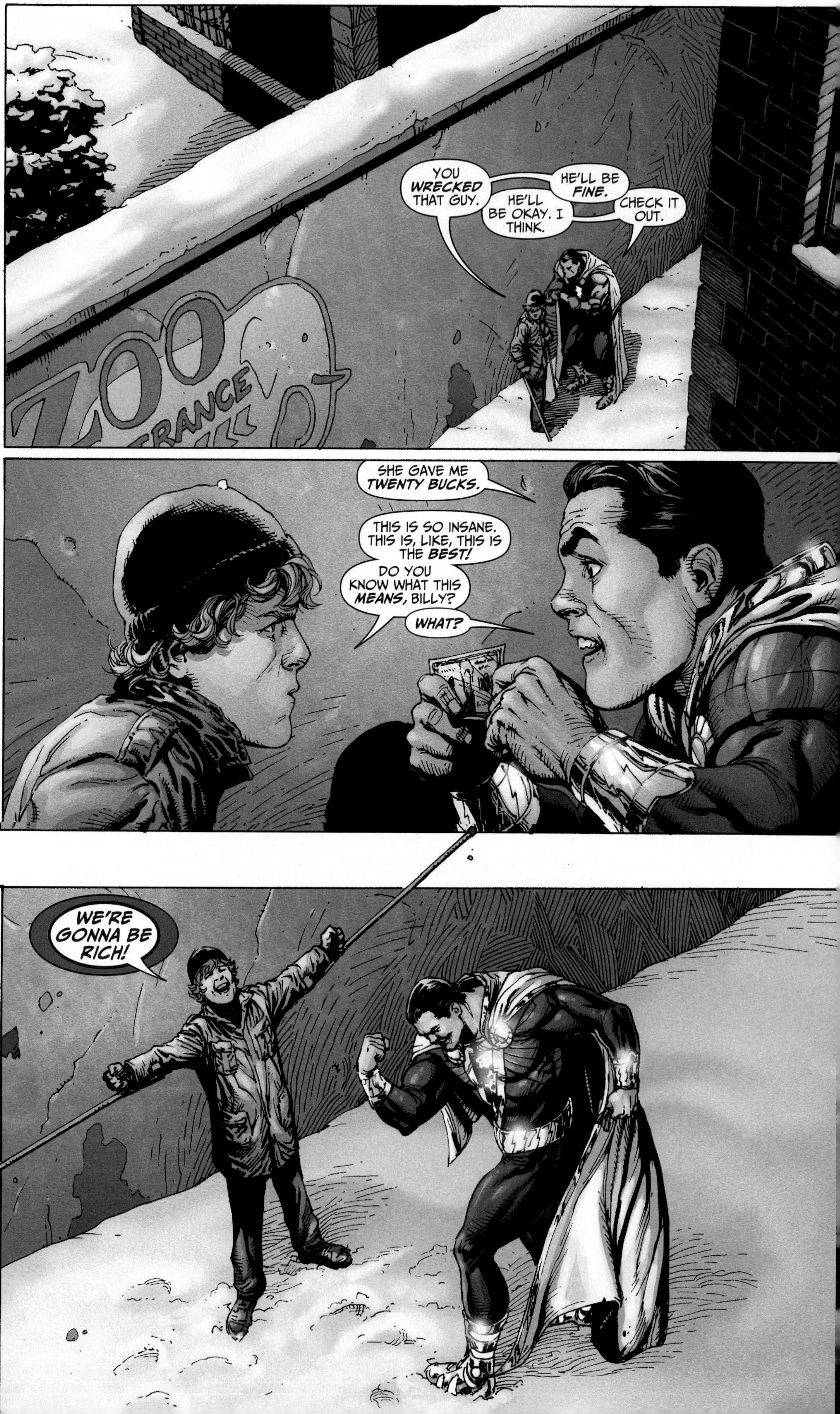

ZOO
TRANCE
YOU WRECKED THAT GUY.
HE'LL BE OKAY. I THINK.
HE'LL BE FINE.
CHECK IT OUT.
SHE GAVE ME TWENTY BUCKS.
THIS IS SO INSANE. THIS IS, LIKE, THIS IS THE BEST!
DO YOU KNOW WHAT THIS MEANS, BILLY?
WHAT?
WE'RE GONNA BE RICH!

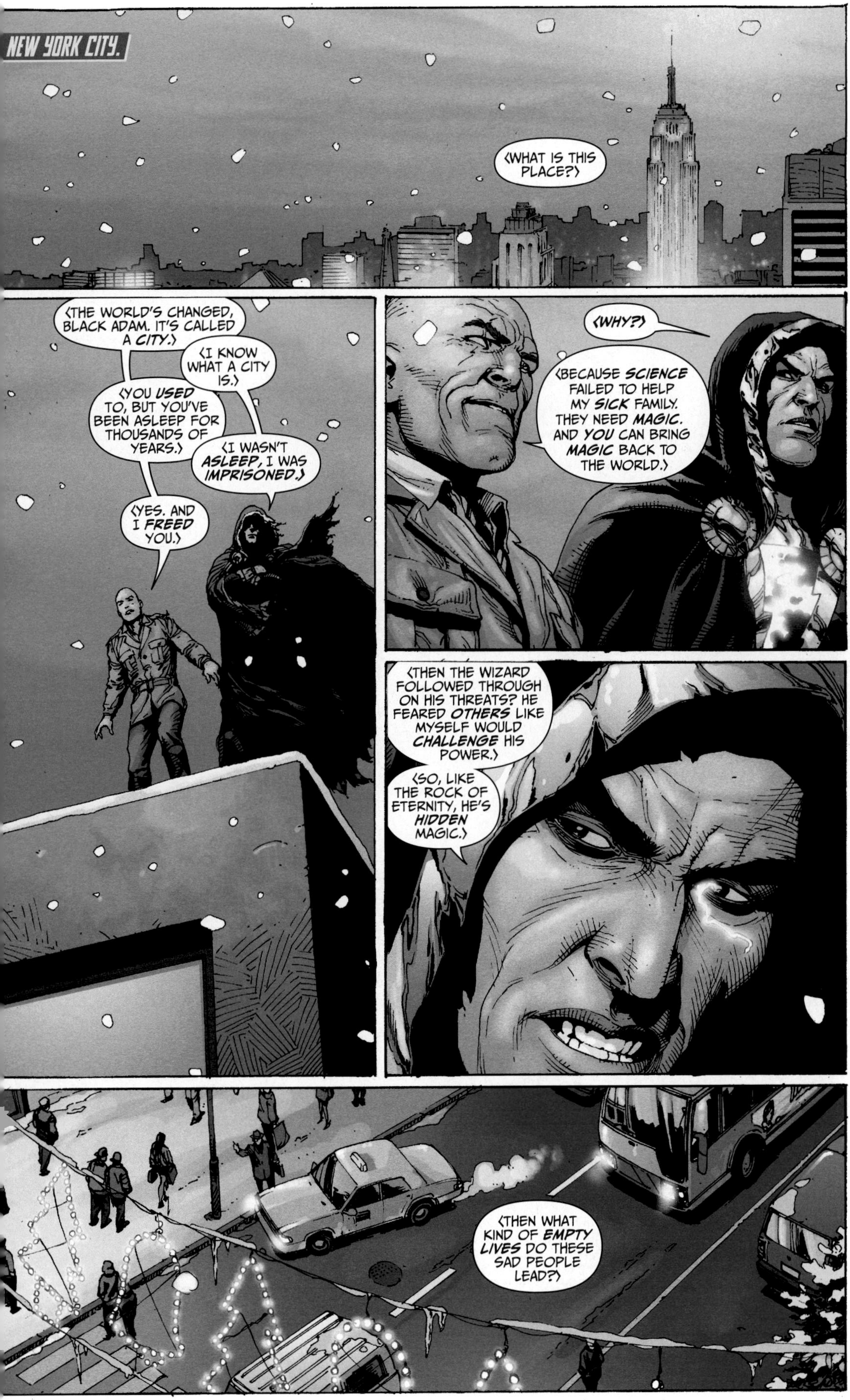
NEW YORK CITY.
⟨WHAT IS THIS PLACE?⟩
⟨THE WORLD'S CHANGED, BLACK ADAM. IT'S CALLED A CITY.⟩
⟨I KNOW WHAT A CITY IS.⟩
⟨YOU USED TO, BUT YOU'VE BEEN ASLEEP FOR THOUSANDS OF YEARS.⟩
⟨I WASN'T ASLEEP, I WAS IMPRISONED.⟩
⟨YES. AND I FREED YOU.⟩
⟨WHY?⟩
⟨BECAUSE SCIENCE FAILED TO HELP MY SICK FAMILY. THEY NEED MAGIC. AND YOU CAN BRING MAGIC BACK TO THE WORLD.⟩
⟨THEN THE WIZARD FOLLOWED THROUGH ON HIS THREATS? HE FEARED OTHERS LIKE MYSELF WOULD CHALLENGE HIS POWER.⟩
⟨SO, LIKE THE ROCK OF ETERNITY, HE'S HIDDEN MAGIC.⟩
⟨THEN WHAT KIND OF EMPTY LIVES DO THESE SAD PEOPLE LEAD?⟩

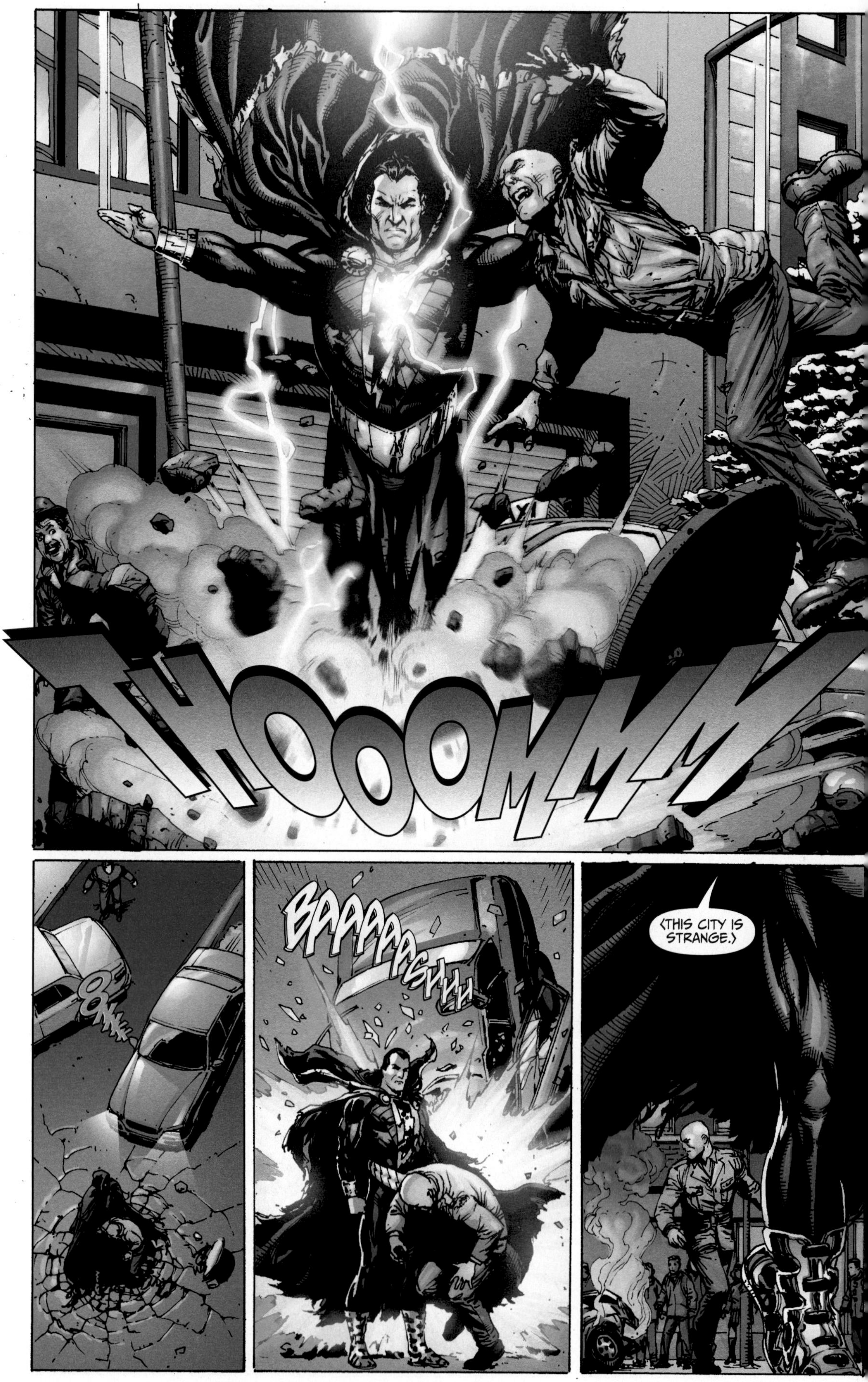
THOOOMMM
BAAAAASHHH
‹THIS CITY IS STRANGE.›

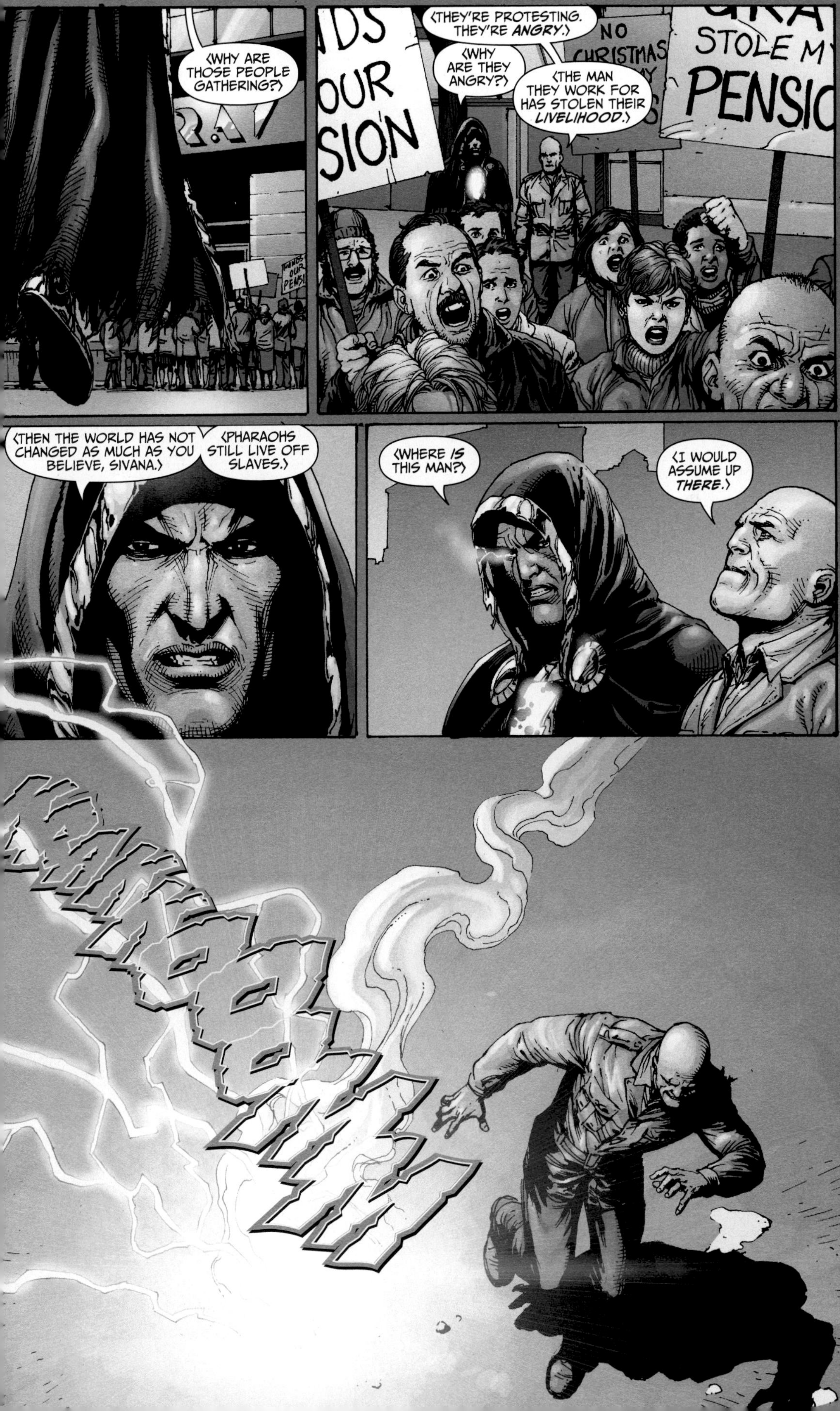

‹WHY ARE THOSE PEOPLE GATHERING?›
‹THEY'RE PROTESTING. THEY'RE *ANGRY*.›
‹WHY ARE THEY ANGRY?›
‹THE MAN THEY WORK FOR HAS STOLEN THEIR *LIVELIHOOD*.›
NO CHRISTMAS
STOLE MY
‹THEN THE WORLD HAS NOT CHANGED AS MUCH AS YOU BELIEVE, SIVANA.›
‹PHARAOHS STILL LIVE OFF SLAVES.›
‹WHERE *IS* THIS MAN?›
‹I WOULD ASSUME UP *THERE*.›

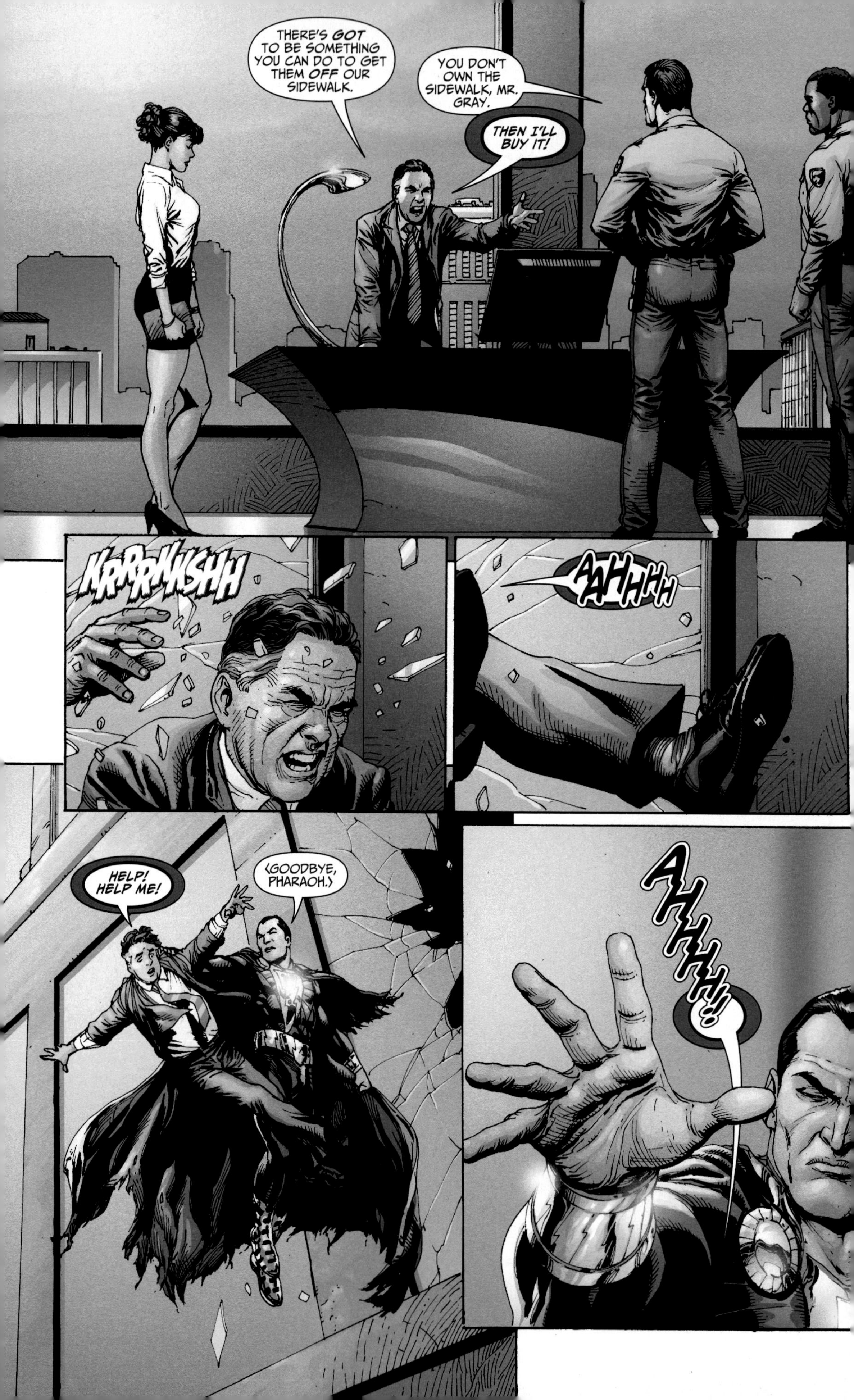
THERE'S GOT TO BE SOMETHING YOU CAN DO TO GET THEM OFF OUR SIDEWALK.
YOU DON'T OWN THE SIDEWALK, MR. GRAY.
THEN I'LL BUY IT!
KRRRKKSHH
AAHHHH
HELP! HELP ME!
‹GOODBYE, PHARAOH.›
AHHHH!!

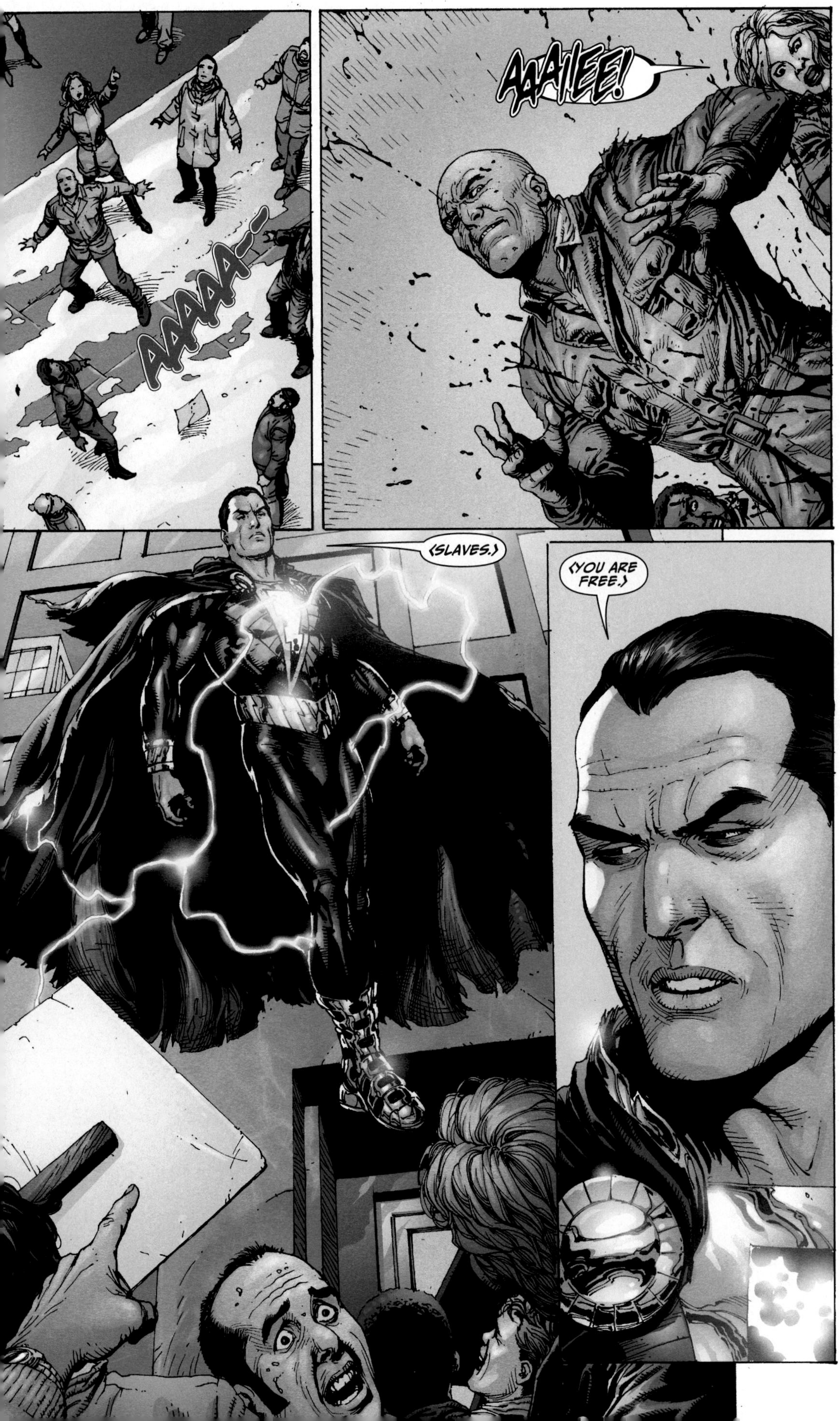
AAAAA--!
AAAIEE!
‹SLAVES.›
‹YOU ARE FREE.›

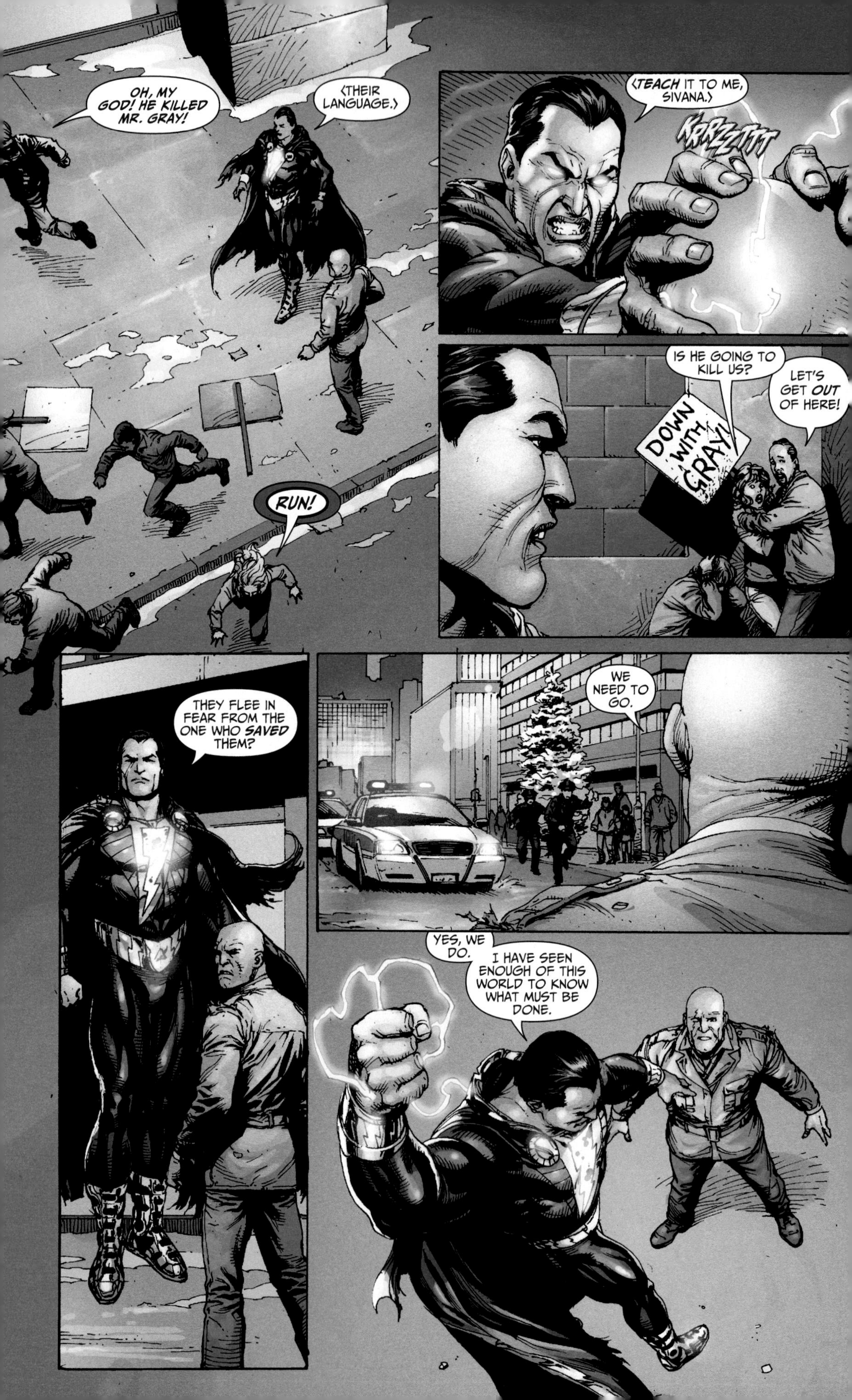
OH, MY GOD! HE KILLED MR. GRAY!
⟨THEIR LANGUAGE.⟩
RUN!
⟨TEACH IT TO ME, SIVANA.⟩
KRRZZTTT
IS HE GOING TO KILL US?
LET'S GET OUT OF HERE!
DOWN WITH GRAY!
THEY FLEE IN FEAR FROM THE ONE WHO SAVED THEM?
WE NEED TO GO.
YES, WE DO.
I HAVE SEEN ENOUGH OF THIS WORLD TO KNOW WHAT MUST BE DONE.

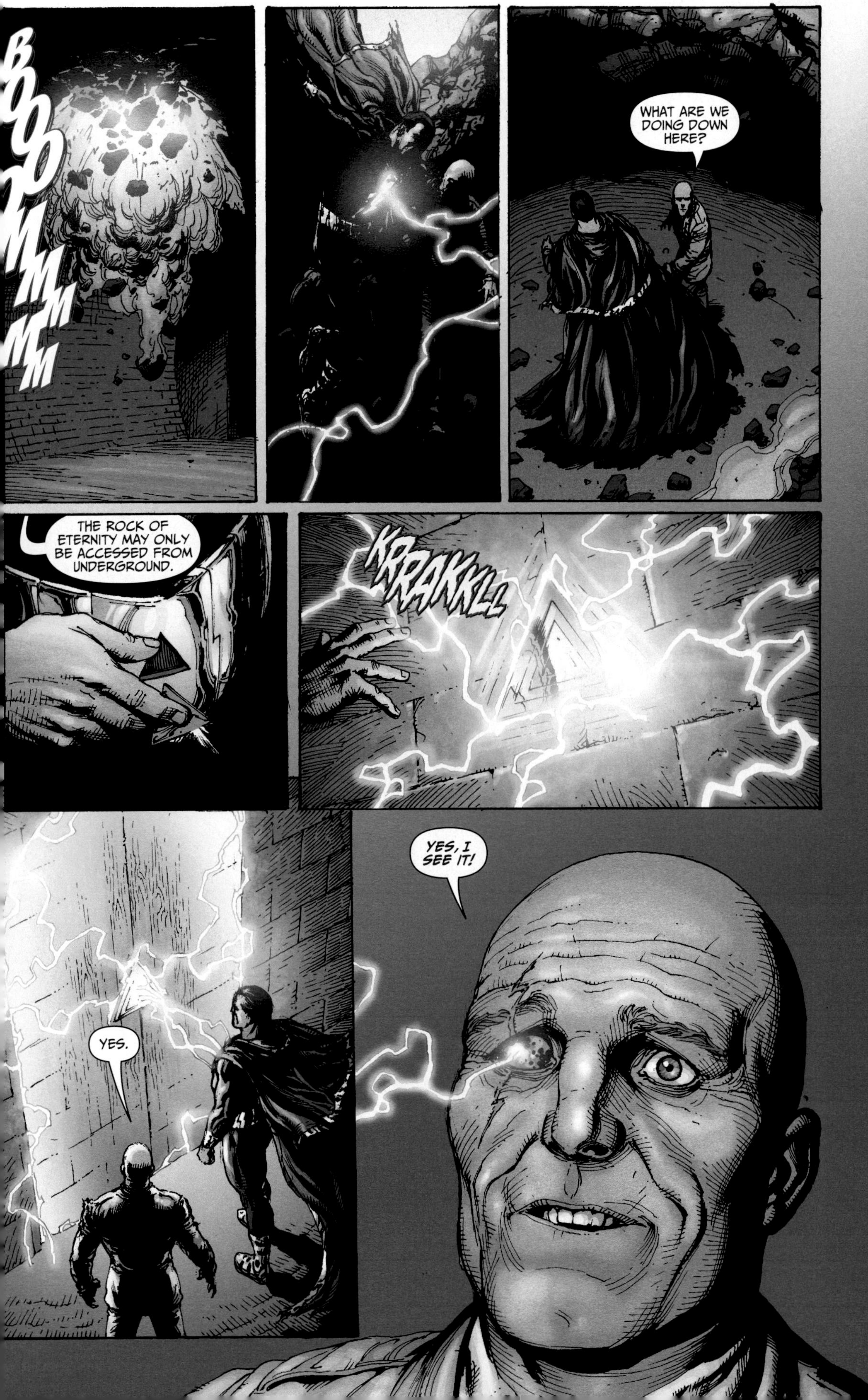
BOOOMMMMMM
WHAT ARE WE DOING DOWN HERE?
THE ROCK OF ETERNITY MAY ONLY BE ACCESSED FROM UNDERGROUND.
KRRAKKLL
YES, I SEE IT!
YES.

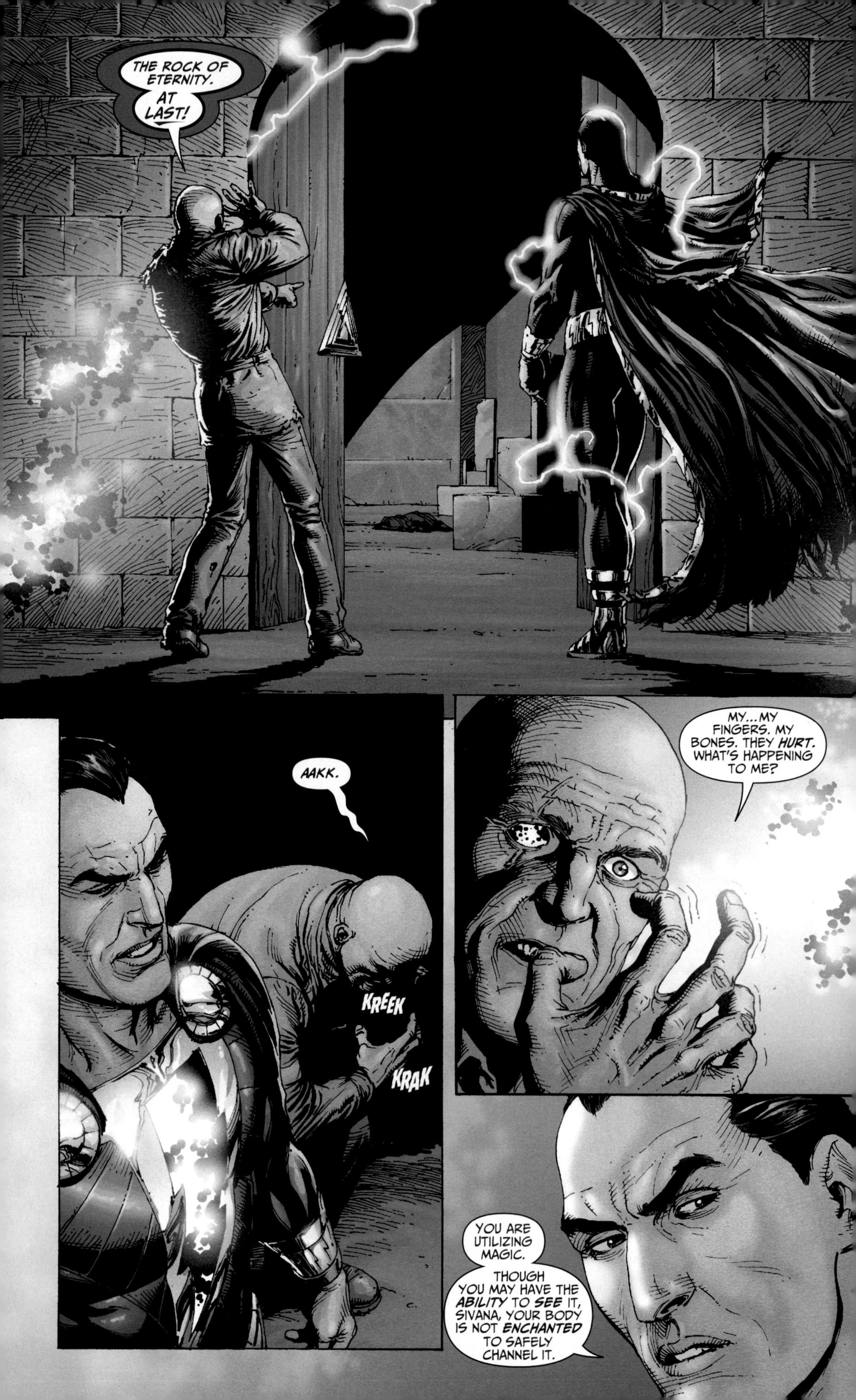
THE ROCK OF ETERNITY. AT LAST!
AAKK.
KREEK
KRAK
MY...MY FINGERS. MY BONES. THEY HURT. WHAT'S HAPPENING TO ME?
YOU ARE UTILIZING MAGIC.
THOUGH YOU MAY HAVE THE ABILITY TO SEE IT, SIVANA, YOUR BODY IS NOT ENCHANTED TO SAFELY CHANNEL IT.

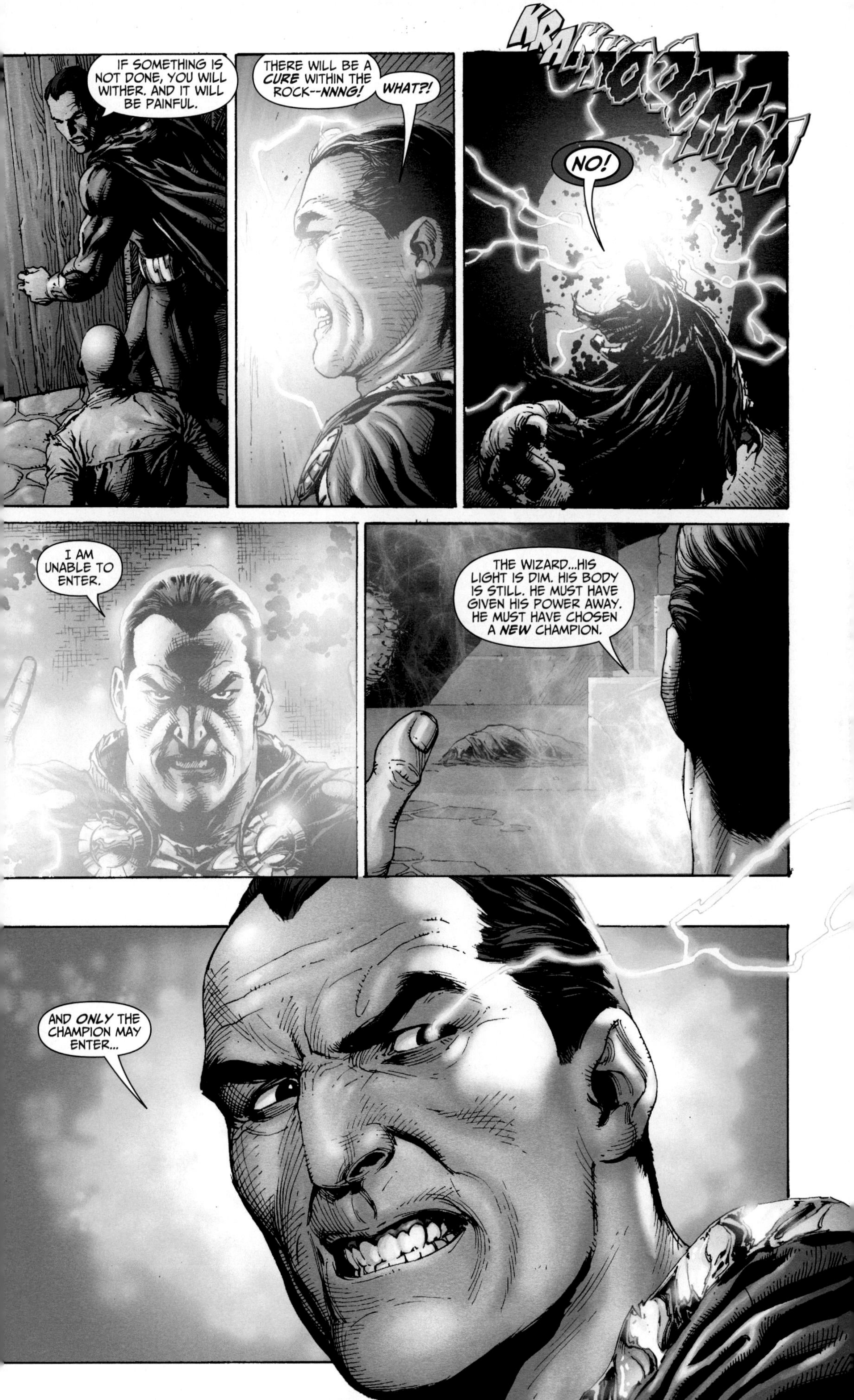
IF SOMETHING IS NOT DONE, YOU WILL WITHER. AND IT WILL BE PAINFUL.
THERE WILL BE A CURE WITHIN THE ROCK--NNNG!
WHAT?!
NO!
I AM UNABLE TO ENTER.
THE WIZARD...HIS LIGHT IS DIM. HIS BODY IS STILL. HE MUST HAVE GIVEN HIS POWER AWAY. HE MUST HAVE CHOSEN A NEW CHAMPION.
AND ONLY THE CHAMPION MAY ENTER...

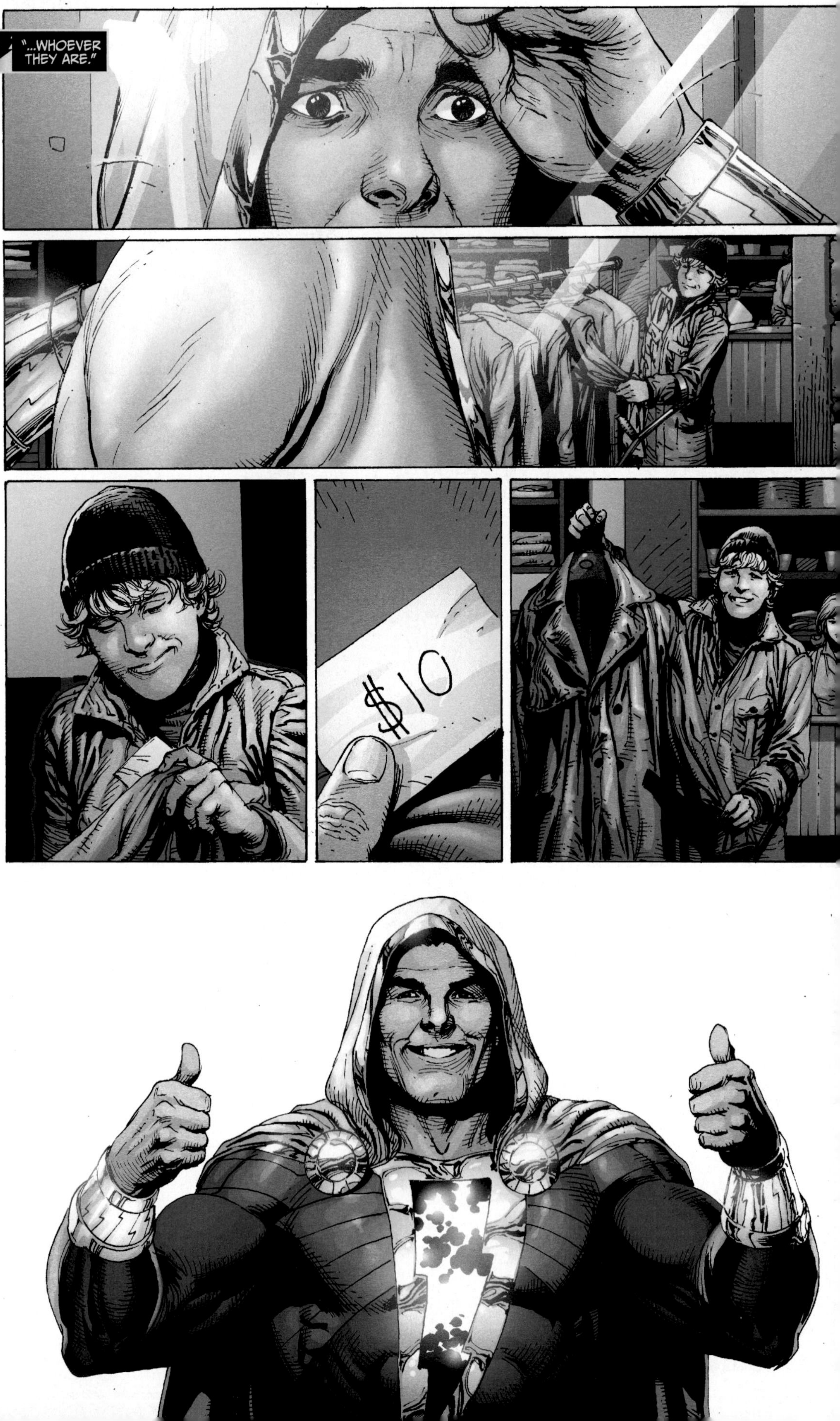
"...WHOEVER THEY ARE."
$10

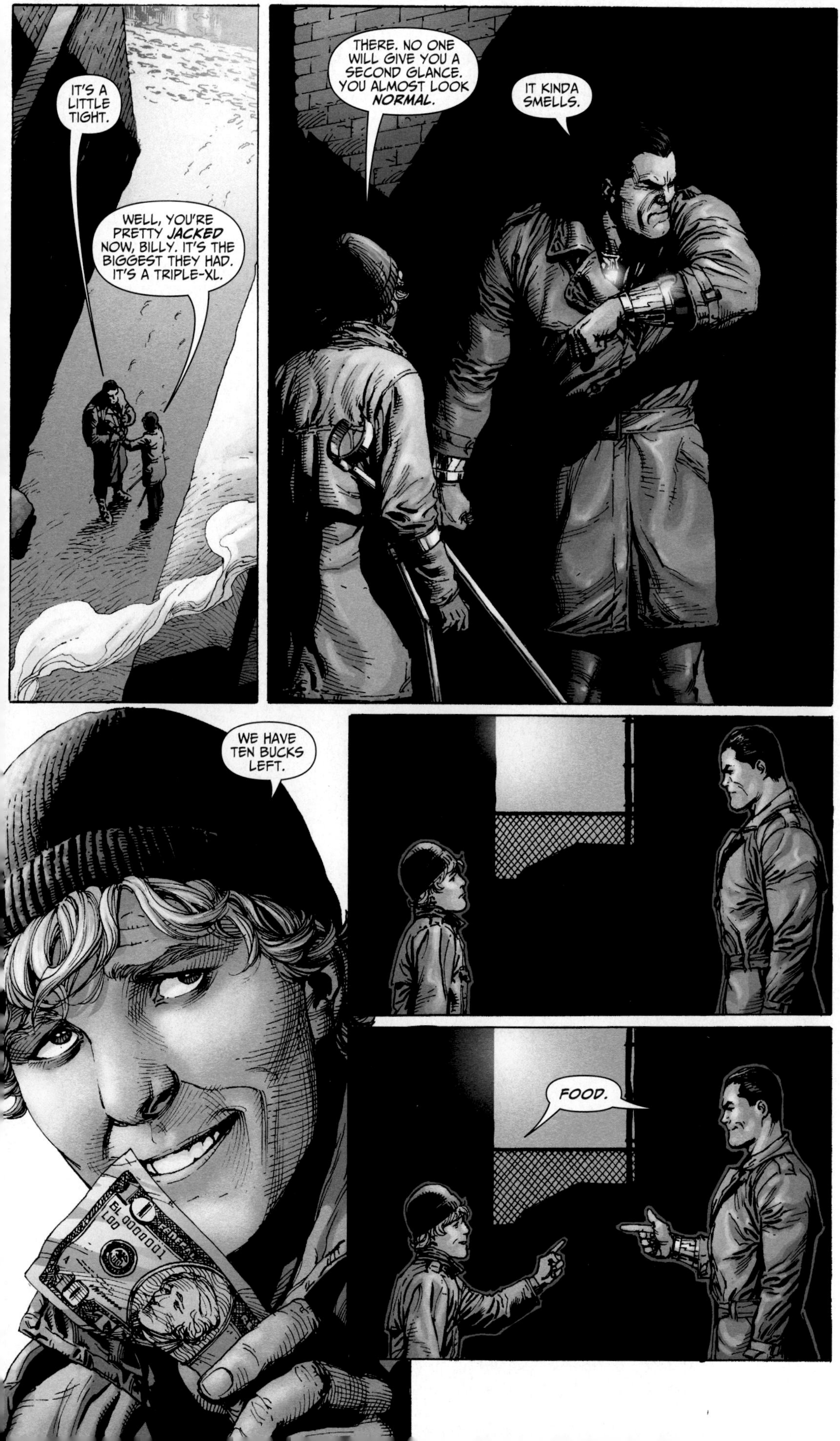
IT'S A LITTLE TIGHT.
WELL, YOU'RE PRETTY JACKED NOW, BILLY. IT'S THE BIGGEST THEY HAD. IT'S A TRIPLE-XL.
THERE. NO ONE WILL GIVE YOU A SECOND GLANCE. YOU ALMOST LOOK NORMAL.
IT KINDA SMELLS.
WE HAVE TEN BUCKS LEFT.
FOOD.

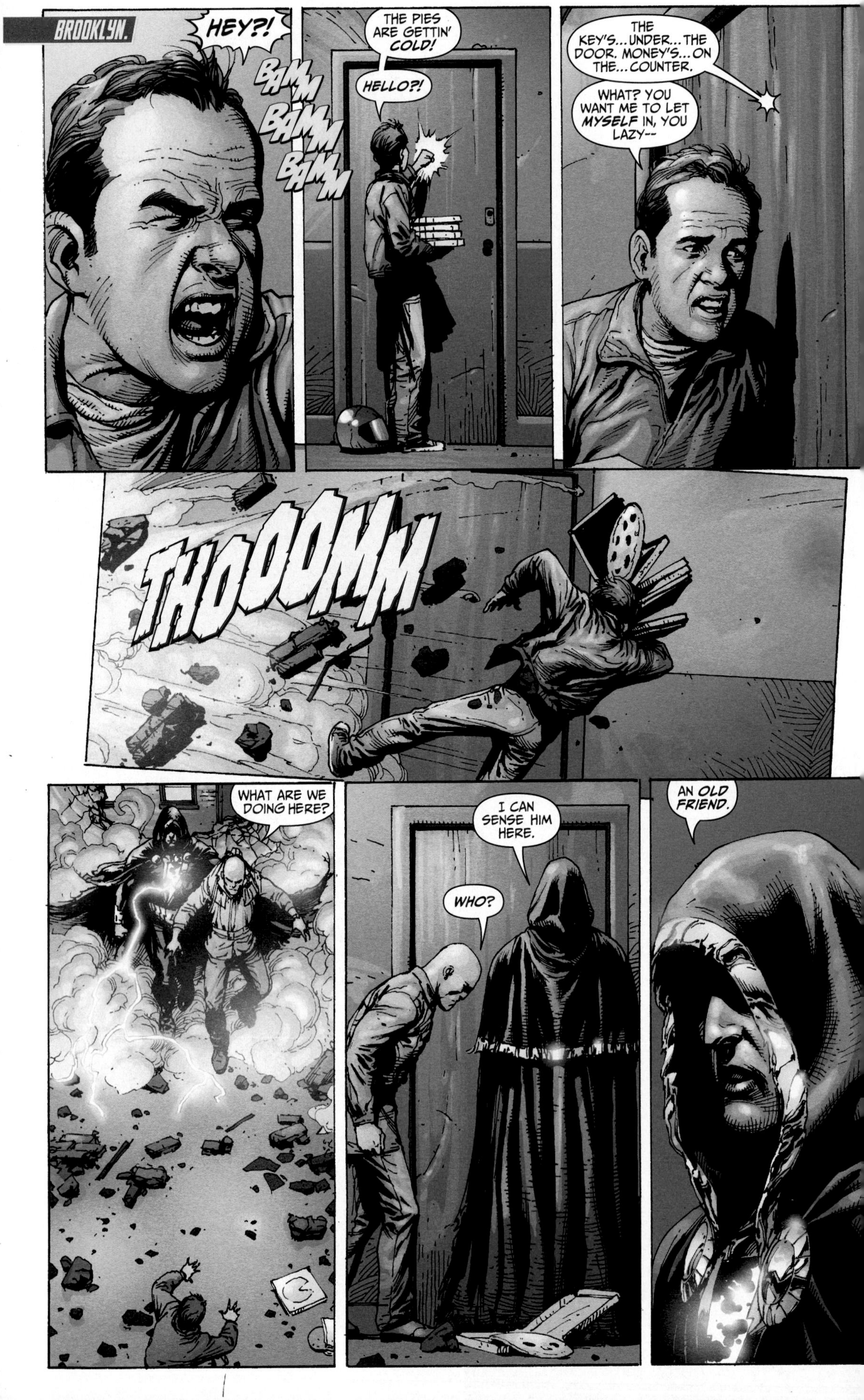
BROOKLYN.
HEY?!
BAMM BAMM BAMM
THE PIES ARE GETTIN' COLD!
HELLO?!
THE KEY'S... UNDER... THE DOOR. MONEY'S... ON THE... COUNTER.
WHAT? YOU WANT ME TO LET MYSELF IN, YOU LAZY--
THOOOMM
WHAT ARE WE DOING HERE?
I CAN SENSE HIM HERE.
WHO?
AN OLD FRIEND.

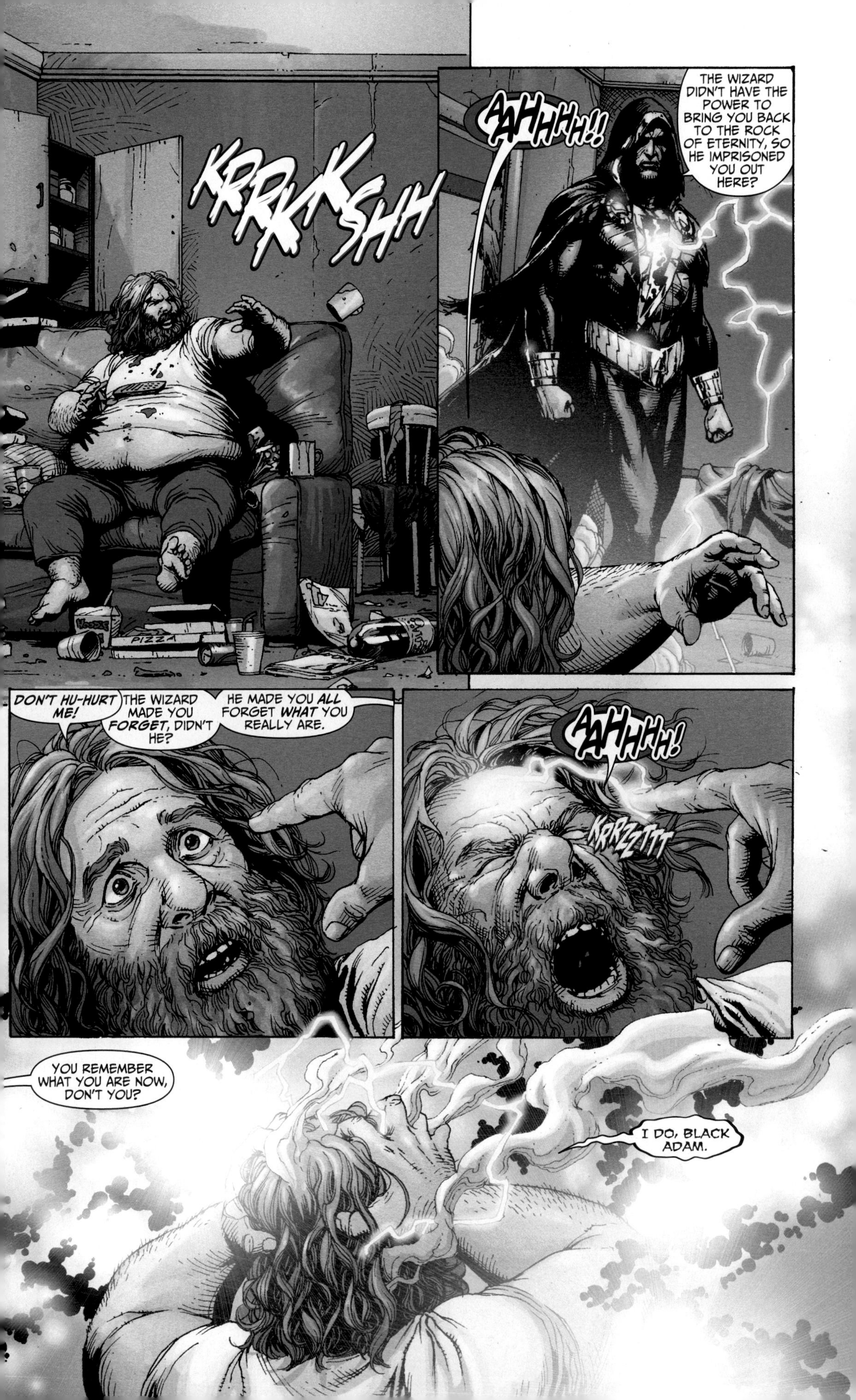
KRRKKSHH
AAHHHH!!
THE WIZARD DIDN'T HAVE THE POWER TO BRING YOU BACK TO THE ROCK OF ETERNITY, SO HE IMPRISONED YOU OUT HERE?
DON'T HU-HURT ME!
THE WIZARD MADE YOU FORGET, DIDN'T HE?
HE MADE YOU ALL FORGET WHAT YOU REALLY ARE.
AAHHHH!
KRRZZTTT
YOU REMEMBER WHAT YOU ARE NOW, DON'T YOU?
I DO, BLACK ADAM.

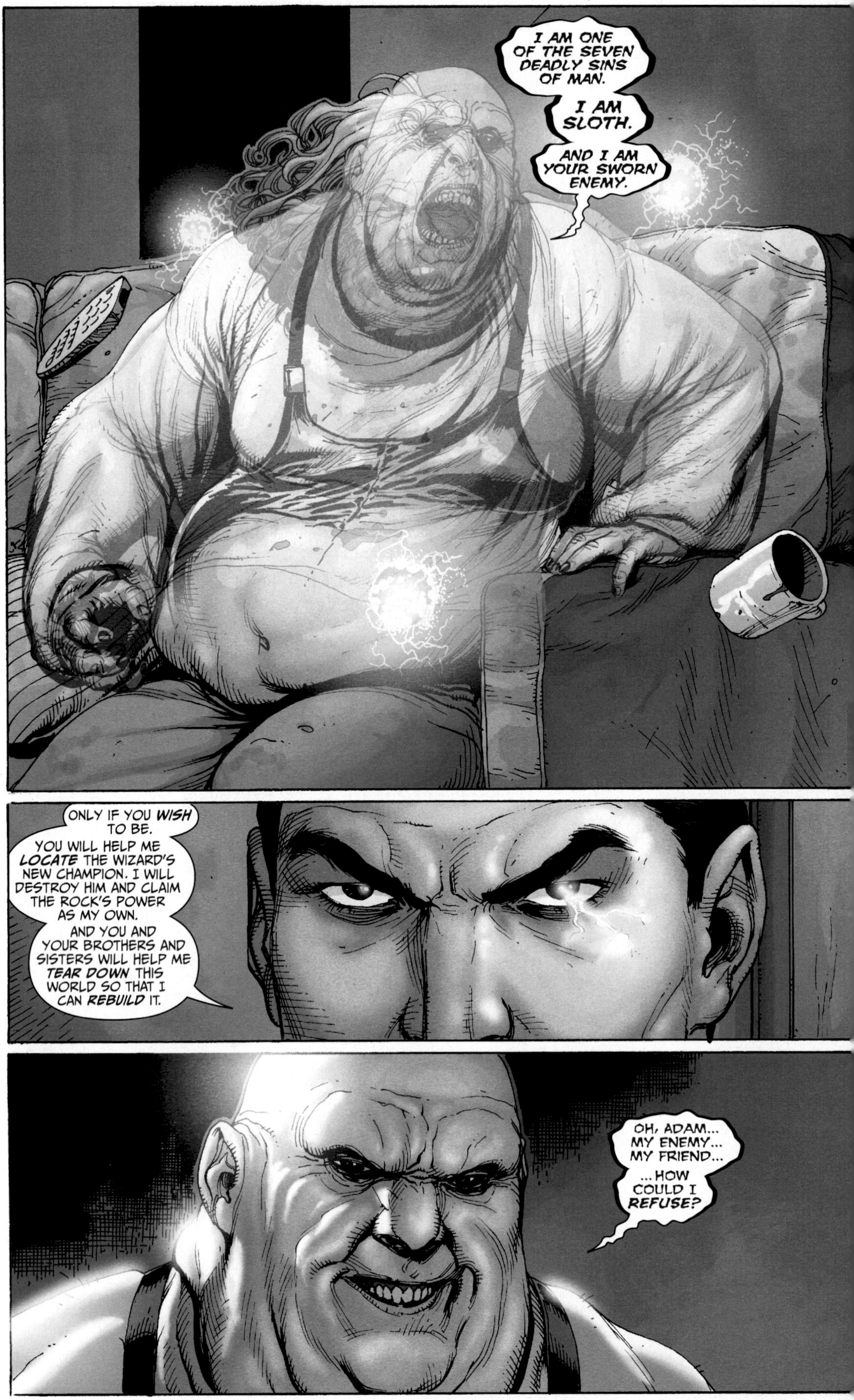
I AM ONE OF THE SEVEN DEADLY SINS OF MAN.
I AM SLOTH.
AND I AM YOUR SWORN ENEMY.
ONLY IF YOU WISH TO BE.
YOU WILL HELP ME LOCATE THE WIZARD'S NEW CHAMPION. I WILL DESTROY HIM AND CLAIM THE ROCK'S POWER AS MY OWN.
AND YOU AND YOUR BROTHERS AND SISTERS WILL HELP ME TEAR DOWN THIS WORLD SO THAT I CAN REBUILD IT.
OH, ADAM... MY ENEMY... MY FRIEND...
...HOW COULD I REFUSE?

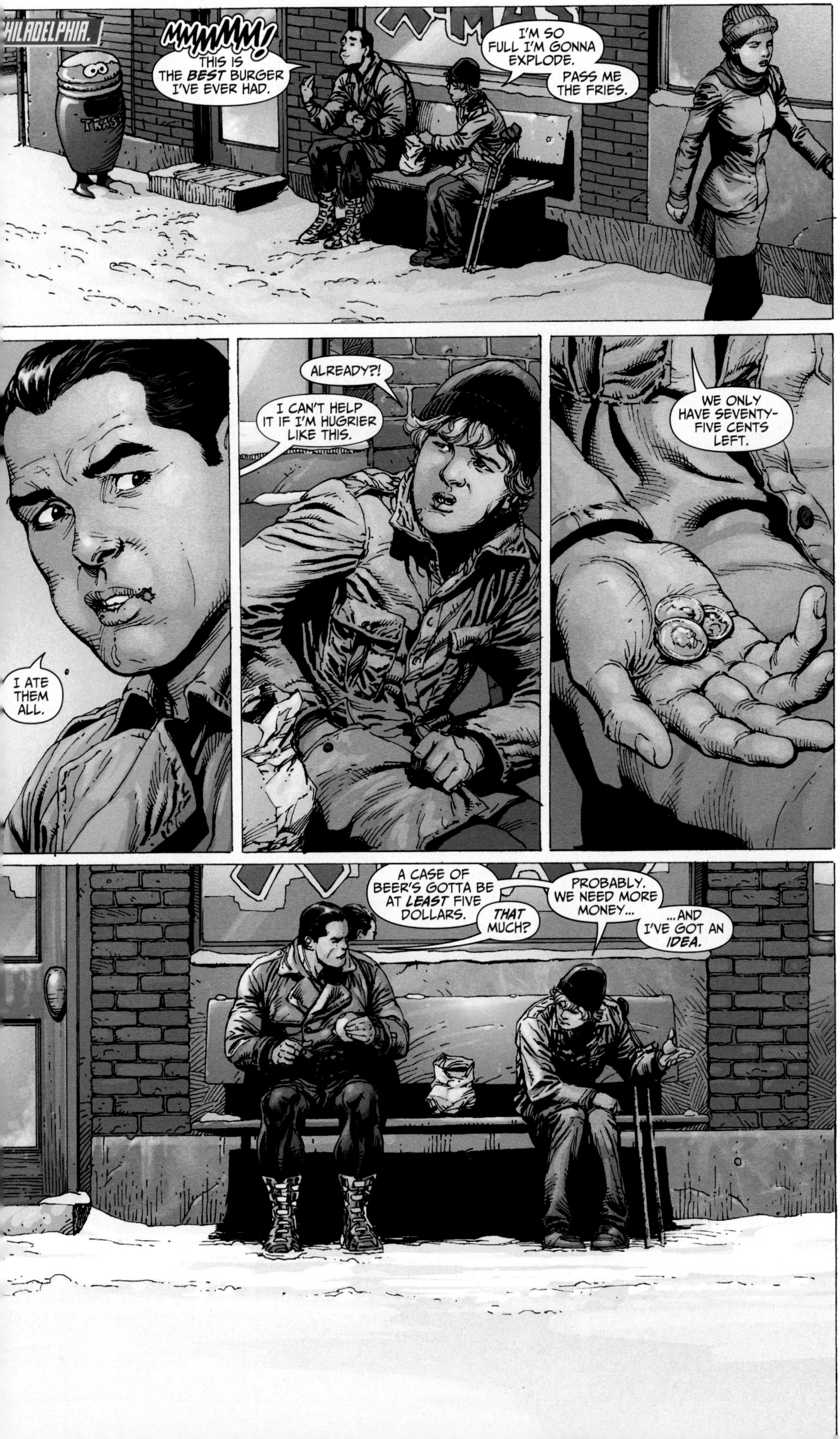
PHILADELPHIA.
MMMMM!
THIS IS THE BEST BURGER I'VE EVER HAD.
I'M SO FULL I'M GONNA EXPLODE.
PASS ME THE FRIES.
TRASH
I ATE THEM ALL.
ALREADY?!
I CAN'T HELP IT IF I'M HUGRIER LIKE THIS.
WE ONLY HAVE SEVENTY-FIVE CENTS LEFT.
A CASE OF BEER'S GOTTA BE AT LEAST FIVE DOLLARS.
THAT MUCH?
PROBABLY. WE NEED MORE MONEY...
...AND I'VE GOT AN IDEA.

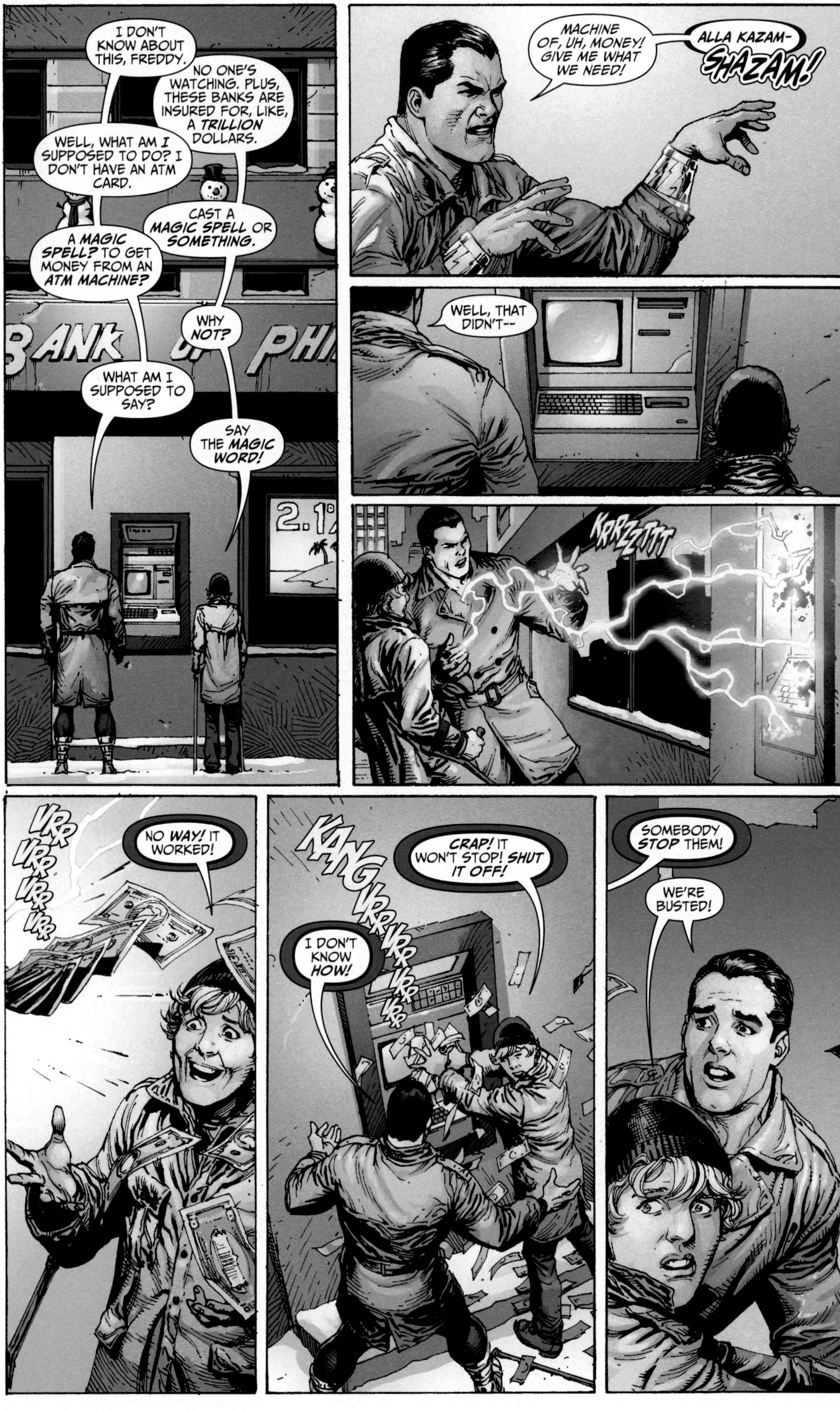
I DON'T KNOW ABOUT THIS, FREDDY.
NO ONE'S WATCHING. PLUS, THESE BANKS ARE INSURED FOR, LIKE, A *TRILLION* DOLLARS.
WELL, WHAT AM *I* SUPPOSED TO DO? I DON'T HAVE AN ATM CARD.
CAST A *MAGIC SPELL* OR *SOMETHING.*
A *MAGIC SPELL?* TO GET MONEY FROM AN *ATM MACHINE?*
BANK
WHY *NOT?*
WHAT AM I SUPPOSED TO SAY?
SAY THE *MAGIC WORD!*
MACHINE OF, UH, MONEY! GIVE ME WHAT WE NEED!
ALLA KAZAM-
SHAZAM!
WELL, THAT DIDN'T--
KRRZZTTT
VRR VRR VRR VRR
NO *WAY!* IT WORKED!
KANG
VRRVRRVRRVRR
CRAP! IT WON'T STOP! *SHUT IT OFF!*
I DON'T KNOW *HOW!*
SOMEBODY *STOP* THEM!
WE'RE BUSTED!

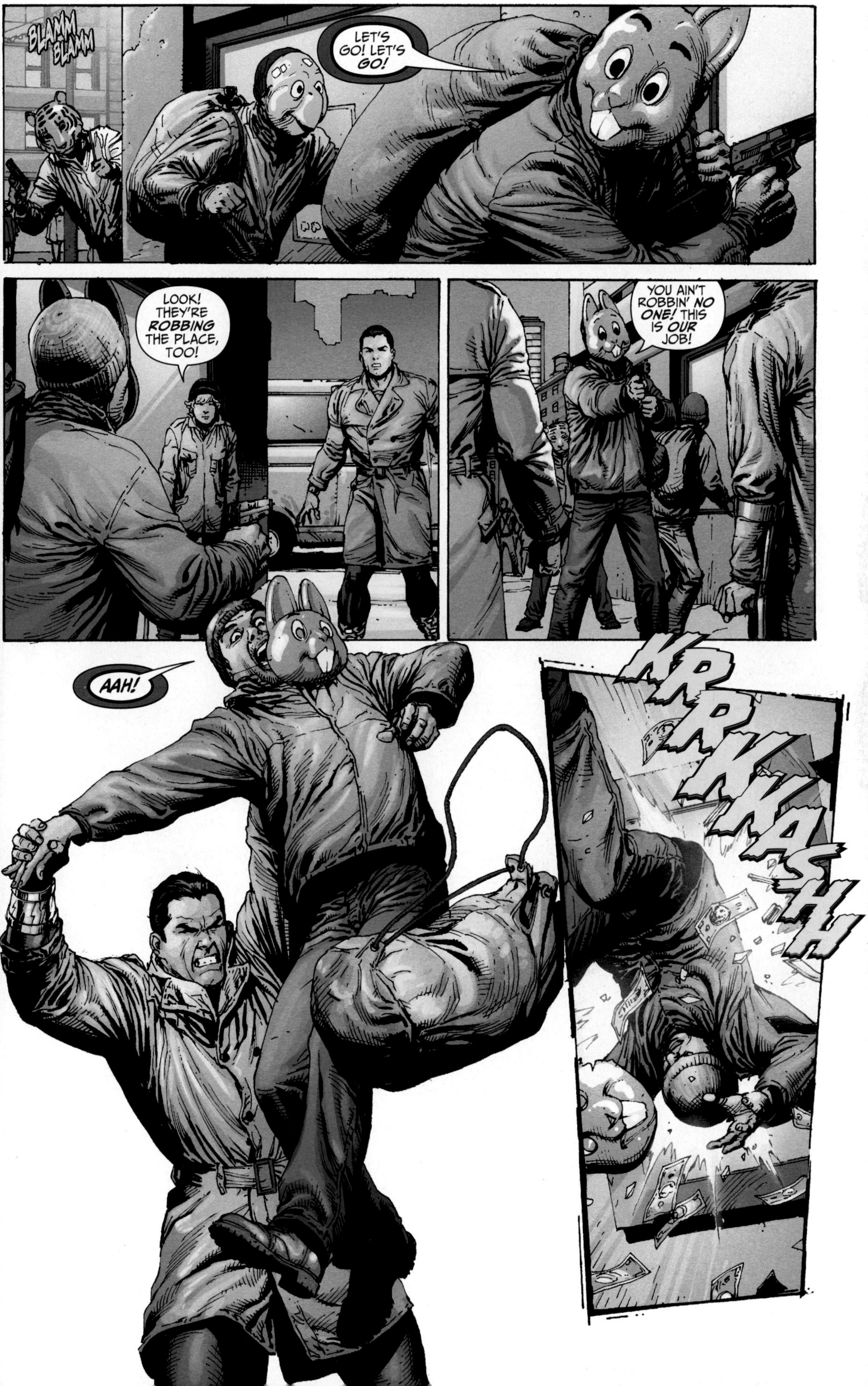
BLAMM BLAMM
LET'S GO! LET'S GO!
LOOK! THEY'RE ROBBING THE PLACE, TOO!
YOU AIN'T ROBBIN' NO ONE! THIS IS OUR JOB!
AAH!
KRKKASH

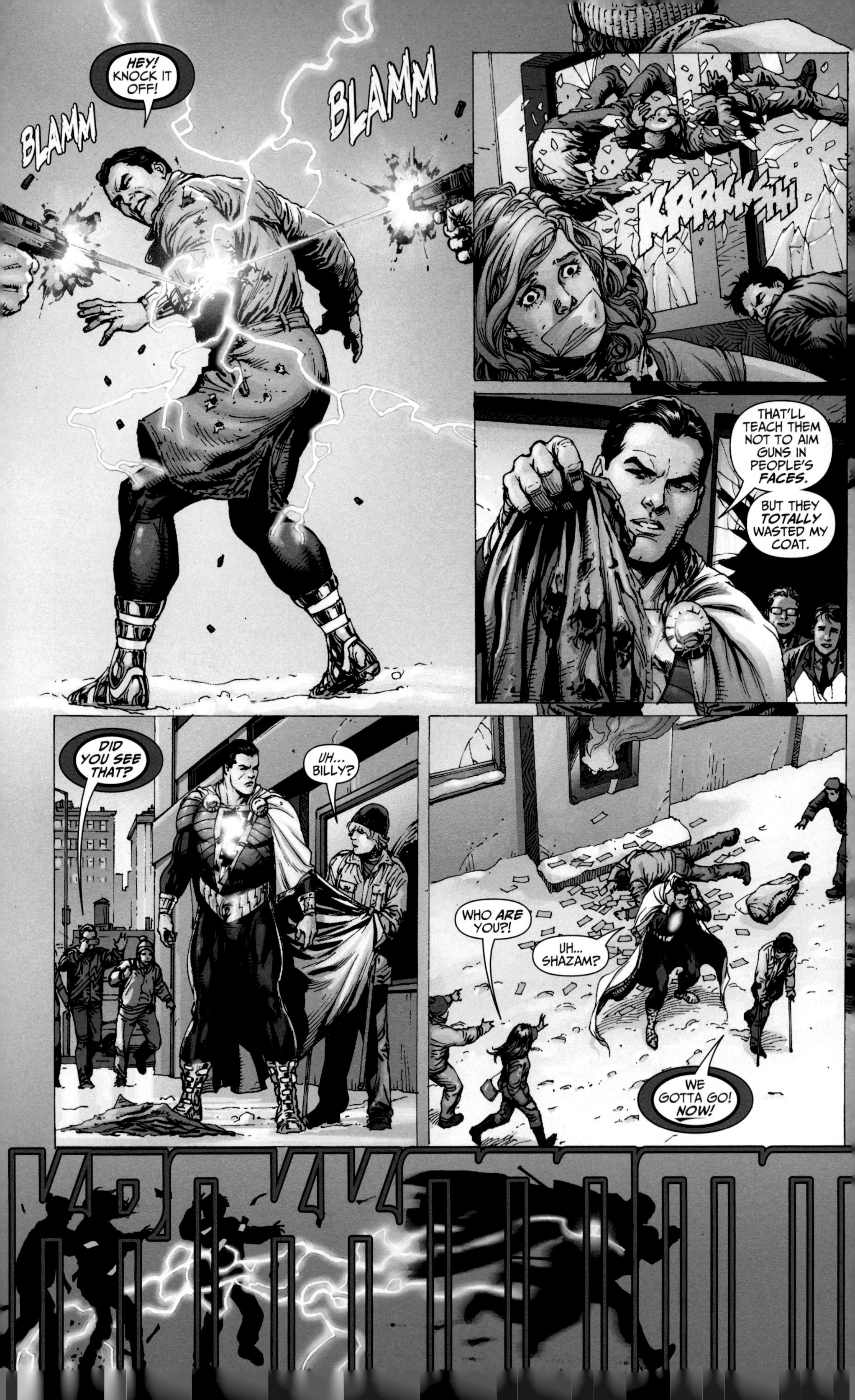
BLAMM
HEY! KNOCK IT OFF!
BLAMM
THAT'LL TEACH THEM NOT TO AIM GUNS IN PEOPLE'S *FACES.*
BUT THEY *TOTALLY* WASTED MY COAT.
DID YOU SEE THAT?
UH... BILLY?
WHO *ARE* YOU?!
UH... SHAZAM?
WE GOTTA GO! *NOW!*

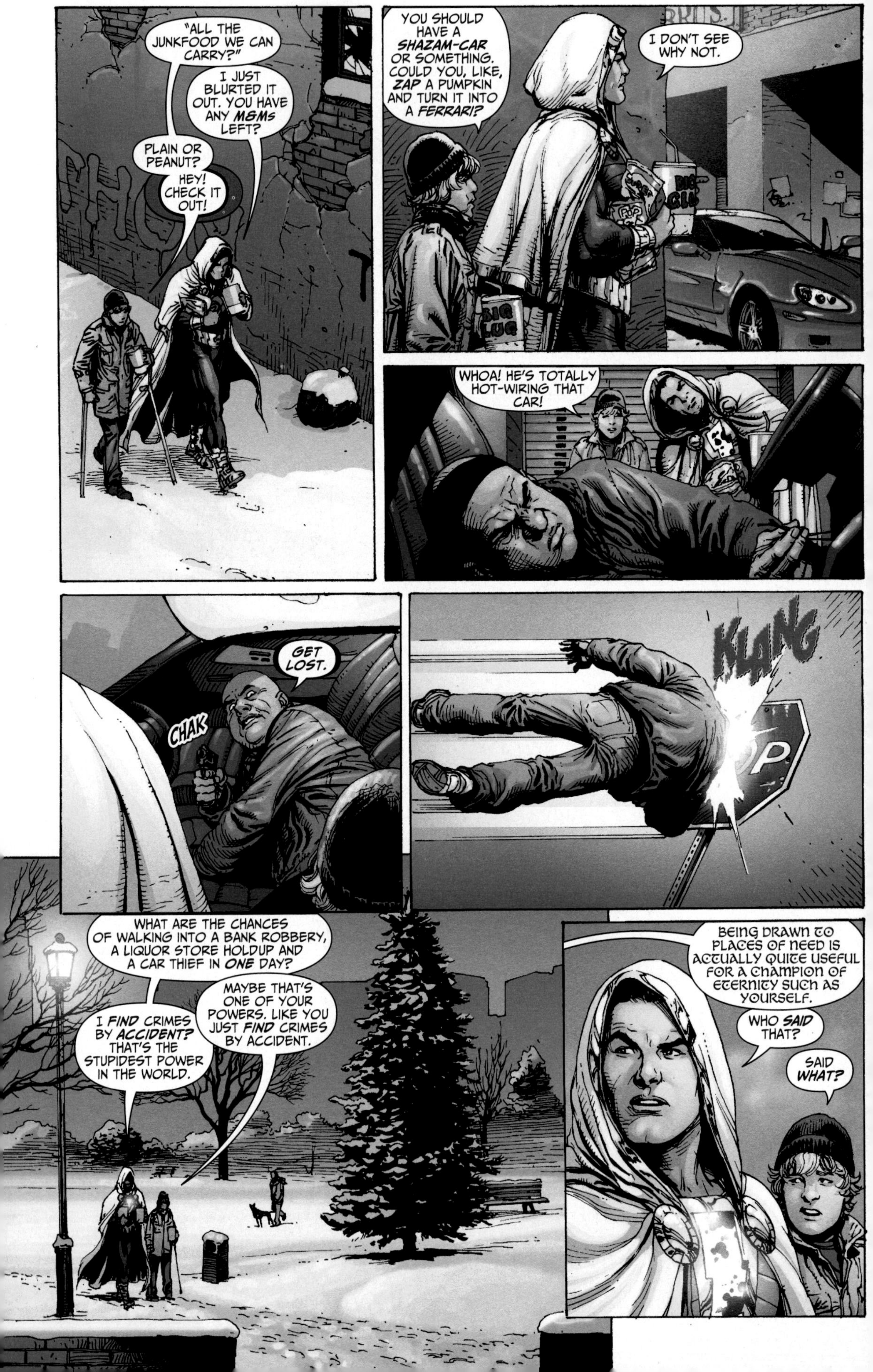
"ALL THE JUNKFOOD WE CAN CARRY?"
I JUST BLURTED IT OUT. YOU HAVE ANY M&Ms LEFT?
PLAIN OR PEANUT?
HEY! CHECK IT OUT!
YOU SHOULD HAVE A SHAZAM-CAR OR SOMETHING. COULD YOU, LIKE, ZAP A PUMPKIN AND TURN IT INTO A FERRARI?
I DON'T SEE WHY NOT.
BIG GLUG
WHOA! HE'S TOTALLY HOT-WIRING THAT CAR!
GET LOST.
CHAK
KLANG
WHAT ARE THE CHANCES OF WALKING INTO A BANK ROBBERY, A LIQUOR STORE HOLDUP AND A CAR THIEF IN ONE DAY?
MAYBE THAT'S ONE OF YOUR POWERS. LIKE YOU JUST FIND CRIMES BY ACCIDENT.
I FIND CRIMES BY ACCIDENT? THAT'S THE STUPIDEST POWER IN THE WORLD.
BEING DRAWN TO PLACES OF NEED IS ACTUALLY QUITE USEFUL FOR A CHAMPION OF ETERNITY SUCH AS YOURSELF.
WHO SAID THAT?
SAID WHAT?

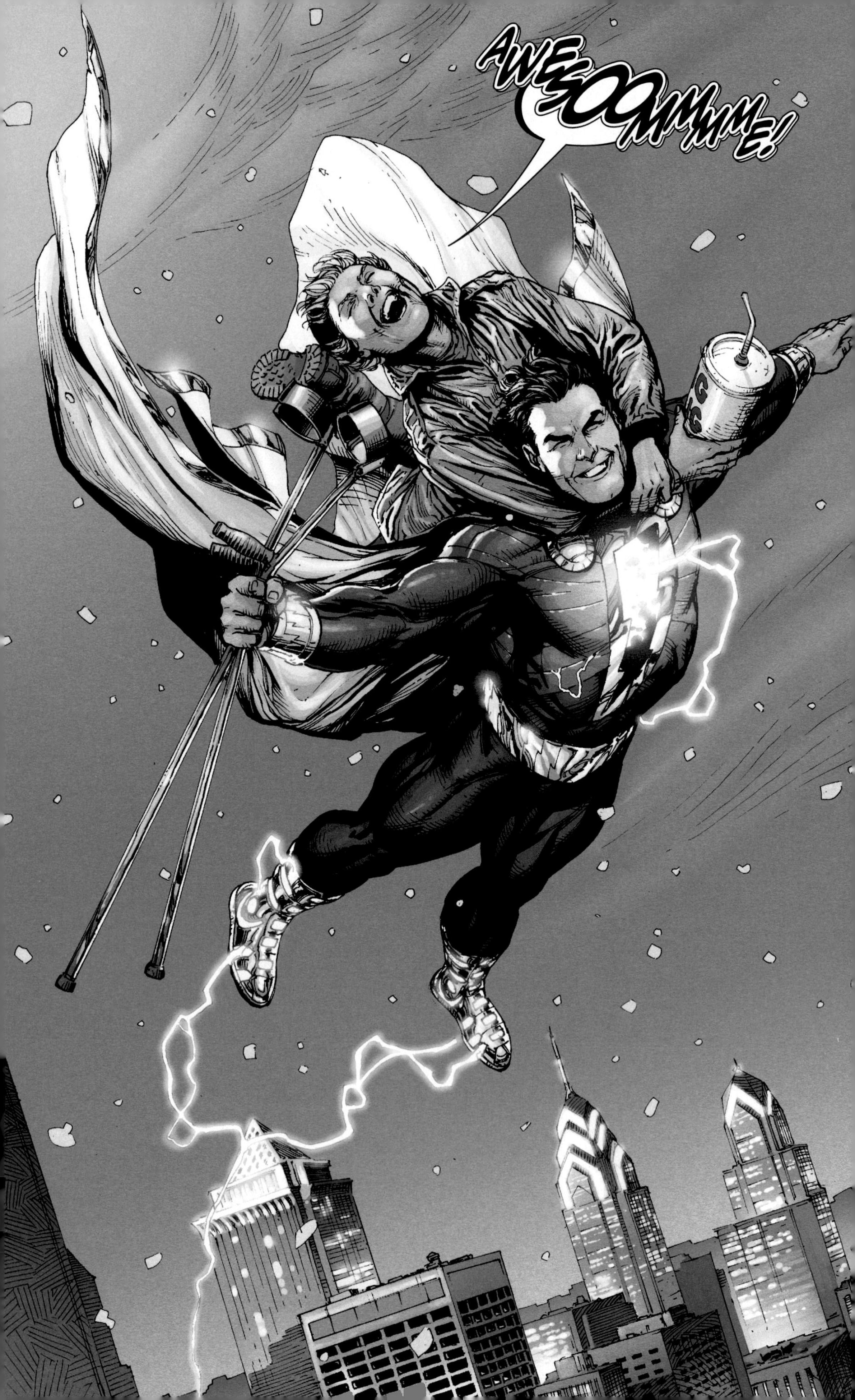
AWESOOMMMMME!

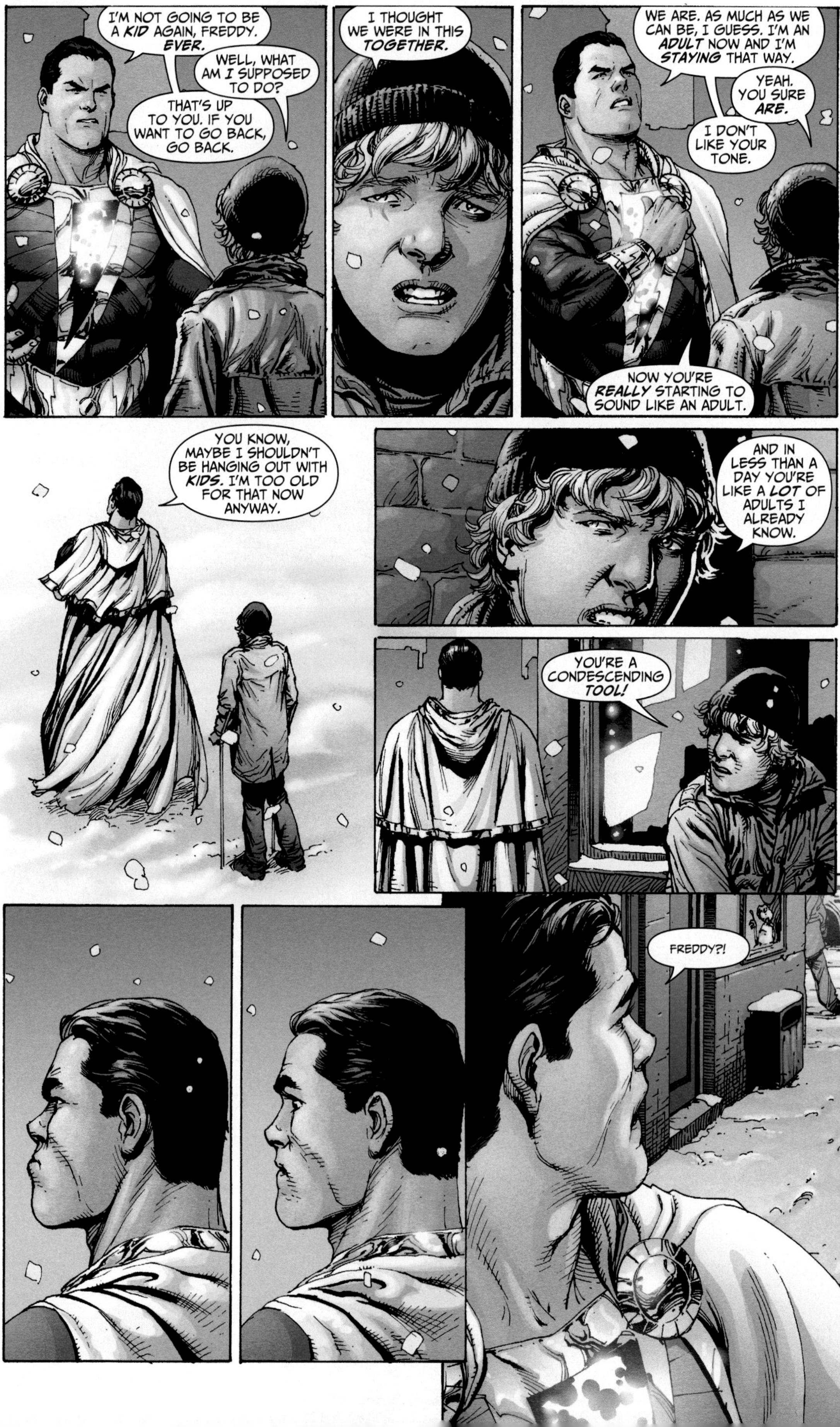
I'M NOT GOING TO BE A KID AGAIN, FREDDY. EVER.
WELL, WHAT AM I SUPPOSED TO DO?
THAT'S UP TO YOU. IF YOU WANT TO GO BACK, GO BACK.
I THOUGHT WE WERE IN THIS TOGETHER.
WE ARE. AS MUCH AS WE CAN BE, I GUESS. I'M AN ADULT NOW AND I'M STAYING THAT WAY.
YEAH. YOU SURE ARE.
I DON'T LIKE YOUR TONE.
NOW YOU'RE REALLY STARTING TO SOUND LIKE AN ADULT.
YOU KNOW, MAYBE I SHOULDN'T BE HANGING OUT WITH KIDS. I'M TOO OLD FOR THAT NOW ANYWAY.
AND IN LESS THAN A DAY YOU'RE LIKE A LOT OF ADULTS I ALREADY KNOW.
YOU'RE A CONDESCENDING TOOL!
FREDDY?!

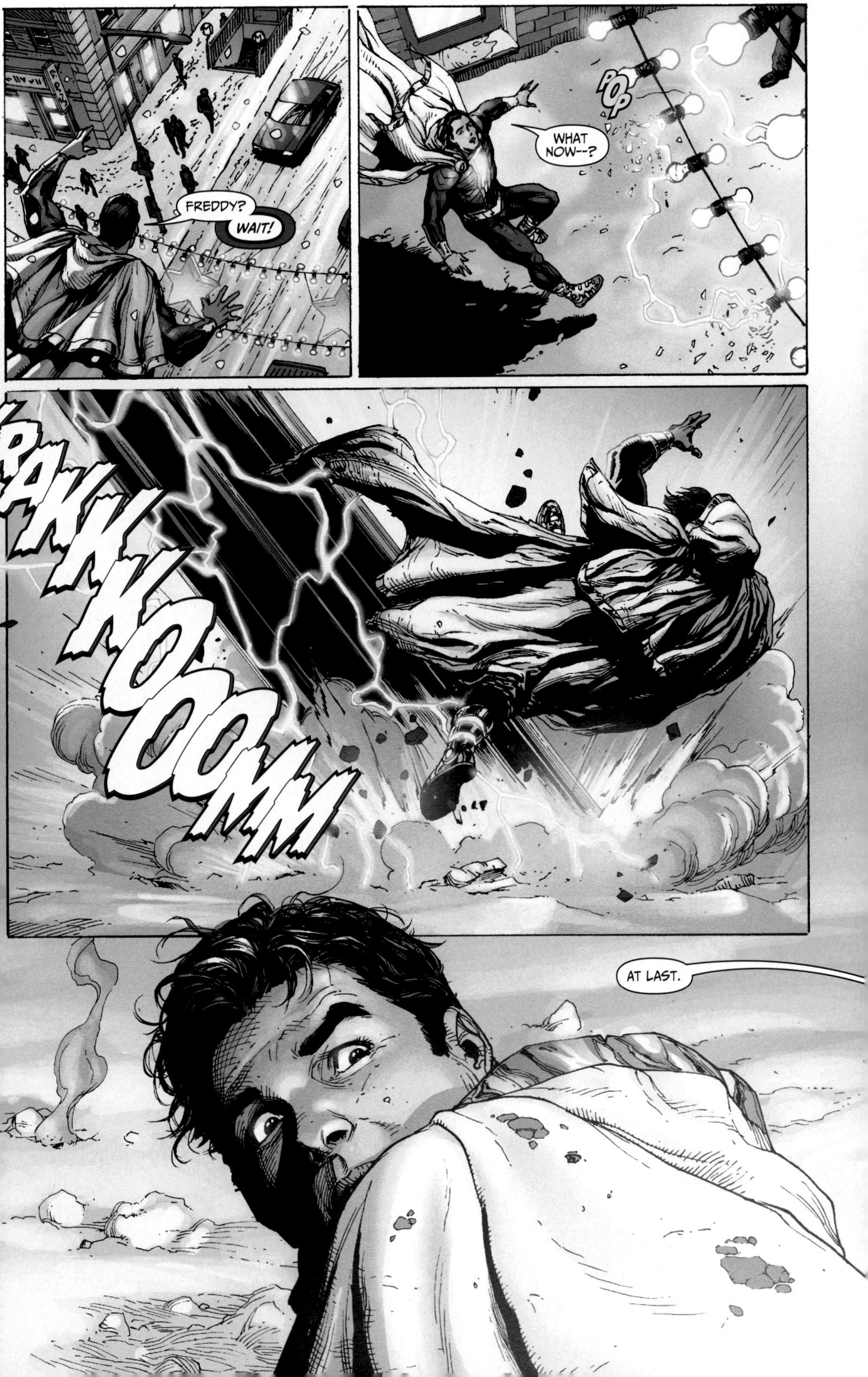
FREDDY?
WAIT!
POP
WHAT NOW--?
KRAKKOOOMM
AT LAST.

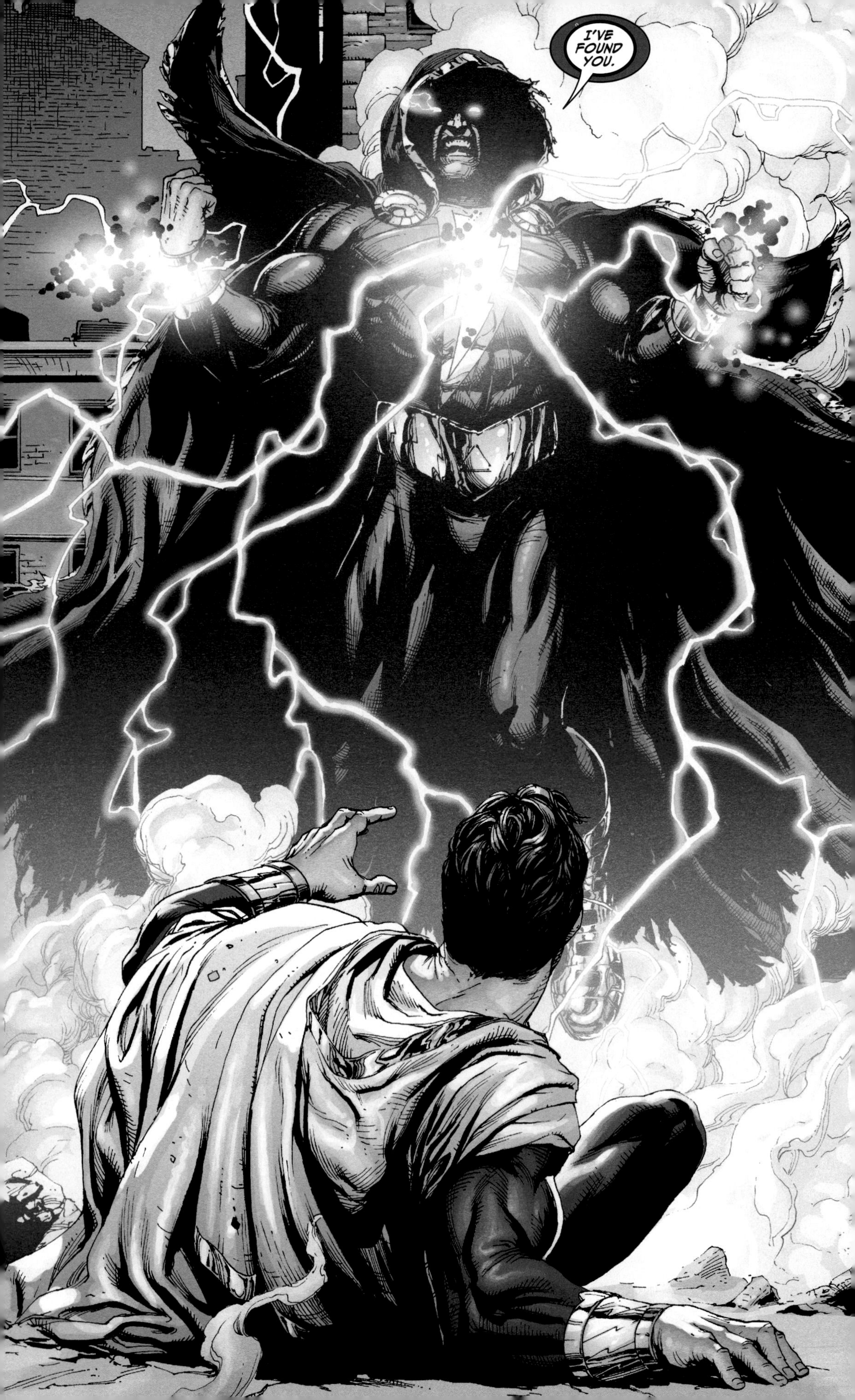
I'VE FOUND YOU.

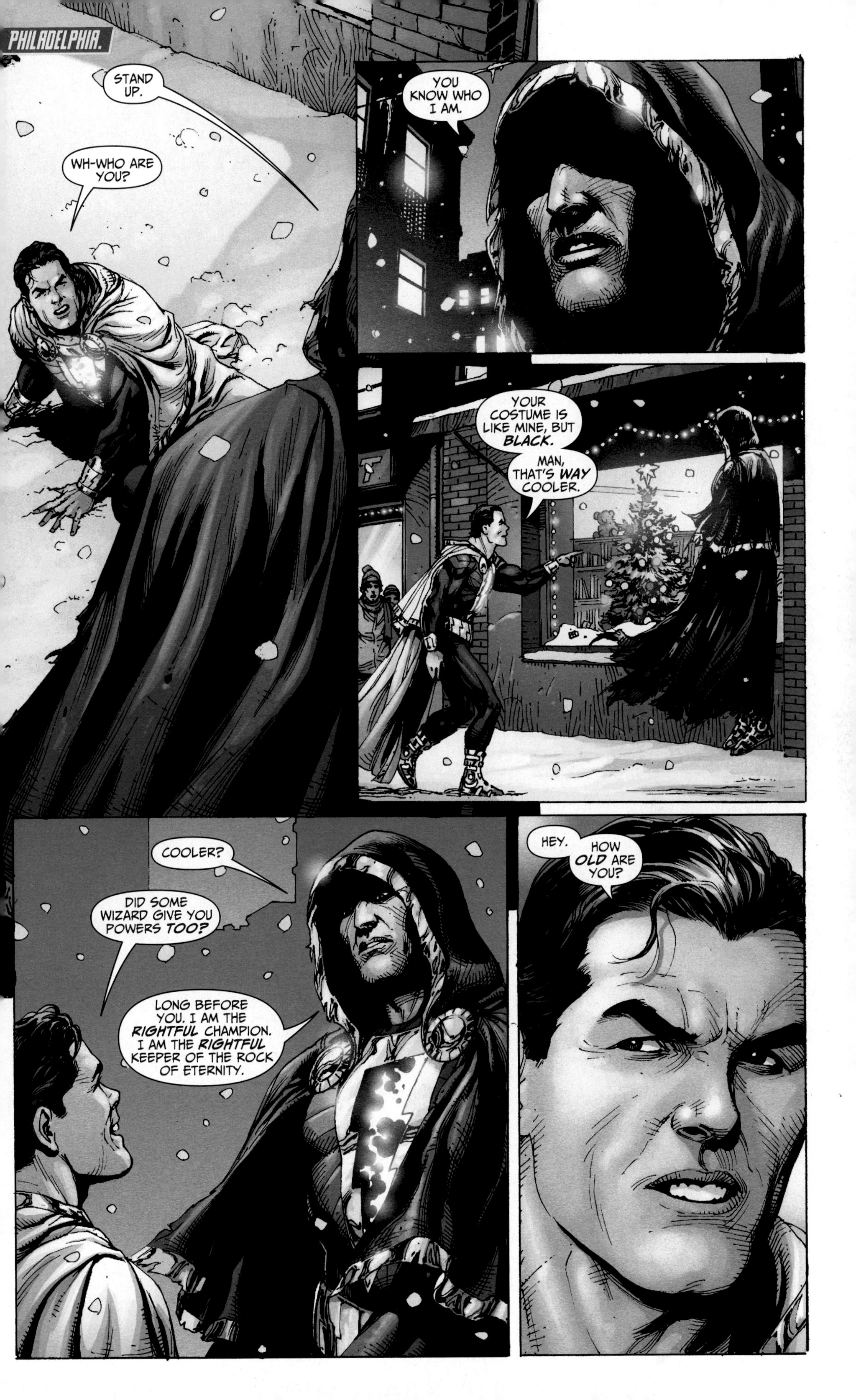
PHILADELPHIA.
STAND UP.
WH-WHO ARE YOU?
YOU KNOW WHO I AM.
YOUR COSTUME IS LIKE MINE, BUT BLACK.
MAN, THAT'S WAY COOLER.
COOLER?
DID SOME WIZARD GIVE YOU POWERS TOO?
LONG BEFORE YOU. I AM THE RIGHTFUL CHAMPION. I AM THE RIGHTFUL KEEPER OF THE ROCK OF ETERNITY.
HEY. HOW OLD ARE YOU?

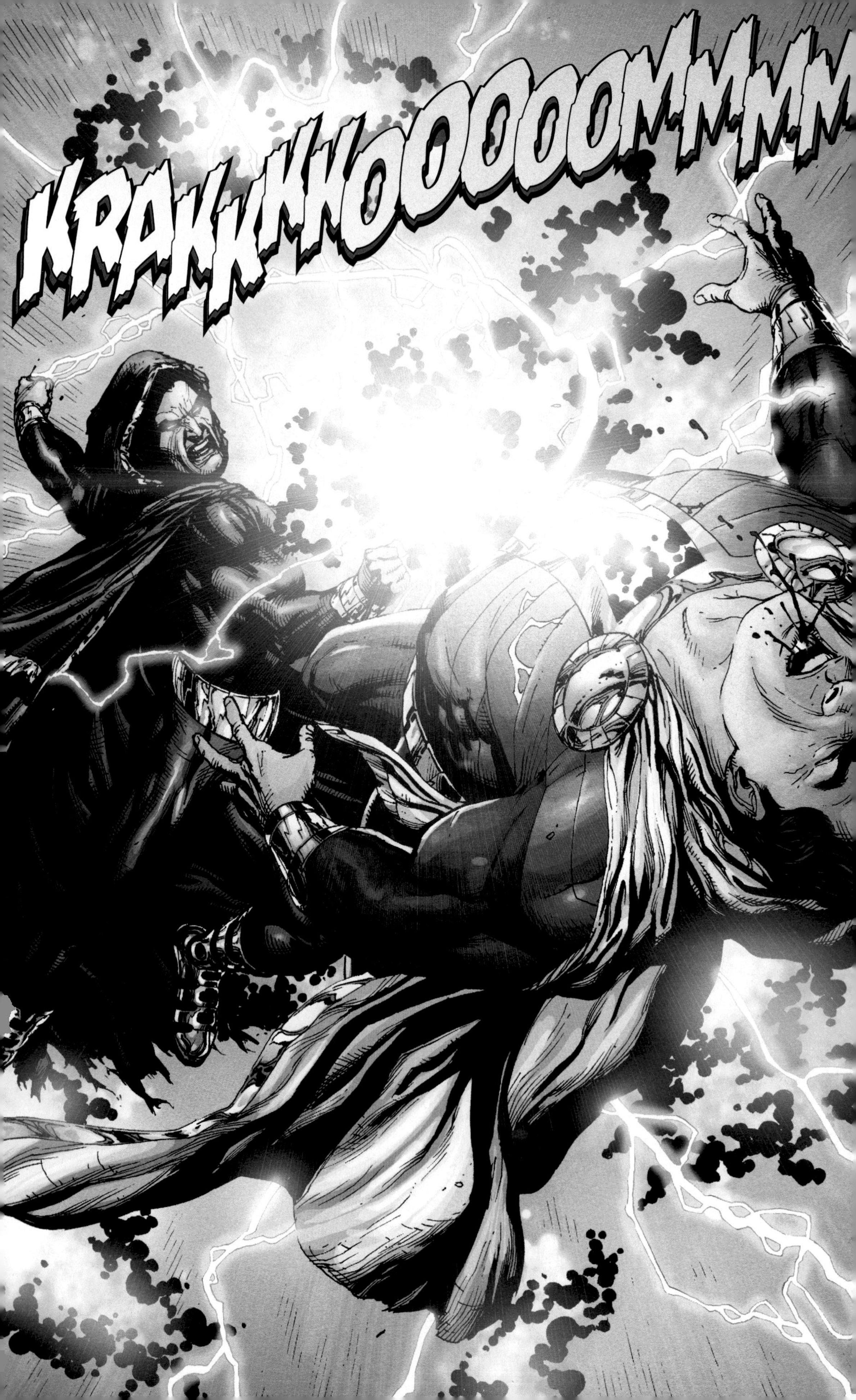
KRAKKKHOOOOOOMMMM

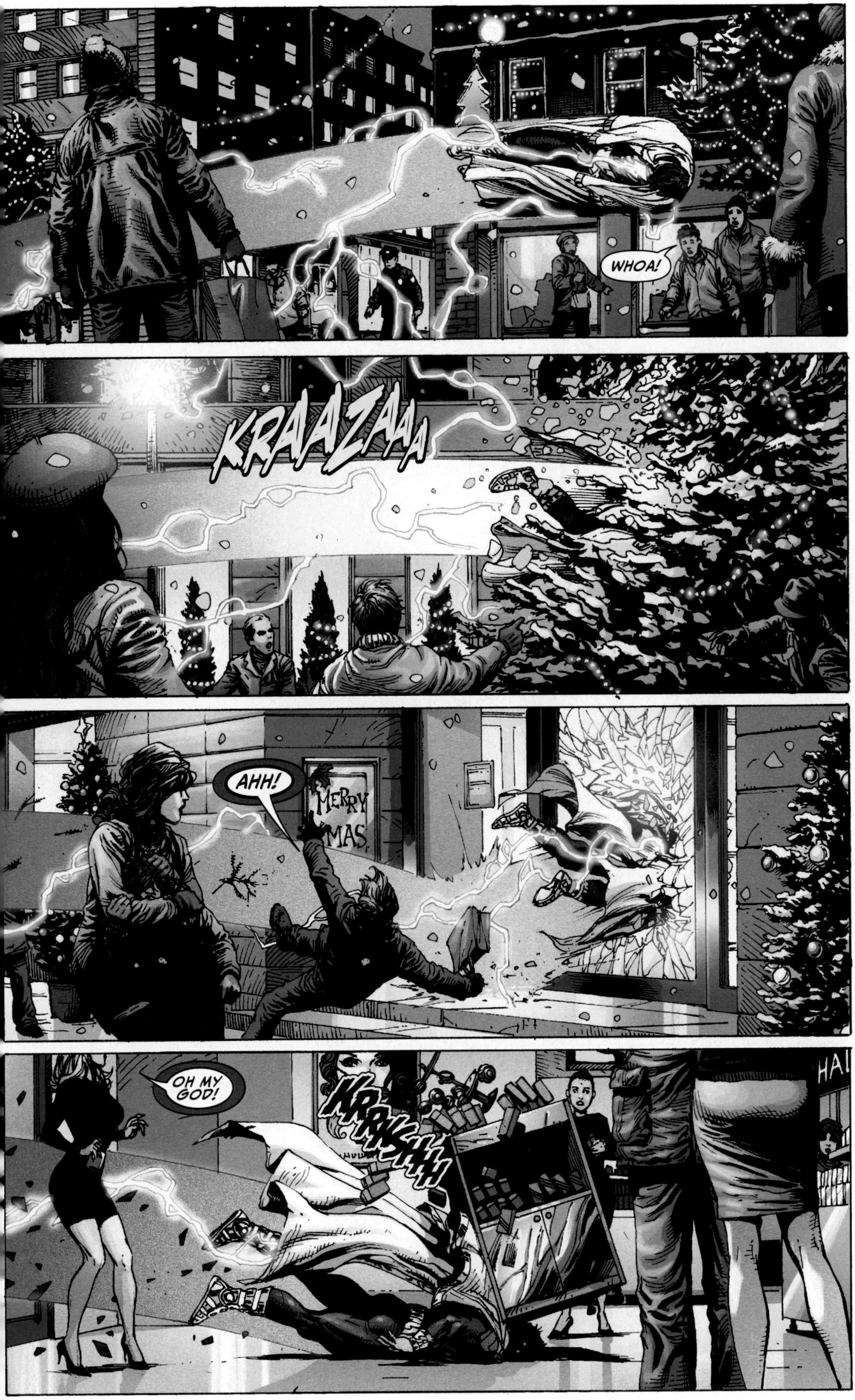
WHOA!
KRAAZAAA
AHH!
MERRY
XMAS
OH MY GOD!
KRRASHHH

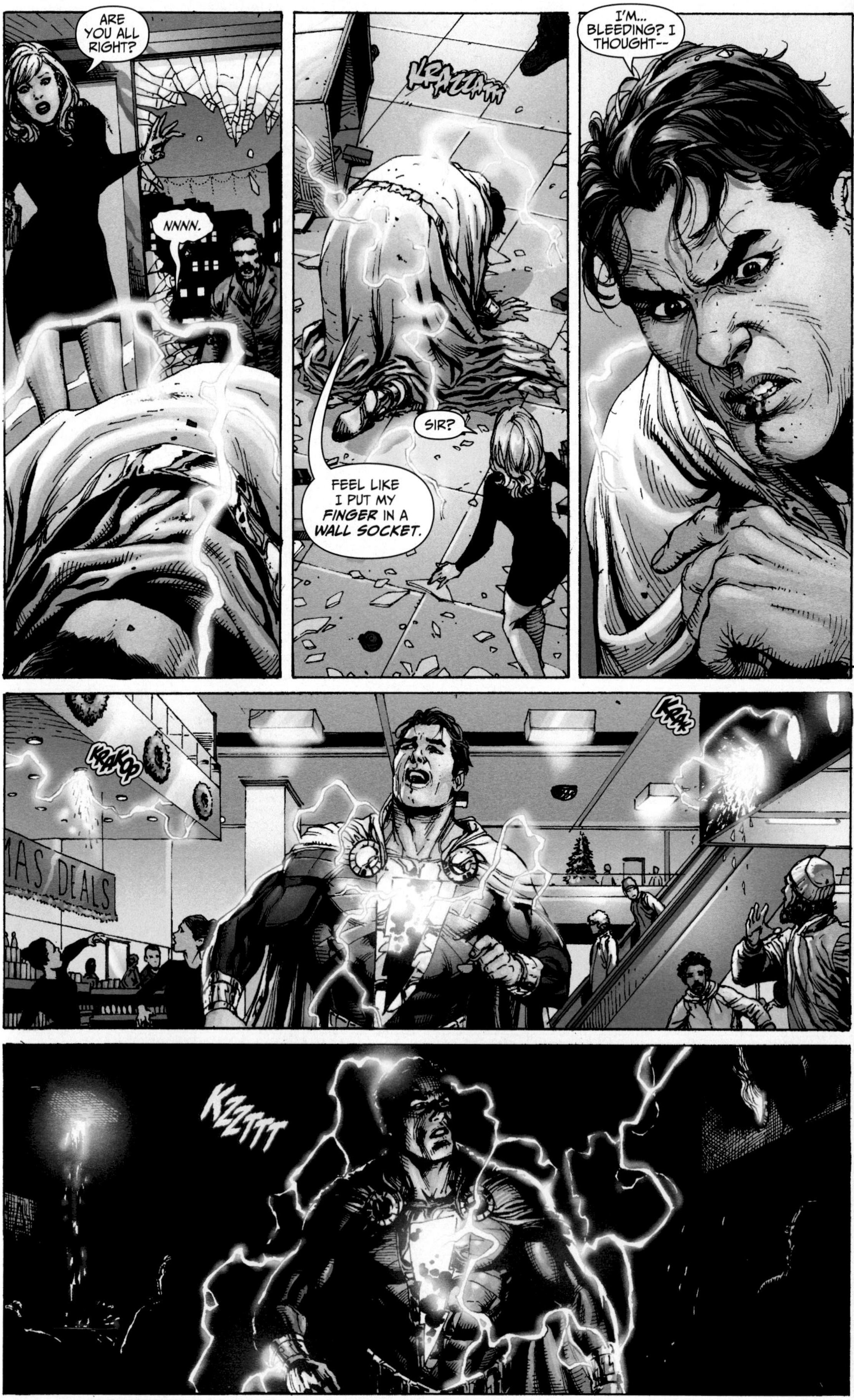
ARE YOU ALL RIGHT?
NNNN.
SIR?
FEEL LIKE I PUT MY *FINGER* IN A *WALL SOCKET*.
I'M... BLEEDING? I THOUGHT--
MAS DEALS
KRAK
KZZTTT

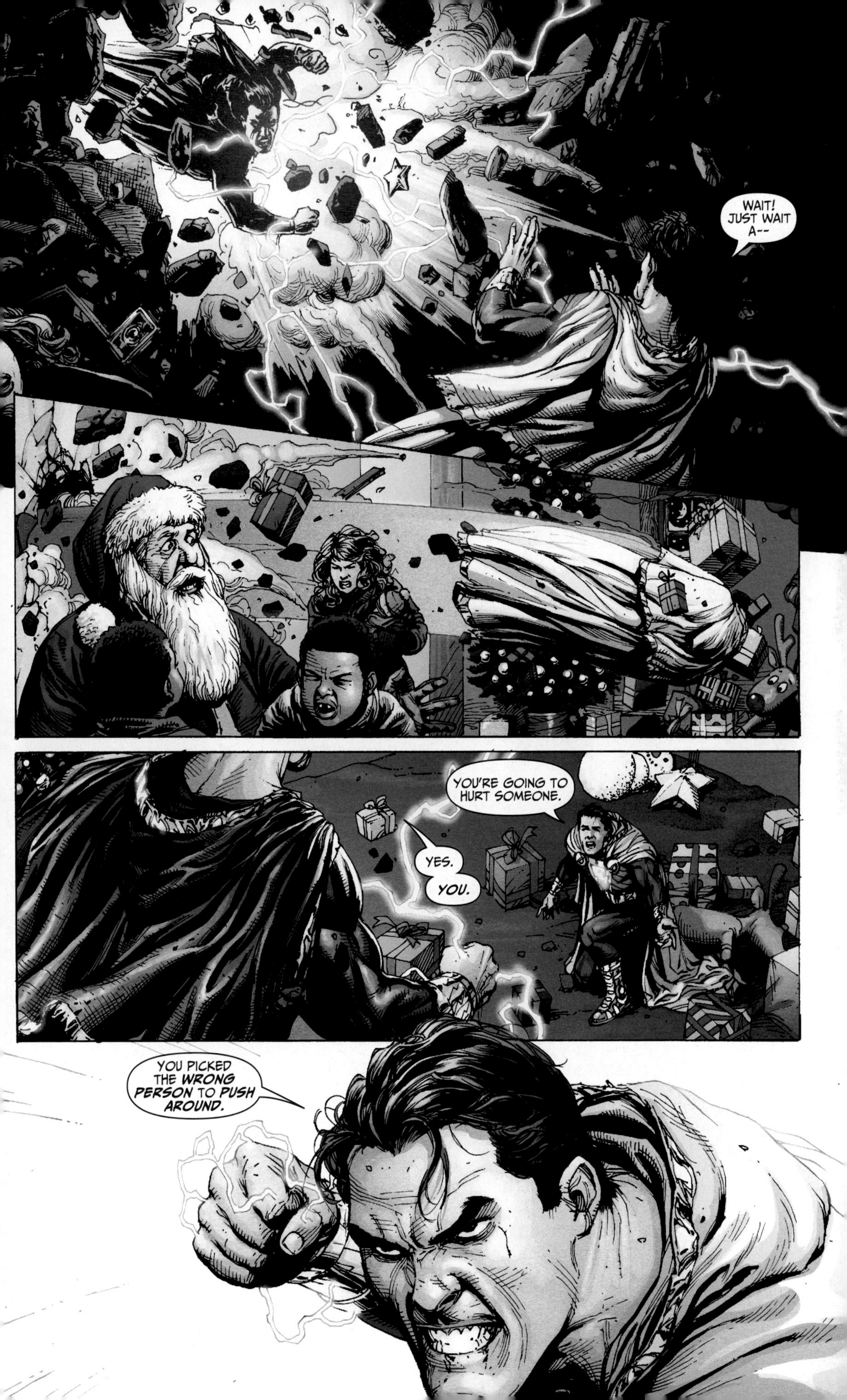
WAIT! JUST WAIT A--
YOU'RE GOING TO HURT SOMEONE.
YES.
YOU.
YOU PICKED THE WRONG PERSON TO PUSH AROUND.

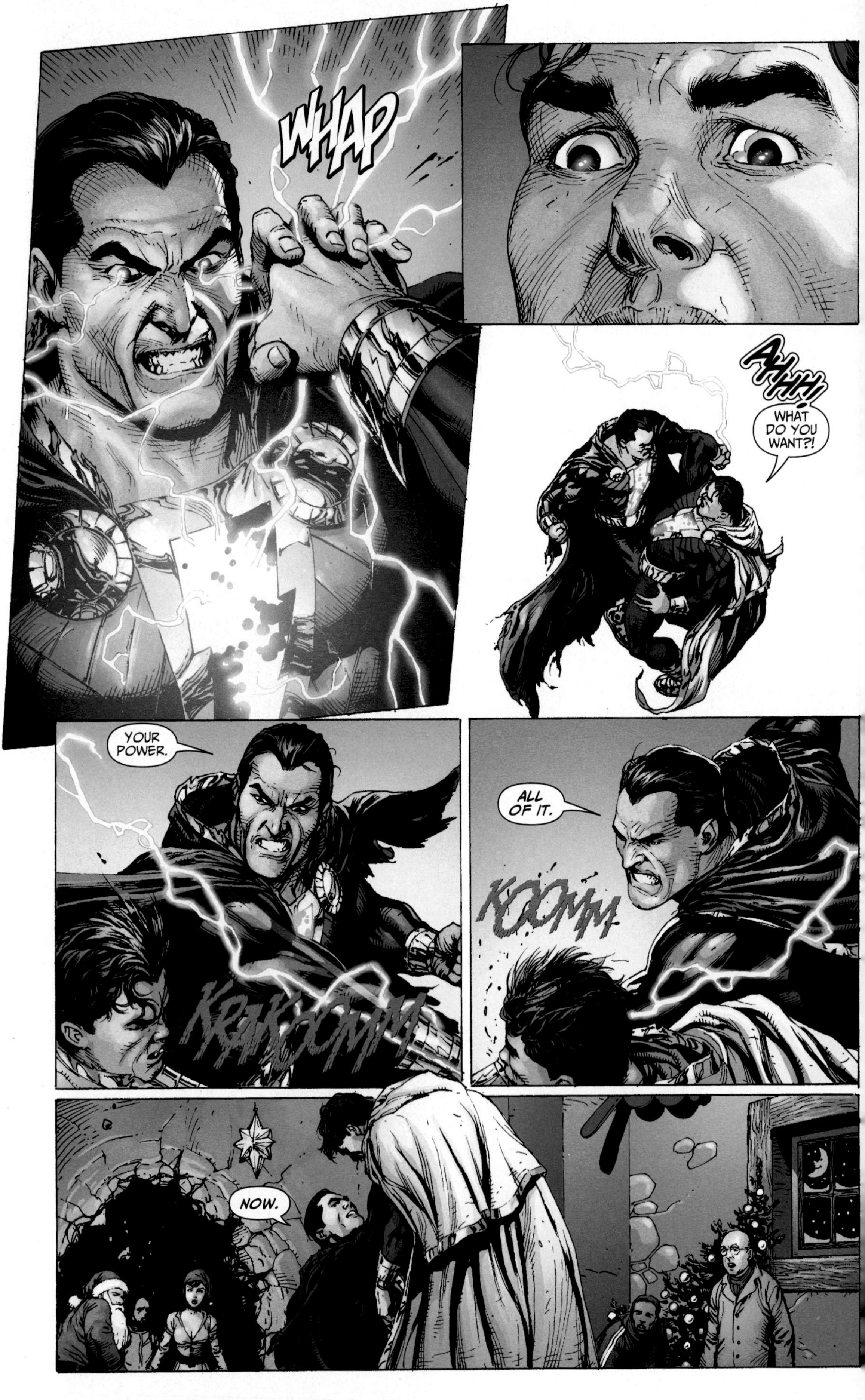
WHAP
AHHH!
WHAT DO YOU WANT?!
YOUR POWER.
KRAKOOMM
ALL OF IT.
KOOMM
NOW.

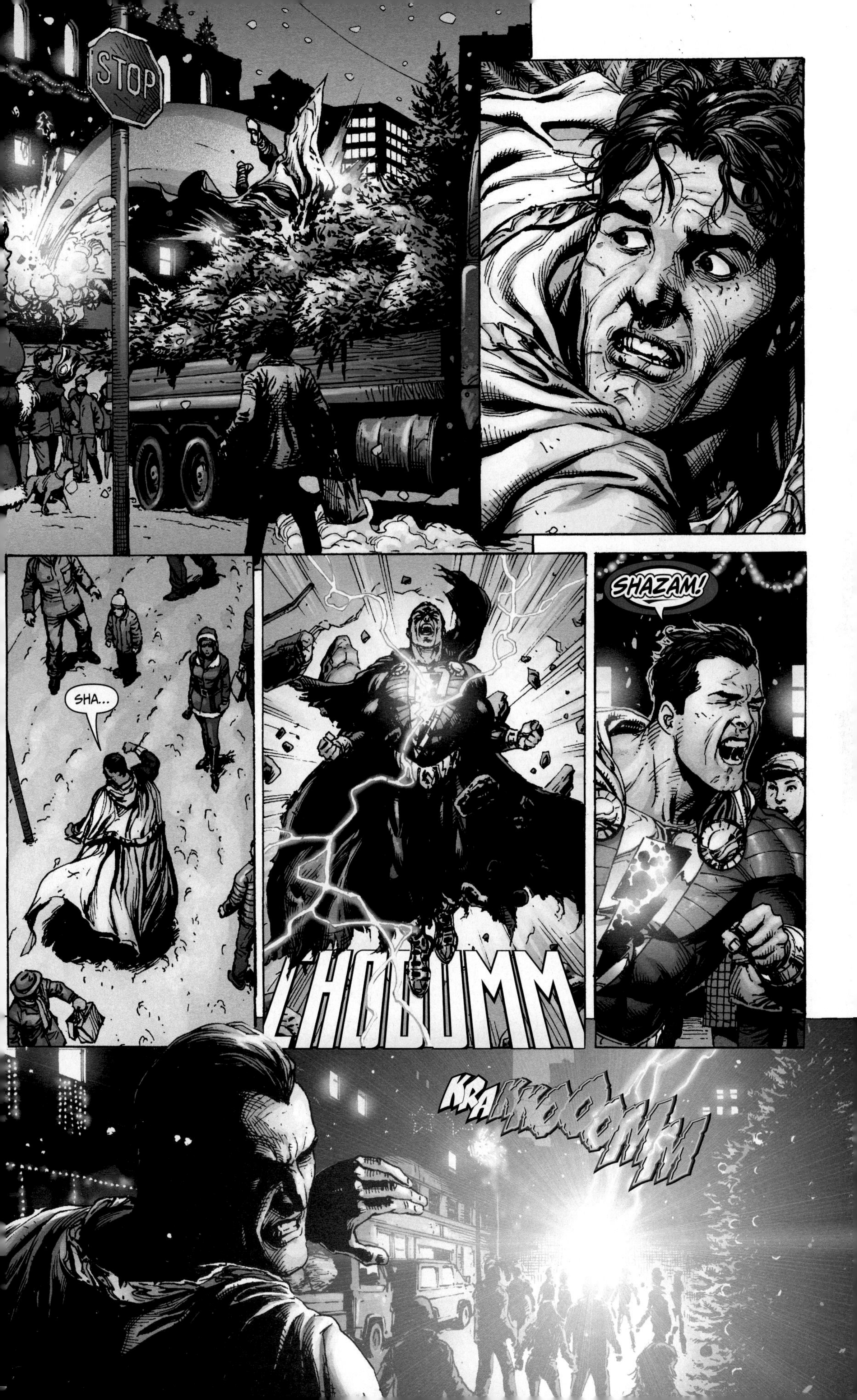
STOP
SHA...
CHOOOMM
SHAZAM!
KRAKOOOMM

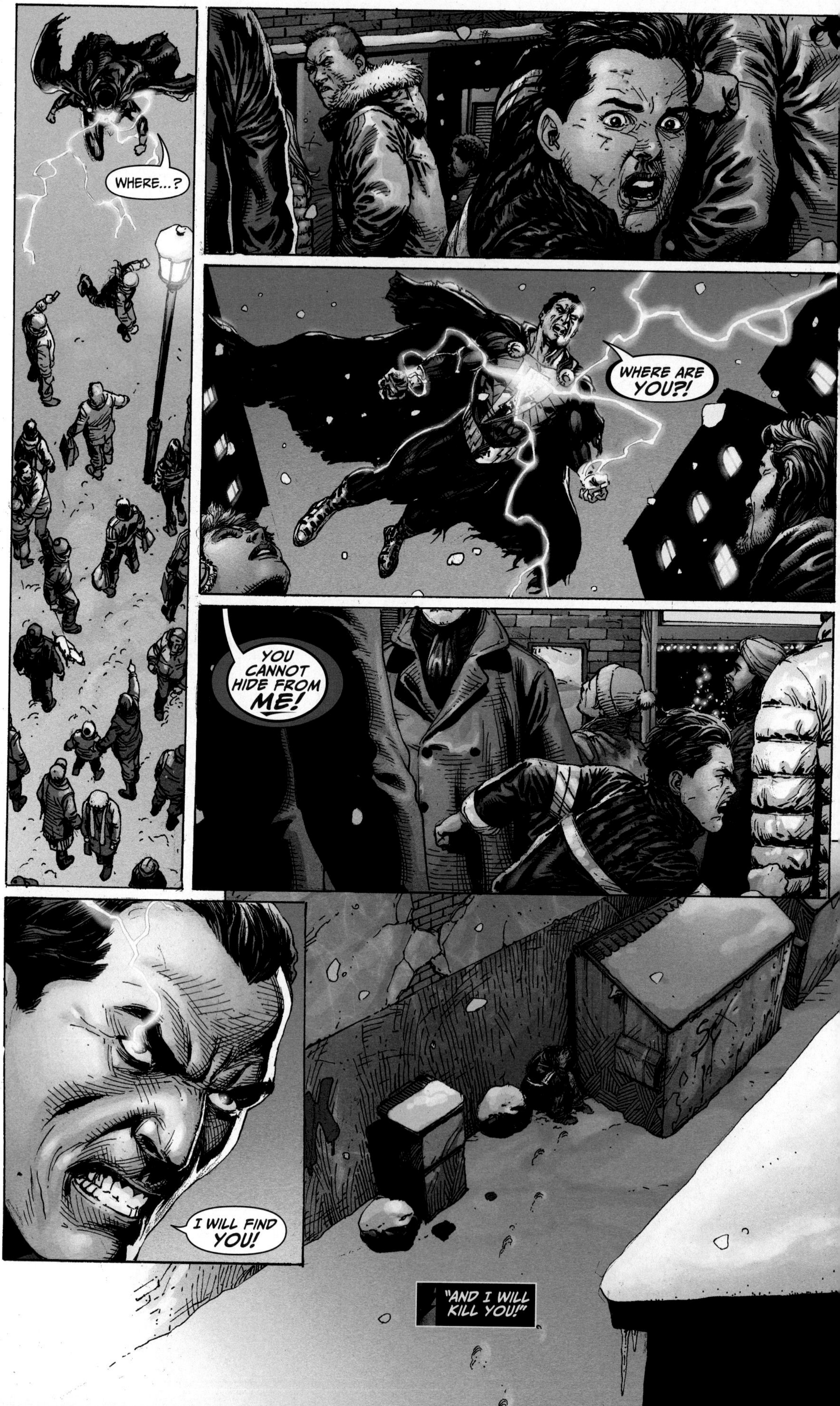
WHERE...?
WHERE ARE YOU?!
YOU CANNOT HIDE FROM ME!
I WILL FIND YOU!
"AND I WILL KILL YOU!"

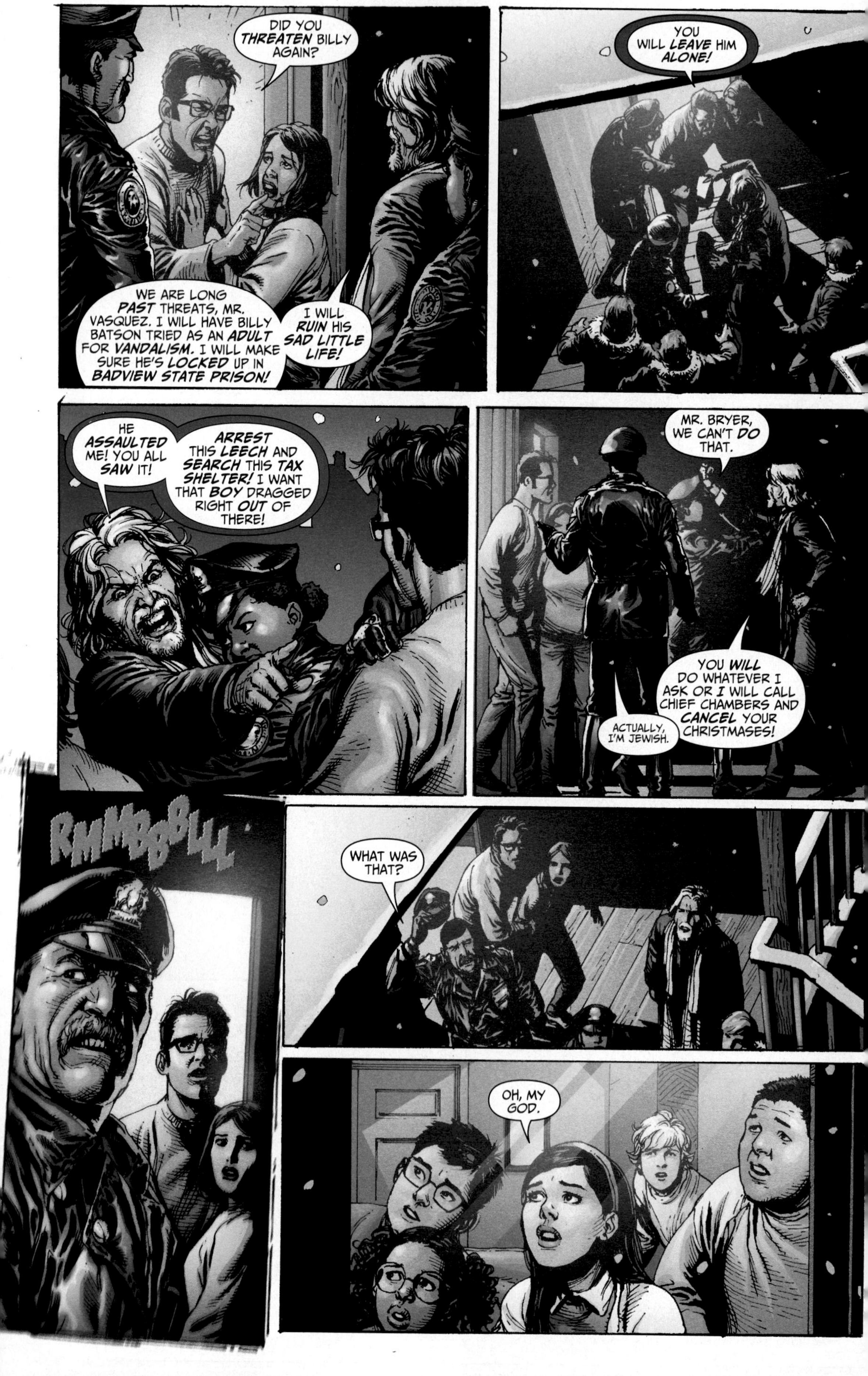
DID YOU THREATEN BILLY AGAIN?
WE ARE LONG PAST THREATS, MR. VASQUEZ. I WILL HAVE BILLY BATSON TRIED AS AN ADULT FOR VANDALISM. I WILL MAKE SURE HE'S LOCKED UP IN BADVIEW STATE PRISON!
I WILL RUIN HIS SAD LITTLE LIFE!
YOU WILL LEAVE HIM ALONE!
HE ASSAULTED ME! YOU ALL SAW IT!
ARREST THIS LEECH AND SEARCH THIS TAX SHELTER! I WANT THAT BOY DRAGGED RIGHT OUT OF THERE!
MR. BRYER, WE CAN'T DO THAT.
YOU WILL DO WHATEVER I ASK OR I WILL CALL CHIEF CHAMBERS AND CANCEL YOUR CHRISTMASES!
ACTUALLY, I'M JEWISH.
RMMBBBLLL
WHAT WAS THAT?
OH, MY GOD.

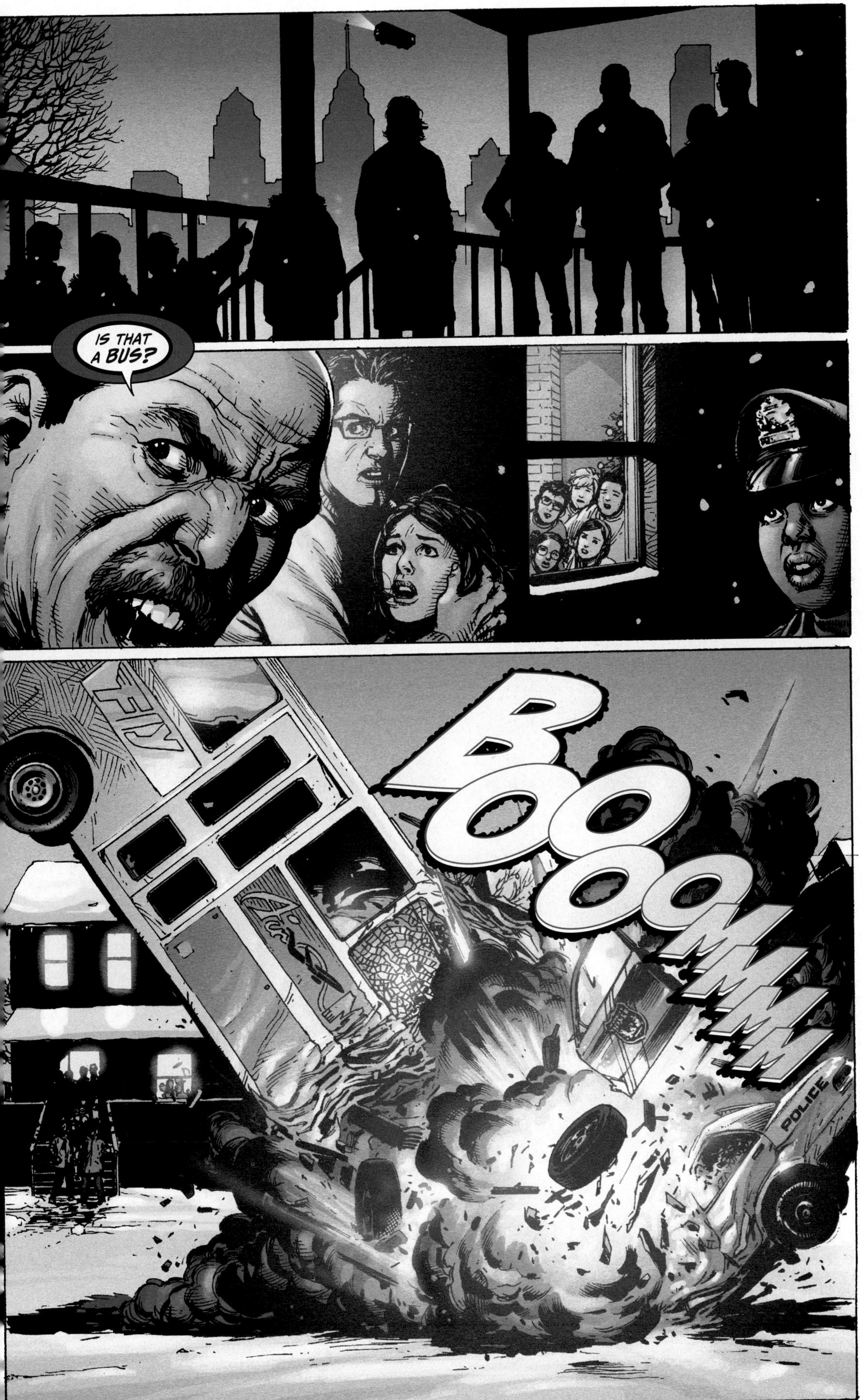

IS THAT A BUS?
BOOOOMMM
POLICE

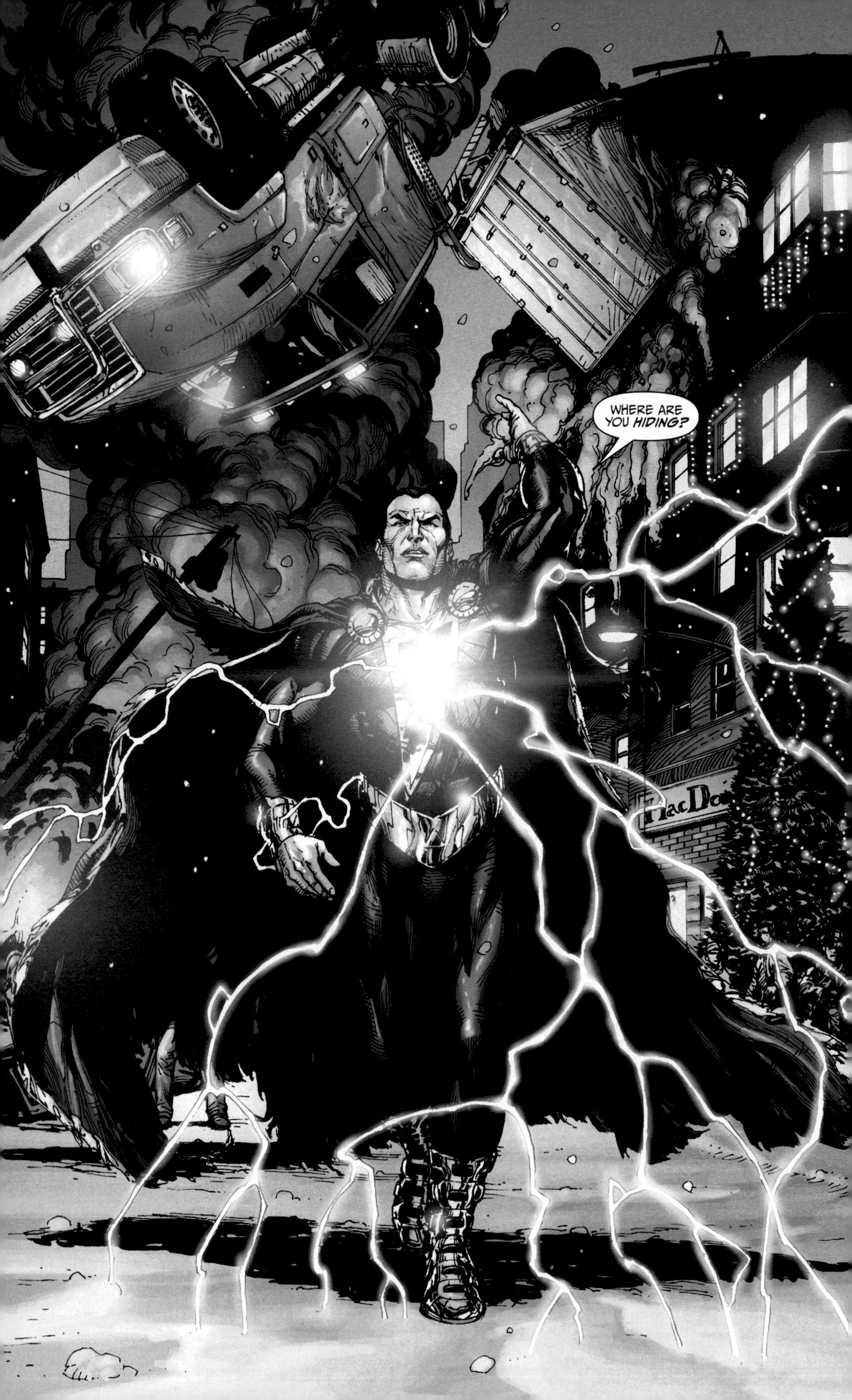
WHERE ARE YOU *HIDING?*
MacDo

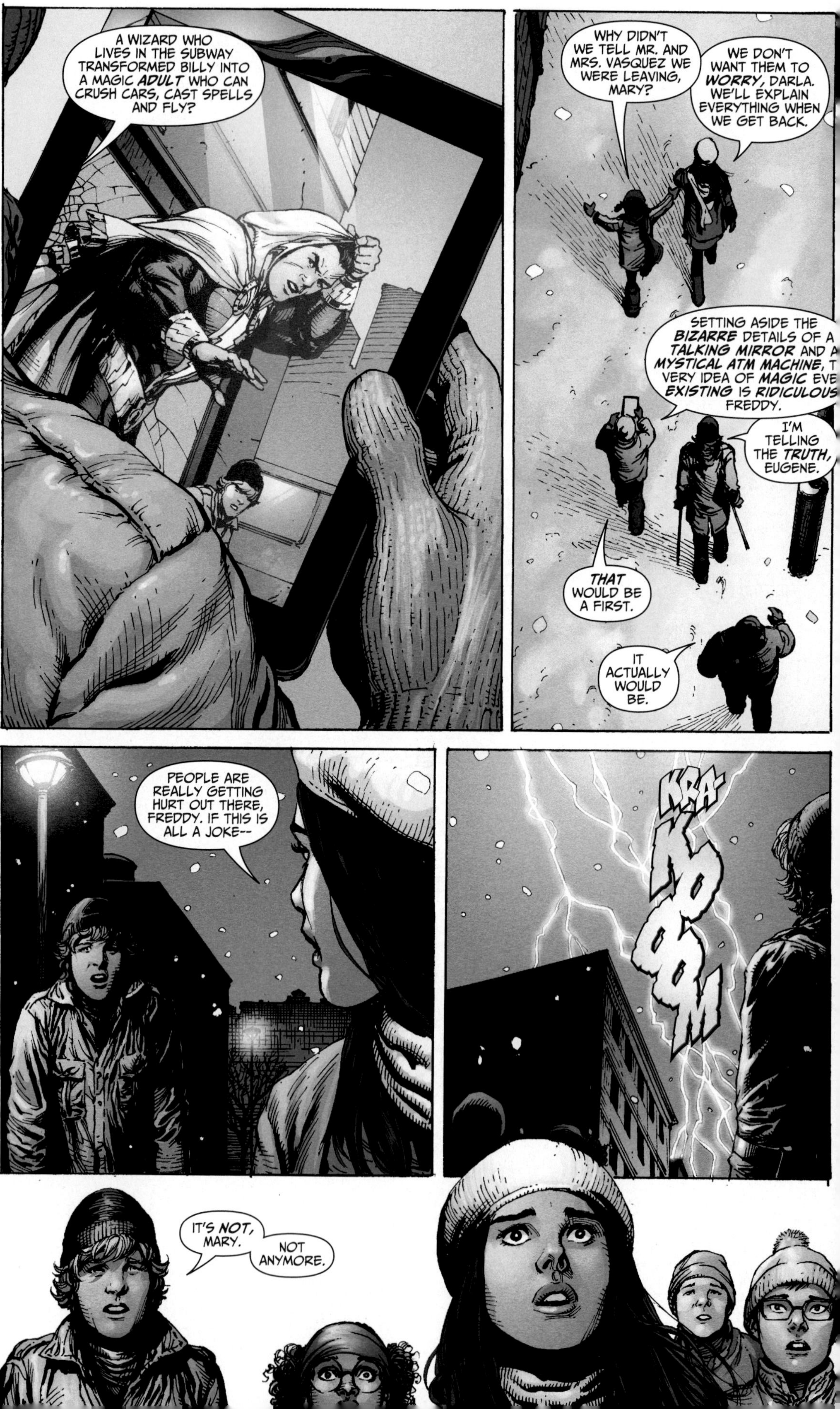

A WIZARD WHO LIVES IN THE SUBWAY TRANSFORMED BILLY INTO A MAGIC *ADULT* WHO CAN CRUSH CARS, CAST SPELLS AND FLY?
WHY DIDN'T WE TELL MR. AND MRS. VASQUEZ WE WERE LEAVING, MARY?
WE DON'T WANT THEM TO *WORRY,* DARLA. WE'LL EXPLAIN EVERYTHING WHEN WE GET BACK.
SETTING ASIDE THE *BIZARRE* DETAILS OF A *TALKING MIRROR* AND A *MYSTICAL ATM MACHINE,* T VERY IDEA OF *MAGIC* EVE *EXISTING* IS *RIDICULOUS* FREDDY.
I'M TELLING THE *TRUTH,* EUGENE.
THAT WOULD BE A FIRST.
IT ACTUALLY WOULD BE.
PEOPLE ARE REALLY GETTING HURT OUT THERE, FREDDY. IF THIS IS ALL A JOKE--
KRA-KOOOM
IT'S *NOT,* MARY.
NOT ANYMORE.

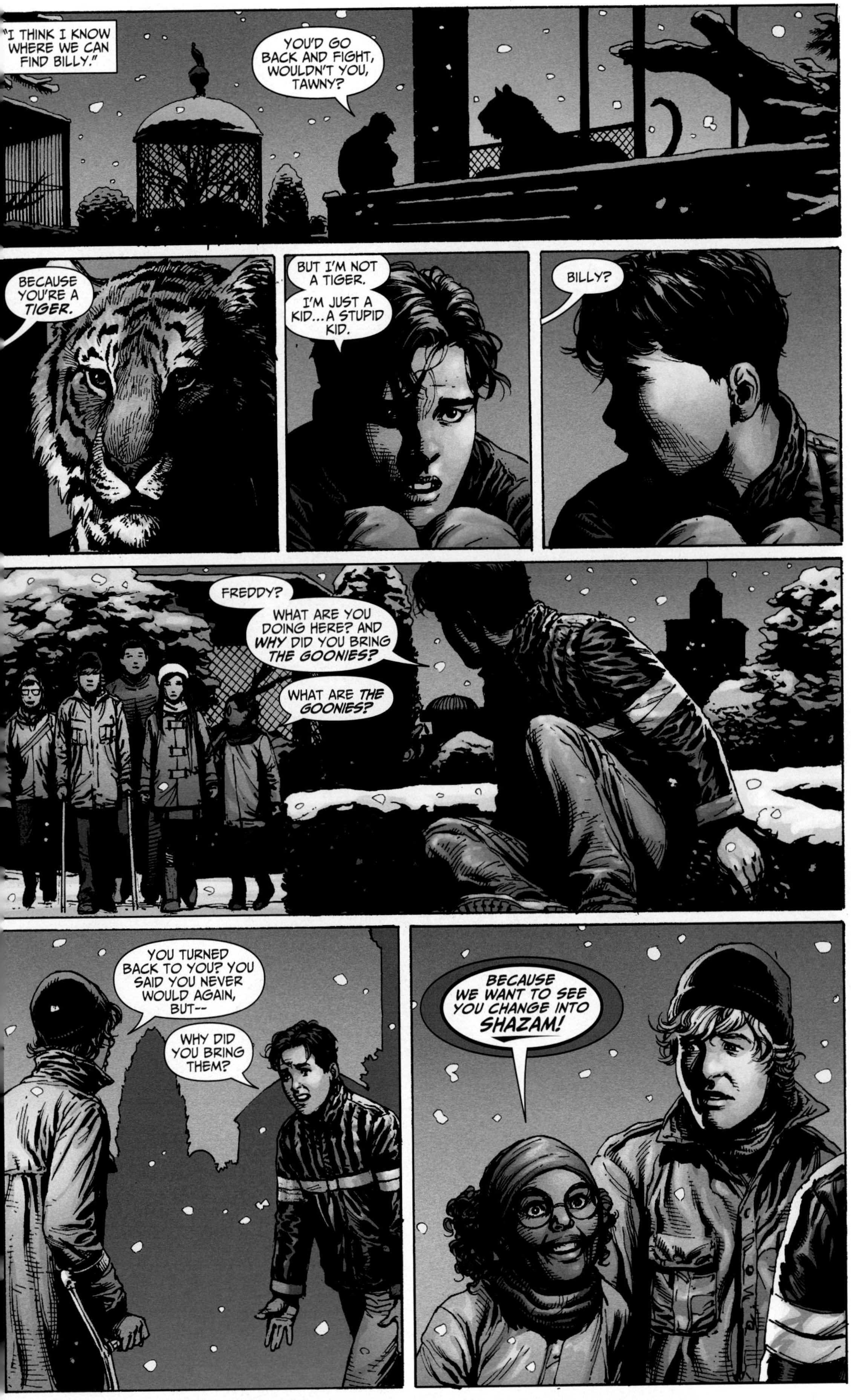
"I THINK I KNOW WHERE WE CAN FIND BILLY."
YOU'D GO BACK AND FIGHT, WOULDN'T YOU, TAWNY?
BECAUSE YOU'RE A *TIGER.*
BUT I'M NOT A TIGER.
I'M JUST A KID... A STUPID KID.
BILLY?
FREDDY?
WHAT ARE YOU DOING HERE? AND *WHY* DID YOU BRING *THE GOONIES?*
WHAT ARE *THE GOONIES?*
YOU TURNED BACK TO YOU? YOU SAID YOU NEVER WOULD AGAIN, BUT--
WHY DID YOU BRING THEM?
BECAUSE WE WANT TO SEE YOU CHANGE INTO SHAZAM!

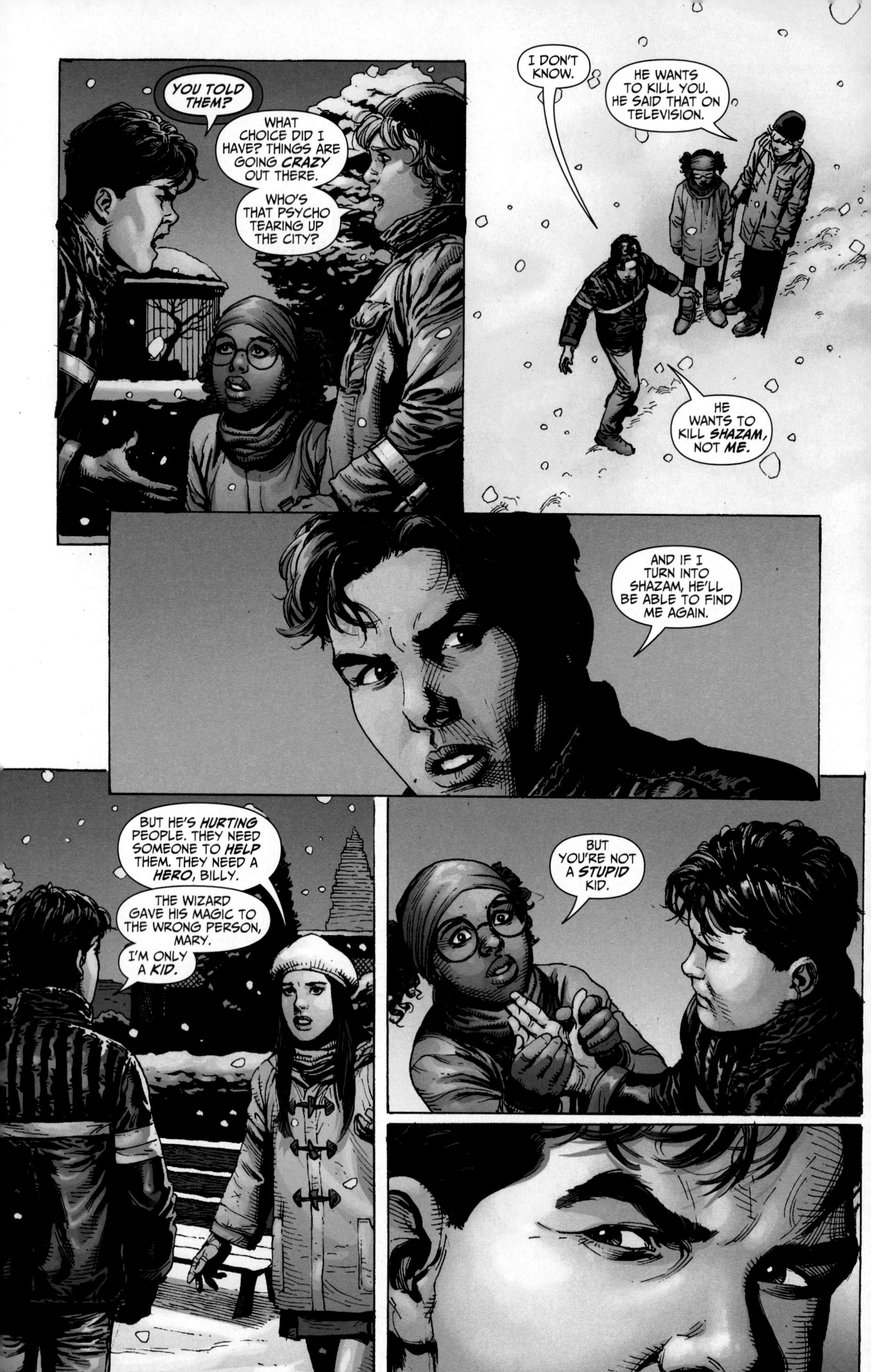
YOU TOLD THEM?
WHAT CHOICE DID I HAVE? THINGS ARE GOING CRAZY OUT THERE.
WHO'S THAT PSYCHO TEARING UP THE CITY?
I DON'T KNOW.
HE WANTS TO KILL YOU. HE SAID THAT ON TELEVISION.
HE WANTS TO KILL SHAZAM, NOT ME.
AND IF I TURN INTO SHAZAM, HE'LL BE ABLE TO FIND ME AGAIN.
BUT HE'S HURTING PEOPLE. THEY NEED SOMEONE TO HELP THEM. THEY NEED A HERO, BILLY.
THE WIZARD GAVE HIS MAGIC TO THE WRONG PERSON, MARY.
I'M ONLY A KID.
BUT YOU'RE NOT A STUPID KID.

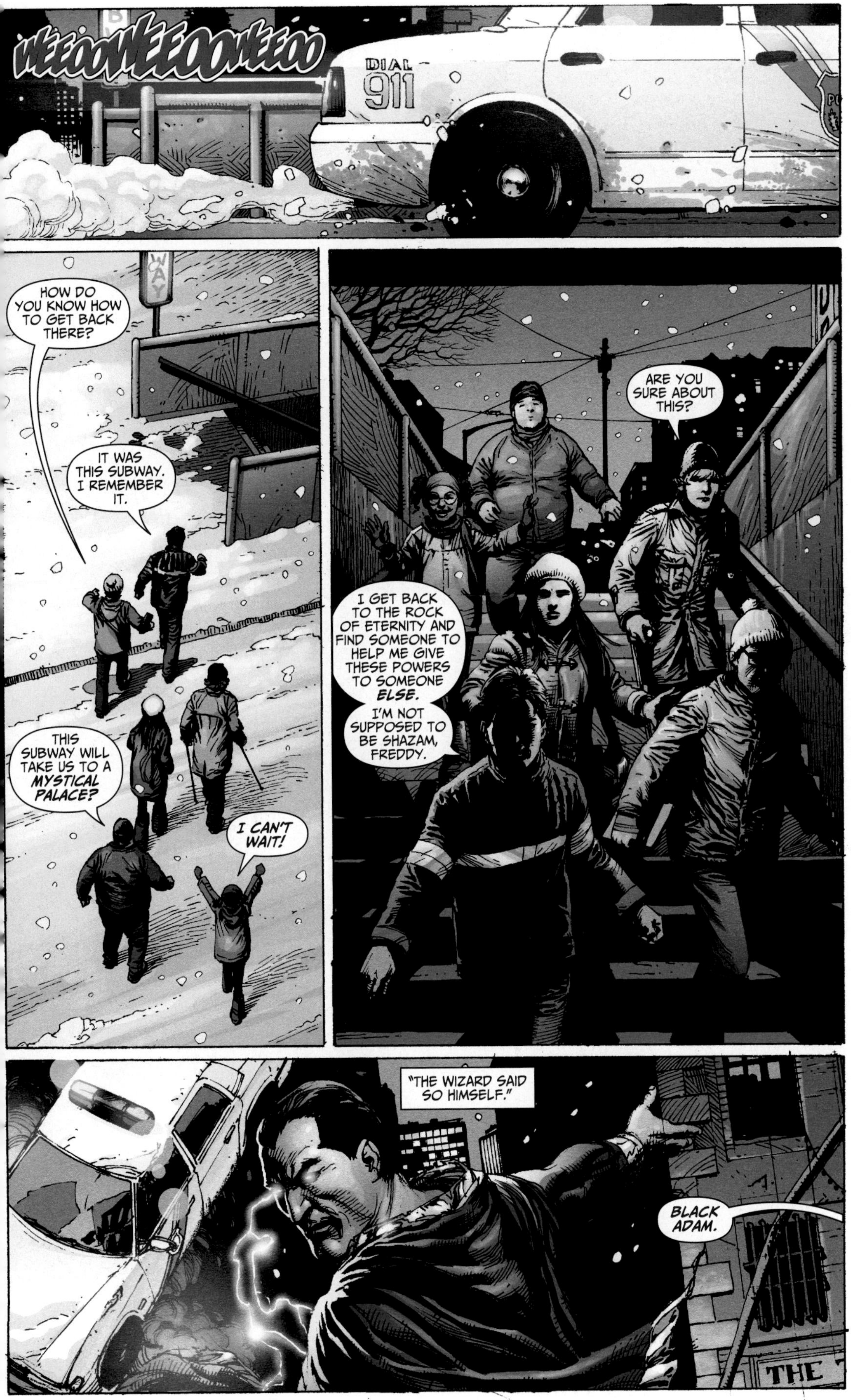
WEEOOWEEOOWEEOO
DIAL 911
HOW DO YOU KNOW HOW TO GET BACK THERE?
IT WAS THIS SUBWAY. I REMEMBER IT.
THIS SUBWAY WILL TAKE US TO A *MYSTICAL PALACE?*
I CAN'T WAIT!
ARE YOU SURE ABOUT THIS?
I GET BACK TO THE ROCK OF ETERNITY AND FIND SOMEONE TO HELP ME GIVE THESE POWERS TO SOMEONE ***ELSE.***
I'M NOT SUPPOSED TO BE SHAZAM, FREDDY.
"THE WIZARD SAID SO HIMSELF."
BLACK ADAM.
THE

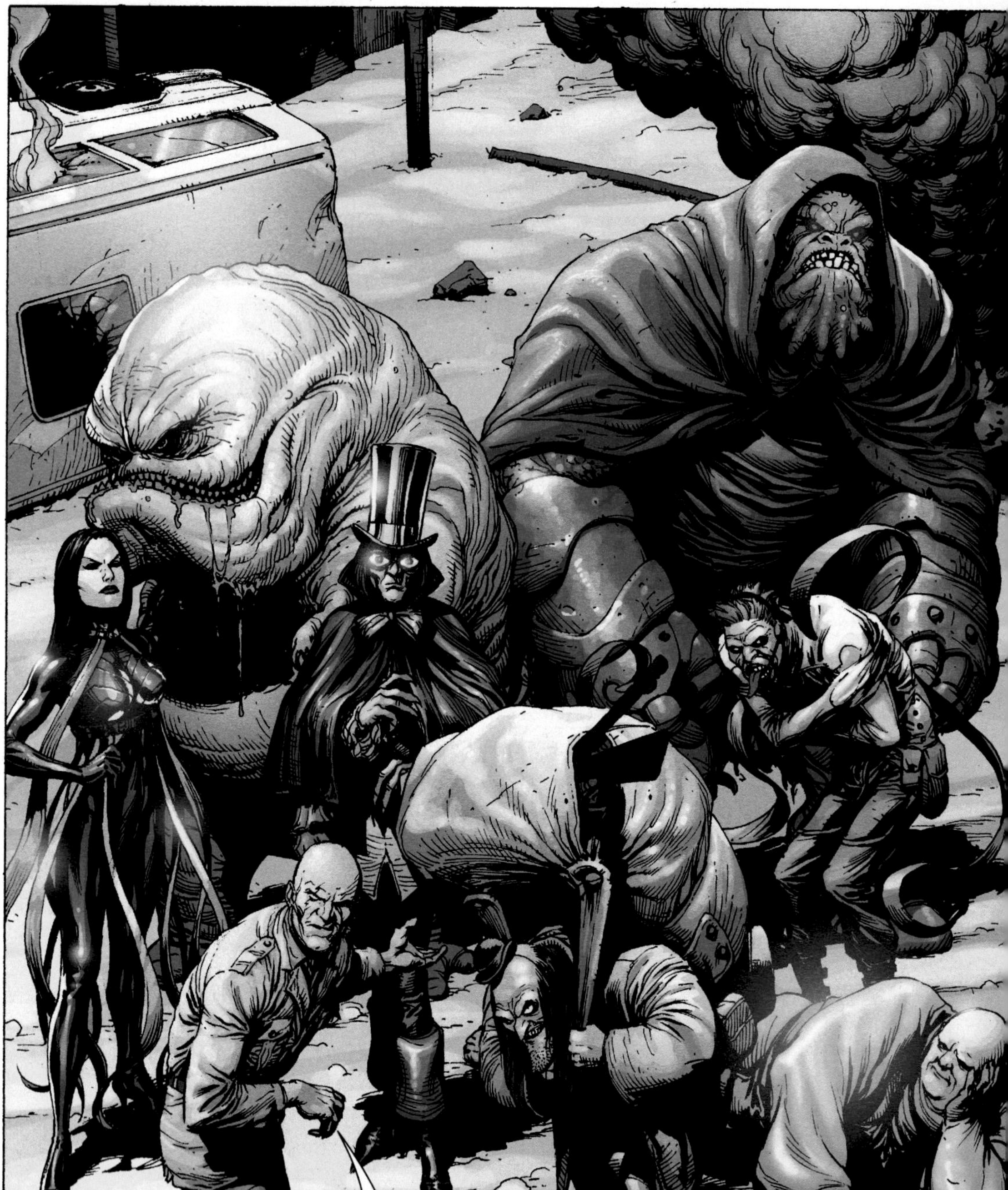
THE SEVEN SINS HAVE GATHERED.

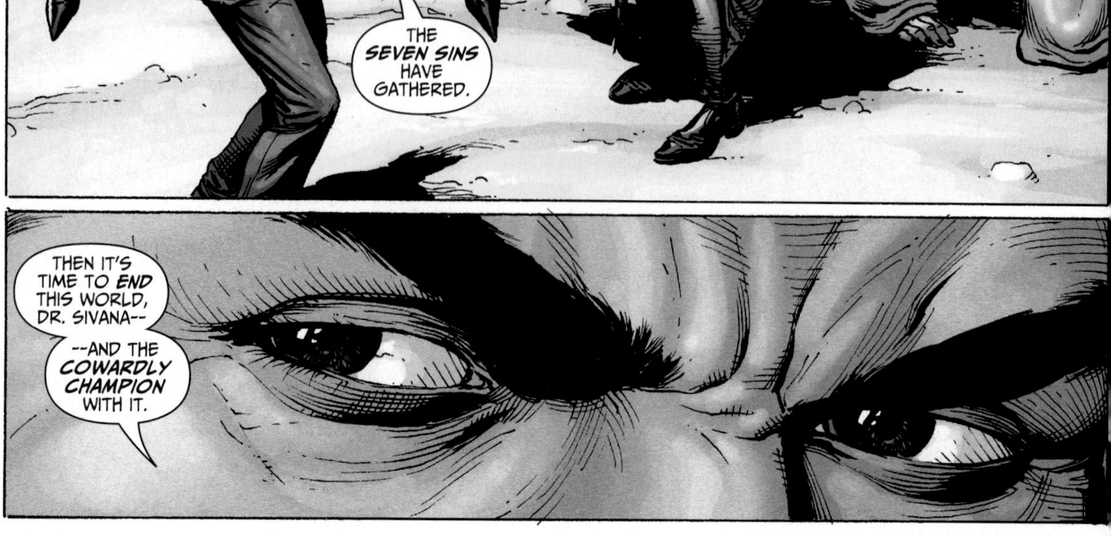
THEN IT'S TIME TO END THIS WORLD, DR. SIVANA--
--AND THE COWARDLY CHAMPION WITH IT.

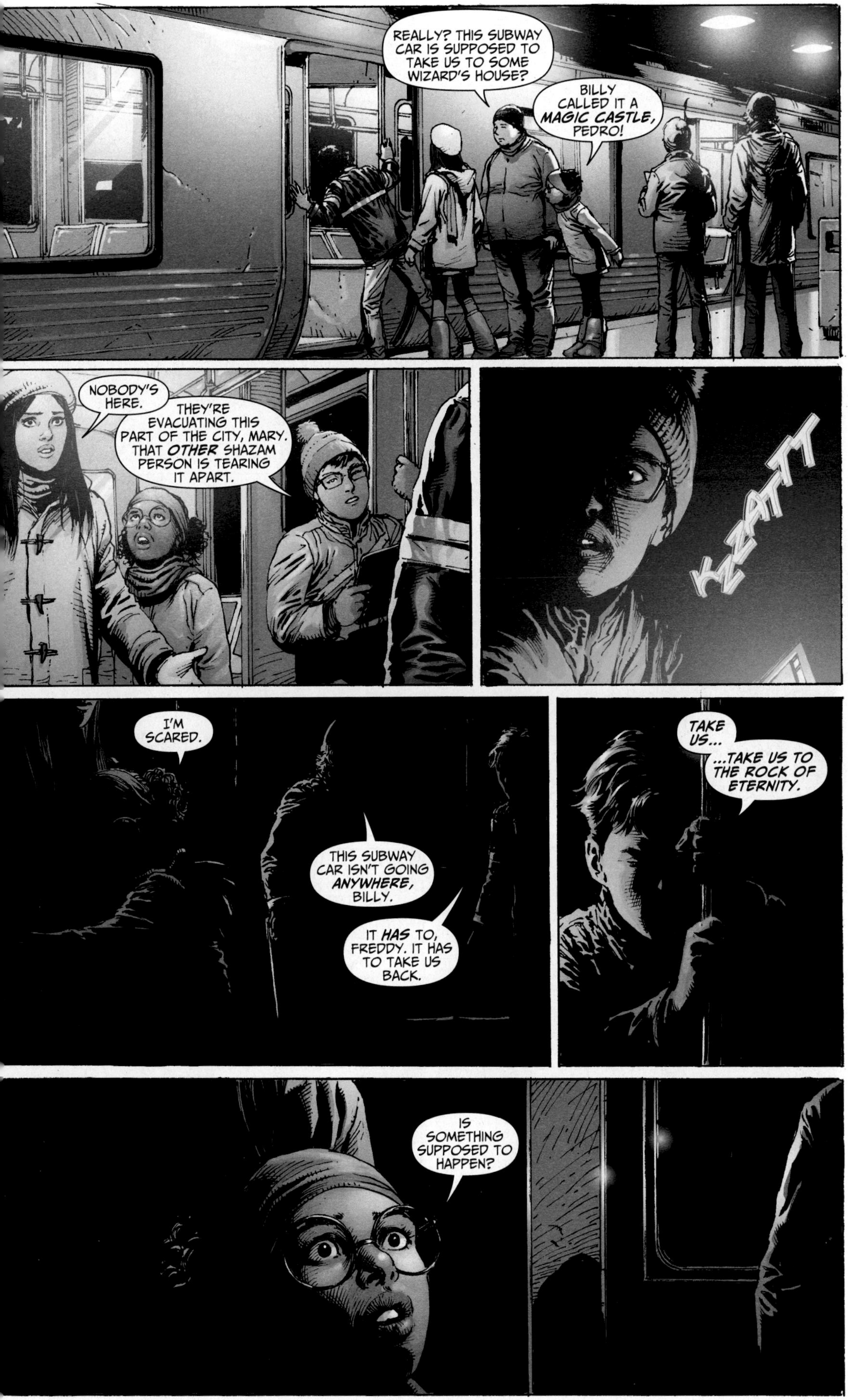
REALLY? THIS SUBWAY CAR IS SUPPOSED TO TAKE US TO SOME WIZARD'S HOUSE?
BILLY CALLED IT A *MAGIC CASTLE,* PEDRO!
NOBODY'S HERE.
THEY'RE EVACUATING THIS PART OF THE CITY, MARY. THAT *OTHER* SHAZAM PERSON IS TEARING IT APART.
KZZATTT
I'M SCARED.
THIS SUBWAY CAR ISN'T GOING *ANYWHERE,* BILLY.
IT *HAS* TO, FREDDY. IT HAS TO TAKE US BACK.
TAKE US...
...TAKE US TO THE ROCK OF ETERNITY.
IS SOMETHING SUPPOSED TO HAPPEN?

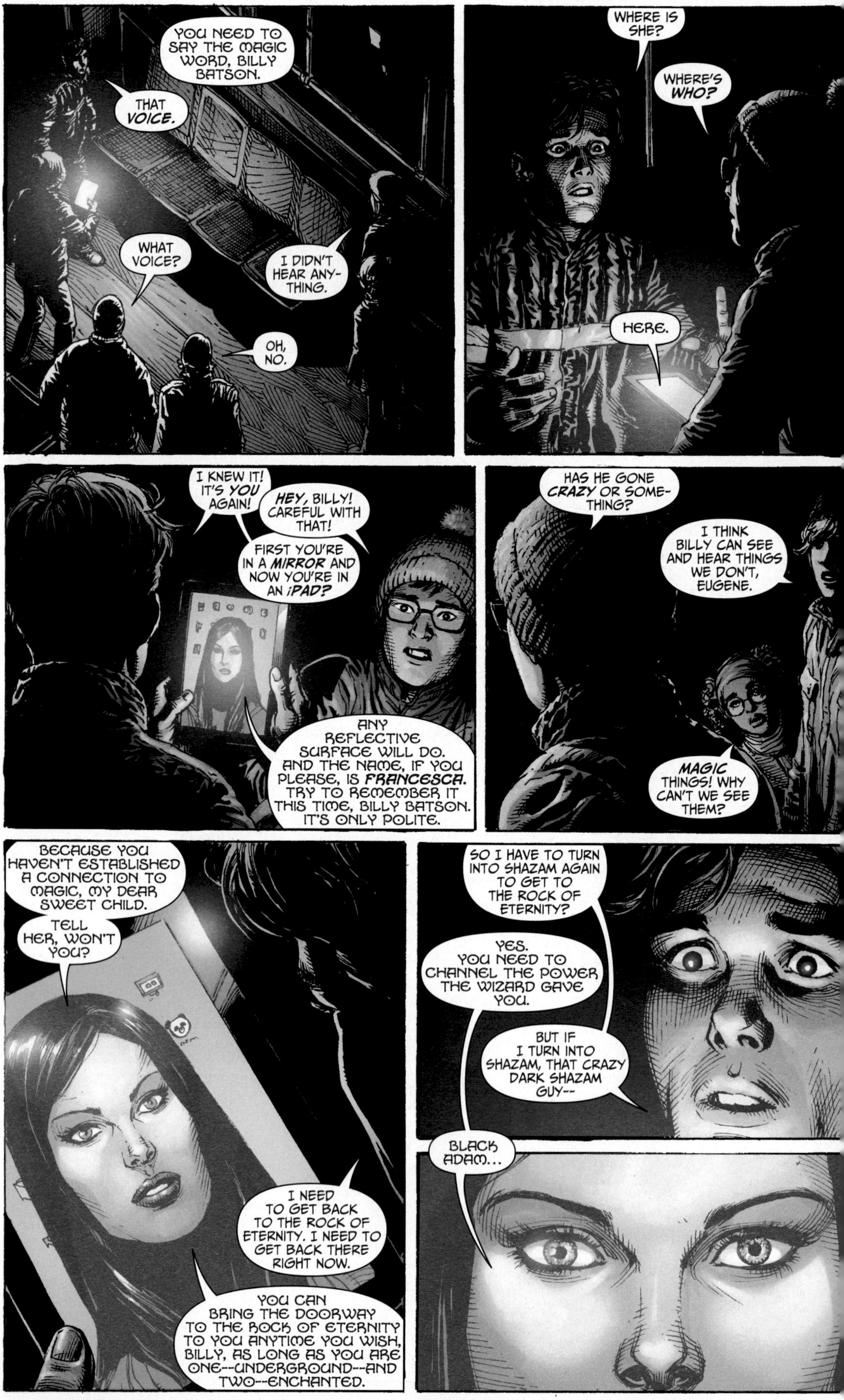
YOU NEED TO SAY THE MAGIC WORD, BILLY BATSON.
THAT *VOICE.*
WHAT VOICE?
I DIDN'T HEAR ANY-THING.
OH, NO.
WHERE IS SHE?
WHERE'S *WHO?*
HERE.
I KNEW IT! IT'S *YOU* AGAIN!
HEY, BILLY! CAREFUL WITH THAT!
FIRST YOU'RE IN A *MIRROR* AND NOW YOU'RE IN AN *iPAD?*
ANY REFLECTIVE SURFACE WILL DO. AND THE NAME, IF YOU PLEASE, IS *FRANCESCA.* TRY TO REMEMBER IT THIS TIME, BILLY BATSON. IT'S ONLY POLITE.
HAS HE GONE *CRAZY* OR SOME-THING?
I THINK BILLY CAN SEE AND HEAR THINGS WE DON'T, EUGENE.
MAGIC THINGS! WHY CAN'T WE SEE THEM?
BECAUSE YOU HAVEN'T ESTABLISHED A CONNECTION TO MAGIC, MY DEAR SWEET CHILD.
TELL HER, WON'T YOU?
I NEED TO GET BACK TO THE ROCK OF ETERNITY. I NEED TO GET BACK THERE RIGHT NOW.
YOU CAN BRING THE DOORWAY TO THE ROCK OF ETERNITY TO YOU ANYTIME YOU WISH, BILLY, AS LONG AS YOU ARE ONE--UNDERGROUND--AND TWO--ENCHANTED.
SO I HAVE TO TURN INTO SHAZAM AGAIN TO GET TO THE ROCK OF ETERNITY?
YES. YOU NEED TO CHANNEL THE POWER THE WIZARD GAVE YOU.
BUT IF I TURN INTO SHAZAM, THAT CRAZY DARK SHAZAM GUY--
BLACK ADAM...

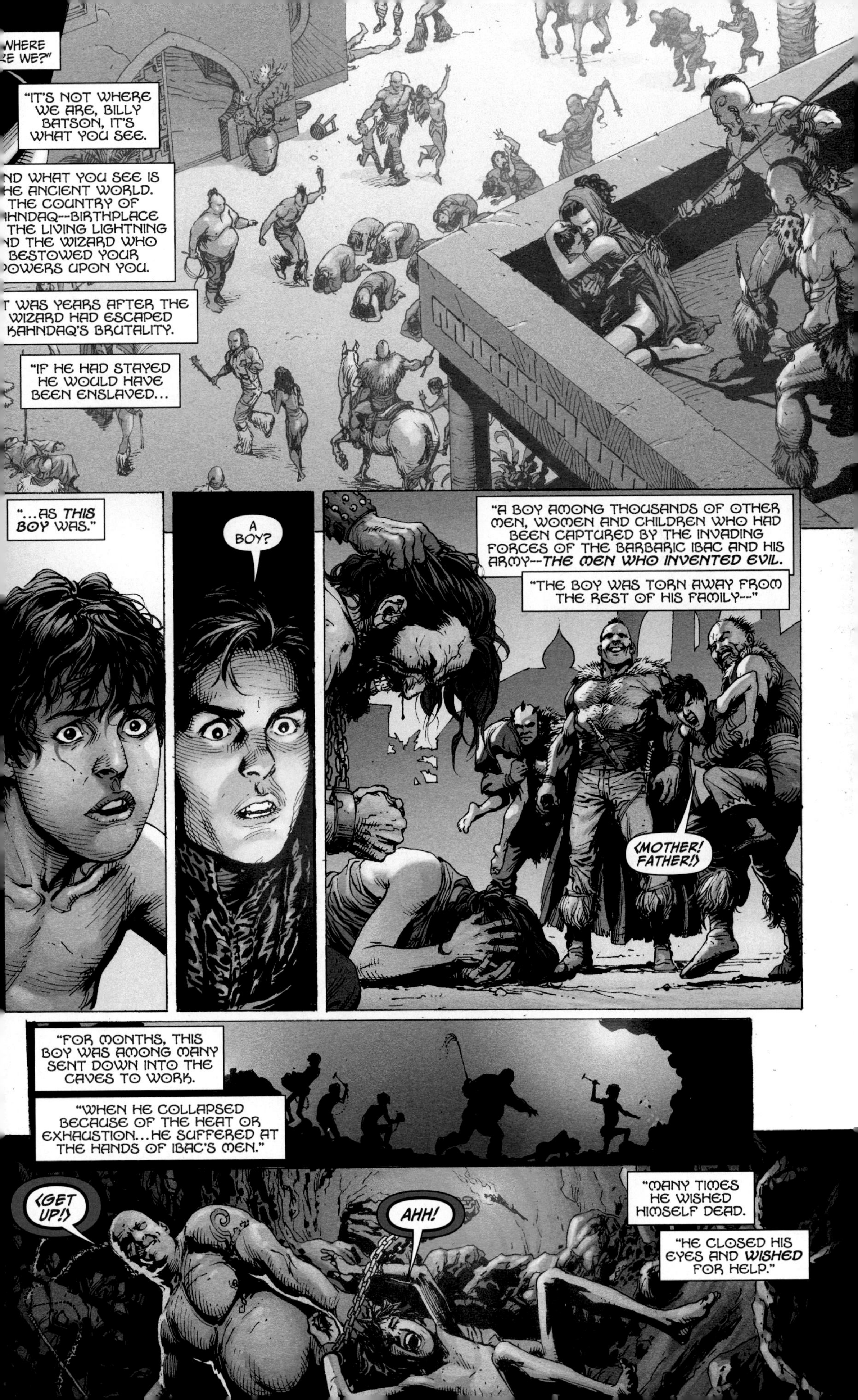

WHERE ...E WE?"
"IT'S NOT WHERE WE ARE, BILLY BATSON, IT'S WHAT YOU SEE.
...ND WHAT YOU SEE IS ...HE ANCIENT WORLD. ...THE COUNTRY OF ...HNDAQ--BIRTHPLACE ...THE LIVING LIGHTNING ...ND THE WIZARD WHO BESTOWED YOUR ...OWERS UPON YOU.
...T WAS YEARS AFTER THE WIZARD HAD ESCAPED KAHNDAQ'S BRUTALITY.
"IF HE HAD STAYED HE WOULD HAVE BEEN ENSLAVED...
"...AS THIS BOY WAS."
A BOY?
"A BOY AMONG THOUSANDS OF OTHER MEN, WOMEN AND CHILDREN WHO HAD BEEN CAPTURED BY THE INVADING FORCES OF THE BARBARIC IBAC AND HIS ARMY--THE MEN WHO INVENTED EVIL.
"THE BOY WAS TORN AWAY FROM THE REST OF HIS FAMILY--"
<MOTHER! FATHER!>
"FOR MONTHS, THIS BOY WAS AMONG MANY SENT DOWN INTO THE CAVES TO WORK.
"WHEN HE COLLAPSED BECAUSE OF THE HEAT OR EXHAUSTION...HE SUFFERED AT THE HANDS OF IBAC'S MEN."
<GET UP!>
AHH!
"MANY TIMES HE WISHED HIMSELF DEAD.
"HE CLOSED HIS EYES AND WISHED FOR HELP."

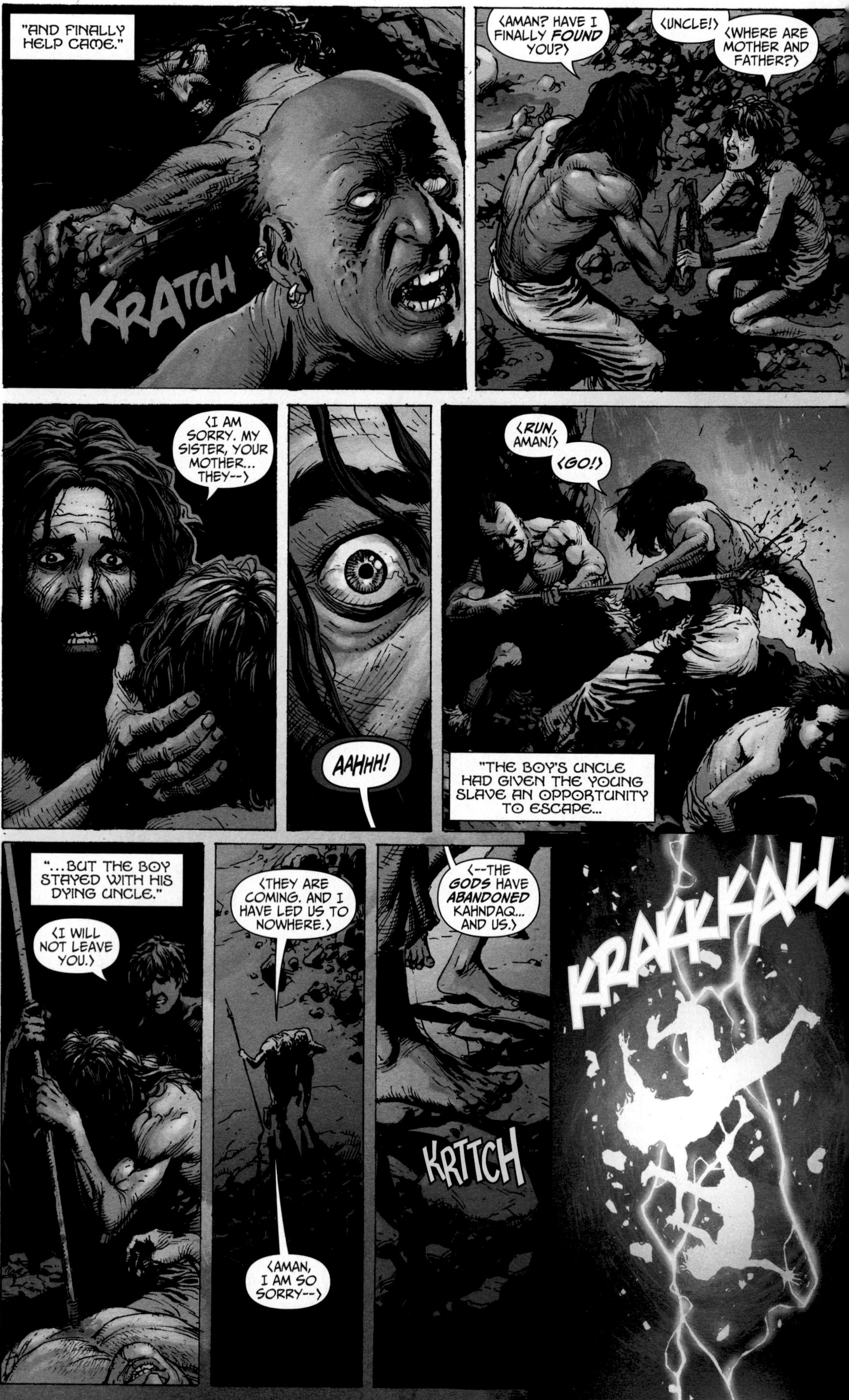
"AND FINALLY HELP CAME."
KRATCH
‹AMAN? HAVE I FINALLY FOUND YOU?›
‹UNCLE!›
‹WHERE ARE MOTHER AND FATHER?›
‹I AM SORRY. MY SISTER, YOUR MOTHER... THEY--›
AAHHH!
‹RUN, AMAN!›
‹GO!›
"THE BOY'S UNCLE HAD GIVEN THE YOUNG SLAVE AN OPPORTUNITY TO ESCAPE...
"...BUT THE BOY STAYED WITH HIS DYING UNCLE."
‹I WILL NOT LEAVE YOU.›
‹THEY ARE COMING. AND I HAVE LED US TO NOWHERE.›
‹AMAN, I AM SO SORRY--›
‹--THE GODS HAVE ABANDONED KAHNDAQ... AND US.›
KRTTCH
KRAKKALL

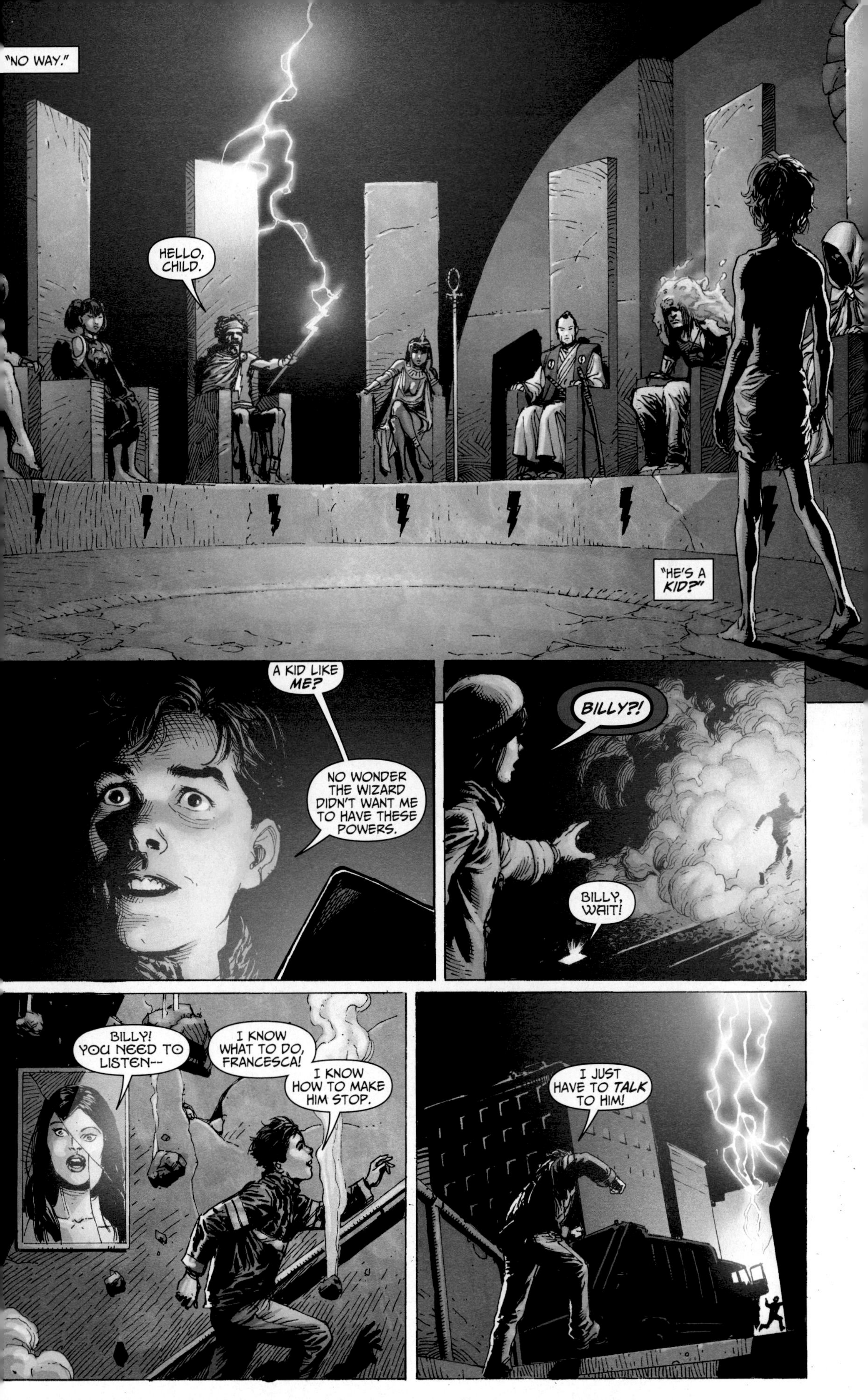
"NO WAY."
HELLO, CHILD.
"HE'S A KID?"
A KID LIKE ME?
NO WONDER THE WIZARD DIDN'T WANT ME TO HAVE THESE POWERS.
BILLY?!
BILLY, WAIT!
BILLY! YOU NEED TO LISTEN--
I KNOW WHAT TO DO, FRANCESCA!
I KNOW HOW TO MAKE HIM STOP.
I JUST HAVE TO TALK TO HIM!

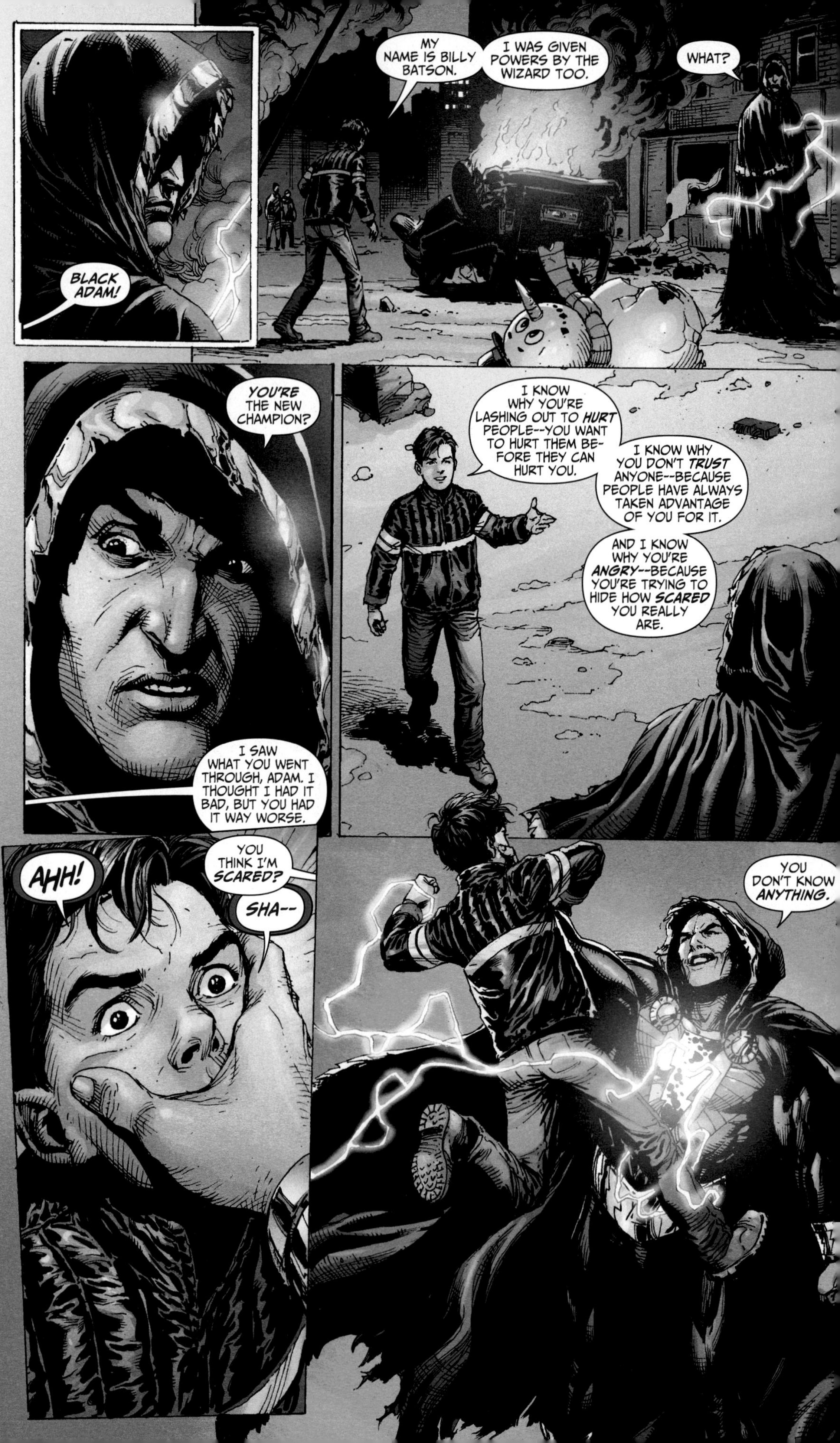
BLACK ADAM!
MY NAME IS BILLY BATSON.
I WAS GIVEN POWERS BY THE WIZARD TOO.
WHAT?
YOU'RE THE NEW CHAMPION?
I SAW WHAT YOU WENT THROUGH, ADAM. I THOUGHT I HAD IT BAD, BUT YOU HAD IT WAY WORSE.
I KNOW WHY YOU'RE LASHING OUT TO HURT PEOPLE--YOU WANT TO HURT THEM BEFORE THEY CAN HURT YOU.
I KNOW WHY YOU DON'T TRUST ANYONE--BECAUSE PEOPLE HAVE ALWAYS TAKEN ADVANTAGE OF YOU FOR IT.
AND I KNOW WHY YOU'RE ANGRY--BECAUSE YOU'RE TRYING TO HIDE HOW SCARED YOU REALLY ARE.
AHH!
YOU THINK I'M SCARED?
SHA--
YOU DON'T KNOW ANYTHING.

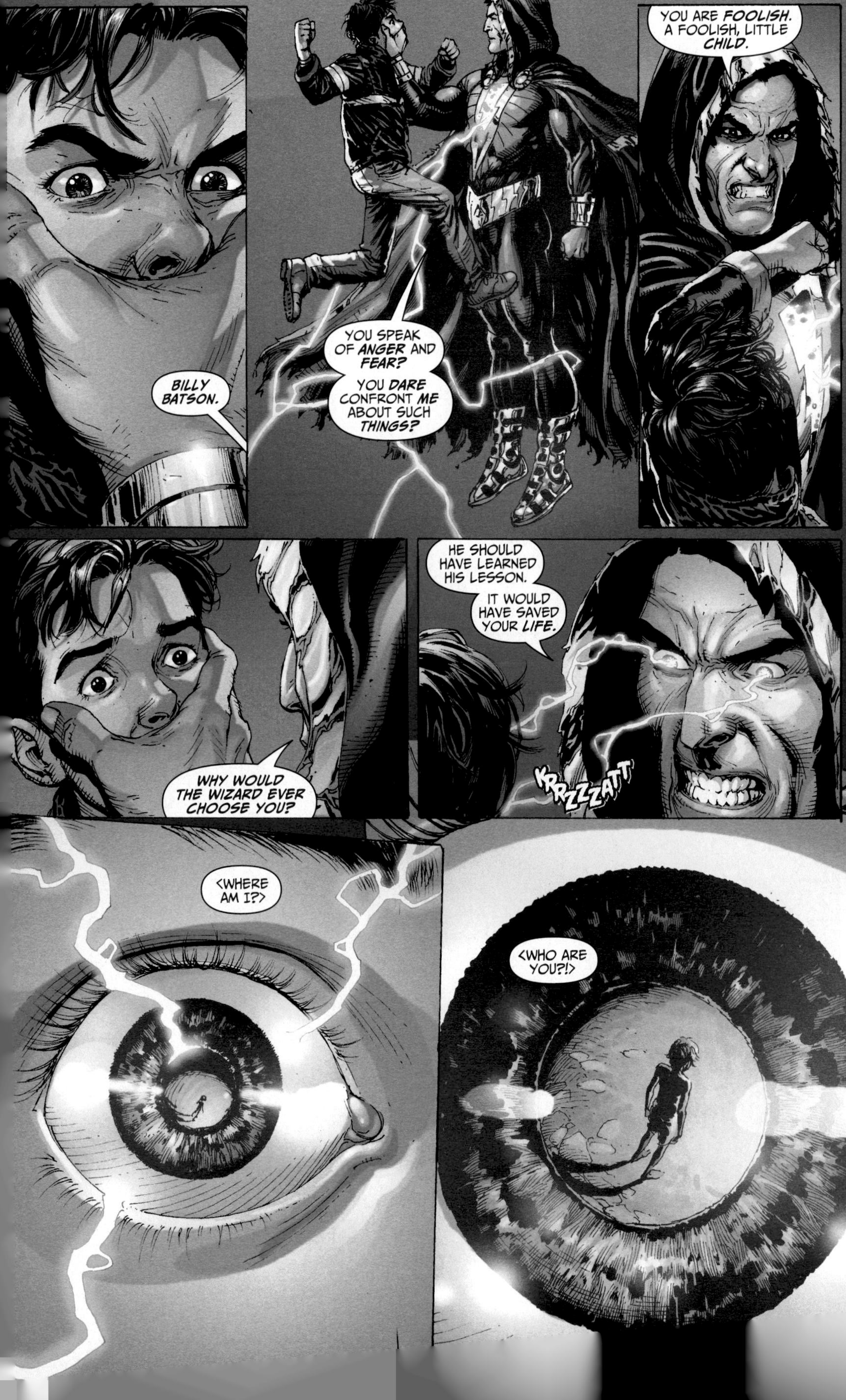
BILLY BATSON.
YOU SPEAK OF ANGER AND FEAR?
YOU DARE CONFRONT ME ABOUT SUCH THINGS?
YOU ARE FOOLISH. A FOOLISH, LITTLE CHILD.
WHY WOULD THE WIZARD EVER CHOOSE YOU?
HE SHOULD HAVE LEARNED HIS LESSON.
IT WOULD HAVE SAVED YOUR LIFE.
KRRZZZATT
<WHERE AM I?>
<WHO ARE YOU?!>

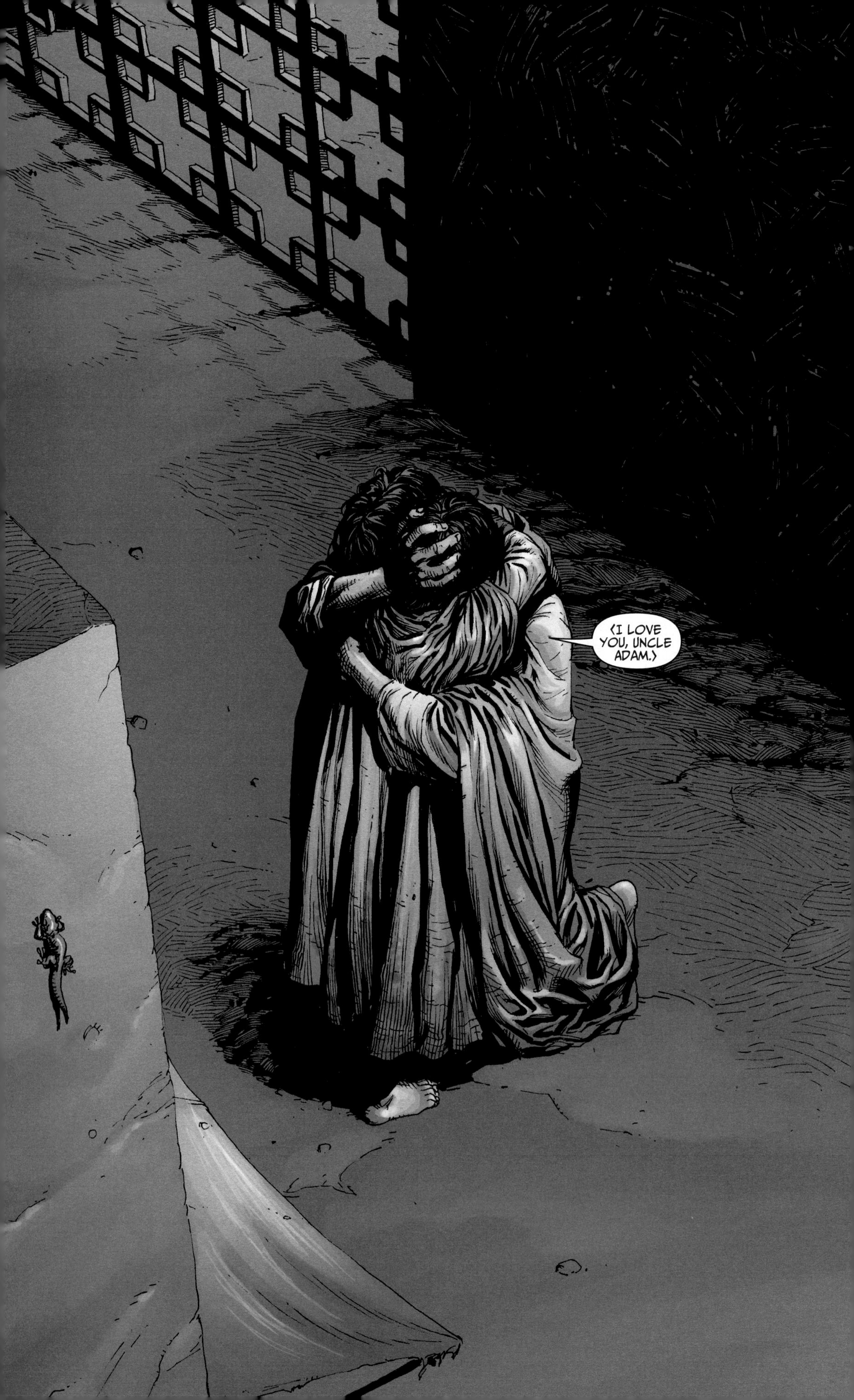
<I LOVE YOU, UNCLE ADAM.>

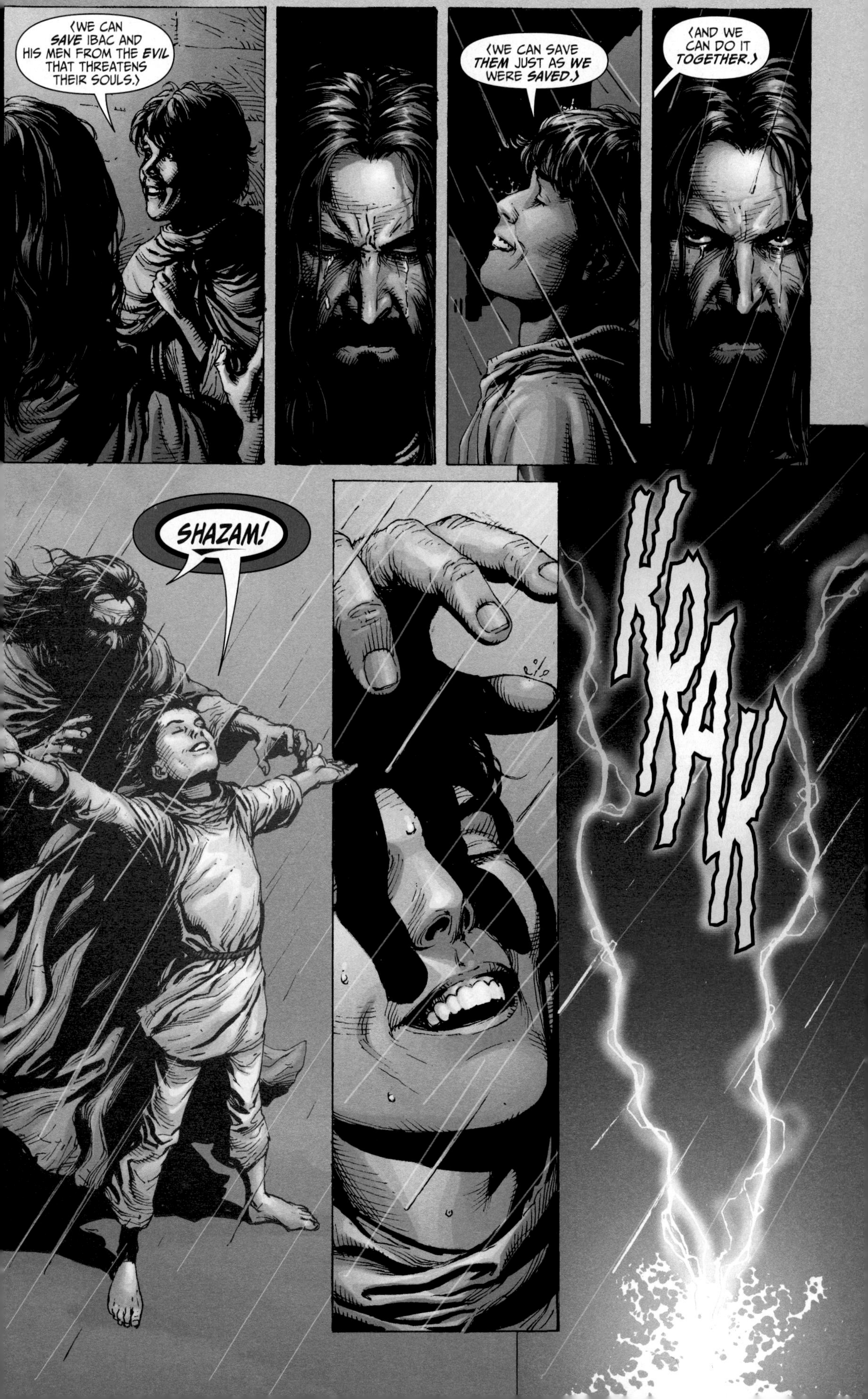
‹WE CAN SAVE IBAC AND HIS MEN FROM THE EVIL THAT THREATENS THEIR SOULS.›
‹WE CAN SAVE THEM JUST AS WE WERE SAVED.›
‹AND WE CAN DO IT TOGETHER.›
SHAZAM!
KRAK

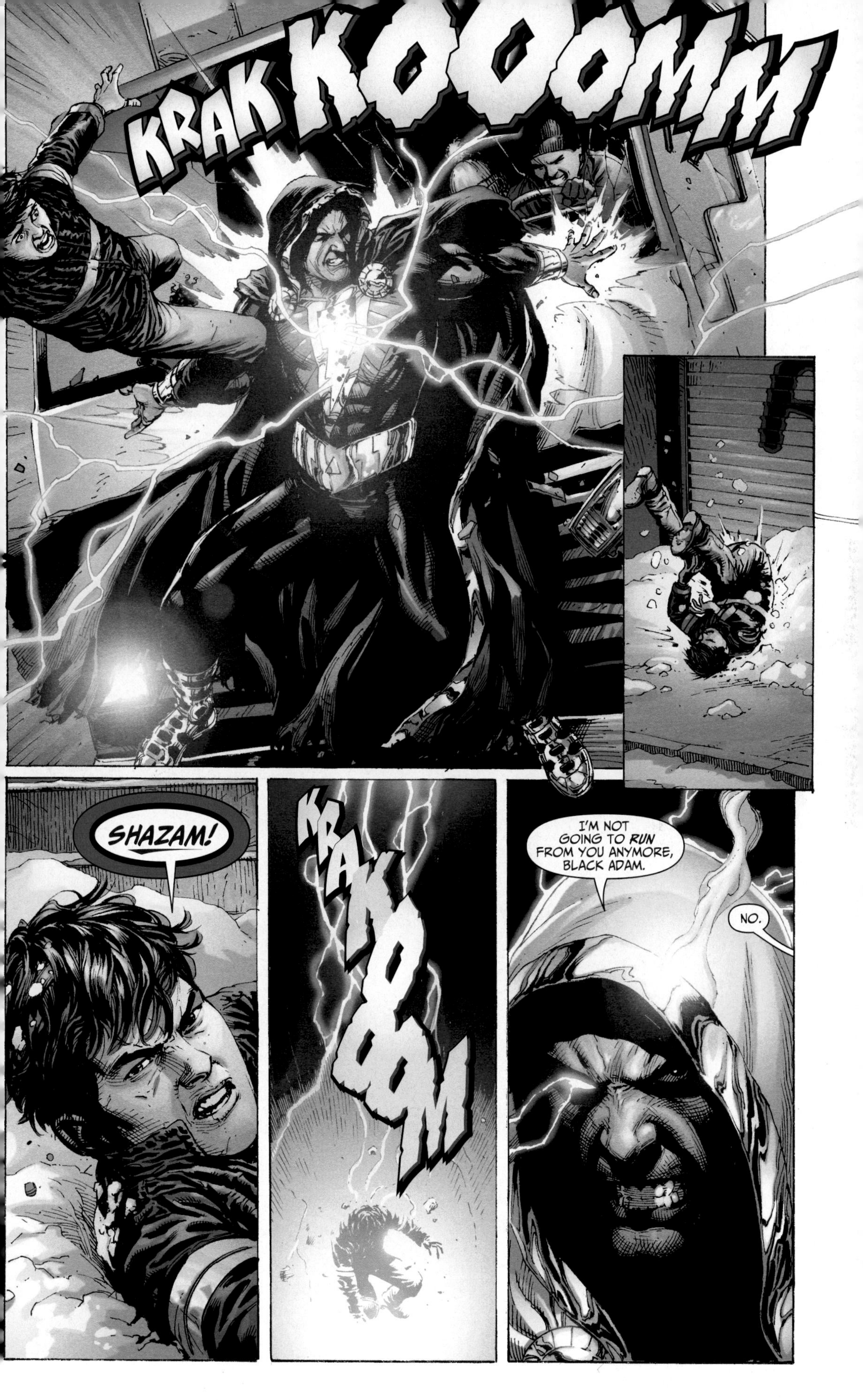
KRAK KOOOMM
SHAZAM!
KRAKOOM
I'M NOT GOING TO RUN FROM YOU ANYMORE, BLACK ADAM.
NO.

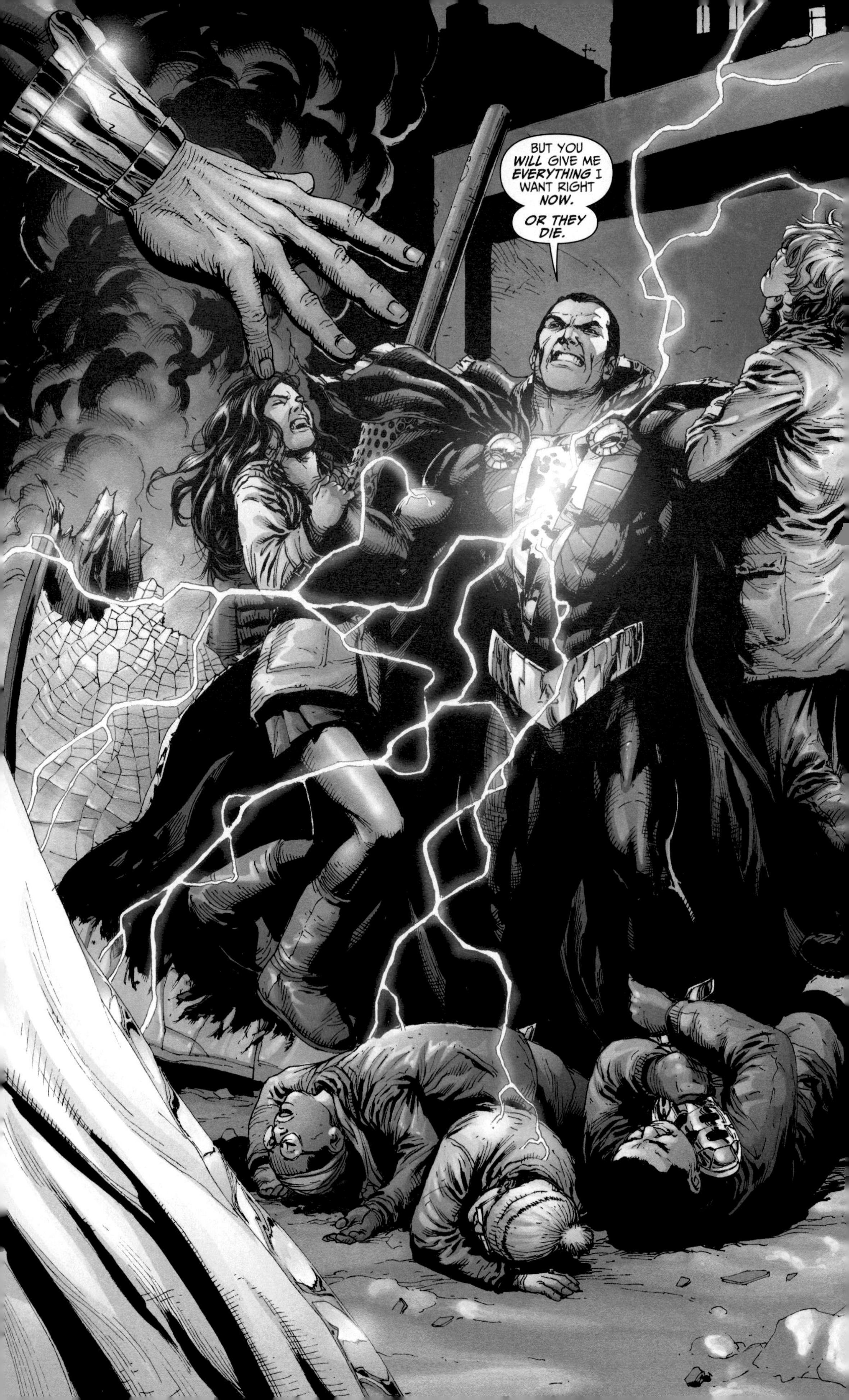
BUT YOU WILL GIVE ME EVERYTHING I WANT RIGHT NOW.
OR THEY DIE.

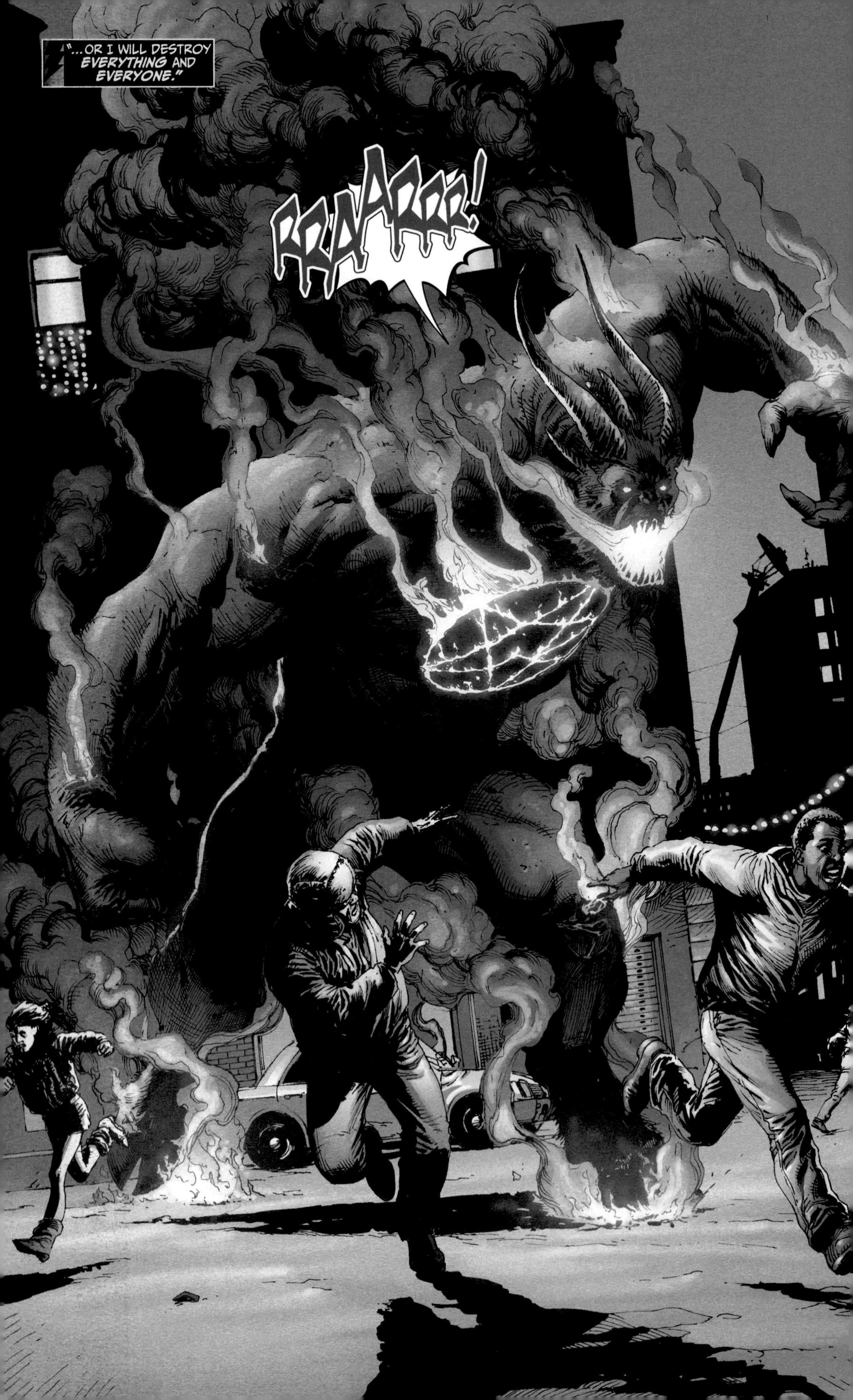
"...OR I WILL DESTROY EVERYTHING AND EVERYONE."
RRAARRR!

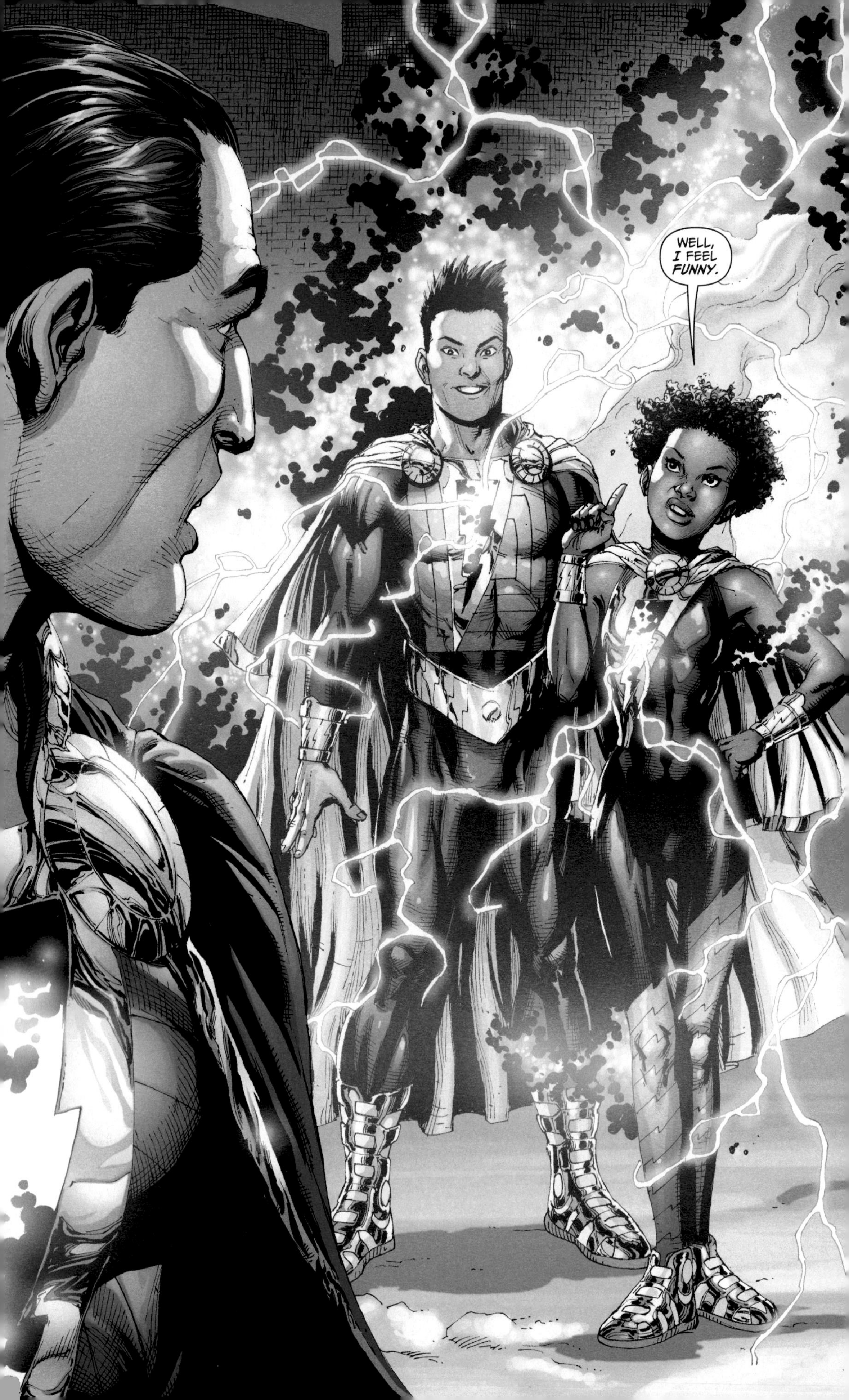
WELL, I FEEL FUNNY.

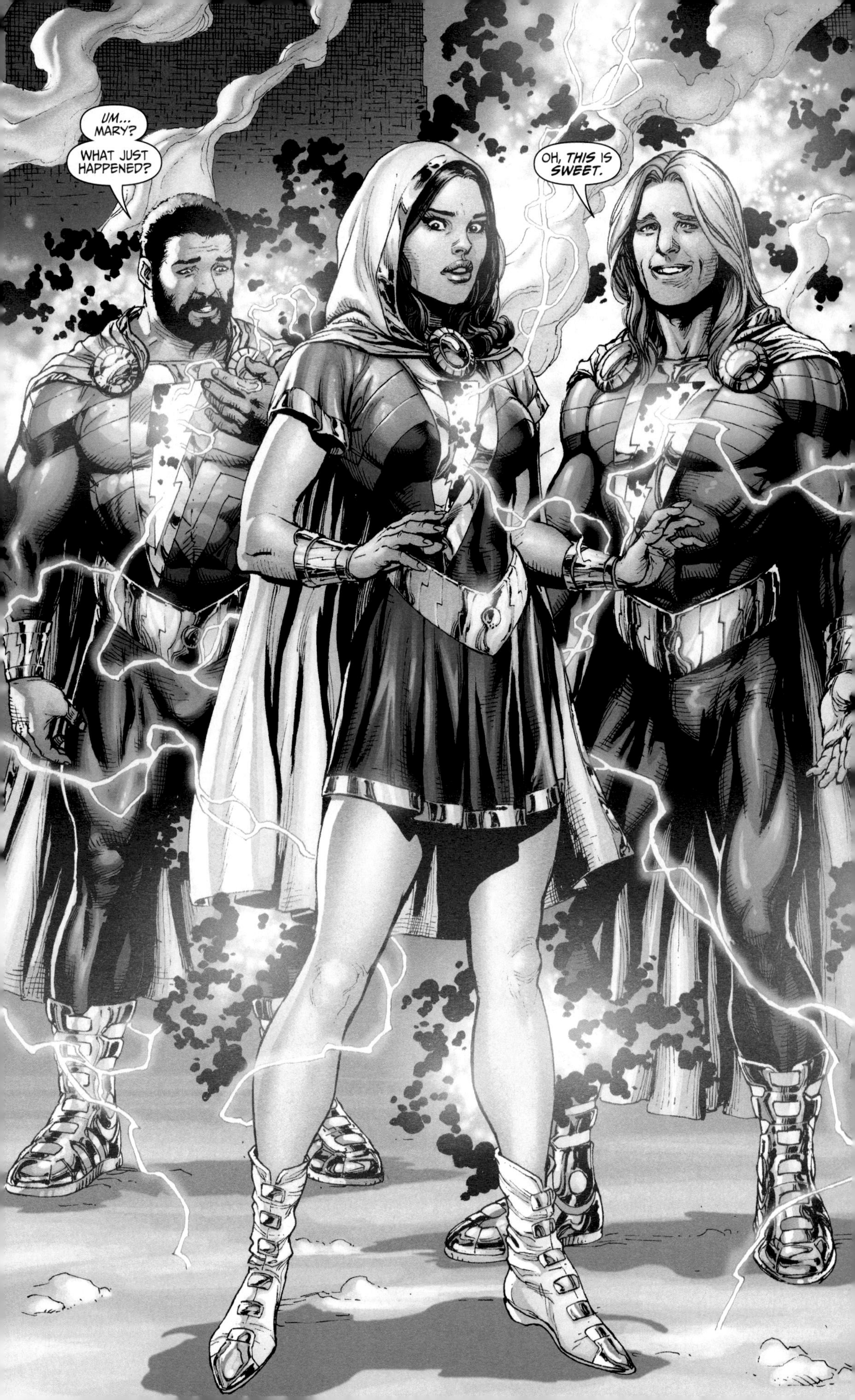
UM... MARY?
WHAT JUST HAPPENED?
OH, THIS IS SWEET.

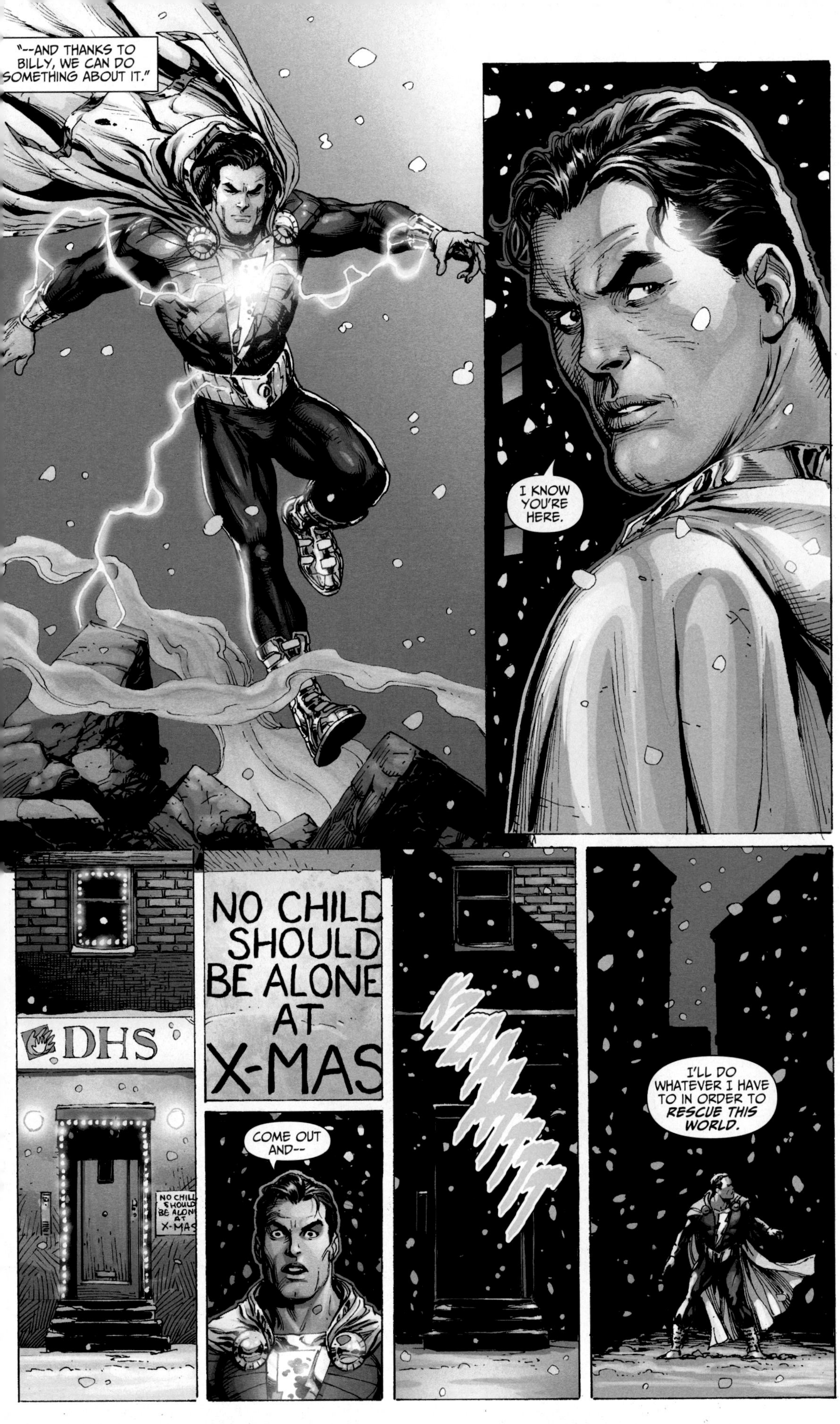
"--AND THANKS TO BILLY, WE CAN DO SOMETHING ABOUT IT."
I KNOW YOU'RE HERE.
DHS
NO CHILD SHOULD BE ALONE AT X-MAS
NO CHILD SHOULD BE ALONE AT X-MAS
COME OUT AND--
KZAAKTTT
I'LL DO WHATEVER I HAVE TO IN ORDER TO *RESCUE THIS WORLD.*

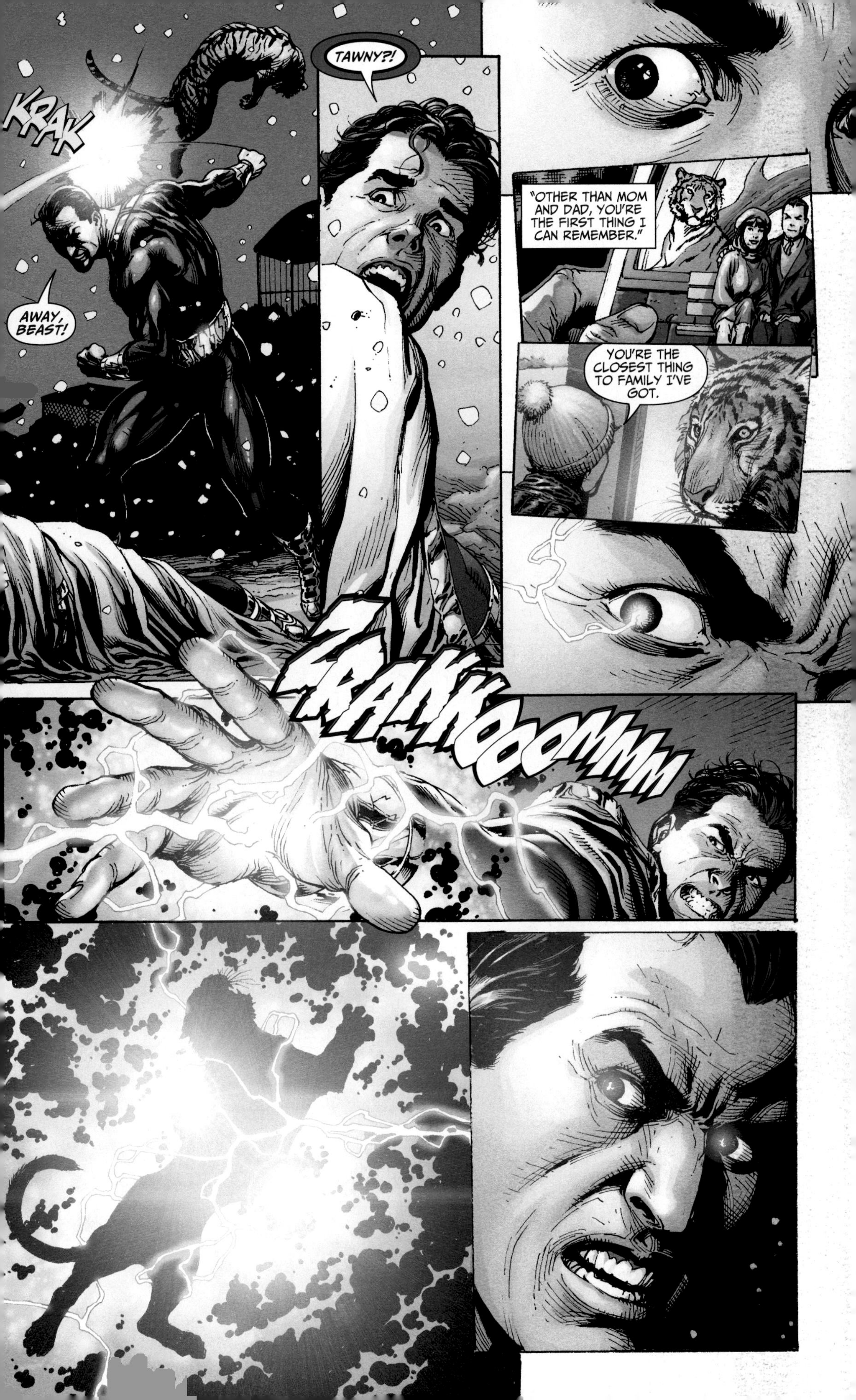
KRAK
AWAY, BEAST!
TAWNY?!
"OTHER THAN MOM AND DAD, YOU'RE THE FIRST THING I CAN REMEMBER."
YOU'RE THE CLOSEST THING TO FAMILY I'VE GOT.
ZRAKKOOMMM

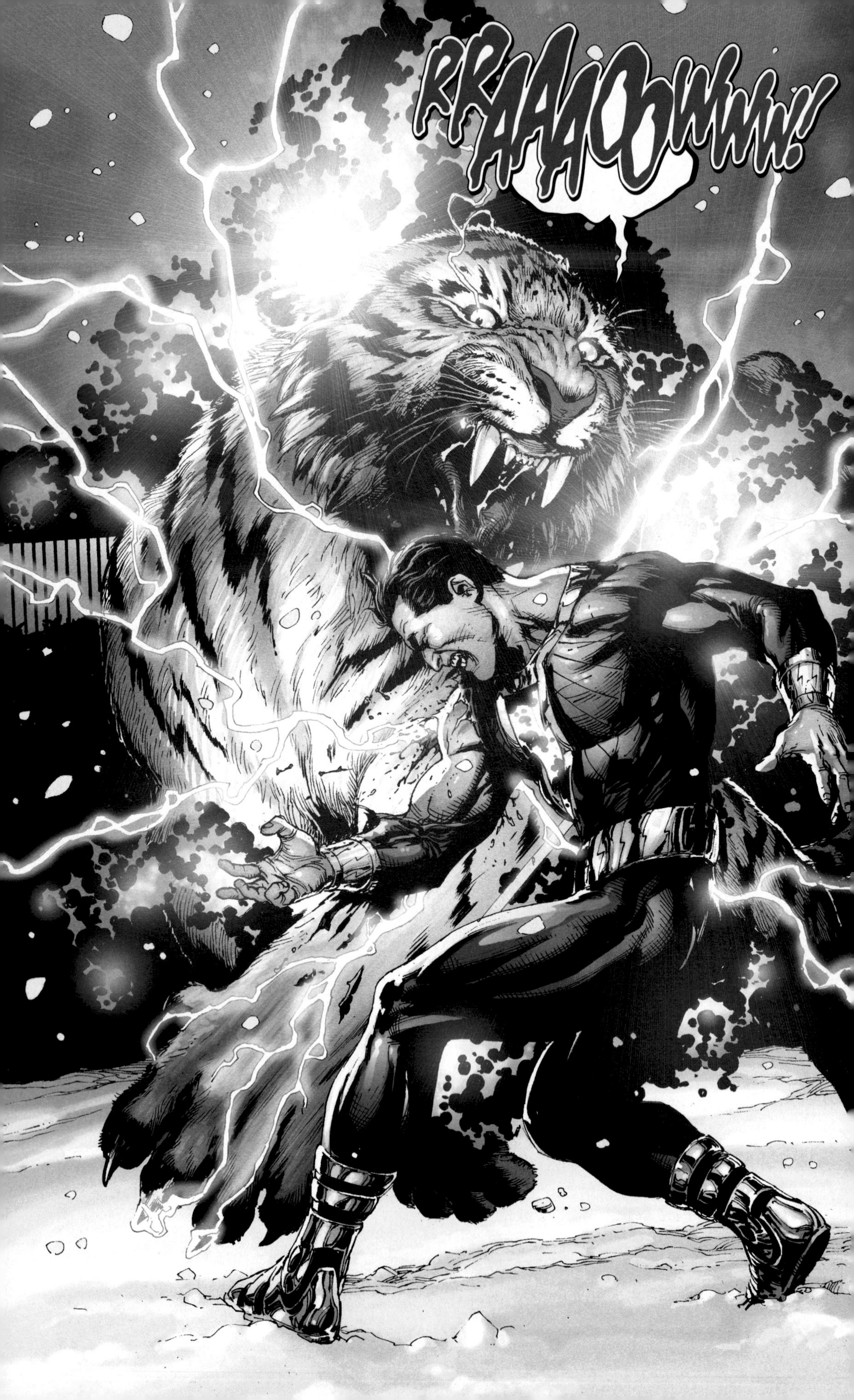
RRAAAOWWW!

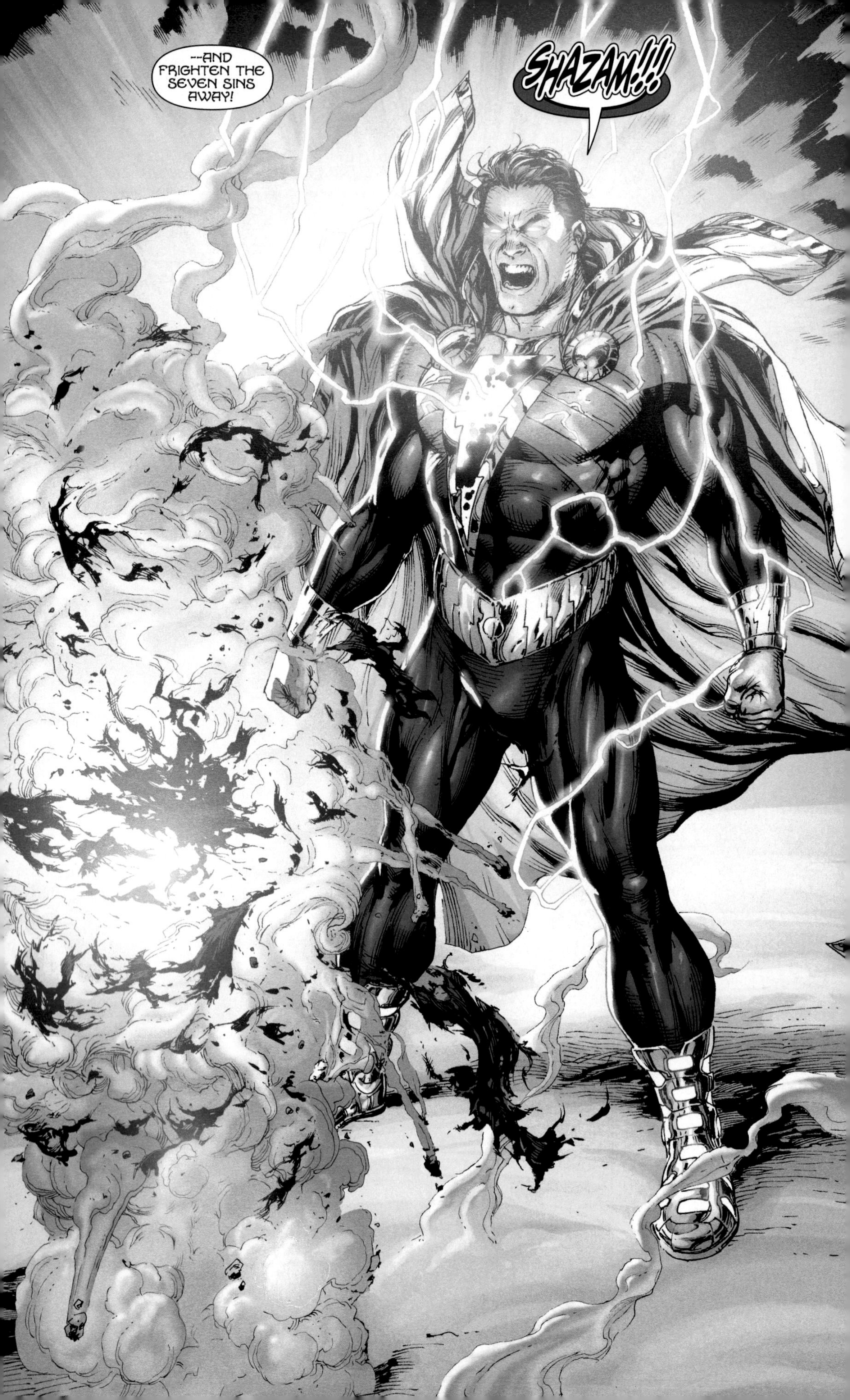
--AND FRIGHTEN THE SEVEN SINS AWAY!
SHAZAM!!!

THE BEGINNING

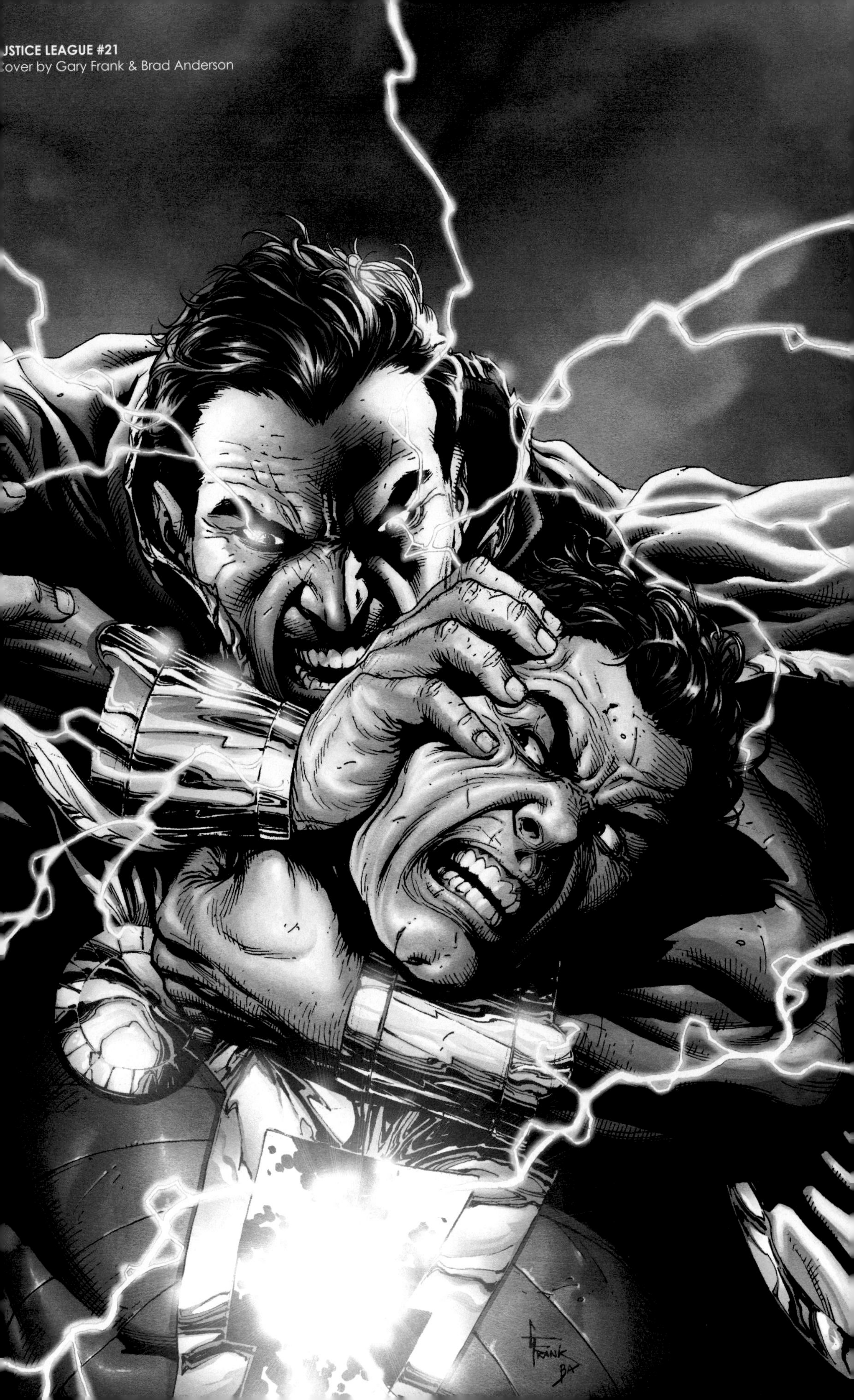

JSTICE LEAGUE #21
Cover by Gary Frank & Brad Anderson

JUSTICE LEAGUE #21
Variant cover by Shane Davis, Michelle Delecki & Alex Sinclair

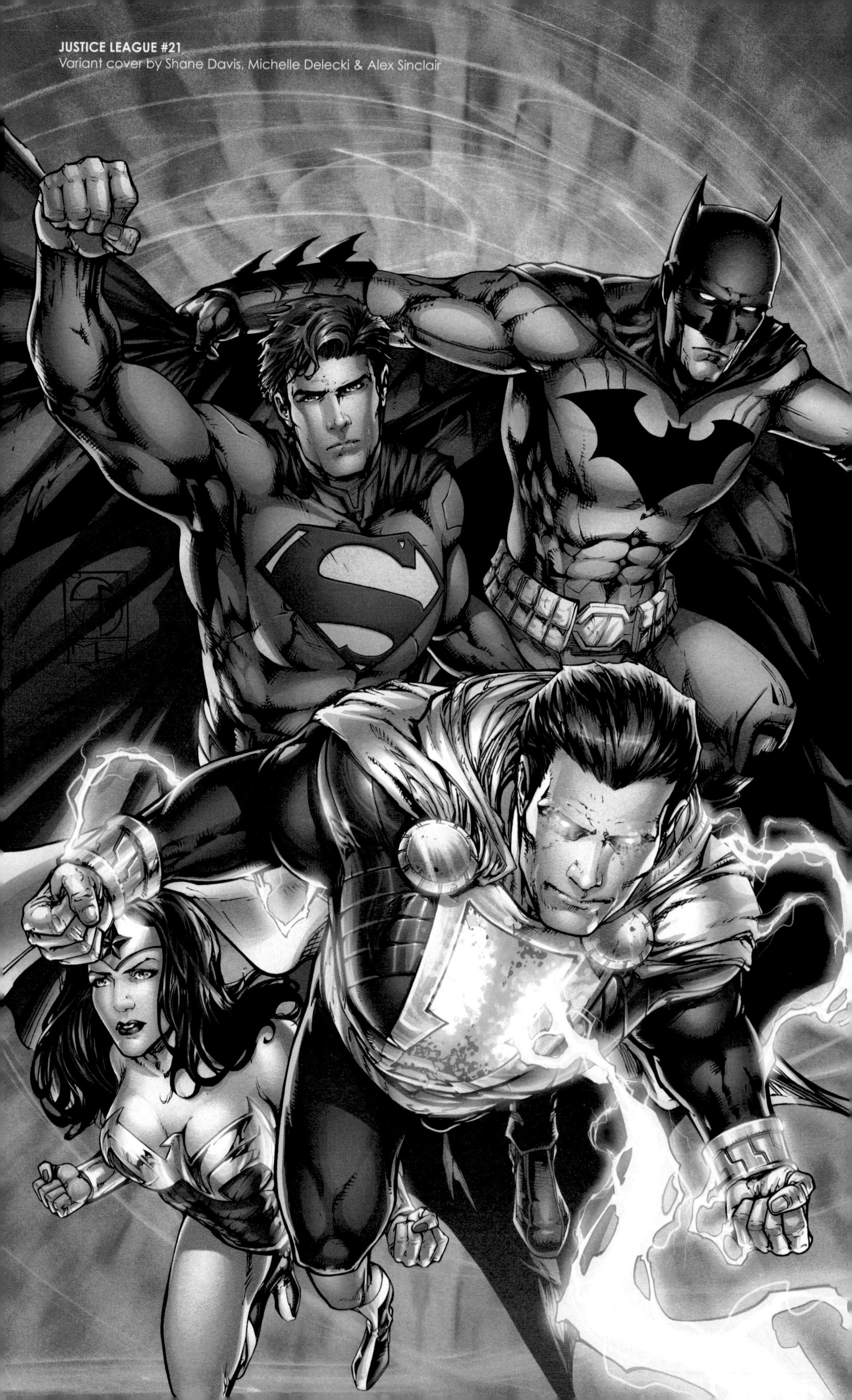

JUSTICE LEAGUE #0
Variant cover by Ivan Reis, Joe Prado & Rod Reis

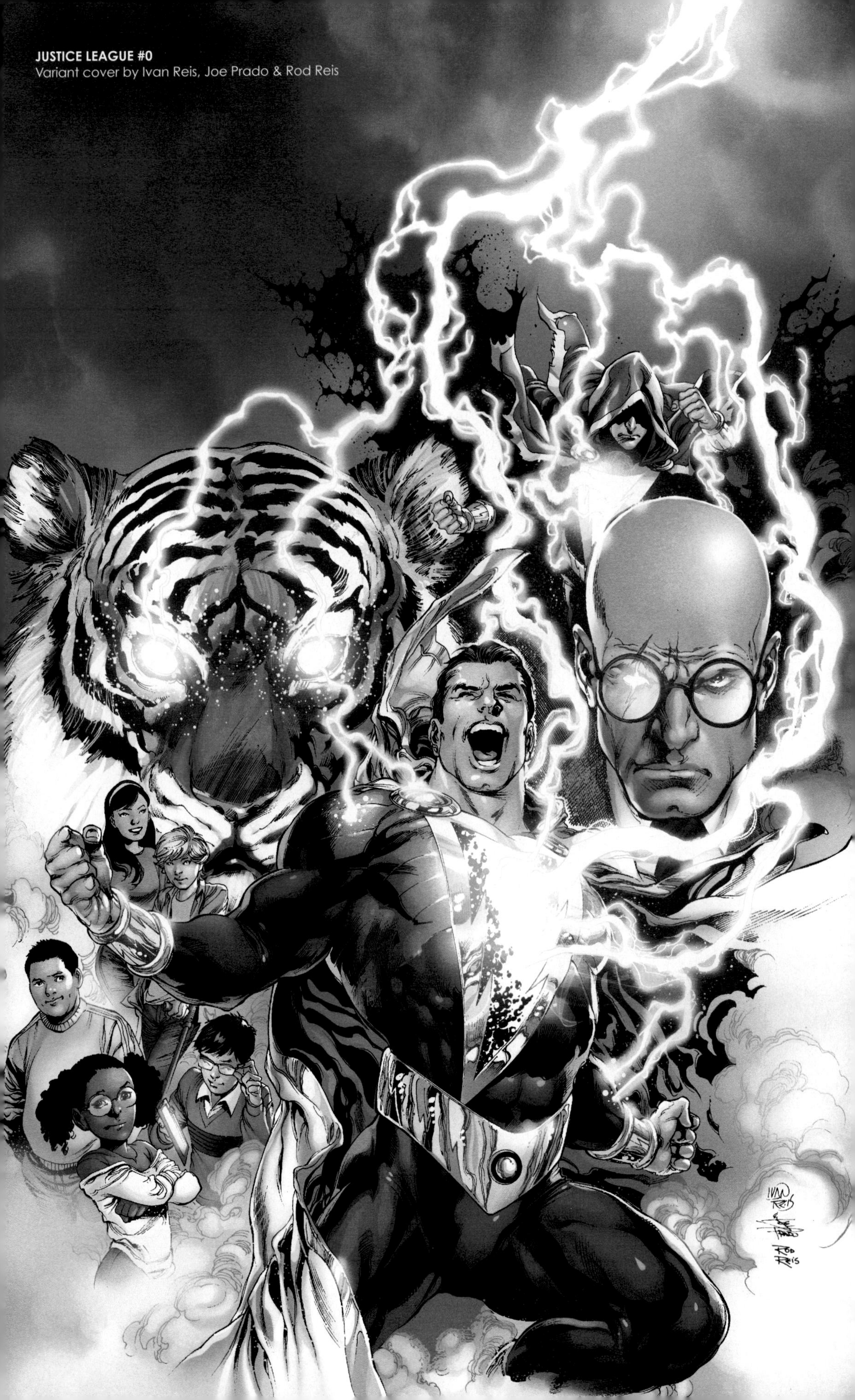

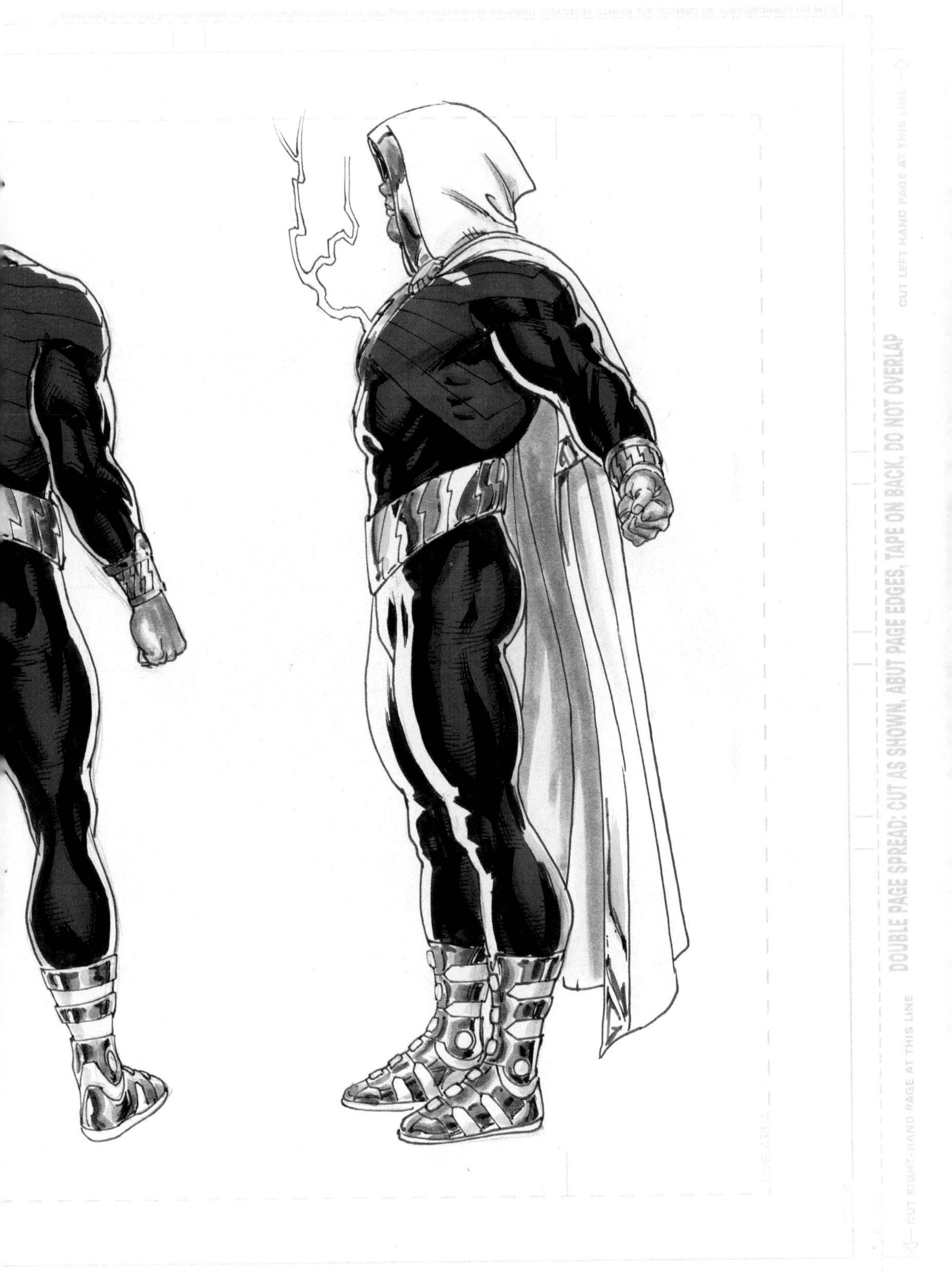
DOUBLE PAGE SPREAD: CUT AS SHOWN, ABUT PAGE EDGES, TAPE ON BACK, DO NOT OVERLAP
CUT LEFT HAND PAGE AT THIS LINE
CUT RIGHT-HAND PAGE AT THIS LINE

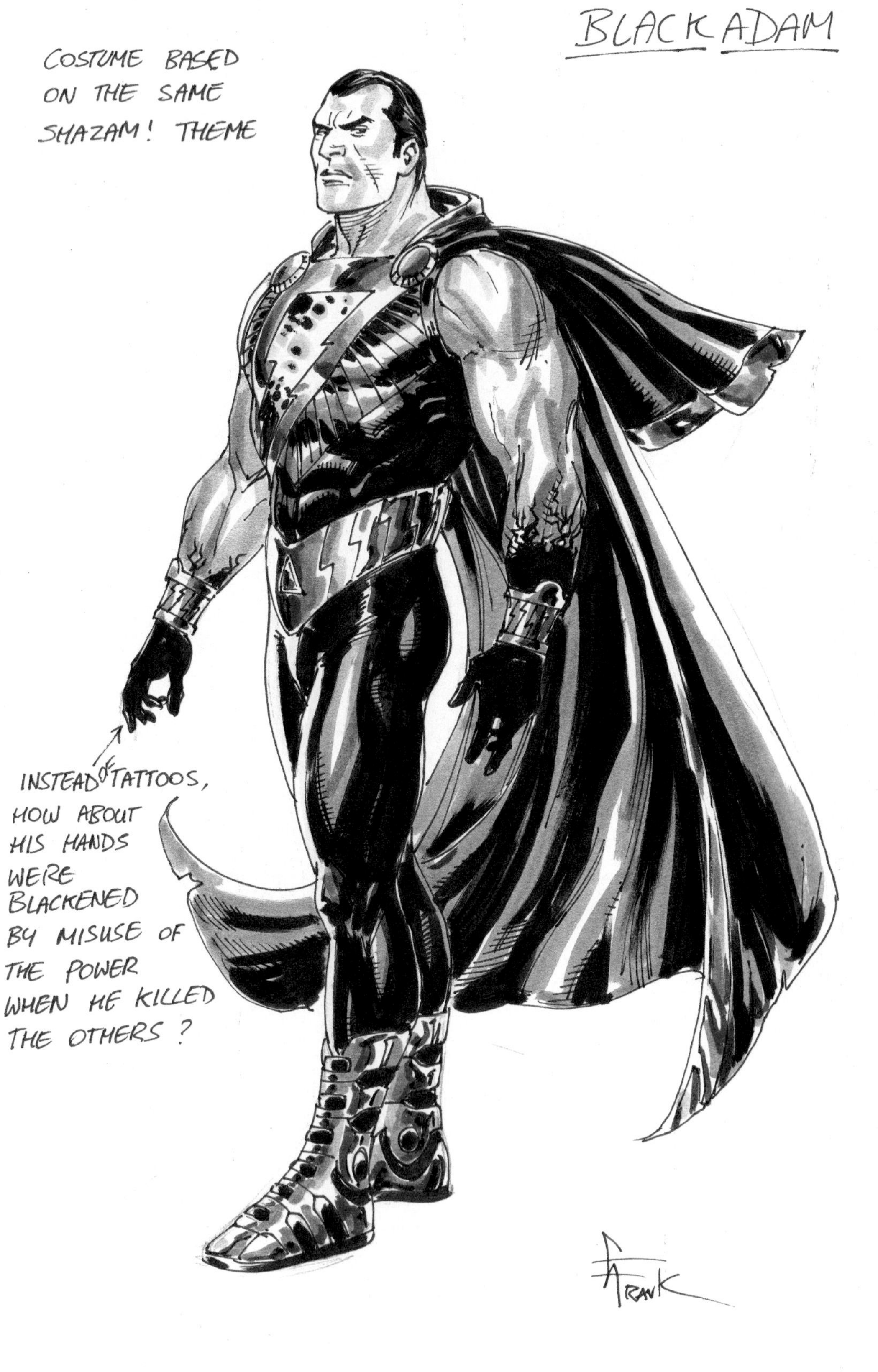
BLACK ADAM
COSTUME BASED ON THE SAME SHAZAM! THEME
INSTEAD of TATTOOS, HOW ABOUT HIS HANDS WERE BLACKENED BY MISUSE OF THE POWER WHEN HE KILLED THE OTHERS ?
FRANK

MARY

HOW I IMAGINE
SHAZAM'S TWIN SISTER
WOULD APPEAR.
SKIRT/SLEEVES
RETAINED FROM
ORIGINAL.

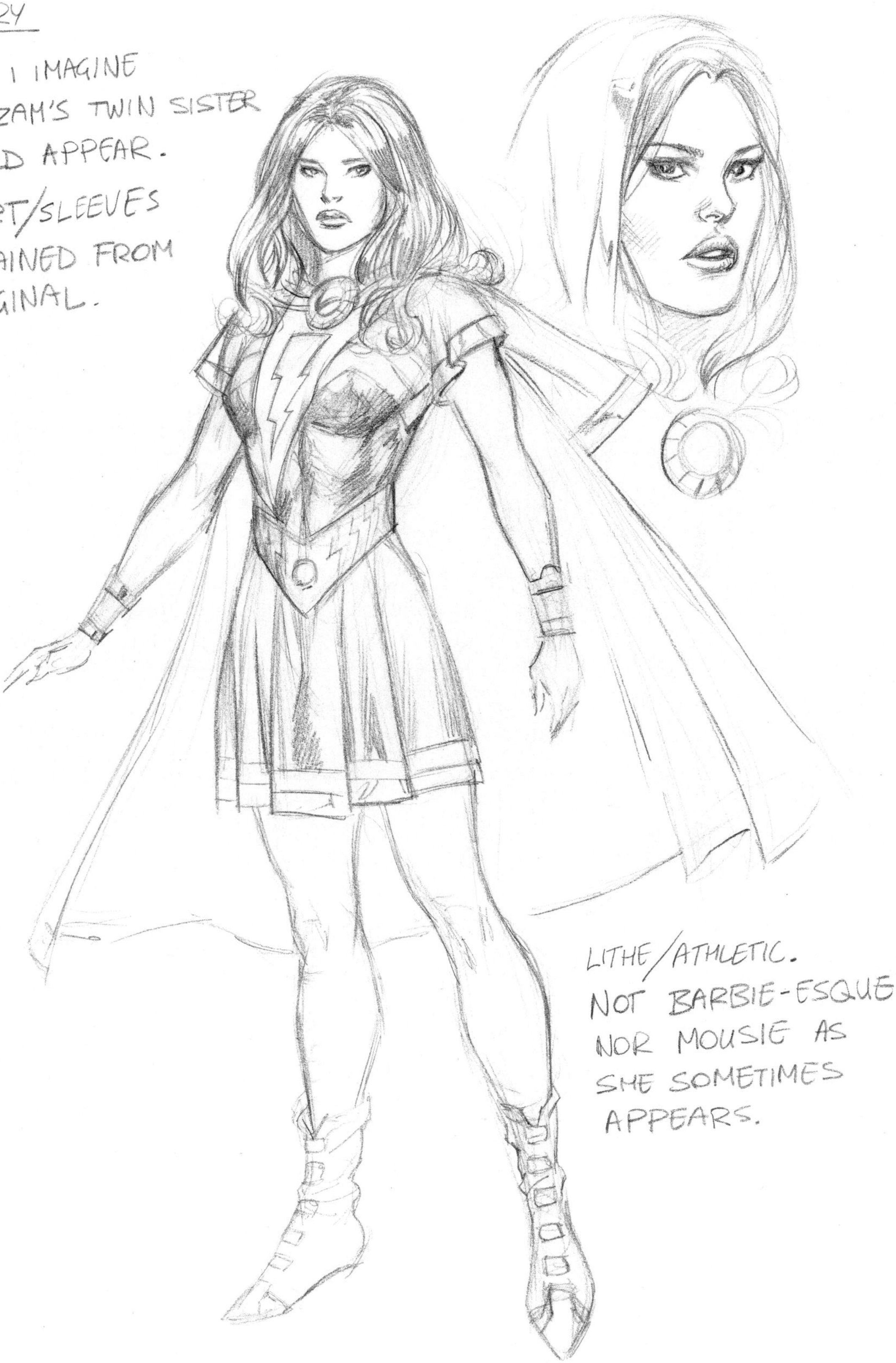
LITHE/ATHLETIC.
NOT BARBIE-ESQUE
NOR MOUSIE AS
SHE SOMETIMES
APPEARS.

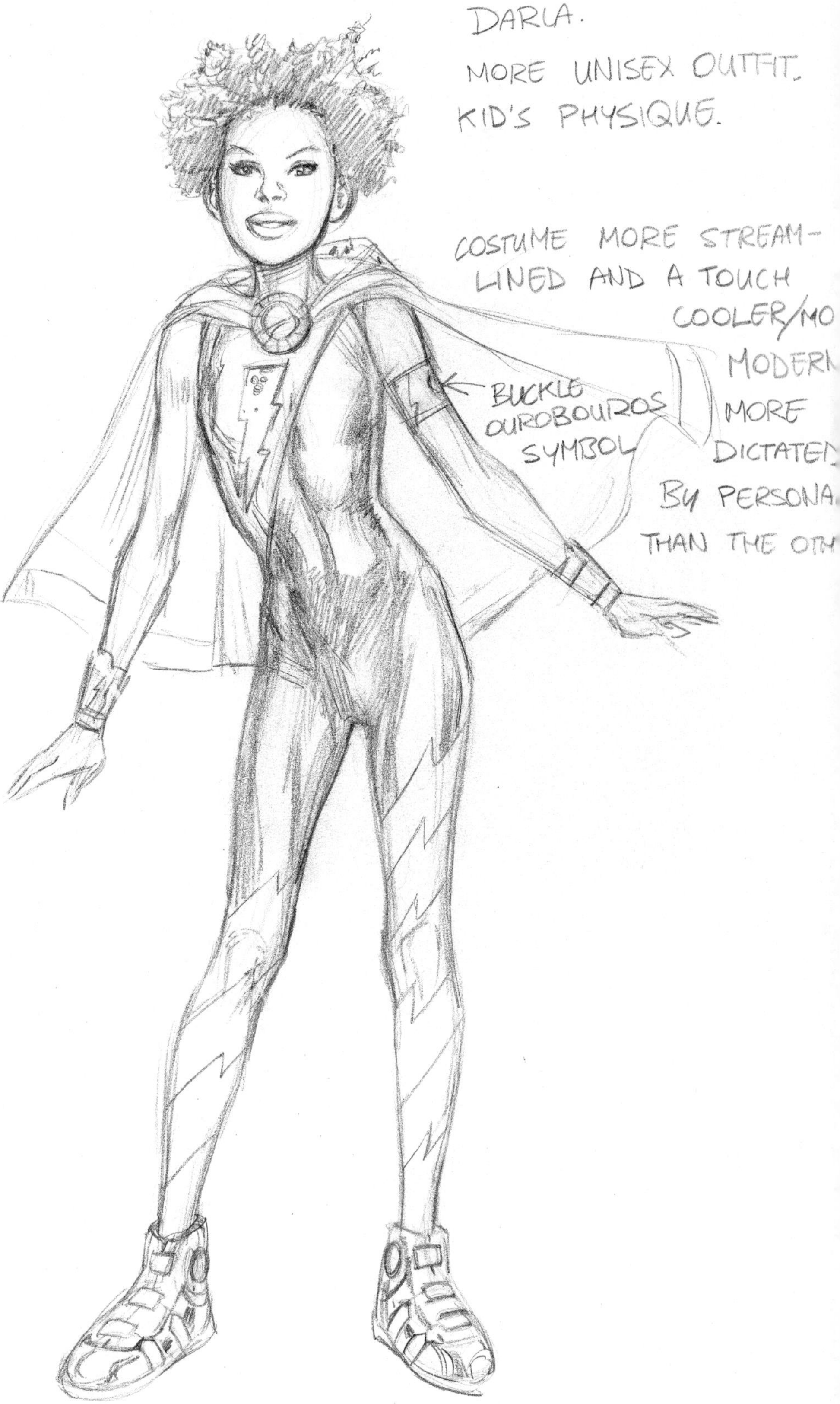
DARLA.
MORE UNISEX OUTFIT.
KID'S PHYSIQUE.
COSTUME MORE STREAM-
LINED AND A TOUCH
COOLER/MO
MODERN
MORE
DICTATED
BY PERSONA
THAN THE OTH
BUCKLE
OUROBOUROS
SYMBOL

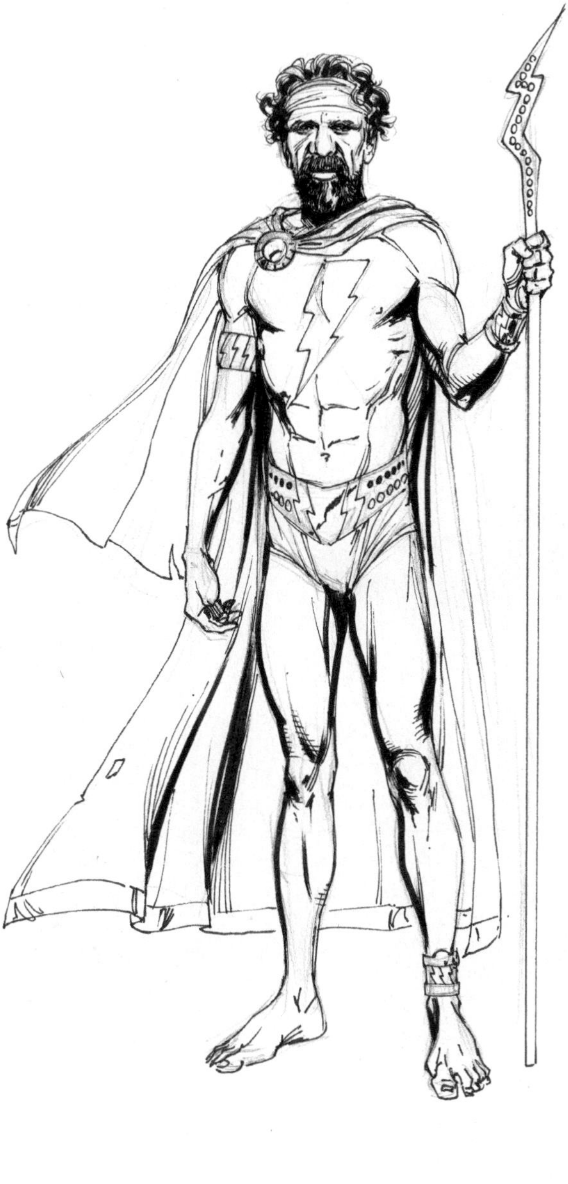

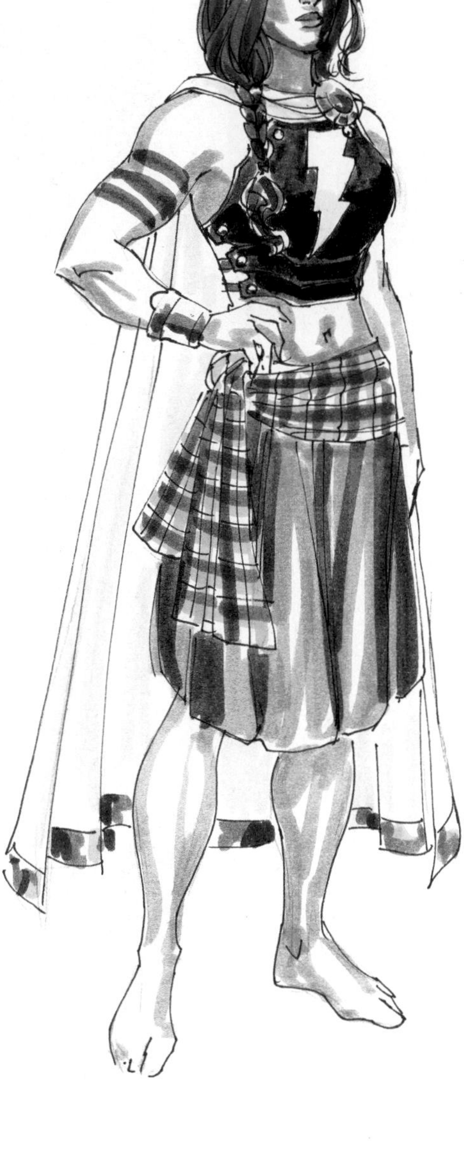

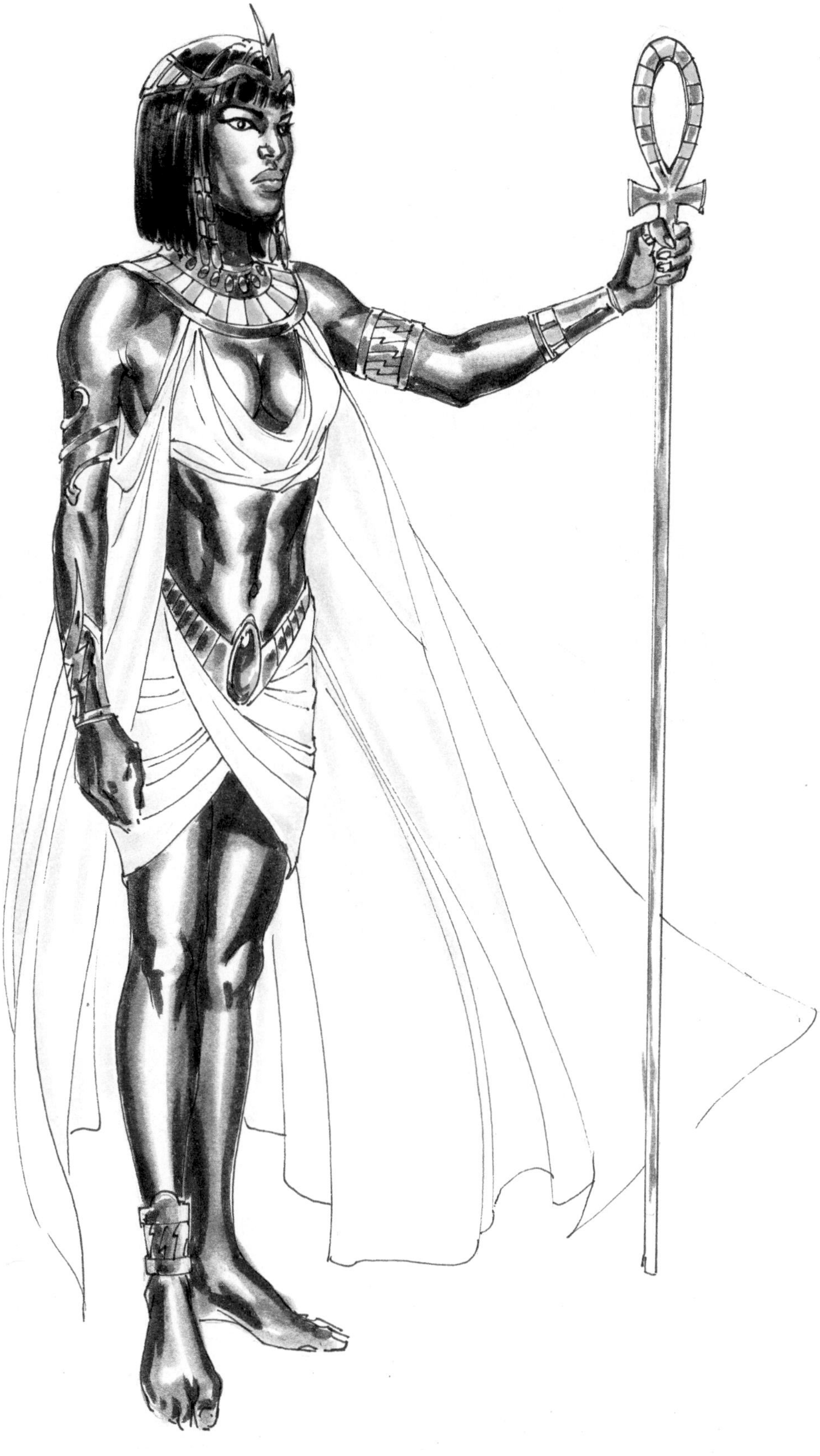

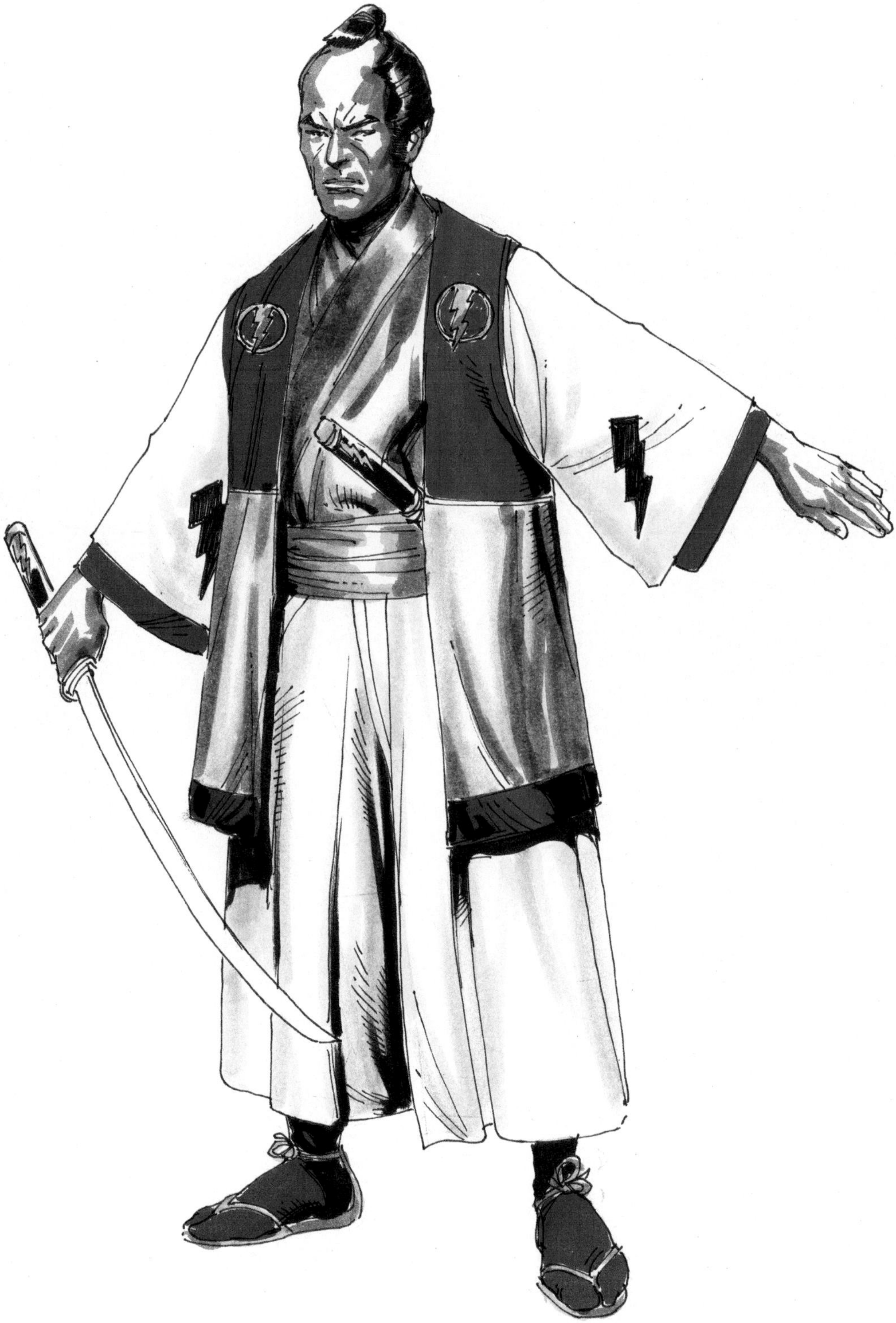

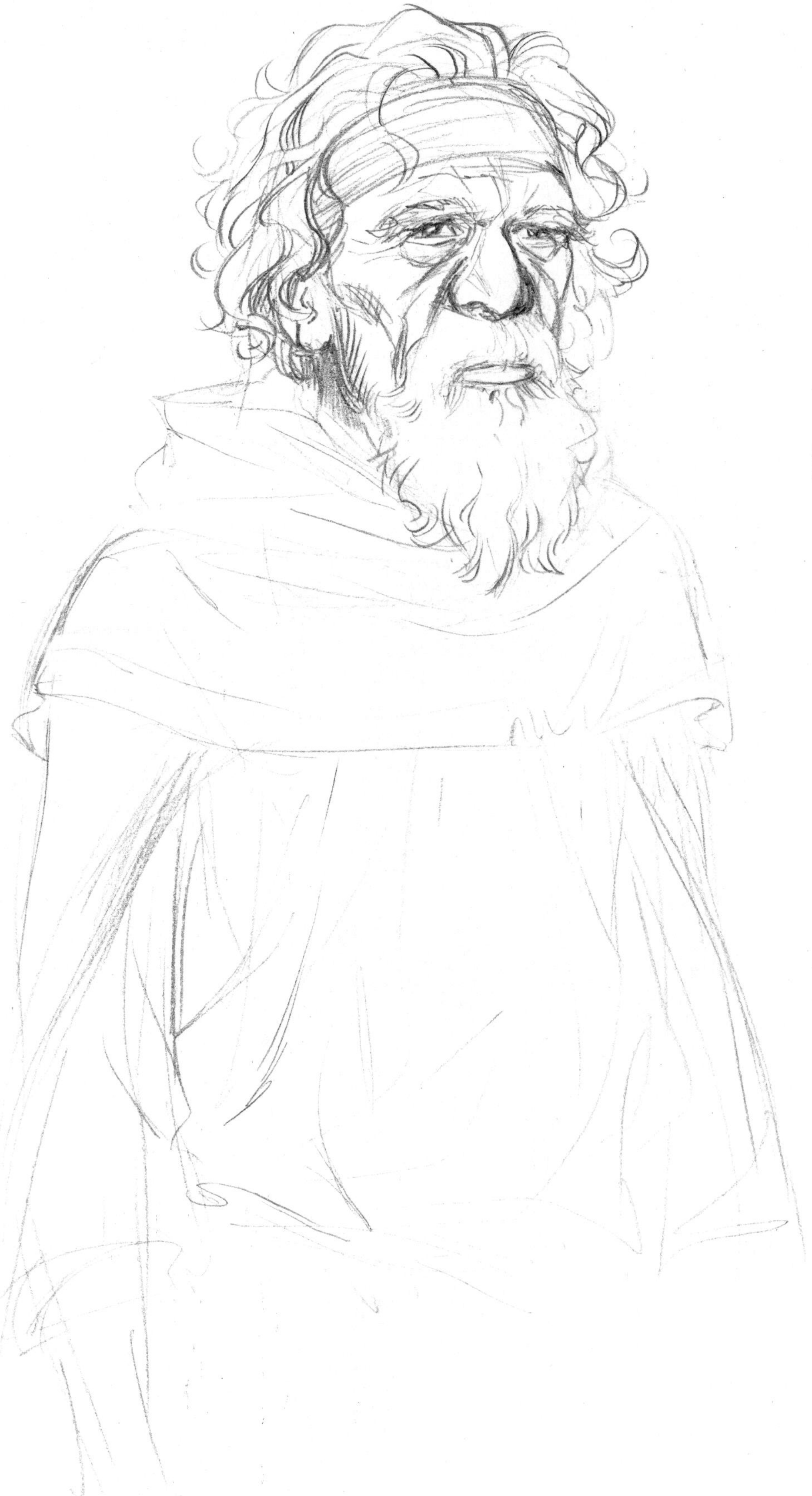